Portraits of Conflict

JOSEPH R. GARZA
copy print of ambrotype

Portraits of Conflict

A PHOTOGRAPHIC HISTORY

OF TEXAS

IN THE CIVIL WAR

Carl Moneyhon and Bobby Roberts

Portraits of Conflict Series

The University of Arkansas Press
Fayetteville   1998

02   01   00   99   98   5   4   3   2   1

Designed by Alice Gail Carter

☉ The paper used in this publication meets the minimum require-
ments of the American National Standard for Permanence of Paper
for Printed Library Materials   z39.48–1984.

Library of Congress Cataloging-in-Publication Data

Moneyhon, Carl H., 1944–
     A photographic history of Texas in the Civil War / Carl Moneyhon
     and Bobby Roberts.
          p.   cm. — (Portraits of conflict)
     Includes bibliographical references (p.   ) and index.
     ISBN 1-55728-533-0 (alk. paper)
     1. Texas—History—Civil War, 1861–1865—Pictorial works.
     2. Texas—History—Civil War, 1861–1865.   I. Roberts, Bobby Leon.
     II. Title.   III. Series.
     E532.M66   1998
     976.4'05'0222—dc21   98-8827
                                                     CIP

This volume is dedicated to the Moneyhon, Hofmann, Keller, and Valliant families of Texas, whose lives have been a part of their state's history for so long.

Preface and Acknowledgments

This is the sixth volume in a series of photographic histories of the South in the Civil War. As in the previous books, this volume uses the surviving photographic evidence to broaden and hopefully deepen the appreciation of the human and personal character of this war. Readers should remember that, when compared to Civil War–era documents, the number of extant photographs is quite small. All historians are limited by the documents that are left, and our primary sources—namely photographs—are severely limited. It is, therefore, impossible to provide images for every important event in which Texans participated, and the story we tell from the photographs is regrettably uneven. The authors offer no new interpretations of the history of Texas in this great national conflict. However, the surviving photographs, when integrated with appropriate primary and secondary documents, do remind the reader that this war was ultimately about individuals who, for whatever reason, gave up something of themselves, and in some cases their lives, to this titanic struggle. As always, we have relied heavily on the compiled service records of the soldiers to provide basic, primary information about the men. These sources have been supported by other primary materials and selective secondary works that are appropriate to the topic under discussion.

As in the past volumes of *Portraits of Conflict*, the obligations of the authors have been numerous. We appreciate the support of public and private institutions around Texas and the nation, private collectors, and individuals who shared images of their family members. Without them the collection of photographs presented here would not be possible.

We owe a particular debt of gratitude to Peggy Fox of the Harold B. Simpson Confederate Research Center at Hill College, Hillsboro, Texas. Peggy has always been supportive of this work and helped us use the wonderful collections under her direction.

Many other public institutions provided photographs for this work and we appreciate their help. We are indebted to many members of their staffs, but we would like to offer special thanks to John Slate, former head of the Photograph Collections, and Ralph Elder, an old friend from reference, at the Center for American History at the University of Texas at Austin. John Anderson and Donaly Brice, another old friend, with the Archives Division of the Texas State Library were both valuable in their suggestions and aid in securing materials from that repository. Alice E. Sackett and Diane Bruce of the Institute of Texan Cultures at San Antonio proved invaluable with their help during a research trip to that collection and in subsequent correspondence. The authors would also like to thank Rickie Brunner at the Alabama Department of Archives and History for locating several important photographs.

There are other institutions that have repeatedly helped us with this and other volumes in the series. Corrine P. Hudgins located many important images in the Museum of the Confederacy. Our friend, Art Bergeron, found several interesting Texas images in the Louisiana and Lower Mississippi Valley Collection at Louisiana State University, Baton Rouge; we would like to thank him and also Judy Bolton for helping provide copies to us. The photographic curators at the United States Army Military History Institute at Carlisle Barracks, Pennsylvania, and the United States Naval History Center in Washington, D.C., have offered repeated help over the years. The Library of Congress and the National Archives have also been of immeasurable assistance. We would especially like to think Mary Ison of the Library of Congress and Michael Winey and Randy Hackenberg of Carlisle Barracks for their almost decade long assistance on this series.

We also appreciate the help of archivists, curators, and reference specialists at many other institutions who went out of their way to help us locate Texas-related Civil War materials in their collections. Among these were Les Smith of the San Jacinto Museum of History at La Porte, Shannon Simpson of the Ellis County Museum, Susan Sudweeks of the Dallas Historical Society, Carrie Griffin of the Sam Houston Regional Library and Research Center of the Texas State Library at Liberty, Claire Maxwell, Photographs Curator of the Austin History Center of the Austin Public Library, Mrs. Charlie Burns, curator of the Jefferson Historical Society Museum, Martha Gilliland Long and the Llano County Museum, Nina Nixon-Mendez of the Webb County Heritage Foundation, David J. Mycue of the Hidalgo County Historical Museum, and Erin Wardlow, the Huntington Library, San Marino, California. Finally, we wish to thank the staffs at the Smith County Historical Society in Tyler and at the Rosenberg Library at Galveston for their considerable assistance.

A large number of individuals generously shared photographs and images from their private collections. J. Dale West of Longview has been a supporter of this project almost from its inception and again allowed us to use images from his collection. Dale also put us in contact with several collectors. Other long-time supporters of the Portraits project continue to assist us in our research. We would like to thank especially Dale Snair of Atlanta, Don W. Scoggins of Longview, Texas, Gary Hendershott of Little Rock, Arkansas, George Esker of Metairie, Louisiana, and Roger Davis of Keokuk, Iowa, for their contributions to this volume.

We also owe a debt to many new friends who offered their use of Texas materials. These include Martin Callahan (San Antonio), Gary Canada (Keller, Texas), Gregg Gibbs (Austin), Milo Mims (San Antonio), and Dr. Larry L. Smith (Longview, Texas). The authors would especially like to thank Martin Callahan who has given us his unwavering support and advice since we began this project almost four years ago. Martin not only provided many excellent photos and much information for this volume, but he also helped us obtain images from other Texas collectors.

We would also like to thank June Tuck of Sulphur Springs, who shared materials that she had collected on Hopkins County soldiers. Jerry Thompson from Texas A&M International University at Laredo, the unquestioned expert on the war on the Rio Grande, shared his photographs and expertise. Anne Bailey of Georgia State College and University at Milledgeville provided useful images and help in finding information on them.

We also appreciate many individuals who shared pictures of their family members. David Smith of Garland, whose own work on the Texas frontier during the Civil War was particularly useful in preparing this book, provided the image of Anderson Augustus King. Others who allowed us to use images were Alvin Young Bethard (Lafayette, Louisiana), Mary Boone (Shreveport, Louisiana), Mrs. Richard Davis, (Canton), Martha Durst (Mason), Minetta Altgelt Goyne (Arlington), Michael Jones (Iowa, Louisiana), Judge David D. Jackson (Dallas), Max S. Lale (Fort Worth), Judson Milburn (Stillwater, Oklahoma), Roger Pinckney, (Llano), Jeneal Riley (Rogers, Arkansas), Leland E. Stewart (Spring), Warner Wallace (Hughes Springs), Don A. Schroeder (Dallas), and Jenece Waid-Hurst (Dewey, Arizona). Having access to such photos was particularly important to our research.

Thanks to Louise Lester and Natalie Morgan of the Kendall County Public Library for their help in running down information on Unionists who served in central Texas. Nancy I. Detlefsen provided us with useful information on her great-great-grandfather John E. Chaffin, her great-grandfather Francis A. Taulman, and her great-great-uncle John Crist. Finally, our thanks to Tim Burgess of White House, Tennessee, for helping us locate several images of Texans who served in the Franklin-Nashville Campaign.

We would like to acknowledge the continuing assistance of Linda Pine of the University of Arkansas at Little Rock Archives and Special Collections. Her collections are always invaluable for these works, and Linda allows us to continue to use the department's darkroom.

The University of Arkansas Press remains a real gem of presses to work with. They have continued to push for quality in these books, both in content and production. Kevin Brock has become virtually the permanent copyeditor, even as his duties have changed within the Press. Beth Motherwell in marketing has been a source of never ending faith in the value of these books.

Of course none of these volumes would be possible without the support and forbearance of our wives, Patricia Moneyhon and Kathy Roberts. For years now they have put up with research trips, social conversation that always included too much about history, and most troublesome of all, moody historians who were trying to meet deadlines. Bobby gives a special thanks to Kathy for reading, critiquing, and correcting the four chapters written by him.

CARL MONEYHON
BOBBY ROBERTS

Key to Photographic and Archival Locations

Archives Division, TSL: Archives Division, Texas State Library, Austin, Texas

CAH: Center for American History, University of Texas at Austin, Austin, Texas

CRC: Harold B. Simpson Confederate Research Center, Hill College, Hillsboro, Texas

ITC: Institute of Texan Cultures, San Antonio, Texas

LLMVC: Louisiana and Lower Mississippi Valley Collection, Hill Memorial Library, Louisiana State University, Baton Rouge, Louisiana

MOC: Museum of the Confederacy, Richmond, Virginia

U.S.A.M.H.I.: The United States Army Military History Institute, Carlisle Barracks, Pennsylvania. MOLLUS, Mass., refers to the Military Order of the Loyal Legion of the United States–Massachusetts Commandery Collection.

Contents

Portraits of Conflict

Chapter 1

Civil War Photography in Texas

Equal any in the Confederacy
—WILLIAM W. BRIDGERS

In the autumn of 1861, William W. Bridgers advertised that his Photographic Gallery at Austin was open for business and promised his patrons photographs that would "equal any in the Confederacy."[1] A native North Carolinian, Bridgers had moved to Texas about 1856 to ply his trade as a photographer and opened his first studio on Pecan Street in Austin. He represented one of a small number of men and women who captured images of Texas and Texans as they went to war. The legacy of their work, although small, nonetheless serves as important documentation of a state and its people engaged in the great national Civil War.

As with other states of the Trans-Mississippi Confederacy, the Civil War experience of Texas was not well documented visually. There was no one comparable to Mathew Brady, Alexander Gardner, or the hundreds of others who accompanied the Federal armies into the South and photographed the region's battlefields, people, and scenery. The state had no Jay D. Edwards, as did Louisiana, to provide a glimpse of the Confederate side. Yet photographers did work in the state, and through the individual portraits and the few exterior scenes that they captured, they did produce a body of work that provides a sense of the people and the state at war.

When the Civil War broke out, photography was a well-established trade in Texas. In December 1843 a Mrs. Davis, certainly among the first photographers in the state, advertised in the Houston *Morning Star* that she had established a studio at the Houston House, where she would "take likenesses" using the daguerreian process. In the years that followed Mrs. Davis's introduction of photography, hundreds of photographers practiced their craft. In 1860, on the eve of war, the census reported sixty-one photographers and artists in Texas, all men. Such a figure must be considered only approximate, however, since it is known that at least one woman, Mary Collins of Marshall, worked in the state at that time.[2]

The photographers who worked Texas in 1860 typically were older than those in many other Southern states. The average age of twenty-six photographers identified in the census of that year was thirty-three years old. John H. Stephens Stanley, who operated a studio at Houston, was the oldest at sixty-one. John M. Hill of Tyler and Milton Jones of Meridian, both age nineteen, were the youngest.

Almost all of the photographers were newcomers to Texas. In 1860 only one, thirty-year-old Milam Collum from Palo Pinto, was a native-born Texan. Of the twenty-seven whose birthplace could be identified, six were foreign-born, three were Northerners, six (including Collum) were from the Lower South, and twelve were from the Upper South.

Advertisements indicated that Texas photographers were up to date in basic technology, offering all of the known photographic techniques. Among contemporary photographers there were four major photographic techniques commonly in use. The oldest was the daguerreotype, which was produced by exposing images onto light-sensitized silver-plated sheets, then developing and fixing the plates. This process produced remarkably detailed images, although the reversal of the image was a drawback. Daguerreotypes also were expensive, a fact that restricted somewhat the market. While some photographers still made daguerreotypes in 1861, this process had been largely supplanted by others.

In 1851 photographers had developed a technique for binding photo-sensitive chemicals to glass or other surfaces with the use of collodion. When applied to glass, the photo-sensitive salts produced a negative image that when placed against a black background created a positive image. The resulting picture was known as an ambrotype and had wide currency throughout the United States and certainly in Texas by the mid-1850s. The ambrotype solved the problem of image reversal typical of the daguerreotype, but these pictures remained expensive.

The use of collodion, however, paved the way for two breakthroughs on the eve of the Civil War that reduced the price of photography (which may account for the large number of images that ultimately were made). The first technique was the use of collodion to apply a silver-halide emulsion to a black-lacquered iron plate. Introduced after 1856, the melainotype, or tintype, was durable, lightweight, and inexpensive and opened up a whole new market for photographers.

The second breakthrough was the discovery of a technique for holding photographic salts to paper with albumin, thus making possible the creation of paper prints from glass negatives. In Texas, albumen printing was advertised prior to the war, although advertisements do not indicate that the particularly popular technique of attaching paper prints to calling cards, *cartes de visite,* was widespread in Texas before the war. During the war, however, photographers began producing this style of image.

Advertisements in 1860 and 1861 indicate that the daguerreotype had been largely displaced by the ambrotype and tintype. In the larger towns photographers also offered paper pictures. A. G. Wedge's September 1861 advertisement of his "Lone Star Gallery of Art" at the corner of Tremont and Market in Galveston advised patrons that he could produce tintypes, ambrotypes, photographs (plain or colored in oil), and all other photographic styles "in the most perfect manner."[3] R. E. Curlee, owner of the Sky Light Ambrotype Gallery at Tyler, informed patrons that he could provide them with "likenesses on patent leather or paper as cheap, if not a little cheaper, and equal to anybody's pictures."[4] William H. Howe offered patrons at Clarksville "first-class pictures," including a "Velovotype, on purple glass."[5] Frank Naghel's Dollar Gallery at San Antonio simply offered "Photograph's Plain and Colored."[6]

The heart of the photographer's business was the personal portrait, and they made every effort to appeal to the sentiments of the public in order to attract customers. One of the more blatant of these appeals was that of Vivier & Fagersteen in San Antonio, asking "Mothers! Fathers! Brothers!

Sisters and Friends" what they would not give to have the "image of the *absent . . .* smile upon you as in life!" The photographers urged patrons to "delay not. 'Leave the substance ere the shadow fade.'"[7] John M. Hill at Tyler made a special appeal to women to see him for portraits, promising that his rooms were well-furnished, with all of the "conveniences of a parlor."[8]

Advertisements suggest, however, that the portrait business alone might not have been enough to sustain operations. Photographers offered a wide variety of other services as well. Vivier & Fagersteen offered to make albumen copies of old daguerreotypes.[9] William W. Bridgers and M. W. Townsend at Austin and E. T. Dudley at Clarksville also sold photographic supplies to other artists.[10] Dudley even offered to work on watches, clocks, and jewelry.[11]

Only a few photographers had attempted to make money by producing images of public figures for sale in the manner of Mathew Brady or Edward and Henry T. Anthony. William DeRyee and R. E. Moore photographed members of the Eighth Legislature in 1860 and then published these pictures as *The Texas Album of the Eighth Legislature 1860.* DeRyee and Moore printed images for each volume, tipping or gluing them onto the pages. William W. Bridger set up his photographic studio on Pecan Street in Austin in the autumn of 1861 specifically to take advantage of the opportunities presented by the meeting of the state legislature. In his advertisement Bridger invited members of the legislature to come by his shop and judge his work for themselves. However, there is no indication that he attempted a wider public sale.[12]

During the secession crisis DeRyee realized that many people might be interested in purchasing images of the individuals taking the lead in this momentous event. In April 1861 DeRyee offered "Sam Houston's Picture!!" which "Has been taken from life during his late Farewell Address at Austin." The image had actually be made by Charles G. Ivonski, but DeRyee had then "chemically multi-plied" it. Seeking a mass market, the enterprising photographer offered his prints to customers for fifty cents per copy.[13]

Despite the apparent quantity of work being done, few photographs from the era remain. This is the case in part because there are no collections of images belonging to the individual photographers, as may be found in some other states. The transitory nature of the these artists may account for their failure to hold onto their negatives. Photography in antebellum Texas was an itinerant trade, with most of the artists traveling from town to town, setting up their studios, taking pictures until the market was exhausted, then moving on. E. T. Dudley offered his services to the people of Clarksville in the spring of 1861 for only a "short time."[14] Most of them probably returned periodically to the towns where they had done well. William H. Howe, who also worked the Clarksville area in 1861, indicated in his advertisements that he had been there before and that he had done well. Howe announced that he was pleased to be back and looked forward to seeing his "old friends."[15]

The outbreak of the Civil War brought about several changes in photographic work in the state, some of which further reduced the number of photographs taken. For some, it forced them to settle in one town and appears to have encouraged them to make clear their Southern sympathies. R. E. Curlee, a native of South Carolina, announced that he had resided in Texas for several years and indicated that "now that Texas has seceded, he expects to remain right here."[16]

Others apparently joined the army. E. T. Dudley of Clarksville encouraged patrons who wanted their picture made to hurry by, because he belonged to Gould's Regiment which would be called up soon.[17] Dudley in fact joined the 23d Texas Cavalry, State Troops, as a member of the Clarksville Light Infantry. It is impossible to tell with certainty how many of the photographers at work in Texas in 1860 ultimately joined the army, but men with the same names as nineteen of the forty-one photographers identified from 1860 were found in Texas military units. The unique names of some of these individuals suggests that at least some were the same men. Rudolph Cordes of Galveston, for example, joined Company H, 2d Texas Infantry, and Ambrose Hardin of Palo Pinto was in the 5th Texas Cavalry.

It is worth noting that none of the Northerners who were working in the state in 1860 appear to have joined the Confederate forces. These possibly left the state, depleting further the stock of photographers.

Still, photographic work appears to have continued within the state throughout much of the war, even though there are few images that clearly come from this period. This was made possible partly by the fact that Texas photographers never seemed to have suffered from the lack of photographic supplies experienced elsewhere in the South. William Bridger appealed to Southern patriotism when he advertised that he had obtained photographic supplies in May 1861. Promising to fill orders with dispatch, Bridger indicated that he could provide photographic stock and chemicals for sale at reasonable prices. He believed that those wanting to purchase small orders could do better by ordering from him than sending to the North and having to pay charges.[18] As late as September 1862, E. T. Dudley announced at Clarksville that he had received a new supply of ambrotype stock.[19]

Even though able to secure supplies, as the war progressed the number of Confederate photographers who continued working was small, and most of their advertisements end in the autumn of 1861. R. E. Curlee of Tyler was still advertising in the Tyler *Reporter* in August 1861. Bridger's advertisements end in November 1861. Dudley's last ad appeared in the fall of 1862.

Even so, photography continued. H. C. Medford, a Texas cavalryman at Houston, noted in his diary on January 21, 1864, that he had gone to an "artist's room, where I have a picture taken for which I pay thirty dollars."[20] The Houston artist is unknown, although at least one *carte de visite* of a member of Gen. John Magruder's staff is identified as being from the studio of Louis de Planque, who in addition to a studio at Matamoras operated one on Houston's Main Street. A. G. Wedge of Galveston also is known with certainty to have continued taking pictures throughout the war years, and given the conditions in that blockaded city, he may also have had a studio at Houston.

While other Southern states experienced an influx of photographers with the arrival of Federal armies, Texas did not suffer extensive enemy invasion. Union forces were at Galveston only for a short time and remained along the southern border for a somewhat longer period; photographers probably accompanied these latter units. The short period involved, however, weighed against any major accumulation of images, and few remain that can be identified as having come from 1861–1865.

The years immediately after the war were the real bonanza for photographers. Returning soldiers seem often to have had their images made. Photographers also specialized in making inexpensive paper prints of ambrotypes or tintypes that either veterans could share or family members could use to remember those who did not return.

Historian David Haynes has rightly observed of photography in nineteenth-century Texas that it would be difficult to convince anyone that the state was "a hotbed of photographic experimentation and progress, [but] it would be equally inaccurate to dismiss the state as a scientific and artistic backwater."[21] Photographers in Texas never produced the quantity of work achieved by their colleagues elsewhere, but they nonetheless left a rich legacy. Their photographs helped record the state's participation in the Civil War, capturing the images of the individuals who served and at least a few contemporary scenes. Their legacy is all the more surprising because it is so little expected.

JOHN HENRY BROWN AND DAUGHTERS
ambrotype

This image of John Henry Brown is a good example of the photographic work done in Texas at the beginning of the war and was probably made in late 1861. Brown was editor of the *Civilian and Galveston Gazette* and a member of the Secession Convention before he left home as a member of the staff of Gen. Benjamin McCulloch. The image is an ambrotype, with the negative fixed on a glass plate and placed over dark backing. Like most such photographs, it was then put into a decorative case (such as this one) made from either light wood or gutta-percha, a plastic-like substance that could be molded into elaborate forms. Typical of most Texas images of this type, the photographer is unknown. *Photo courtesy of CAH, John Henry Brown Papers, CN 03223*

Durant Duponte
carte de visite
A. G. Wedge

Photography changed significantly within Texas during the war, although there are only a few images remaining that were made by identified local photographers. A. G. Wedge of Galveston was one of these artists. Little is known about Wedge: he began to advertise in Galveston newspapers in the spring of 1861 and continued to make pictures in the city at least through the arrival of Gen. John B. Magruder in 1863. This photograph of Capt. Durant Duponte, an aide to Magruder, was probably made sometime after the reoccupation of Galveston in January 1863. Shortly thereafter, Duponte went on a mission to Cuba in an effort to procure weapons. *Photo courtesy of LLMVC*

WEDGE BACKMARK

Wedge's *cartes de visite* at times had no backmark at all and are identifiable only by the setting that appeared in the image. A few, however, displayed the distinctive mark shown here. The flag, a rough approximation of the Confederate national flag, is not representative of any official banner. *Photo courtesy of LLMVC*

HUNTSVILLE
carte de visite
F. B. Bailey

One of the only other reputed wartime images that can be attributed to a particular photographer is this *carte de visite* of the town square in Huntsville. The picture is reported to have been made sometime during the war by F. B. Bailey of Navasota. Bailey, a native of South Carolina, probably had come to Texas in the 1850s and operated a studio, known as the Bayou City Ambrotype Rooms, with Hiram Hand in 1856 and 1857. Exactly where Bailey was working during the war is unknown, but in the 1870s he had a studio at Navasota and in the 1880s one at Palestine. *Photo courtesy of U.S.A.M.H.I.*

IMMACULATE CONCEPTION CATHOLIC CHURCH
carte de visite

Among the few other exterior images specifically attributed to the war years are several *cartes de visite* of Brownsville, including this image of Immaculate Conception Church supposed to have been made in 1862. The photographer has not been identified, although C. A. Rand, who was associated with the C. H. Washburn studio of New Orleans, was the only photographer known to be in Brownsville at the beginning of the war. *Photo courtesy of ITC*

UNIDENTIFIED SOLDIER,
6TH U.S. CAVALRY
carte de visite
Hamilton B. Hillyer

War-related photography continued into the immediate postwar years. This *carte de visite* was made by Hamilton B. Hillyer, a native of Georgia who moved to Texas in 1848 and settled on a ranch along the San Antonio River. Hillyer bought equipment to make ambrotypes from Anderson & Blessing of New Orleans in 1857 and began making photographs. Little is known of him until the late 1860s, but he was in Austin by either 1865 or 1866. This photograph can be attributed to that time period since the 6th U.S. Cavalry was in the state capital from the autumn of 1865 through the spring of 1866. *Photo courtesy of J. Dale West*

12

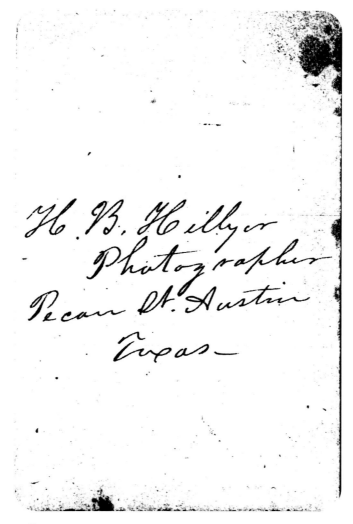

BACKMARK

Reflecting the difficulties encountered by photographers immediately after the war, Hillyer was unable to secure printed cards on which to mount his *carte de visite* prints. Hillyer hand wrote his imprint on the back of the previous picture, identifying his studio as being on Pecan Street—present 6th Street—in Austin. *Photo courtesy of J. Dale West*

WILLIAM W. HEARTSILL
print from *Fourteen
Hundred and 91 Days in
the Confederate Army*

There are no photographs of individual photographers, but there is one image of an individual who helped to preserve at least part of the photographic legacy of the war. William W. Heartsill joined Sam Richardson's company (Company F), 2d Regiment Texas Mounted Rifles, at Marshall in April 1861. He was on detached duty during the New Mexico campaign, and his company was transferred to Morgan's Regiment of cavalry in 1862. Heartsill was captured at Arkansas Post, imprisoned at Camp Butler, and exchanged in 1863, returning to the 2d Cavalry. In 1874 Heartsill began writing his history of the regiment, and in the process requested his fellow soldiers to send in personal photographs. They were copied to paper prints and individually glued into the final work, providing more images of any individuals in any single unit from Texas (excluding those that served in the Army of Northern Virginia).

WILLIAM H. GASTON
cabinet card
Clifton Church

The photographic legacy of the Civil War in Texas also was preserved in the postwar years by photographers who made copies of original one-of-a-kind ambrotypes or tintypes. This copy, made by Clifton Church of Dallas, of an image of William H. Gaston was produced from an original made in 1861, when Gaston went east to join what became the 1st Texas Infantry. The twenty-one-year-old Gaston left the family farm in Anderson County as a member of A. T. Rainey's "Texas Guards." Gaston's brother wrote to their mother and father from New Orleans on July 10, 1861, to let them know about the picture: "Billy & I had our ambrotypes taken yesterday and we will send them by the same mail, by which we send this letter."[22] William Gaston survived the war, as did the ambrotype, and this copy probably was made sometime after Church opened his studio in Dallas in 1891. *Photo courtesy of the Dallas Historical Society*

Chapter 2

Texas Goes to War

I feel that our cause is just.

— W. W. HEARTSILL

In the spring of 1861, W. W. Heartsill, a clerk in a mercantile store at Marshall, concluded that he had no choice but to join a military unit being organized in Harrison County. As he started a war diary that he hoped would provide a history of his unit, the W. P. Lane Rangers, he agreed with many other Texans that the election of Abraham Lincoln as president of the United States had produced a situation that was intolerable for the South. Secession was the only answer. In noting the reasons for his own enlistment, Heartsill probably also captured the motives of many others who rushed to the colors in 1861. "I was prompted to enlist," he recorded, "because of a strict sense of duty and because I feel that our cause is just."[1] With such feelings thousands of Texans went to war.

In Texas as elsewhere in the South, the election of Abraham Lincoln in the autumn of 1860 produced a governmental crisis. At least some Texas political leaders considered the results of the polls to be a clear indicator that the slave states of the South would be unable to live in peace within the national Union. Led by men such as Hardin R. Runnels, Francis R. Lubbock, and Richard B. Hubbard, the Democrats had adopted a platform in their 1860 state convention charging the Republican Party with carrying out a conflict against them and asserting their right to withdraw from the Union and reestablish independence should the Republicans win the national election. Lincoln's victory precipitated a crisis as the state's rights Democrats pushed for action and more conservative forces within Texas urged caution.

Unionists such as Gov. Sam Houston argued that while Lincoln's election might pose a threat, anything that he did could be resisted better within the Union than outside of it. Houston conceded Lincoln's constitutional election and concluded that "no alternative is left to me but to yield to the Constitution."[2] Among those supporting the governor were Congressman Andrew J. Hamilton, former governor Elisha M. Pease, and the politically prominent northwesterner, James W. Throckmorton. Houston, in control of the state government, delayed any action that would promote immediate action.

Radical secessionists, however, acted to force the issue. On December 3 in Austin, a group of secessionists, including Justice Oran M. Roberts of the state supreme court, Guy M. Bryan, George M. Flournoy, William S. Oldham, and John Marshall of the *State Gazette,* issued an address to the people of Texas that called on voters in each legislative district to hold an election on January 8, 1861, and select two delegates to a state convention scheduled for January 28 to consider the state's future in the Union. Houston was forced to call a special session of the legislature to meet with this emergency. The legislature authorized the convention but required that any ordinance of secession be submitted to the people of the state for approval.

The state convention met at Austin. Oran M. Roberts was easily elected president. On January 29, the second day, the delegates approved a resolution endorsing secession and provided that the ordinance be submitted to the voters on February 22. Only eight of the attending delegates voted against the ordinance. The negative vote of James W. Throckmorton was met with a hiss from among the delegates and the galleries. Throckmorton responded: "Mr. President, when the rabble hiss well may patriots tremble."[3]

Before the convention adjourned on February 5, the delegates agreed to send seven members—John H. Reagan, Louis T. Wigfall, John Hemphill, Thomas N. Waul, John Gregg, W. S. Oldham, and William B. Ochiltree—to Montgomery, Alabama, to take part in the formation of a new government, even though voters had yet to decide if Texas would secede from the Union. They also sent ambassadors to various Indian tribes in order to secure cooperation and friendship. The delegates agreed to reconvene on March 2, the date on which secession would take effect if approved by the citizens. In the meantime, the convention appointed a committee on public safety to prepare for secession and to deal with the approximately three thousand Federal troops in Texas (most of which were posted along the frontier). This body, headed by John C. Robertson, included many prominent Texans.

The Committee on Public Safety continued to meet in secret session after February 5 to coordinate efforts at securing the state from Federal authorities. Members of the committee assumed secession was inevitable and aggressively worked to secure the local military situation by demanding the surrender of the 2,700 United States troops within the state, commanded by Maj. Gen. David E. Twiggs. They appointed a subcommittee consisting of Samuel A. Maverick, Thomas J. Devine, Philip N. Luckett, and James H. Rogers to confer with Twiggs. Sympathetic to the Southern cause, Twiggs offered little resistance. He reported to Washington that "If an old woman with a broomstick should come with full authority from the state of Texas to demand the public property, I would give it to her."[4] However, he did delay. Seeking to force the issue, the Texans called in a force of four hundred men that had been raised by Benjamin McCulloch and authorized for use in San Antonio. This force arrived on February 15 and was joined by as many as seven hundred armed citizens. Three days later, Twiggs agreed to evacuate all Federal fortifications in Texas.

Following Twiggs's surrender, Henry E. McCulloch was commissioned by the Committee of Public Safety to raise a cavalry force and to seize Federal installations along the northern Indian frontier. John S. Ford was given authority to take troops to the Rio Grande, where he was to take over Federal properties and to protect that frontier. Ford's task was deemed extremely important, since Texas authorities feared a possible attack out of Mexico by Juan Cortina, a formidable outlaw who had raided along the Rio Grande border during the 1840s and 1850s. Ford's troops, some five hundred men, gathered at Galveston and were sent to Brazos Santiago on board the *General Rusk,* commanded by Capt. Leon Smith.

In the end, the audacity of the Committee of Public Safety proved justified, for Texans handily approved secession. Unionists throughout the state vigorously opposed the ordinance, but with little success. At the polls the secessionist vote was 46,153 against a pro-Union vote of 14,747. Only ten

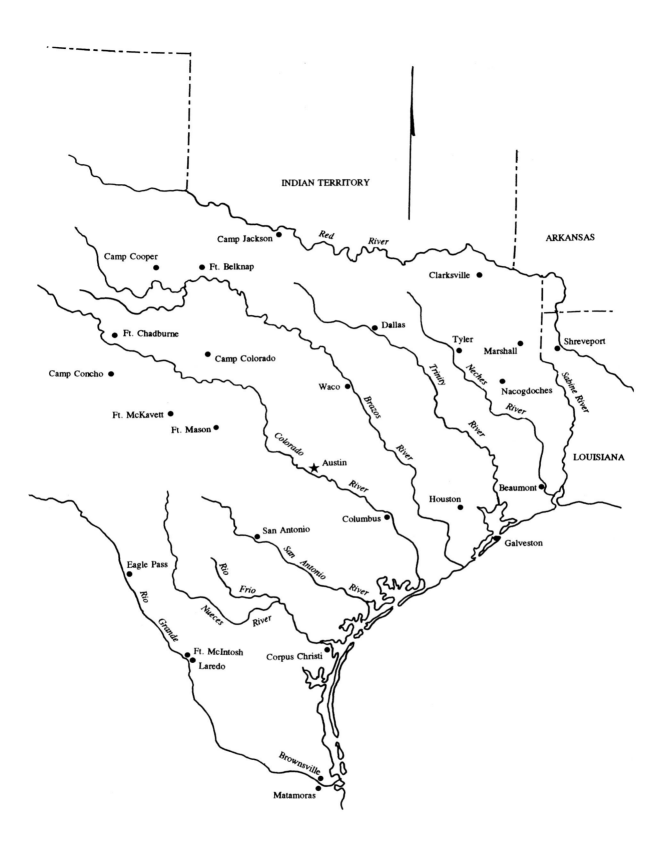

INDIAN TERRITORY

ARKANSAS

Camp Jackson • *Red   River*

Camp Cooper •   • Ft. Belknap

Clarksville •

Ft. Chadburne •   • Dallas

Tyler •   Shreveport •

Camp Colorado •   Marshall •

Camp Concho •   Waco •   *Trinity*   *Neches*   Nacogdoches •

Brazos   *River*   *River*

Ft. McKavett •   LOUISIANA

Ft. Mason •   *Colorado*

★ Austin   Beaumont •

River   Houston •

Columbus •

San Antonio •   Galveston •

Eagle Pass •   *Rio*   *San*

Frio   *Antonio*

Rio   *Nueces*   *River*   *River*

Grande

Ft. McIntosh •   Corpus Christi •
Laredo

Brownsville •

Matamoras •

19

counties in central Texas and eight in northern Texas gave anti-secession majorities.

When the convention reassembled on March 2 after the election, the members directed the delegates in Montgomery to ask for admission to the Confederacy, although the Confederate Congress had already acted to admit Texas to the new Confederacy. The convention also passed a resolution demanding that state officers take an oath of allegiance to the new government. Governor Houston refused to take the oath on the grounds that the convention had no authority over him. On March 16, 1861, the convention declared the office of governor vacant and named Lt. Gov. Edward Clark to fill the post. The convention, in cooperation with the legislature, continued to prepare for war until it adjourned on March 25, at which point the legislature resumed full authority.

Under Governor Clark, supported by the convention and then by the legislature, the state actively prepared for war. On March 18, state authorities authorized the organization of the first regiment of state troops—commanded by John S. Ford, with John R. Baylor and Edwin Waller as his junior officers. After the legislature adjourned on April 9, Clark continued the creation of new regiments, encouraged by Gen. Earl Van Dorn, who had been sent by the Confederate government to get regiments organized. On April 17, Clark announced plans to raise 3,000 troops and organized the state into six military districts from which these soldiers would be enrolled. Eight days later he called for 5,000 more troops to resist a potential Federal invasion following Fort Sumter and Lincoln's call upon the states for troops to suppress the insurrection.

There was an initial reluctance to commit these troops to Confederate service, however, and the first units clearly designated for the Confederate Army were not raised until August, when 2,000 men were called to serve in regiments being raised to fight in Virginia. At that time, the state responded with the creation of the 1st, 4th, and 5th

Texas Infantry Regiments—the basic elements that would later constitute Hood's Texas Brigade.

Through the first year and a half of war, Texans joined the newly formed units readily and in large numbers. Governor Clark reported at the end of 1861 that some 25,000 Texans were in Confederate service. Approximately 8,000 of these were organized into seven infantry regiments and four infantry battalions. The rest were formed into sixteen regiments and three battalions of cavalry.

Such numbers could be explained as a result of the general enthusiasm of many for what appeared to be an exciting adventure. Few of these men knew quite what to expect in 1861. At the beginning, the war seemed like it was going to be a lark. Ralph J. Smith, who joined the 2d Texas Infantry in the autumn of 1861 from Texana in Jackson County, later remembered those days when he wrote:

I wish I were able to describe the glorious anticipation of the first few days of our military lives, when we each felt individually able to charge and annihilate a whole company of blue coats. What brilliant speeches we made and the dinners the good people spread for us, and oh the bewitching female eyes that pierced the breasts of our grey uniforms, stopping temporarily the heartbeats of many a fellow that the enemies bullets were destined soon to do forever.[5]

With such expectations it was not surprising that some men joined who had no business in the army. Some were underage. Others were too old to withstand the rigors of a military campaign. Within the first year many of the initial volunteers would go home. The army sent back those who were too young. The infirm often went home on their own.

The men who volunteered either for state service or for the Confederate army usually came together in companies principally organized in individual counties. Sometimes the core of these units were prewar militia companies. Other units were raised and sometimes supplied by a prominent local citizen, and many of these named themselves after their patron. Frequently they simply took on the names of their communities, and companies such as Bastrop County Rawhides, Crockett Southrons, Grimes County Greys, Grimes County Rangers, Henderson Guards, Panna Marie Grays, Polk Rifles, Sabine Pass Guards, and San Elisario Spies testified to the units' local origins.

These companies were outfitted by the communities where they were raised. They arrived for mustering-in clothed in homemade uniforms of every shade of gray, decorated with piping and trim of every possible military color. Individual companies often possessed two or more different types of weapons—rifles of different gauges, muskets, and even shotguns. A soldier's camp equipment often consisted of what he could rummage from his own household goods.

When organizing into regiments, company names were exchanged for company letters. The Walter P. Lane Rangers, for example, became Company A, 2d Texas Mounted Rifles. Some regiments began to receive basic instruction in tactics. Others were rushed to positions, where action seemed imminent, as soon as enough companies arrived; their training would take place in the field.

The initial enthusiasm for service died quickly among many of the men as they confronted the realities of military service. Army life produced enemies many had never expected. Camp life proved tedious and boring. Robert Hodges of Company H, 8th Texas Cavalry, wrote from Kentucky in the autumn of 1861:

[Our] boys are anxious for a fight. I myself am tired of lazing in camps and doing nothing and wouldn't mind a little brush with the Yanks, just for a change if nothing else. Jack, I tell you what's a fact. This soldiering is poor business. I don't think I ever would like it if I had to do as I have done heretofore, lay in camp.[6]

In addition, many who joined to fight Yankees discovered that the more immediate threat came from epidemic diseases such as measles and small-pox. These ailments wreaked havoc among the new troops. From Nashville, Tennessee, John W. Rabb

of the 8th Cavalry informed his sister that after hard winter campaigning in 1861, the Texas Rangers "got Measles & neumonia in camp which thined the companys down so that each company could not send more than fifty or sixty on a scout."[7] Another member of Rabb's regiment estimated that in this particular epidemic more men died than were killed in all its battles. Ultimately, for every one Southern soldier who died in battle, approximately two would die from disease.

Following the initial enthusiasm, volunteering fell off in Texas and throughout the rest of the Confederacy, and in the spring of 1862 the Confederate government imposed conscription. In the law passed that April, all men ages eighteen to thirty-five were eligible to service. By September the upper limit had been raised to forty-five years old. In February 1864 the age range was expanded to include men between seventeen and fifty. Conscription caused problems among soldiers, who did not want to be joined by men forced to fight. It was also resisted by many at home who did not want to fight.

Nonetheless, thousands of Texans ultimately joined the Confederate Army—as did W. W. Heartsill—out of a sense of duty and for what they considered a just cause. Texas sent twenty-two regiments and five battalions of regular infantry to the war, twenty-eight regiments and four battalions of regular cavalry, and sixteen batteries of light artillery. Approximately two-thirds of Texas Confederates fought in the Trans-Mississippi—that is, in Arkansas, Indian Territory, western Louisiana, or Texas itself. Only three infantry regiments served with the Army of Northern Virginia. The rest were in the Army of Mississippi or the subsequent Army of Tennessee.

In the end, between 60,000 and 90,000 Texans may have seen service in either Confederate or state units. Given the state's military population of 92,145 in 1860 and 110,000 when including those who came of age during the war, the number who ultimately served represented a remarkable proportion of the state's men.

HARDIN R. RUNNELS
albumen print
William DeRyee

The principal supporters of secession in Texas included many distinguished leaders of the Democratic Party. Of these men Hardin Runnels, who had been elected governor over Sam Houston in 1857 only to lose to him in 1859, was one of the most prominent. Runnels, a wealthy planter and slaveowner from Bowie County, had been prominent in the Democratic Party during the 1850s and had served in the Texas House and as lieutenant governor. As governor, he was a strident spokesmen for an aggressive Southern policy against the North. He even favored a renewal of the slave trade. In his farewell address to the state legislature in December 1859, Runnels had said: "It is now clearly demonstrated by the history of the past five years that a deep unchangeable determination exists in the Northern States to assail our dearest political rights, and if possible, destroy our domestic institution. . . . The time has surely arrived when the South should look to her defences."[8] The election of Lincoln as president was the final straw, and Runnels and others took the lead in seeking the state's withdrawal from the Union. *Photo courtesy of Archives Division, TSL*

22

ORAN M. ROBERTS
albumen print

The direction the state would take when the state convention met in January 1861 was clear almost from the beginning. The majority of members were strongly pro-secession and elected Oran M. Roberts as the president of the convention. Roberts, shown in a picture taken between sessions of the convention, came to Texas in 1841 and was a successful lawyer at San Augustine. He was on the state supreme court in 1856. In more recent years, he had become an ardent secessionist and was one of the men who had signed the call for a state convention in 1861. His election indicated that the secessionists controlled the meeting, and they quickly produced an ordinance taking Texas out of the Union. Its wording indicated both the anger and fear of Texans, declaring that the Federal government had failed to protect the citizens of Texas on the frontier; was in violation of the constitutional compact; and now had fallen into the hands of an interest that would use the Federal government as "a weapon with which to strike down the interests and prosperity of the people of Texas and her sister slave-holding States, instead of permitting it to be, as was intended, our shield against outrage and aggression."[9] On February 2, the majority put the ordinance before the convention for a vote. *Photo courtesy of CAH, Oran M. Roberts Papers, CN 08135*

SEVEN WHO VOTED AGAINST SECESSION. *Top:* A. P. SHUFFORD, JAMES W. THROCKMORTON, LEMUEL H. WILLIAMS, JOSHUA JOHNSON; *bottom:* WILLIAM H. JOHNSON, GEORGE W. WRIGHT, THOMAS P. HUGHES
copy print

On the day the convention considered the secession ordinance, the galleries were packed and tension filled the hall of the House of Representatives at the state capitol. The result was a foregone conclusion, but at least some of the members had resisted the strong pressure for decisive action and stood against secession. Applause greeted each vote for secession, but a murmur of disapproval met Thomas P. Hughes of Georgetown when he cast the first "no" vote. When James W. Throckmorton of McKinney cast his nega-tive vote, loud cries issued from the gallery. This friend of Governor Houston refused to vote against the Union, however, and declared that he remained "unawed by the wild spirit of revolution."[10] Seven men, all but Hughes from the northeastern counties of the state, ultimately took their stand against secession. The ordinance carried, however, and the best that the Unionists could achieve was to have it submitted to a vote of the people. *Photo courtesy of Austin History Center, Austin Public Library*

SAMUEL A. MAVERICK
albumen print
William DeRyee

When the convention adjourned to await the vote, it appointed the Committee on Public Safety, which acted immediately to secure the state's military position. One of the committee's more active members was Sam Maverick, a South Carolinian who had come to Texas in 1835. The Yale educated attorney arrived in Texas at the outbreak of the Texas Revolution and was a delegate to the independence convention in 1836. He ultimately established his home in San Antonio and practiced law in that town. He also speculated extensively in Texas land and owned some 300,000 acres at the time of his death. Maverick engaged in politics as well and initially had opposed secession but shifted his allegiances early (as did many other Unionists). In the spring of 1861, he was sent as part of a commission to San Antonio to seek the surrender and removal of Federal troops from the state. On February 8, along with Thomas J. Devine and P. N. Luckett, Maverick met with Gen. David E. Twiggs, commander of the Department of Texas. After the initial meeting, the commissioners were uncertain that Twiggs would surrender peaceably and asked Col. Benjamin McCulloch, who had been authorized by the Committee on Public Safety to raise a cavalry force, to come to San Antonio. Maverick and the others clearly were ready to use force to achieve their ends, and on February 18 General Twiggs finally surrendered his men and agreed to their removal from Texas. *Photo courtesy of Archives Division, TSL*

BENJAMIN E. BENTON
carte de visite

Benjamin E. Benton was one of the recruits who joined Ben McCulloch's Texas state cavalry. A nephew of Ben and Henry McCulloch and a grandnephew of Thomas Hart Benton of Missouri, Ben Benton had moved to Texas with his family while still a child. When only sixteen, he had accompanied the Callahan expedition into Mexico in 1855. In 1861 at the age of twenty-two, Benton joined his uncle at San Antonio, where the hastily enlisted soldiers expected a fight. Twiggs's surrender, however, confronted the Texans with a new problem as Federal troops began to pull out of their frontier posts. McCulloch's command was soon dispersed to patrol the frontier until more permanent arrangements could be made. Benton was sent to Fort Mason to receive the surrender of Capt. Edmund Kirby Smith, and then commanded that post until April. When Henry McCulloch was authorized to organize the 1st Texas Mounted Rifles for frontier duty, Benton enlisted as a private in Company B. *Photo courtesy of LLMVC*

26

SAM HOUSTON
albumen print
William DeRyee

Gov. Houston had opposed secession all along, and while the Committee on Public Safety proceeded to take control of the military situation within the state, the governor campaigned actively against secession. His opposition had complex roots, but at least in part he thought the South could never win a war with the North. A few days before the vote on secession, Houston spoke at Galveston.

Some of you laugh to scorn the idea of bloodshed as a result of secession, and jocularly propose to drink all the blood that will ever flow in consequence of it! But let me tell you what is coming on the heels of secession. The time will come when your fathers and husbands, your sons and brothers, will be herded together like sheep and cattle at the point of the bayonet; and your mothers and wives and sisters and daughters, will ask, Where are they? and echo will answer, where?[11]

The tide ran against Houston, however, and on February 23, voters approved the ordinance of secession by a vote of 46,153 to 14,747. Houston stayed in office, trying to play a moderating role while possibly attempting to once again establish Texas as an independent nation. In March, however, the convention determined that state officers should swear an oath of allegiance to the new Confederate government. While he was loyal to his state, Houston refused to go back on his oath to uphold the Constitution of the United States and instead stepped down from office. *Photo courtesy of Archives Division, TSL*

27

EDWARD CLARK
albumen print
William DeRyee

Edward Clark, the forty-six-year-old lawyer from Marshall who succeeded Houston as governor, brought considerable talents with him to the organization of Texas for war. Among these was his experience as a staff officer for Gen. J. Pinckney Henderson during the Mexican War. He proved to be an effective administrator and quickly raised supplies, organized troops, and began other preparations for defending the state. Under Clark the first Texas regiments for the Confederacy took shape and moved out to service throughout the South. Despite his abilities, Clark's political future was dark. He had run for lieutenant governor as an independent candidate in 1859 and was not part of the Democratic party's leadership. In the regular election for governor held in the fall of 1861, Clark was defeated by Francis R. Lubbock, who was closely connected with Democratic leaders. *Photo courtesy of Archives Division, TSL*

RICHARD B. HUBBARD
albumen print

From the spring of 1861 through the spring of 1862, Texans in large numbers joined the Confederate Army. They came from all across the state and from all classes. As would be expected, prominent planters and slaveowners played a major role in the mustering of the army. Richard Hubbard, a distinguished lawyer, politician, and planter from Smith County, had been a leading secessionist in 1861 and had run for the Confederate Congress. When he lost, Hubbard determined to raise a regiment and, with David Rusk and Oran Roberts, set about organizing the 22d Texas Infantry at Tyler. When men were slow to join, he complained to the military commander in Texas that the lagging enlistments resulted from the facts that his regiment was infantry and that the term of service was three years or the war. To A. A. G. Samuel B. Davis he wrote, "Our people are somewhat unfortunately infatuated on the subject of *Cavalry* and 12 month's service."[12] *Photo courtesy of CRC*

EDWARD CURRIE
copy print

Edward Currie was another of the popular community leaders who took the lead in raising the army. Currie was a well-known physician at Crockett before the war, and in April 1861 he recruited an independent company in Houston County known as the Crockett Southrons. His company was among the first five thousand men who volunteered for service. The Southrons mustered in at New Orleans on August 9, 1861, where they became Company I, 1st Texas Infantry. Currie was elected captain but never saw action. On December 20, 1861, he resigned his commission for unknown reasons and returned home to Texas. *Photo courtesy of CRC*

WILLIAM B. DUNCAN
quarter-plate tintype

William Duncan of Liberty County also came from a well-known plantation family. A native of Louisiana, Duncan immigrated to Texas with his family in 1824 and at the age of eighteen participated in the Texas Revolution. Duncan subsequently served as Liberty County sheriff, tax collector, and county clerk. When the war broke out, it was expected that he would play a role. In 1862 he left behind his wife and six children to join Capt. Ashley Spaight's cavalry company, the Moss Bluff Rebels, comprised primarily of militia from Liberty and Chambers Counties. The company became a part of the 11th Battalion of infantry and cavalry and in June, when Spaight was named lieutenant colonel; Duncan was elected captain. Duncan's unit was virtually wiped out in July 1862 when yellow fever was introduced to Sabine Pass, where the 11th Battalion was stationed. An officer of another company recalled that for almost four months "our principal business was to bury the dead."[13] The 11th Battalion never regained its full strength, and Duncan apparently suffered through the rest of the war from the effects of the disease. *Photo courtesy of Sam Houston Regional Library & Research Center, Texas State Library, Liberty, Texas*

HUGH COOKE
copy print

Young men appeared particularly attracted to what initially looked to be a tremendous adventure. Hugh Cooke, the son of a planter in Waller County, was only seventeen years old when he joined in 1861. Even though he was under the required age, Cooke was accepted for six months service in Company A, 3d Battalion Texas Volunteer Infantry and Cavalry. His unit was sent into Louisiana early in 1862 to try to prevent the Federal capture of New Orleans, and in a skirmish near that city he was left holding the horses so that he would not be hurt. Cooke apparently wanted to fight and called out to his captain: "Cap'n come 'here. They've got me here holding horses; I didn't come here to hold horses. I came here to shoot Yankees."[14] Having fulfilled his term of service, Cooke was mustered out in April 1862, but he soon reentered the army, enlisting in Company C, Waller's Battalion, in April 1864 (in time to see service at the end of the Red River campaign). He remained with the unit through the end of the war. *Photo courtesy of Archives Division, TSL*

EDWIN P. ERATH
quarter-plate ambrotype

Edwin P. Erath was even younger than Hugh Cooke when he joined. Erath had been born in Falls County and was only sixteen years old when he joined the army in March 1862. Special allowances may have been made for him since his company was commanded by his father, George B. Erath. Erath's Company became a part of Speight's 15th Texas Infantry when it mustered into Confederate service at Waco in March 1862. Before Edwin saw battle, however, he was discharged. The surgeon's certificate written that August listed as the reason Erath's "immature age & imperfect development."[15] *Photo courtesy of CAH, George B. Erath Papers, CN 08739*

33

WILLIAMSON MILBURN
copy print

While many of those who rushed to join the army were young, Confederate patriotism was not restricted to youth. Williamson Milburn was too old. A Baptist minister in Smith County, Milburn was fifty-three years old when he joined D. Y. Gaines's Company in Smith County in June 1861. At Dallas the company was mustered in for twelve-months service as Company K, 3d Texas Cavalry. Milburn proved to be a leader in the company, organizing preaching while it was at Dallas, and he was elected 1st lieutenant. When the regiment was reorganized in the spring of 1862 under provisions requiring a longer period of service, many of the younger and older men left—207 of them in all, including Milburn. He returned to Smith County and to his church. Smith County proved more dangerous than the army, though, for Milburn was killed shortly after his return in an argument with a neighbor over a dog. *Photo courtesy of Judson Milburn*

34

EVAN VAN DEVANDER DOUTHET
quarter-plate ambrotype

Ultimately, the majority of soldiers were in their twenties and thirties and, as would be expected, most were neither slaveholders nor planters. Evan Douthet was typical. A native of Tennessee, Douthet had come to Texas about 1850 and worked as a wagoner at Pruitt's Tan Yard in Anderson County in 1860. The census that year showed him possessing only two hundred dollars in personal property. On March 6, 1862, the thirty-four-year-old father of five children enlisted in Company K, 22d Texas Infantry. If he had expected glory, Douthet and his fellow soldiers soon found it in abundantly short supply. From Houston, another member of the regiment described the conditions in a military camp, warning his brother-in-law not to enlist. "My advice to him is, while he has good parents, stay with them and not change a feather bed for the cold ground—mud, water, filth and everything else bad in a camp life, to say nothing of the forty millions of fleas that we are troubled with."[16] For the rest of the war, Douthet and hundreds of others struggled with conditions such as these, conditions that took as great a toll among the soldiers as battle. *Photo courtesy of Dale Snair*

WESLEY COLLINGS
tintype

While the majority of those who joined the army came from the South, an interesting phenomenon was the sizable number of transplanted Northerners who went with their adopted state in secession. Wesley Collings had moved to Red River County with his family from Indiana in 1850. The family owned no slaves and operated only a small farm, but when the war broke out Wesley's brother Robert joined the 1st Mounted Rifles and served on the frontier. Wesley was only sixteen years old in 1861, but he enlisted in the Rosalie Guards, a local militia company at Clarksville. We know nothing of what motivated the young Collings brothers, but Robert served the full term of his enlistment and Wesley probably joined a regular army unit in the Trans-Mississippi later (although there is no record of that service). *Photo courtesy of Mada B. West and Leland E. Stewart*

STOKES'S COMPANY, 4TH CAVALRY, ARIZONA BRIGADE
copy print

The only image of a unit of Texas Confederate soldiers is this photograph of William J. Stokes's company of the 4th Cavalry Regiment, Arizona Brigade. Stokes recruited for the regiment, which had been authorized in February 1863, in Ellis County during the spring of 1864, and this picture is supposed to have been made at that time. The regiment served primarily along the Red River boundary between Texas and the Indian Territory to the end of the war, but it was engaged in no major battles. Some companies of the 4th Cavalry became notorious in Cooke County for depredations carried out against the civilian population, and at the war's end Confederate authorities had been forced to send other cavalry units into that area to suppress the activities of these men. *Photo courtesy of Ellis County Museum*

The Texas volunteers of 1861 and 1862 probably never envisioned what they were about to encounter, but by 1865 the toll that had been taken among them clearly demonstrated the horrors they had faced. Among the first to enter the Confederate service were these men of the "Star Rifles," Company D, 1st Texas Infantry. The company was raised at Linden in Cass County by a Dr. Clopton. Cornelius Curtright's nineteen-year-old bride presented the company with a flag when it left for Jefferson to be mustered in. This image was taken at New Orleans in the summer of 1861 as the 1st Texas was being transported to Virginia. Of these men John and Henry Oliver died from pneumonia at Fredericksburg in 1862, while William Oliver died of wounds received at Chickamauga. Thomas was wounded in the head in 1864 but survived to be paroled at Appomattox along with Absalom. Curtright left the unit in 1862, although he apparently served elsewhere. Of the six men shown here, three are known to have died, 50 percent of this small band of friends. *Photo courtesy of CRC*

"STAR RIFLES." *Standing:* LT. CORNELIUS R. CURTRIGHT, ABSALOM CARTER OLIVER, HENRY OLIVER; *Seated:* JOHN OLIVER, WILLIAM OLIVER, THOMAS FRANCES OLIVER
copy print

Chapter 3

The New Mexico Campaign

And after all our toils and losses of good and noble officers & men, and of wagons and in fact everything save our guns, we have to return to Texas without having benefitted our country one dime's worth.

—WILLIAM L. ALEXANDER

In May 1862 Capt. William Alexander of Company H, 4th Texas Cavalry, wrote to a friend of his in Nacogdoches County of the recently completed Confederate campaign in New Mexico. Of the one hundred men in his company, he had only ten fit for duty. Seven of his men had died in New Mexico and sixteen were prisoners of war. The tale told by Alexander was not a happy one. Defeat had followed what had promised to be inevitable victory, and Alexander blamed his commanding officers for the failure. Their *"masterly* inactivity" had allowed the enemy to concentrate a superior force, and in the end the Confederate captain found "after all our toils and losses of good and noble officers & men, and of wagons and in fact everything save our guns, we have to return to Texas without having benefitted our country one dime's worth."[1]

The New Mexico campaign had been the product of ambitious plans for the expansion of Confederate power in the Southwest. In the summer of 1861, Confederate and Texas authorities consolidated their position within the state and turned to other matters. While ultimately many Texas troops would be shuttled to battlefields east of the Mississippi or to protect the frontiers of the state, many of the first troops mustered in would be used in the West. There, some authorities believed that only a modest force could push Confederate territory to the Pacific and secure for the new nation the three northern states of Mexico. The idea of Manifest Destiny had driven Americans westward for at least four decades by the time of the Civil War. Southerners had held their own unique view of this idea of conquest and occupation and in the 1850s looked to the west and south for new lands for slavery. Under the new Confederacy, these designs took tangible shape in the form of the New Mexico campaign.

Initially, the New Mexico Territory appeared a likely first step for expansionists. In the spring of 1861, the Texas Convention sent Simeon Hart and Phil Herbert as commissioners to New Mexico to negotiate relations with the territory. Both Hart and Herbert were received well by New Mexicans, many of whom were originally from the South. But Federal troops in New Mexico, unlike those within Texas itself, showed no sign of surrendering. Instead, this force of approximately two thousand men began to dig in at Forts Fillmore, Craig, and Union to hold on to New Mexico for the Union.

The first stage of the South's campaign in the West began in May, when Gen. Earl Van Dorn ordered men of the 2d Texas Mounted Rifles under Lt. Col. John R. Baylor from San Antonio to Fort Bliss, where they were to secure the munitions and supplies that had been surrendered by the Federal garrison. When the ambitious Baylor arrived, however, he prepared to do more than the stated mission. He quickly set out to consolidate the Confederate hold over the area and on July 23, 1861, led a small force of 258 men against Fort Fillmore, upriver in the vicinity of Mesilla. The Confederates failed to take the fort but did occupy the town. Two days later the Federals, commanded by Maj. Isaac Lynde, tried to push Baylor's force out of Mesilla but were unable to move the well-positioned Confederates. On July 27, following the loss of his horses in a night raid, Lynde abandoned Fort Fillmore only to be overtaken by the pursuing Confederates. The fall of the fort and the capture of its garrison of nearly 500 men represented a major first step toward seizing control of the region. On August 1, Baylor declared martial law, began to organize the Confederate Territory of Arizona, and proclaimed himself governor. Baylor had been more successful than he originally hoped, but his victory was hardly secure, for he faced the continued presence of Federal forces assembling further upriver at Fort Craig and the hostility of Indians. Only an increase in Confederate military strength could maintain his gains.

The troops necessary ultimately came, but they were not to be in his hands. In June, Henry H. Sibley, who had resigned from the United States Army in New Mexico, reached Richmond with his own plans for a Confederate empire in the West.

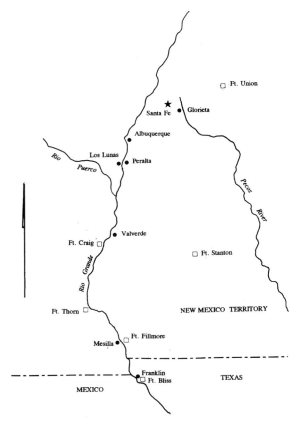

NEW MEXICO CAMPAIGN

Sibley met with Pres. Jefferson Davis and proposed a plan for conquering New Mexico and opening the way to California. The plan was simple: with volunteers raised in Texas, Sibley intended to invade New Mexico from El Paso, using the Rio Grande River as his highway to move against Union positions all the way to Santa Fe. Sibley believed thousands would join his column, and with these reinforcements he planned to move from Santa Fe on to California. In July, Sibley received his commission and command of the Department of New Mexico.

Sibley returned to San Antonio and began to recruit the force he needed for the invasion. The general had hoped to move quickly, but he found Texas military organization to have proceeded slowly and no men available for his use. Units that he organized were recruited specifically for the New Mexico campaign. Encamped along Salado Creek, the general brought together the men who would constitute the 4th, 5th, and 7th Texas Mounted Rifles. They drilled while he struggled to complete the brigade's organization and secure the supplies necessary for a campaign in the inhospitable western country. The brigade did not begin its march to El Paso until October 23, 1861.

General Sibley arrived at Fort Bliss on December 13, having passed his regiments enroute. Sibley found conditions in the Territory of Arizona in considerable disarray. After his initial military successes, Baylor had become convinced that he faced an overwhelming Union force converging on him and was preparing to retreat into Texas as far as Fort Davis. Baylor also was unable to handle the political difficulties that emerged at Mesilla. After being welcomed initially, local inhabitants began to see the Confederate army, busy impressing supplies to maintain itself, as a burden. When he murdered a popular newspaper editor in a street fight, Baylor found that he had lost most local support. Sibley, as a result, was forced to repair civilian affairs as well as plan his invasion.

The last of Sibley's regiments did not reach their camps in New Mexico until the end of January 1862, when companies of the 7th Texas Mounted Rifles finally joined him. Baylor's troops were also integrated into Sibley's command, and the bitter Baylor was shoved aside. Sibley was unable to do much to make his peace with local citizens. As he prepared for his invasion, he was forced to rely on local supplies, just like Baylor, and Sibley's men systematically plundered the surrounding countryside.

Sibley also pursued a diplomatic initiative with the northern Mexican states of Chihuahua and Sonora. Col. James Reily of the 4th Mounted Rifles, a man not particularly popular among his men, was sent to Chihuahua City on January 2, 1862. His mission was to secure promises that Federal troops would not be allowed to move through the state and to negotiate an agreement that would allow Confederate troops to pursue raiding Indians into Mexico. Reily also sought commercial agreements with the Chihuahuan government for the purchase of supplies. Returning with at least some agreements, Reily, with an armed escort of one hundred men, then departed for Sonora (by way of Tucson) for negotiations with the governor of that state.

Early in January, 1862, Sibley ordered his Army of New Mexico to occupy Fort Thorn, forty miles north of Mesilla. It was from this position that he intended to launch his invasion. At Fort Thorn, however, Sibley's men suffered seriously from disease and also from privation as the inadequacy of the army's logistics became obvious. One member of the 5th Mounted rifles recognized that the situation was not good when he wrote to his wife that he hoped for a fight soon. If they had to pursue the enemy northward in the winter he believed that the army would "be worn out and our transportation entirely exhausted before we could overtake them."[2]

Sibley's invasion finally got underway on February 7, 1862, when Tom Green's 5th Mounted Rifles left Fort Thorn. Their goal was Fort Craig, one of the points at which Col. Edward R. S. Canby, the resourceful commander of Federal troops in New Mexico, had begun to concentrate his forces. In the months between Baylor's arrival in the El Paso area and the beginning of Sibley's campaign, Canby had been busy. He virtually had to build an army, since many of his troops were being removed east. Canby had decided to place his remaining force along the approaches to Santa Fe—at Forts Craig, Fillmore, and Union. Canby supplemented the regular troops he retained with regiments of New Mexico volunteers. In all, he had a combined force of approximately 8,000 men to oppose Sibley, whose army never exceeded 3,700 soldiers.

While Canby appeared to have the numerical advantage, he necessarily had to spread his men out to counter any potential Confederate move. This meant that if Sibley could strike before Canby figured out his line of march, he could defeat in detail the scattered Federal garrisons. This was the situation as the Confederates approached Fort Craig. Sibley's column, minus those left behind sick, occupying garrisons, or despatched for special duties, numbered about 2,500 men. Canby's force at Fort Craig was too strong to take in a frontal assault, but at the same time it was ill-trained and probably not much of a match for the Confederates in an open-field fight. By February 16, Tom Green had pushed to within a thousand yards of the fort, trying to get Canby to come out. A skirmish with New Mexico volunteers halted any further advance, though, and that evening Sibley decided to try to flank Canby by moving around the fort on the eastern side of the Rio Grande and regain the main road north after recrossing the river at Val Verde.

On February 19, Sibley's army crossed the Rio Grande at Paraje. After a perilous march through difficult countryside, the Confederates were just to the north of Fort Craig by late afternoon the next day. Canby, recognizing that Sibley was trying to place himself on the Federal line of retreat, sent a small force east of the river on February 20 that engaged the Confederates but failed to stop them. He then decided to try and stop the Rebels from recrossing the Rio Grande at Val Verde. A small advance force left Fort Craig that evening, followed by Canby and the larger portion of the garrison the next morning.

Early on February 21, the Confederate vanguard approached the fords at Val Verde and encountered companies of the 1st and 3d U.S. Cavalry reinforced by New Mexico militia; the 3d New Mexico Infantry joined these units before the main engagement began. Charles L. Pyron's Battalion, at the head of the Confederate column, ran head long into the Federals. Canby brought his main force east of the river, while Sibley's troops hurried to the scene. The 4th Mounted Rifles were the first to arrive; Canby countered by committing more of his own men to

the fight. Sibley did not order in companies of the 7th and 5th Texas until after noon, when it appeared the Federals might turn his right flank. In part, the Confederate effort suffered because Sibley, ill from kidney disease, was unable to move forward and personally direct his units. The resulting frustration of the Texans on the battlefield reached its climax when Capt. Willis Lang's lancer company attacked Canby's lines without any support and was practically destroyed.

That afternoon the battle was renewed when Tom Green arrived and assumed command of the Confederate forces engaged. At the same time, Canby decided to personally direct the Federal forces in battle and ordered an attack aimed at dislodging the Confederate left. The assault seemed on the verge of success when Green ordered an infantry counterattack on the batteries anchoring the left of the Federal line. The Texans succeeded in taking Capt. Alexander McRae's battery in a wild charge and turned the tide of battle. Canby, not willing to risk his command and seeing nearly half of his men already retreating from the field, ordered the rest to return to Fort Craig. The battle had been indecisive, although the Confederate volunteers had managed to drive an army composed largely of Federal regulars from the field. The Confederates lost thirty-three soldiers dead and one hundred and fifty wounded, about 10 percent of the men engaged. The Federals suffered one hundred and ten killed and two hundred and forty wounded. For the Confederates, the most costly loss was that of some one thousand animals—these could not be replaced.[3]

Sibley resumed command that evening. His demand for Canby to surrender Fort Craig was met with a refusal. Canby had not been decisively defeated, and Sibley could not dislodge him from his fortifications. Running low on food and forage, Sibley decided to leave Canby's force in place rather than renew the battle. On February 23, he ordered his column northward again, hoping to seize enough supplies on his advance to sustain the army. Sibley chose to place himself between two enemy forces and effectively cut himself off from his own line of supply in hopes of seizing the rest of New Mexico.

Initially, Sibley's daring move appeared to be working. Little stood in the way of the advancing Army of New Mexico. However, retreating Union forces did what they could to deprive the Confederates of much-needed supplies. On March 2, the Rebel army arrived at Albuquerque to find the place abandoned and desperately needed supplies torched by the Yankees as they left. A member of Sibley's command later remember that on seeing the flames at Albuquerque he "thought of Napoleon and Moscow."[4] The Federals clearly were fighting a battle designed to turn the isolation of New Mexico to their advantage and to deprive the Confederates of much needed provisions.

At Albuquerque, Sibley discovered that the Union forces in New Mexico had all withdrawn to Fort Union, about sixty miles east of the capital. If he was going to consolidate his territorial gains, the Confederate commander had to take Fort Union, but his command was in dire straits. At Albuquerque they husbanded what supplies they could find. On March 8 Sibley ordered nine companies of the 4th Mounted Rifles and five companies of the 7th Mounted Rifles, all under the command of Lt. Col. William Scurry, to the area of Galisteo. There the soldiers' mounts could regain their strength while the detachment blocked the road from Fort Union to Fort Craig. Maj. Charles Pyron was sent on to Santa Fe. The 5th Texas and Green's regiment were to stay in the vicinity of Albuquerque and recover. These units then would move toward Fort Union by crossing the Sandia Mountains. However, Green showed little desire to implement that order. Sibley's goal was to bring all three of these columns together at Fort Union at the end of March.

That spring in New Mexico was hard on the ill-equipped Confederates. When Pyron's command reached Santa Fe on March 10, they discovered that the much-needed supplies they had expected to use had been burned, just like in Albuquerque. Disease and discontent ran rampant among the members of the army. The Yankees added to their problems, for Canby believed that Sibley's army was vulnerable, and although cautious, he urged Federal action to drive the Rebels out of New Mexico. On March 22 Canby began to send patrols north from Fort Craig along the Confederate line of march while a force of some 1,300 men under Col. John P. Slough of the 1st Colorado Volunteers left Fort Union.

Sibley immediately ordered troops at Santa Fe to respond. Green's regiment went south to see investigate Canby's actions while Pyron took a force from Santa Fe east on the Santa Fe Trail to find Slough. On March 25 he reached the western entrance to Glorieta Pass (Apache Canyon), the Trail's route through the Sangre de Cristo Mountains.

On March 26 the two sides met in battle at Glorieta Pass. The previous day, Pyron had discovered the approach of Maj. John Chivington's command. A picket guard posted on a summit of the pass was surprised and captured. Chivington, with about four hundred men, then launched an unexpected attack on Pyron's three hundred Confederates. At first the Texans were uncertain of the size of the enemy force. They apparently confronted only a detachment of cavalry that they outnumbered, and so established a line of battle across the canyon floor and prepared to repel the Federals. Instead, they soon realized that the advancing cavalry had been a feint to force the Confederates to reveal their position. Union infantry, consisting primarily of the 1st Colorado, had moved up the sides of the canyon and now poured a flanking fire into the Rebel line. The Confederates fell back to a dry stream bed to resist the Federals, but a cavalry attack broke through this line and forced the Texans to retreat. While the Union force lost only nineteen men, the Confederates lost twenty-four killed and wounded and another seventy-five captured.

Both sides rushed their main forces to Apache Canyon and on March 28, two days after the initial clash, they came together in the Battle of Glorieta Pass. Scurry reinforced Pyron and, with Green coming up, decided to move into the Pass believing that the Federals had retreated back toward Fort Union. At 11:00 A.M., just past the summit, the Confederate column ran into a Federal line of battle. The terrain provided no room for maneuver, so the two armies ran head long against each other in a five-hour battle during which Scurry's men slowly pushed the Federals back down the Santa Fe Trail. By nightfall the Federals had established a new line in the valley, and Scurry's men made a final charge that failed to break the Union line. That evening, Slough's men fell back ten miles farther down the Trail. The day's casualties had amounted to forty-six dead and sixty wounded Confederates with forty-six dead and sixty-four wounded Federals.

Scurry had won the day, but during the battle Major Chivington's force had found the Confederate supply train at the entry to the Pass. Chivington had already realized the battle was not going as Slough had planned, so he attacked and overwhelmed the three hundred men with the wagons. The Federals then destroyed eighty wagons with much of the hard-won supplies gathered by Sibley, along with a two-gun battery. Scurry, realizing that he could not sustain his army, had little choice but to retreat. Leaving the wounded behind, Scurry's men fell back to Santa Fe.

Sibley regrouped his command at Santa Fe to face what he feared would be a major attack by Slough. At first he received word that Scurry had achieved a great victory at Glorieta, but it quickly became clear that with the loss of the wagon train, Scurry would be forced to retreat. Sibley expected the Federals to follow. He was in danger, but not from Slough, who had retreated to Fort Union. Rather, the threat came from Canby, who had advanced as far north as Socorro by April 2.

At Santa Fe it was clear that the Confederate army was about to disintegrate. Wounded filled the hospitals, and there was little medicine with which to treat them or enough food to feed them. All of the men suffered in the cold evenings because they had no blankets and their clothing was falling apart. Sibley's dream was turning into a nightmare, for there was no place from which supplies could be secured. Worse, the Federals were beginning to press in from the south and the northeast.

Canby arrived at Albuquerque on April 8. He greatly outnumbered the Confederates there but approached cautiously. His timid advance allowed reinforcements under Tom Green to arrive. Canby did not want a general engagement, however, and withdrew into the Sandia Mountains. By doing so, he put himself in a position to be reinforced from Fort Union. While Canby was operating around Albuquerque, Federals at Fort Union, now under the command of Col. Gabriel Paul, began to move into the Santa Fe area. Sibley reacted quickly, withdrawing his entire command from Santa Fe and retreating to Albuquerque. There, he found the situation almost as bleak: the Rebels had supplies enough for only ten days, Canby was about to bring together a greatly superior force, and Sibley's own command was badly depleted by disease and battle. On April 12 he ordered the Army of New Mexico to retreat to Mesilla, where it could await reinforcements he had urgently begged Richmond to send.

The retreat began leisurely enough. Neither the commander nor his men thought the Federals would make any effort to stop them except at Fort Craig. They were wrong. On the evening of April 14, Canby brought his combined forces within striking distance of the Confederates along the eastern bank of the Rio Grande at Peralta. The next morning the Federals attacked. Canby soon realized that the Confederate position was too strong and refused to waste his men in a fruitless assault. Probing for a weakness, skirmishers and artillery encountered a spirited Rebel defense. Sibley realized that Canby had only been feeling out the Confederate position and that he faced an army that in manpower and resources was now far superior to his own. As a result, on the evening of April 15 he moved all of his troops west of the river and put them on the march southward.

Canby showed little hurry after Peralta and opted to shadow Sibley's force as it moved south. In fact, he had no need to hurry for Sibley's force was moving into several potential traps along the river. On April 17 at Rio Puerco, the Rebel column abandoned almost all of its equipment and supplies, taking a mountain trail that led away from the pursuing Federals and around Fort Craig. Canby let them go and moved his force to Fort Craig. The Texans who abandoned the Rio Grande near Socorro faced a one-hundred-mile march before they linked back with the river and the main road. The movement took ten days and involved incredible suffering. Sibley's force finally reached Mesilla on April 24, with only 1,800 of the 2,500 men who had left that town two months before.

The situation was not much better there. Col. William Steele, who had been left in command at Mesilla, had found it difficult to secure enough supplies to maintain even his small command; what he did obtain had been by seizing civilian property. As a result, relations with New Mexican civilians were low, and his foraging parties sometimes met armed opposition. It was clear that Sibley's demoralized command could not be sustained in New Mexico. In June, the Confederates began the difficult march across western Texas headed for San Antonio. On July 12 Colonel Steele and the companies of the 7th Mounted Rifles left behind to hold the territory, by then involved in a virtual civil war with local inhabitants and threatened by the growing presence of Federal forces nearby, also marched back to Texas.

All the effort and all the lives lost had been for nothing. In a report dated March 4, Sibley summed up the prospects for the Arizona Territory, his experiences colored his attitudes. "Except for its geographical position," he concluded, "the Territory of New Mexico is not worth a quarter of the blood and treasure expended in its conquest. As a field for military operations it possesses not a single element, except in the multiplicity of its defensible positions. The indispensable element, food, cannot be relied on."[5] The South would not return to the dream of empire in the Far West.

JOHN ROBERT BAYLOR
copy print

John Baylor, a Texan since 1845 who had dabbled at farming, ranching, law, and Indian fighting, was lieutenant colonel of the 2d Texas Mounted Rifles when ordered to El Paso to take Fort Bliss as the first step to bringing Arizona under Confederate control. He left San Antonio with four companies in June. By July 1 he had secured the surrender of Fort Bliss. An aggressive leader, Baylor then began plans for further operations up the Rio Grande, and on July 23 his forces took the town of Mesilla on the western bank of the river, across from Fort Fillmore. When the fort's garrison tried to retake the town, Baylor showed his combative spirit with his reply: "If you wish the town and my forces, come and take them!"[6] The Federals did not and the following day he attacked Fort Fillmore. The garrison fled, only to be run down and captured as they retreated toward Fort Stanton: a force of nearly four hundred regulars was taken by less than three hundred volunteers. On August 1, Baylor proclaimed martial law, claimed the territory for the Confederacy, and appointed himself military governor. He had ambitious plans to organize an army to move against Tucson, but fear of Federal attacks ultimately paralyzed his efforts. In December, his role in New Mexico ended with the arrival of Gen. Henry H. Sibley and the 4th, 5th, and 7th Texas Mounted Rifles. Sibley assumed command of all forces, and while he remained governor, Baylor's military plans had come to an end. *Photo courtesy of CAH*

48

ARTHUR PENDLETON BAGBY
quarter-plate ambrotype

When Sibley moved upriver against Federal troops at Fort Craig in January 1861, he left Col. William Steele as acting governor of Arizona at Mesilla and Maj. Arthur P. Bagby of the 7th Mounted Rifles in command of a force to protect his line of advance and the Mesilla Valley from Indian raids. Bagby, a native of Alabama, was well suited for the assignment. A graduate of West Point, he had seen service on the Texas frontier at Fort Chadbourne. He had resigned his commission, however, returned to Alabama, and then moved to Gonzales, Texas, in 1858. Perhaps General Sibley's confidence in Bagby was well placed, but the general did his subordinate no favor. The line was protected, but Bagby began to drink. In April one of his captains, Hiram M. Burrows, preferred charges against the major for being intoxicated to the point that he could not perform his duties and for drawing a gun on Burrows. A court of inquiry was not held until after Sibley had been forced to retreat back into the interior of Texas, and by then qualified officers were in too much demand to cashier from the army for drunkenness. A scholar would later observe of Bagby's situation in the Mesilla Valley and subsequent career that "if an officer possessed Bagby's innate warrior characteristics, drinking on duty, or even getting drunk, was no deterrent in gaining promotion and recognition in the Confederate Army."[7] *Photo courtesy of Milo Mims*

THOMAS DUNCAN
carte de visite

In the meantime, Sibley headed toward Fort Craig, the first Federal garrison in the way of a march toward Santa Fe. Rather than trying to take this well-protected fort, Sibley decided to go around the position by marching down the eastern bank of the Rio Grande and recrossing the river at Val Verde. He would then have his army positioned on the Federal line of retreat. Col. Edward R. S. Canby, the Union commander at Fort Craig, sent his troops out to stop the Rebels at Val Verde. Maj. Thomas Duncan, with four companies of the 1st and 3d U.S. Cavalry along with companies from the 3d New Mexico Infantry and the New Mexico militia, advanced to block the Confederates. The first Confederate troops to reach the fords were part of the 2d Texas Mounted Rifles under Maj. Charles L. Pyron. Major Duncan was a veteran of the regular army, having served in the Mexican War, the Navajo Expedition of 1858, and on the frontier throughout the 1850s. He recognized his overwhelming superiority in numbers and aggressively attacked the Confederates, driving Pyron's men back from the river. Across the river, however, Duncan became confused as to how he should proceed and lost the tactical advantage when he dismounted his men and unnecessarily placed them on the eastern bank. *Photo courtesy of U.S.A.M.H.I.*

JOHN WILLIAMS
pastel drawing

Sgt. John Williams of Company E, 4th Mounted Rifles, was among the men that Col. William R. Scurry hurried forward to support Pyron's battalion and to extend the Confederate line to the right. Twenty-two years old, Williams had moved from Georgia to Milam County in 1860. On June 16, 1861, he had enlisted in W. A. Sewell's Milam Guards at Cameron. On the march to New Mexico, his captain had written that John and his brother Tom "are the only ones who make music for us. They fiddle and the boys dance."[8] The captain of another company of the 4th Texas described the situation Williams and the rest of Scurry's men encountered as they moved forward: "Volley after volley met our advance. . . . As we came into line the balls greeted us with the viper's hiss. . . . The enemy's cannon balls came just over our heads, tearing the trees and cutting the limbs. . . . Their minnie muskets were whizzing by in rapid succession, clipping the trees. Now, for the first time, did I fully realize the terror of the battlefield."[9] Despite the heavy fire they encountered, the Texans pushed forward and threatened to flank the Federal position. *Photo courtesy of Don A. Schroeder*

BENJAMIN S. ROBERTS
carte de visite

Lt. Col. Benjamin S. Roberts, another veteran of the regular army, had been sent from Fort Craig by Canby to hold the fords. His five-hundred-man column arrived on the scene as Scurry threatened Duncan's position. Like Duncan, Roberts was a capable officer and quickly grasped the tactical situation. Deploying his artillery on the western bank of the Rio Grande, he advanced infantry over the river on his left to counter Scurry's extension of the Confederate line. Federal fire pinned Scurry's men down and Canby, sensing victory, committed more of his force. Colonel Roberts, reinforced by Federal regulars and two regiments of New Mexico volunteers, was not a man to miss an opportunity. He ordered a general advance along the line that continued to push back the Confederates away from the river, while pouring a merciless fire into their position. *Photo courtesy of U.S.A.M.H.I.*

CHRISTOPHER "KIT" CARSON
(STANDING)
carte de visite

Following a lull in the battle at noon, while both sides replenished ammunition and ate what food they had with them, the Union advance east of the river began again. Canby arrived on the field and assumed personal control of Federal forces. His plan was to wheel his command on the left flank, which was positioned on the Rio Grande. The attack was designed to break the Confederate line and drive the Rebels to the north. At the center of the attack were four companies of the 5th U.S. Infantry and the 1st New Mexico Infantry, composed largely of Spanish-speaking natives of New Mexico and commanded by Col. "Kit" Carson, the well-known mountain man and explorer. Carson had been with his regiment since its formation and had proven to be a strong leader. At Val Verde it was one of the best-trained units at Canby's disposal. The 1st New Mexico had occupied Canby's left through the morning, and now supported with deadly artillery fire they moved forward and hit the left of the Confederate line. The Confederate units collapsed. Sgt. Alfred B. Peticolas of the 4th Mounted Rifles recorded that the men began to fall back, "The close, heavy cannonading on the left showed us that our men could not long hold their lines against the galling fire."[10] "Kit" Carson's men appeared on the verge of breaking through the Confederate position. *Photo courtesy of U.S.A.M.H.I.*

53

TOM GREEN
albumen print

The battle was going badly for the Texans. General Sibley, suffering from kidney disease and possibly incapacitated by the alcohol that he drank for the pain, had withdrawn from the field. At about 1:00 in the afternoon, Col. Tom Green of the 5th Texas Mounted Volunteers, a veteran of the Texas War for Independence, the Mexican War, and two decades of Indian fighting, assumed command and confronted Canby's advance. Extremely popular among his men, Green had a reputation for decisive action and moved quickly. Realizing that the Federal left, held by the battery of Capt. Alexander McRae, was the key to stopping the attack, Green began to concentrate his men on his right, leaving only token resistance under Maj. Henry Raguet on the left. *Photo courtesy of Archives Division, TSL*

THOMAS KENNEDY
sixth-plate ambrotype

Green's right was reinforced at about 3:30 P.M. by six companies under the command of Lt. Col. John S. Sutton. Pvt. Tom Kennedy of Company I, 7th Mounted Rifles, was with this force. Kennedy, nineteen years old, was from Anderson County and had joined the regiment the previous October. As Green watched Canby reinforce the Federal right in order to push back Raguet's troops, he realized that the Federal left was only thinly supported. At this point he ordered the troops he had concentrated on his right to attack McRae's battery. Tom Kennedy joined the mad dash across some six hundred yards of open space toward the Federal cannon. Case shot plowed paths through the attacking Confederates, but they still moved forward. Within forty yards of the battery, they opened fire with shotguns, cutting down the Federal gunners. The effect of the shotgun fire rallied the Confederates who poured onto the battery. When Canby was unable to retake the guns, he decided to withdraw to Fort Craig rather than continue to fight with his disorganized force, ending the fighting that afternoon. Canby decided not to renew the attack the following day, uncertain about his men. Sibley decided to move north, leaving Fort Craig and its garrison in his rear.

As Federal units fled before Sibley's column, they destroyed supplies that were essential for the Confederate army's survival. Nonetheless, by March 23 the Army of New Mexico had reached Santa Fe. *Photo courtesy of J. Dale West*

55

JOHN POTTS SLOUGH
carte de visite

At Santa Fe, Sibley's army still was in the presence of a sizable enemy force, with Federals to the east at Fort Union and Canby's troops still behind him at Fort Craig. The immediate threat appeared to be from those at Fort Union, and Sibley sent the 2d and 5th Texas to Apache Canyon to the block the road along which any attacking force would have to march. On March 26 these Confederates entered the canyon at Glorieta Pass, just as the vanguard of a Federal column arrived. Skirmishing that day was followed by a lull on March 27, while both sides waited for reinforcements to arrive. The Union commander was Col. John P. Slough of the 1st Colorado Infantry, who was every bit as aggressive as his Confederate adversaries. He prepared to move part of his force up the canyon the next morning, while sending four hundred men under Maj. John Chivington to flank the Confederate position. If the plan had worked, Slough would have brought a superior force against the Confederates west of Glorieta Pass. Instead, the Confederates themselves moved forward at about 11:00 A.M. As a result, Slough encountered them much earlier than planned; Chivington would not be in the enemy's rear for hours, and now he had to fight a force that outnumbered his own. As soon as he saw enemy cavalry, the colonel ordered his companies into line of battle across the narrow canyon. Their first volley stopped the Confederate approach, but the Rebels quickly formed for battle and began to push the Federals back. *Photo courtesy of U.S.A.M.H.I.*

56

ISAAC ADAIR
copy print of original tintype

Under the command of Lt. Col. William R. Scurry, men of the 4th, 5th, and 7th Mounted Rifles along with Maj. Charles L. Pyron's Battalion were thrown at the Federal line. The fight quickly turned into a bloody brawl. The terrain was so rough that it was impossible to maintain the integrity of the units, and men from various companies became intermingled. Nonetheless, by mid-afternoon the Federals had been pushed back to a position at Pigeon's Ranch, where they made a vigorous stand. Capt. Isaac Adair of Company H, 7th Mounted Rifles, apparently was with Maj. John Shropshire's column when ordered against the enemy left. Adair, thirty-five years old and a veteran of the United States Army during the Mexican War, had been District Clerk at Crockett in Houston County and had left his wife and three children there when he joined the army. As his column advanced, it was broken up by the rugged terrain and men fell behind. Those who moved forward finally ran into the Federal left, but did not see the Colorado troopers until within only thirty yards of them. The Union soldiers leveled a volley at them that cut down their commander and forced a rapid retreat. Captain Adair fell wounded and was captured by the enemy. *Photo courtesy of CRC*

SAMUEL F. TAPPAN
carte de visite

Lt. Col. Samuel F. Tappan commanded the Federal left flank that Shropshire's men had attacked. Tappan, an abolitionist newspaperman and veteran of the war in Kansas, had been ordered by Slough to hold at all costs a small hill to the west of Pigeon's Ranch that protected the Federal artillery batteries and train. Tappan scrounged up about one hundred men to carry out the assignment. Watching the approach of Shropshire's men, Tappan ordered his men to hold their fire, uncertain at first whether the column might be Chivington's men. He had already mistaken a previous group of Confederates as Colorado Volunteers. When the Federals opened fire, one of Tappan's skirmishers killed Major Shropshire and captured Capt. Denman Shannon. The fire of Tappan's skirmishers "was directed against the head of the still advancing column with such rapidity and effectiveness that the enemy was compelled to retire."[11] Despite Tappan's successful defense of the Federal left, Scurry's attackers had pushed the center farther down the valley, and Tappan was forced to abandon his position to avoid being cut off. *Photo courtesy of U.S.A.M.H.I.*

58

THOMAS H. FENTRESS
ambrotype

With the repulse of Shropshire, the focus of the battle shifted to Pigeon's Ranch, where the Federals had established a strong position, using the ranch buildings as fortifications. Colonel Scurry sent his own men directly at the Federal line while ordering Maj. Henry W. Raguet and Col. Charles L. Pyron to advance on the left and try to flank the enemy position. Thomas H. Fentress of Company A, 4th Mounted Rifles, probably was with Raguet's command as it advanced. Fentress, who was twenty-one years old, was the son of a prosperous slaveowning planter at Prairie Lea in Caldwell County. As was befitting his position in society, he had attended college. The young man left school to be a part of the New Mexico campaign. The fighting on the Confederate left was intense and the terrain made movements difficult. The Federal commander observed that it caused the whole engagement to be "of the bushwhacking kind."[12] Scurry observed that Raguet's and Pyron's men eventually reached the high ground above Pigeon's Ranch and "opened a galling fire upon their left from the rock on the mountain side." Young Fentress, however, was badly wounded in the assault and carried to the rear. *Photo courtesy of CAH, Cased Photograph Collection, CN 05603*

59

WILLIAM READ SCURRY
carte de visite

While Raguet and Pyron moved on the left, Scurry took personal command of the Confederate forces in the center, determined to drive the Federals from Pigeon's Ranch. Scurry, known as "Dirty Shirt" to his men, was another veteran of the Army of the Republic and the Mexican War and, like many other of the Texas commanders, an aggressive leader. The Union position was a strong one, protected by the adobe buildings of the ranch and a heavily stockaded corral, but Scurry unleashed a frontal assault. Faltering at first, the attack pushed forward when Raguet and Pyron began to fire down on the enemy position. The Federals pulled back to a new line, but Scurry, despite receiving several wounds, continued to drive his men headlong against Slough's men who unleashed, in Scurry's words, "a furious fire of grape, canister, and shell upon our advancing troops."[13] *Photo courtesy of Library of Congress, LC-B812-8841*

ALBERT G. WILKINSON
ninth-plate tintype

In the midst of Scurry's savage assault were men such as Albert Wilkinson, 2d sergeant of Company F, 5th Texas Mounted Rifles. The Yegua Notch Cutters, as the company was originally known, was probably named for its member's optimistic belief that they would be notching their guns for Yankees killed and for Yegua Creek in Burleson County, where most of the men came from. Wilkinson was a twenty-three-year-old farmer when he joined the unit in 1861. As he and his comrades continued their advance through Glorieta Pass, the fighting became furious as the Federals made another desperate stand after pulling back from Pigeon's Ranch. Scurry reported that his "brave soldiers, heedless of the storm, pressed on, determined if possible to take their [the enemy's] battery." Despite the determined effort of the Confederates to reach their goal, the Federals successfully pulled their artillery from the field and retreated from what Scurry called "the hardest contested fight it had ever been my lot to witness."[14] The Texan clearly believed that he also had won the day. *Photo courtesy of Martin L. Callahan*

61

JOHN M. CHIVINGTON
carte de visite

The Confederate success at Pigeon's Ranch was a Pyrrhic victory, though. All that the Texans had accomplished in the main fighting was undone when John Chivington's flanking column stumbled upon Scurry's supply train. Chivington, a native Ohioan, strident abolitionist, and presiding elder of the Rocky Mountain Methodist Conference in Colorado when the war broke out, had determined that he could not assist in the battle and pushed his flankers toward the Confederate rear. Surprised by the sudden appearance of the Yankees, the three hundred men guarding the train were quickly driven away, and the Federals destroyed eighty wagons containing Scurry's ordnance and quartermaster supplies as well as the clothing and equipment of the men, ruined two 6-pounder guns, and drove away almost five hundred mules and horses. Scurry had no choice but to fall back on Santa Fe, and Sibley was compelled to abandon his entire enterprise. He had failed to destroy the Union force, which continued to grow, while he was short of supplies. *Photo courtesy of U.S.A.M.H.I.*

62

WILLIAM STEELE
albumen print

It was left to Col. William Steele of the 7th Texas Mounted Rifles to commit the final act of frustration in the campaign. Steele had been left behind at Mesilla to guard Sibley's base of operations. This West Point graduate and veteran of frontier warfare during the 1850s had been left out of the campaign, but the men from his regiment pressed their complaints about General Sibley to their colonel. As a result, Steele forwarded charges against Sibley to the War Department, accusing him of drunkenness, inhumane treatment of the sick and wounded, cowardice, and misappropriation of confiscated goods. The campaign begun with hope and promise ended in a spiritual as well as a military defeat. *Photo courtesy of MOC*

Chapter 4

Hood's Texas Brigade

I'm going to smite them hip and thigh. We ain' guerillas. We're the Army of Northern Virginia.

— PRAXITELES SWAN

It became clear one bleak evening in March of 1861 that he must fight even though he was a Methodist minister and man of peace. Once the decision was made he stopped pacing to tell his wife; she replied simply, "Yes, Mr. Prax. I thought you would." The next day the preacher left for Houston to join the army. He was soon in Virginia where battles on scales that exceeded anything that had occurred in North America waited in his future. The preacher was not much given to philosophizing about why he went to war, but after the Battle of the Wilderness, the question did come up. The preacher was now a captain; he was tired and leaned on his sword as he spoke softly about the matter. ". . . when I came up here, in '61, I had State's Rights on my mind. . . . Now I don't know." Then, his voice grew strong and he added "A Man's bound to fight . . . For what he believes in. He's bound to keep on fighting—that part of it's with him. But whether he wins or not—that's with God."[1]

Rev. Praxiteles Swan is a fictional character in John W. Thomason Jr.'s *Lone Star Preacher,* but his wartime life is a composite of the experiences and spirit of the more than 4,000 Texans who traveled to Virginia to fight. We shall meet the spirit of Praxiteles Swan again among many of the men from the Lone Star State who went east to fight with Gen. Robert E. Lee.

Large numbers of nonfictional Texans began arriving in Richmond, Virginia, in the spring and summer of 1861. The initial eight companies became the nucleus of the 1st Texas Infantry, with four more companies added later. The 4th and 5th Texas Infantry Regiments, totaling twenty companies, began arriving late that summer. None of the Texas companies fought at the First Battle of Bull Run on July 21, 1861.[2]

In the months following First Bull Run, many curious Virginians came out to the Texans' camps near Richmond because they assumed they were going to see a set of wild frontiersmen. The westerners sometime obliged onlookers with a Comanche war-whoop, but it was nothing more than theatrics, since most of the men came from settled counties in east and central Texas. However, the frontier was still close enough to influence their lives so that most of the recruits were familiar with firearms and outdoor living. Many had some rudimentary military training through membership in one of the various militia groups that proliferated after the election of Lincoln.[3] Certainly civilian skills and militia experience were useful, but they were no substitute for the hard training that created disciplined soldiers who acted together as a military unit. That training began in earnest in camps around the Confederate capital in the fall of 1861.

The organizational beginnings of the Texas Brigade in Virginia really started on October 21, 1861, when Louis T. Wigfall, a former U.S. senator and colonel of the 1st Texas Regiment, received his promotion to brigadier general. The next day he assumed command of the three Texas regiments, and sometime in mid-November the units bivouacked near Dumfries, Virginia. It was the first time that all the Texans were physically together; they were later joined by the 18th Georgia Infantry, which became part of the brigade. It soon became common knowledge among most of the men that Wigfall was an untalented officer whose real interest was in politics. On February 21, 1862, he assumed a seat in the Confederate Senate, a post to which he won election on November 16, 1861. Thirty-year-old John Bell Hood, the man whose name would be forever associated with the Texas Brigade, then assumed command of the four regiments. Hood's connection to the Lone Star State began in the mid-1850s when, as a young lieutenant in the 2d United States Cavalry, he fought Indians on the Texas frontier. Since September 30, 1861, Hood had been colonel of the 4th Texas Infantry and had already established himself as a talented regimental commander. On March 6, 1862, he was promoted to brigadier general. Hood soon developed a well-earned reputation as one of the Confederacy's most aggressive generals, and the troops he commanded became respected as hard-hitting infantrymen.

Since coming to Virginia, the Texas regiments had seen little action beyond a few scouts and several minor skirmishes along the Occoquan River in Northern Virginia. Like most soldiers during the winter of 1861–1862, the men were ravaged by disease, but by that spring they seemed fit and as ready for combat as most of the largely untried troops in both armies.

The Texans were in their first real fight on May 7, 1862, at Eltham's Landing. Earlier, Maj. Gen. George B. McClellan, commander of the Federal Army of the Potomac, finally tried to seize the initiative in his campaign on the Virginia Peninsula and began his long-awaited advance against Richmond on April 4, 1862. However, he quickly became bogged down in front of the Rebel defenses strung across the Peninsula at Yorktown. McClellan's adversary, Gen. Joseph E. Johnston, kept the timid Federal commander in place for a month. On May 3, 1862, Johnston ordered a retreat because he feared that McClellan was about to use the amphibious mobility available through the U.S. Navy to flank the Rebel position. Once McClellan understood that Johnston was withdrawing, he did attempt such a flanking maneuver by sending Brig. Gen. William Franklin's division up the York River to Eltham's Landing, where he hoped to ambush Johnston's supply trains moving toward Richmond. Hood's soldiers led the column that Johnston sent to counter the move. On May 7 the Texans played the prominent role in driving Franklin's Federals back to the river and their U.S. Navy support. The encounter cost the Texas regiments fifteen dead and twenty-five wounded.[4]

Hood's aggressive attack ensured the safety of Johnston's supplies, but the retreat continued. By mid-May, Johnston had established a new defensive line a few miles from Richmond, and McClellan's men were preparing for another siege. Hood's brigade settled in a few miles northeast of the capital near the little village of Mechanicsville. Johnston had extracted his men from a dangerous situation, but the Union army was in sight of Richmond, an intolerable situation to the Rebel government.

Johnston, after much prodding by Pres. Jefferson Davis, finally decided to launch a limited offensive. He attacked early on the morning of May 31 near Seven Pines, but almost from the beginning his plan misfired. The most important result of the battle was the wounding of Johnston that evening. He was replaced by Gen. Robert E. Lee, who quickly saw the futility of continuing the offensive and broke off the battle around noon the next day. The Texas Brigade came under artillery fire on May 31 and was engaged in minor skirmishing the next day, but the regiments suffered only twenty-one casualties in the failed offensive at Seven Pines.

Lee's disengagement did not mean that he planned to abandon offensive operations, but rather that the general needed time to develop his own plan. By late June, Lee was ready. On June 25, 1862, his offensive began to unfold against a Union probing attack near Oak Grove. McClellan's troops recoiled from the Confederate advance, but the Federals withdrew in good order. Brig. Gen. Fitz-John Porter, with 30,000 men, blunted Lee's attack on June 26. The next morning he established a particularly strong position on the low ridges overlooking a swampy stream known as Boatswain's Creek. The defensive positions were in the vicinity of Gaines' Mill, and it became the scene of the first of many killing fields for the Texans. Hood's brigade, which had been strengthened by eight companies of South Carolina troops known as Hampton's Legion, arrived on the battlefield around 4:30 P.M; by then the battle was over two hours old. The Texans deployed near the center of the Confederate line and lapped around each side of Col. Evander Law's brigade. Law and Hood's men, in a splendid charge, broke through the Union entrenchments and forced Porter to withdraw. Hood's brigade suffered 571 casualties at Gaines' Mill; most had come during the bloody struggle that ended the day's fighting. The greatest losses were in the 4th Texas, which suffered 253 casualties, and the 18th Georgia, which lost 145 men.[5]

Gaines' Mill was the first clear victory in Lee's offensive and, more importantly, it was a psychological defeat for McClellan, who was now convinced that he had no option but to order a general retreat. Over the next several days, Lee tried to destroy the retreating columns, but actions at Savage's Station and Frayser's Farm were indecisive. The final attack in the offensive occurred on July 1, 1862, when Lee ordered a series of uncoordinated attacks against the impregnable Union positions on Malvern Hill. His columns were repulsed with terrible losses. Hood's battered brigade was not involved at either Savage's Station or Frayser's Farm, and they were held in reserve during the tragic assaults against Malvern Hill. Even so, they did lose 52 soldiers from the withering Federal artillery fire that dominated the Malvern Hill battlefield.[6] In seven days of hard campaigning, Lee's men had driven the Federals from the outskirts of Richmond and had inflicted 16,000 casualties on the enemy. Lee, at a cost of 20,000 casualties, had shown his preference for the offensive, and the performance of Hood's brigade at Gaines' Mill personified that offensive spirit.

Less than a month after the end of the Seven Days' Battles, the divisional commander of the Texans went on sick leave and Hood assumed command of the two-brigade division. Since Hood did not know if or when his superior would return, he maintained temporary control over the Texas Brigade. By then Lee's attention had already turned northward, where a second army under Maj. Gen. John Pope protected the Union capital. Lee, who was between Pope and McClellan's armies, decided to strike before the two forces could unite. During late July and early August, Lee shifted his forces to north-central Virginia. On August 29, 1862, elements of Pope and Lee's armies began fighting near the old Bull Run battlefield. Hood's division, including his Texans, arrived on the battlefield around 10:00 A.M. They were part of Maj. Gen. James Longstreet's troops, who had come to reinforce the outnumbered soldiers of Maj. Gen. Thomas "Stonewall" Jackson. The Texas Brigade filed into line next to Jackson's men and formed the hinge between the two wings of the Rebel army. It took most of the day for the rest of Longstreet's troops to arrive, and around twilight Hood's brigade fought a short but bitter engagement against the enemy. The next afternoon Hood's Texans participated in Longstreet's devastating attack, which crushed the left wing of the Union army and drove everything before it. Again, the Texas Brigade's price for the victory was terrible. The 18th Georgia once more suffered heavily, having 19 men killed and another 114 wounded. The 5th Texas, which had escaped much of the slaughter during the Seven Days' Battles, was not as fortunate at Second Bull Run, where the regiment had 15 soldiers killed and another 224 wounded. The losses sustained by the 5th Texas were the highest of any Rebel unit in the fight. Total casualties for the brigade were 628 men.[7]

Lee had won an impressive victory at Second Bull Run and was now prepared to carry the war into the North. For three days during early September 1862, Confederate infantry crossed the Potomac River and began moving through the Maryland countryside. A strong column under Jackson advanced toward Harper's Ferry and eventually captured the Union garrison there on September 15. The Texans crossed into Maryland on September 6. Hood's command was part of Longstreet's divisions, whose units were eventually strung out between the Potomac River and Hagerstown, Maryland. Meanwhile, on September 13, Lee's campaign was placed in jeopardy when a copy of his marching orders fell into Federal hands. At the time, the Rebel forces were badly scattered, but as soon as Lee learned of McClellan's good luck, he began concentrating the Army of Northern Virginia several miles south of Hagerstown near Sharpsburg on Antietam Creek.

The Texas Brigade, now under the temporary command of Col. William T. Wofford of the 18th Georgia, crossed over Antietam Creek during the early afternoon of September 15, 1862. It eventually took a position on the far left of the line on the Hagerstown Pike, near the Dunkard Church. Late the next day the brigade was engaged in a brief firefight. That evening, Hood's men were withdrawn and placed in reserve, but before they left, the soldiers could already hear Federal reinforcements moving into position.

Early on September 17, 1862, the fighting began with a powerful Union assault against the left wing of Lee's army. The Confederates in that sector were unable to stem the offensive and called for help. Around 6:00 A.M. Hood's division, which contained slightly more than 2,000 effectives, received orders to immediately return to its old position near Dunkard Church. Within a few minutes Hood's men were almost engulfed by "an immense force of the enemy," and by the general's own account, his infantrymen were in "the most terrible clash of arms, by far, that has occurred during the war."[8] The battle raged with great fury until about 9:00 A.M., when the determined defense by the Texas Brigade finally helped blunt the massive attack. Around 10:00 A.M. the remnant of Hood's old brigade withdrew. It had taken 854 men into battle and suffered 519 casualties, or slightly over 60 percent of its numbers. The 1st Texas was practically destroyed, suffering 186 casualties out of 226 men present on the day of the battle. The regiment had lost 82 percent of it soldiers, a percentage that was unmatched by any other regiment either North or South during the war.[9] Lee's army had survived the single bloodiest day of the Civil War, but his offensive was over. On the evening of September 18, the Rebel army, under cover of darkness, began withdrawing to Virginia.

In less than three months and in an equal number of great battles, the Texas Brigade had suffered over 1,700 casualties, representing approximately 43 percent of the unit's authorized numbers.

Throughout the rest of the war, it never again faced such concentrated losses, but the damage was done: Hood's brigade, like other Southern units, could never replace such losses.

After Antietam, Lee reorganized the Army of Northern Virginia's brigades more generally along state lines. He also approved promotions to replace many of the field commanders who either had been casualties of the year's campaign or did not meet Lee's rigorous performance standards. Lee, who had great confidence in Hood's fighting spirit, recommended his promotion to major general and significantly increased the strength of the division by adding two brigades of Georgians. Hood's division remained with James Longstreet, who was promoted to lieutenant general and given command of the First Corps. Col. Jerome B. Robertson, who led the 5th Texas, was promoted to brigadier general and assumed permanent command of Hood's old brigade. Both the 18th Georgia and Hampton's Legion left the brigade, while the only unit from Arkansas, the 3d Infantry, joined the Texans. The Texans and Arkansans remained together in the First Corps until the end of the war.

The four regiments were present on December 13, 1862, during the Battle of Fredericksburg, but they saw almost no fighting as Lee easily defeated the Army of the Potomac. In February 1863, increased Union activity southeast of Richmond forced Lee to detach forces to counter the threat. He sent Longstreet with the divisions of Hood and Maj. Gen. George Pickett to block the Union forces in that area. The next several months Hood and his men operated against the strong Union garrison at Suffolk, Virginia. The siege of Suffolk itself lasted from April 11 until May 4, 1863. Here the Texans had their first taste of sustained trench warfare with its harassing fire and muddy, cramped living conditions. On May 3, 1863, the Texas Brigade finally pulled out of the trenches with orders to return to the Army of Northern Virginia; by then Lee had already sprung a great trap at Chancellorsville and

was in the process of winning his greatest victory against the Federals.

The Texas Brigade was with Lee when the general launched his second invasion of the North. On June 6, 1863, the Texans left camp and soon afterward were slogging through a heavy rainstorm as they marched toward Pennsylvania. The first troops to participate in the greatest battle of the Civil War began concentrating around the little town of Gettysburg on June 30, 1863. At dawn on the next day, July 1, fighting began between Union cavalry occupying the town and the leading elements of Lee's infantry. Shortly after 10:30 A.M. Federal infantry began arriving on the field. The fighting spread as both sides began moving troops toward the expanding battle. The Texas Brigade arrived on the battlefield early on the morning of July 2 and soon took up positions on the right wing of the Rebel army. That morning Lee decided to attack and overwhelm the Federal left. Longstreet and Hood were not pleased with the plan, and their concerns grew when the two saw the actual strength of the Federal positions. Hood especially feared a direct assault and firmly believed that the position could be outflanked; he made three requests to be allowed to make such a maneuver. Each time he was refused.

The Texans were in the first assault line and went into action around 4:00 P.M. On their front was a rock-strewn area known as the Devil's Den; in the distance were two prominent hills known as Round Top and Little Round Top. Both the broken terrain and the furious defense by the Federals threw the attacking formations into disarray, but the jumbled mass of Rebels continued to press on until enemy resistance became too great. Hood was badly wounded early in the attack, and six senior officers of the Texas Brigade also fell. The next day events shifted to the center of the battlefield, where Lee ordered a grand assault of some 12,000 infantry. The attack, commonly called Pickett's Charge, was a slaughterhouse for the Rebels. For the first time

Lee had been badly defeated, and on July 4 he began withdrawing his battered army to Virginia. The fight at Gettysburg had cost the Texas Brigade another 597 casualties; most had occurred in the three-hour fight around the Devil's Den.

The Texas Brigade remained inactive until early September 1863 when it was transferred west. The unit was part of the two divisions from the First Corps that Longstreet took to north Georgia to reinforce Gen. Braxton Bragg's Army of Tennessee. On September 19, 1863, the brigade was heavily engaged in the Battle of Chickamauga, where Bragg's forces made some gains but the fighting was largely indecisive. The next day Longstreet's Texans were among eight Rebel brigades that stumbled into a half-mile gap on the right side of the Federal lines. The attacking Confederates shattered the Union right and sent the broken Federals streaming toward the protection of Chattanooga, Tennessee. However, the stubborn defense on the Federal left prevented their total defeat. The Texas Brigade took approximately 1,300 soldiers into the campaign and lost 570 men in the two-day battle near Chickamauga Creek.[10] Hood, who had barely recovered from his wound at Gettysburg, was struck in the right thigh by a minié ball and subsequently had his leg amputated. The men of the brigade never served under their old commander again.

Bragg had inflicted a decisive battlefield defeat on his opponents but was unable to exploit the success. The First Corps participated in the siege of Chattanooga until early November, when Longstreet's men pulled out of the line and headed east; they were moving toward Knoxville, with the objective of recapturing East Tennessee for the Confederacy. Neither Longstreet nor his subordinates performed well in that campaign. Eventually the First Corps abandoned operations around Knoxville and returned to the Army of Northern Virginia. The five-month campaign did nothing to enhance the reputation of its leaders, but it did wear down the physical, material, and moral conditions of the soldiers.

When the men of the Texas Brigade rejoined Lee, they were without Robertson, who had been removed by Longstreet. His replacement, Brig. Gen. John Gregg, was also a Texan but had never served with these three regiments from the Lone Star State. He would be the last general officer to command the brigade.

On May 5, 1864, Gregg led his men toward the fighting in the Wilderness. It was a long, hard march and around twilight the brigade stopped to rest for the evening. That night they received orders to resume the march so they could reach the battlefield by dawn; they had ten miles to go. On the morning of May 6, 1864, a Federal assault wrecked two Rebel divisions and crumbled Lee's right flank. Two of Longstreet's advancing brigades, including the men from Texas and Arkansas, pushed their way through the retreating Rebels and formed a new battle line. The counterattack of the Texas Brigade began under the watchful eye of Lee who, in the heat of battle, suddenly moved through the advancing troops as if he planned to lead the attack personally. The Texans, fearing that their great chief might be killed, balked and began shouting "Lee to the rear, Lee to the rear!" Lee finally relented, but only after several dozen Texans broke ranks and tried to lead the general's horse away from the front line. The timely arrival and determined counterattack allowed the rest of the First Corps to come up and seal the hole that the Union assault had ripped in the Confederate lines.

On May 7, 1864, the Federals began moving east toward Spotsylvania Court House in the first of several great turning movements against the Army of Northern Virginia. During the following weeks, the Texas Brigade fought at Spotsylvania Court House (May 8–21), North Anna (May 23–26), and Cold Harbor (June 1–3). In each encounter Lee and his troops blunted the Federal assaults, but every battle brought the enemy closer to Richmond. On

June 12, 1864, Lt. Gen. Ulysses S. Grant broke contact with Lee's forces and redeployed the bulk of the Federal army twenty-three miles south of the capital. His objective was the railroad line that ran through Petersburg, Virginia. Lee again managed to block Grant's advance, but now the Rebel army was pinned down in the trenches that protected Richmond and Petersburg.

The Texas Brigade spent the next ten months in the trenches that protected Richmond. Most of that time they were stationed near the capital while the bloodiest fighting in the long siege occurred farther to the south near Petersburg, where Grant applied continuous pressure against the Confederate rail network that kept Lee's army alive. Nevertheless, the brigade was engaged in at least six actions around Richmond which added more names to the casualty list. Their worst fight during the siege occurred on October 7, 1864, in the first engagement at Darbytown Road. There the brigade, numbering no more than 450 men, suffered upwards of 100 casualties.[11] Among the slain was the brigade's commander, Brig. Gen. John Gregg, who was shot through the neck and killed instantly.

On April 1, 1865, Lee's position around Petersburg finally collapsed. The next day he issued orders for what remained of his army to abandon the trenches.

His aim was to break off contact with the pursuing army so he could first resupply his hungry men and then turn south for a junction with Gen. Joseph E. Johnston's Confederate forces in North Carolina. However, the Union pursuit was relentless. Late in the afternoon of April 8, 1865, the leading elements of Lee's army began arriving at Appomattox Court House; the Texas Brigade guarded the rear of the battered force. The next day, word spread through the ranks that the way was blocked by Union infantry and that Lee had decided to surrender. The formal capitulation took place on the morning of April 12, 1865; only 617 men remained with the colors of the Texas Brigade. Since the war began, an estimated 4,346 soldiers had enlisted in the three Texas regiments. Of that number, 736 members were slain in battle while another 643 men died of disease. Non-fatal casualties, including men who were wounded more than once, totaled 1,928. The number of those wounded who were able to return to the ranks is not known, but given the nature of Civil War wounds, many of the injuries probably prevented any further military service. Another 505 men were taken prisoner.[12] The balance of the soldiers were either transferred, discharged, or simply deserted. Hood's Texas Brigade had paid a bloody price for the Confederacy.

JOHN BELL HOOD
copy print

John Bell Hood, who would become the Confederacy's youngest full general, was born in Owingsville, Kentucky, in 1831. Twenty-two years later he graduated from West Point, standing a poor forty-fourth in a class of fifty-two young men. In 1855 he joined the 2d U.S. Cavalry and was soon fighting Indians in Texas. Two days after the surrender of Fort Sumter, Hood, who was angry because his home state had not yet joined the new Confederacy, resigned from the Federal army. On September 30, 1861, he was named colonel of the 4th Texas Infantry, which was one of three units from the Lone Star State that fought with the Army of Northern Virginia. Hood quickly established his reputation as a talented commander, and on March 6, 1862, he was promoted to brigadier general. Four days later

Hood assumed permanent command of the Texas Brigade. He maintained direct command of the brigade for slightly less than five months before receiving temporary control of the division, but during that brief time his men became known as one of Lee's most aggressive units. Hood's offensively-minded temperament later led to disaster when he commanded the Army of Tennessee, but that same aggressiveness made him an excellent leader at both the brigade and division levels. To these men from Texas, he would always be their special leader, and the unit would forever carry the sobriquet of "Hood's Texas Brigade." *Photo courtesy of the Eleanor S. Brockenbrough Library, MOC*

By the late fall of 1861, most of the men on the initial rosters of the three Texas regiments who fought in the East were in Dumfries, Virginia. The winter of 1861–1862 was not much different from most Virginia winters, which could be surprisingly cold, windy, and snowy for a Southern state; it is doubtful if many Texans had experienced such conditions before. Whenever possible, the men built rude huts with mud-chinked log walls and tent roofs to protect them from the elements. What heat they had usually came from small firepits that were vented through stick and mud chimneys. Company officers often required the men to build a more substantial log cabin to serve as a mess. These three messes belonged to men in the 1st Texas Infantry and are typical of such structures. Throughout the history of western armies, small unit messes have commonly served as social institutions that bound soldiers together.

In Civil War camps there was always work to be done. Most soldiers pulled fatigue duty almost daily and guard duty in rotation. If the weather permitted, the men practiced company drill and sometimes trained at the regimental level. After duty hours the soldiers often relaxed in the messes by visiting, playing cards or checkers, and gambling. Soldiers found winter-camp routine boring, but the mess helped make life a bit more tolerable. The men posing for the photographer are probably members of the particular mess seen behind them, and they may have been assigned to cook the meal on the day these photos were taken.[13] *Wigfall's Mess courtesy of Martin Callahan; Beauregard's Mess courtesy of J. Dale West; unknown mess courtesy of The Rosenberg Library, Galveston, Texas*

Wigfall's Mess, Beauregard's Mess, and Unknown Mess
glass negatives

JOHN BEVERLY HENDERSON
copy print

John Beverly Henderson was from Marion County, Texas, and enlisted for one year in the Star Rifles in New Orleans on June 6, 1861. The Star Rifles was one of eight Texas companies that arrived in Richmond, Virginia, during the summer of 1861. They were eventually joined by four more companies to become the 1st Texas Infantry. Henderson's unit became Company D, and he held the rank of 3d corporal. Henderson was present when Hood's brigade fought its first major action of the war at Eltham's Landing on May 7, 1862, but by then he had been reduced to the rank of private. At Eltham's Landing, Hood's brigade was responsible for stopping a Federal effort to ambush the Confederate supply trains that were withdrawing up the Virginia Peninsula toward Richmond. The worst fighting fell on the 1st Texas Infantry, which had twelve men killed and another nineteen wounded. The fight at Eltham's Landing was a small affair and the losses were trifling compared to what lay ahead on future battlefields. Still, the Texans had performed well and their service was duly noted by Pres. Jefferson Davis. Henderson escaped injury in the brigade's first fight, and he would be with his regiment a little over a month later when, at Gaines' Mill, the Texas troops first experienced the real slaughter that occurred during major Civil War battles. *Photo courtesy of CRC*

74

JOHN PORTER SMITH
copy print

John Porter Smith enlisted in Livingston, Texas, on August 24, 1861, as a private in the Polk County Flying Artillery; he had just turned nineteen years old. At the time of his enlistment the Confederacy needed foot soldiers rather than artillerymen, and Smith's unit was accepted into service as Company K, 5th Texas Infantry.

On June 25, 1862, Smith was with the 5th Texas when Lee began his initial advance to drive the Union Army away from Richmond. Two days later, around 4:00 P.M., the 5th Texas and the four other regiments of Hood's brigade neared Gaines' Mill. There, along a low ridge that dominated Boatswain's Creek, an entrenched line of Union soldiers had been holding their own against a series of badly coordinated Rebel attacks that had begun around 2:00 P.M. Lee was by then in the third day of his offensive; he had driven the Federals back but the Army of Northern Virginia had yet to win a clear victory. He had to break the Federal line at Gaines' Mill if the offensive were to continue. Lee selected Hood's command and another brigade to attack the center of the Union line. Hood placed the 5th Texas in the center of his line, and around twilight the infantry moved forward. When the fight ended, the 5th Texas had suffered seventy-five casualties, including thirteen fatalities. Smith was slightly wounded but rejoined the regiment before the next campaign began. *Photo courtesy of CRC*

JOHN MARSHALL
ambrotype

Late on the afternoon of June 27, 1862, Col. John Marshall led the 4th Texas Infantry onto the Gaines' Mill battlefield. Marshall, who was born in Virginia in 1812, had settled in Texas in 1854. Earlier he had lived in Mississippi and had been both a friend and political ally of Jefferson Davis. In Texas, Marshall was active in politics and chaired the Democratic State Convention from 1858 until 1861. He also purchased part of the *Austin State Gazette* and used both the paper and his political office to push for secession. When the war began, Marshall was determined to see Texans go to Virginia, because he knew that the East would be the major theater of operations and that the Lone Star State needed to be well represented there. When the 4th Texas organized in September 1861, Marshall was appointed lieutenant colonel; he became colonel of the regiment when the commander of the 4th Texas, John Bell Hood, was promoted to brigadier general.

At Gaines' Mill, Marshall's men were in reserve when Hood's brigade began advancing. The other assaulting regiments struggled through "dense woods and ugly marsh which totally concealed the enemy."[14] Their attack had hardly begun before Hood saw open ground on his right that ran the entire distance to the Federal entrenchments. Hood assumed direct control of his old regiment and brought the 4th Texas forward to attack through the clearing. Early in the advance, Marshall was on horseback near the head of his troops when he was struck in the neck by a minié ball and died instantly. *Photo courtesy of the Archives Division, TSL*

WILLIAM DAVID ROUNSAVALL
copy print from a
sixth-plate ambrotype

William David Rounsavall enlisted as 3d lieutenant in the Sandy Point Mounted Rifles at Athens, Texas, on July 11, 1861. On September 30, the company mustered into the Confederate service in Richmond, Virginia, as Company K, 4th Texas Infantry. At Gaines' Mill, the 4th Regiment succeeded in breaking the Federal line and helped force the enemy to withdraw. Only six of the unit's thirty-eight company level officers were not wounded or killed in the terrible fight. Rounsavall's right arm was shattered by a shell fragment, and doctors removed the limb on June 29, 1862. He was discharged from the service on September 12, 1862, and returned to Texas. Forty-four of his brother soldiers had died in the assault and another 208 had been wounded. Brigade losses totaled 611 men.[15] It was the bloodiest day of the war for the 4th Texas Infantry. *Photo courtesy of CRC; original image owned by Debra Rounsavall Mueholland*

Just thirty-three days after Gaines' Mill, a different Texas regiment was decimated at the Second Battle of Bull Run. Capt. James Daniel Roberdeau was one of the men who participated in that fight. Roberdeau was born in Fairfax County, Virginia, on February 6, 1830, and moved to Texas in 1858. When the war began, he was living in Colorado County, Texas, and helped raise the volunteers that became Company B of the 5th Texas Infantry. Roberdeau enrolled as 1st lieutenant on July 10, 1861, and was promoted to captain several weeks before Gaines' Mill. Years after the war, a fellow soldier remembered the captain as a disciplinarian who was, nevertheless, fair with his men.[16]

Hood's soldiers, including Roberdeau, arrived on the Bull Run battlefield on August 29, 1862, and suffered a few casualties that day. The next afternoon Captain Roberdeau commanded the 45 men of his company when they and over 25,000 veterans of Longstreet's divisions fell on the left wing of the unsuspecting Federals. When the fighting ended, the 5th Texas had suffered 214 casualties. Company B's losses were put at 26 men, including Roberdeau, who was wounded in the right arm. Much of the slaughter had occurred when the Texans battled the 5th New York Fire Zouaves. The New Yorkers suffered even more than the Texans, losing 297 of their number. When the battle finally ended, the hillside where the two regiments had fought was "literally covered with red jackets and gray uniforms."[17]

JAMES DANIEL ROBERDEAU
copy print from *Confederate Veteran*

ELBERT S. JEMISON
copy print

Eighteen days after Second Bull Run, one of the three regiments of Texas troops in Lee's army was practically destroyed on the Antietam battlefield. One of the soldiers who participated in that fight was 1st Lt. Elbert S. Jemison of Company G, 1st Texas Infantry. Jemison had mustered into the service at Palestine, Texas, on June 23, 1861, and was present until he was slightly wounded in the left breast at Gaines' Mill on June 27, 1862. At that time he commanded Company G. Jemison's wound kept him away until September 12, 1862. When Jemison returned to the 1st Texas, his captain was acting as major of the regiment, so the lieutenant assumed temporary command of his old company.

On the morning of September 17, 1862, the Texas Brigade was in reserve when the Federals attacked in seemingly overwhelming numbers. The Texans quickly came forward to reinforce the line. Jemison led his men as they emerged from the woods and entered a field of clover. Canister and shot tore into the ranks as the 1st Texas crossed the open space, entered a cornfield, and encountered enemy infantry. The commander of the regiment, Lt. Col. P. A. Work, could not restrain his men: they rushed toward the Federals. When the Texans' momentum ended, they were at least 150 yards ahead of any supporting regiment and in danger of being encircled. Fortunately, Work managed to withdraw his men from their precarious position. The 1st Texas had taken 226 soldiers into battle and had lost 186 men and the regimental colors.[18] This loss of 82 percent is the highest of any regiment during the Civil War. Jemison was shot in the hip and thigh; he did not return to his company until shortly after the Battle of Gettysburg. *Photo courtesy of CRC*

RICHARD AND JOHN M. PINCKNEY
quarter-plate ambrotype

Richard and John Pinckney joined the Grimes County Greys on July 19, 1861. The company was accepted into the army at Richmond, Virginia, on September 30, 1861, as Company G, 4th Texas Infantry. Richard became a musician while his brother, John, remained a private. The brothers served with the regiment when it fought at Gaines' Mill and later at Second Bull Run. On September 17, 1862, Richard and John were with approximately 200 other soldiers of the 4th Texas who entered the cornfield on their front. A member of the 4th Texas later recalled that the supply of fresh Union troops "seemed inexhaustible" and that the firing was so intense "the earth and sky seemed to be on fire."

The 4th Texas eventually withdrew from the cornfield and took up defensive positions near Dunkard Church, "where they remained about an hour defiantly waving their flag over empty muskets."[19] Ten men had died and another 97 were wounded in the desperate fight.[20] Richard was not injured; in April 1863 he transferred to the naval cadets but later returned to the regiment. Pvt. John Pinckney was wounded at Antietam; he rejoined the regiment and was injured again at the Battle of the Wilderness on May 6, 1864. John also recovered from this wound and surrendered with the 4th Texas at Appomattox. *Photo courtesy of Roger Pinckney*

80

John Nathaniel Henderson
copy print

John Nathaniel Henderson enrolled in the Dixie Blues on July 19, 1861. Most of the men in the company were from Washington County, Texas. On August 8, 1861, Private Henderson and his comrades were accepted into the service as Company E, 5th Texas Infantry. In May 1862 Henderson was promoted to 3d corporal and was with his men when they marched into the cornfield at Antietam. Less than three weeks earlier, the 5th Texas had endured over 250 casualties at Second Bull Run, and it is doubtful if the regiment took over 175 men into the Battle of Antietam. Even with such reduced numbers, the 5th Texas was powerful enough to defeat two Union attacks in the cornfield, and it withdrew only after most of the brigade had moved back to Dunkard Church. A week later the commander of the regiment reported that 8 men had died and another 78 had been wounded at Antietam.[21] Henderson was badly injured there and lost his arm to amputation. He was furloughed to Texas and subsequently promoted to lieutenant. Henderson ended his military career in Texas, serving on the staff of Brig. Gen. Jerome B. Robertson. *Photo courtesy of CRC*

ROBERT H. GASTON
copy print

Among the dead at Antietam was Lt. Robert H. Gaston of Company H, 1st Texas Infantry. Gaston had originally enlisted as a private on June 24, 1861, and remained with the colors until his death at Antietam on September 17, 1862. After the earlier fight at Gaines' Mill, Robert's brother, William, wrote his parents to tell them that the two were safe. He also remarked that all of the soldiers were so tired that they slept on the battlefield. "Every time we woke up we could hear the shrieks of the wounded and dying, some calling for their regiment, others for their friends and relatives. It seems truly horrible now," he added, "but at the time would excite very little emotion." William was with Robert at Antietam, but he lost contact with his brother as the battle raged around him. On November 28, 1862, he sent a letter to his parents telling them that he had almost given up hope of finding his brother alive. He wrote:

I have been inquiring and hunting for him ever since he was lost. . . . I feel that he was slain although I cannot give him up yet. . . . He may have been badly wounded and still in the hands of the enemy. There has been some of my boys sent back from Maryland that I thought was killed. . . . I have felt miserable since he has been gone and its is with deep regret that I have to communicate his loss to you.[22]

In less than three months the Texas Brigade had distinguished itself in three major battles, but it had suffered over 1,700 casualties and been reduced in numbers to less than a regiment. Veterans like Robert H. Gaston were hard to replace, and the Texas Brigade never really recovered from the bloody months of 1862. *Photo courtesy of the Dallas Historical Society*

82

After Antietam, Lee reorganized his army and promoted dozens of officers. On November 1, 1862, Col. Jerome Bonaparte Robertson of the 5th Texas Infantry received his appointment to brigadier general and took command of Hood's old brigade, which had been under the temporary control of Col. William T. Wofford of the 18th Georgia. Wofford lost the command because Lee had reorganized his army more generally along state lines, which led to the transfer of the Georgians and South Carolinians.

Robertson was born in Kentucky on March 14, 1815, and graduated from medical school at Transylvania University in 1835. The next year he settled in Texas and practiced his trade at Washington-on-the-Brazos. In the antebellum years, Robertson served in the state legislature and, as a member of the Texas Secession Convention, supported leaving the Union. In 1861

Robertson raised the Texas Aides (later Company I , 5th Texas Infantry) and became its captain. An early historian of Hood's brigade (who was a soldier in the 4th Texas Infantry) characterized Robertson as brave and capable but lacking Hood's personal magnetism. He added that Robertson, because of his "democratic ways and a certain fussiness over trifles," became known as "Aunt Pollie." Unfortunately, the general's career with the brigade ended in controversy after he so irritated Longstreet that the latter removed him from command. A court martial later exonerated Robertson, but he never again led his old brigade. The charges did not affect the men's respect for "Aunt Pollie," but the Texans never showed the fondness for Robertson that they did for Hood.[23] *Photo courtesy of MOLLUS, Mass., U.S.A.M.H.I.*

IKE TURNER
copy print

During the Battle of Fredericksburg on December 13, 1862, the Texas Brigade was idle even though the Federals attacked on either side of its position. Only four Texans were wounded in Lee's easy victory. On February 17, 1863, the brigade left winter quarters in a snowstorm and headed south. They were destined to serve in the ill-fated Suffolk campaign. The original goal of the campaign was to counter the Union presence southeast of Richmond by taking Suffolk, Virginia, and perhaps even New Bern, North Carolina.

In 1861 twenty-two-year-old Ike Turner had responded to the call to arms by raising the Polk County Flying Artillery. His father had procured two 6-pounder Napoleons for the unit, but the younger Turner was unable to persuade the government to accept his battery. He subsequently took the men to Virginia, where they enrolled as Company K, 5th Texas

Infantry, and Turner became the youngest captain in the Texas Brigade. By 1863 Turner had a distinguished service record, having been wounded at Seven Pines and again at Second Bull Run. In the latter battle, Turner temporarily commanded his regiment and did so again at Antietam. However, the young captain had a particular talent for leading small detachments of sharpshooters. Shortly after the siege of Suffolk began, Turner was given command of a special detachment of four companies of sharpshooters from the Texas Brigade. On April 14, 1863, Turner was standing on the parapet of the siege line directing the fire of his men against several gunboats, when he was shot in the chest and mortally wounded. He died the next day. Ironically, the bullet had been fired from a distance of 500 yards by a sharpshooter on one of the Union boats.[24] *Photo courtesy of CRC*

Eventually the plan to diminish the Union presence in southeastern Virginia failed, and the men were detailed to scour the rich agricultural countryside for sorely needed supplies for Lee's hungry army. Consequently, the Texas Brigade missed Lee's great victory at Chancellorsville, May 1–4, 1863. For most of the men, life in southeastern Virginia seemed easy when compared to the rigors and dangers of service with the Army of Northern Virginia. However, by mid-May 1863 they were back with Lee and preparing for the second invasion of the North.

Cpl. Miers E. Felder had joined Company E (the Dixie Blues) of the 5th Texas Infantry on July 19, 1861, as a private. On August 30, 1862, he was wounded during the Second Battle of Bull Run and eventually received a discharge at Columbia, South Carolina, on

February 14, 1863. Pvt. Rufus King Felder joined the same company as his brother, Miers. He was frequently sick and missed much of the Suffolk campaign due to illness. Rufus recovered in time to rejoin the regiment when it returned to duty with Lee's victorious army. Felder was with the 5th Texas when it marched into Pennsylvania and fought at Gettysburg. He was slightly wounded in the leg during the regiment's bloody fight on July 2, 1863. A week after the assault, he wrote his mother that "the charge began along the whole line & the fighting was terrible indeed. A part of the enemy['s lines gave way, but the main heights were not taken. It seemed like madness in Lee to have attempted to storm such a position. He came very near loosing his whole army by it."[25] *Photo courtesy of CRC*

VALERIUS CINCINNATUS GILES
copy print from *American
Military Equipage, 1851–1872*

At Gettysburg, the Texas Brigade fought in and around some of the toughest terrain on the battlefield. On their front was a series of bolder-strewn ravines called the Devil's Den, beyond which were two small hills known as Round Top and Little Round Top. The Devil's Den and the two Roundtops dominated the Union army's left wing; even without facing enemy fire it would be hard ground for infantry to cross. Both Longstreet, who commanded Lee's right, and Hood were reluctant to fight there, but Lee had given strict orders. The attack had to be made.

Pvt. Valerius Cincinnatus Giles of the 4th Texas was one of the men who made the attack. Giles was born in Shelby County, Tennessee, on January 26, 1842, and his family had settled on a farm outside of Austin in the late 1840s. When the Civil War began, he joined the Tom Green Rifles, later Company B, 4th Texas. Giles's regiment was cut to pieces at Gaines' Mill, and he was knocked unconscious by a spent grapeshot. He escaped injury during Second Bull Run but probably missed the fight at Antietam.

On July 2, 1863, the brigade began attacking about 5:00 P.M., but the regiments got jammed together and "confusion reigned everywhere." There seemed to be no protection as minié balls poured down on the advancing Texans. Giles's musket became so fouled that the ramrod hung in the barrel; he slammed the gun against a rock, driving the rod and cartridge into the barrel. Giles then laid the weapon on a boulder, ducked, yelled "look out" as the musket roared "like a young cannon" and flew over his shoulder.[26] *(Original owned by Al Sasser)*

86

HUGH DICKSON BOOZER
copy print

Cpl. Hugh Dickson Boozer was born in South Carolina probably in 1842 and was living in Anderson County, Texas, when the war began. He joined the Reagan Guards (later Company G, 4th Texas Infantry) as a private on July 19, 1861, and received his promotion to corporal on October 1, 1862. Boozer was with the colors continuously during the first two years of the war and marched toward the Devil's Den with his regiment on July 2, 1863. That day the 4th Texas moved forward at the double-quick; soon they found enemy skirmishers who put up a stubborn resistance. The regiment covered another two hundred yards before they met the enemy in full force at the edge of the Devil's Den. The 4th Texas managed to drive the enemy back and reach the base of Little Round Top, where the colonel of the regiment, John Key, was mortally wounded. By then so many officers and soldiers were either slain or wounded that it was impossible to continue the assault.[27] The 4th Texas fell back, having suffered 140 losses, among whom 58 men, including Boozer, were prisoners of war. Boozer remained in Federal hands until February 27, 1865, when he escaped; ironically he was being transferred to City Point, Virginia, for exchange. *Photo courtesy of CRC*

WILLIAM L. AND THOMAS HORACE LANGLEY
copy print

William L. and Thomas Horace Langley were brothers who joined the Marshall Guards of Harrison County, Texas, on May 28, 1861. The Guards were accepted into service as Company E of the 1st Texas Infantry. At the time of his enlistment Thomas was a college student in Marshall, Texas. He originally enlisted as a sergeant but contracted typhoid fever in 1862 and was discharged. However on May 3, 1863, Thomas reenlisted as a private in his old company, which was then winding up its service in the Suffolk campaign. Pvt. William Langley apparently missed Second Bull Run but was otherwise with the regiment in its other battles.

The brothers were with Company E when it went into battle on July 2, 1863. They advanced along the north edge of the Devil's Den alongside the 3d Arkansas. The Arkansans became hotly engaged and were forced to withdraw about 150 yards. The 1st Texas's left flank was now exposed, and when elements of the 15th Georgia arrived to fill the gap, they became intermingled with the 1st Texas. The jumbled regiments moved forward together until Union artillery forced them to withdraw about 100 yards. The artillery fire continued to tear into the men and "many were killed and wounded, some losing their heads and others so horribly mutilated and mangled that their identity could scarcely be established. . . ."[28] The 1st Texas lost 125 men at Gettysburg. Thomas survived the battle but his brother, William, died there. The brigade's loss of 706 men was the highest figure for the unit during the war.[29] Pickett's Charge occurred the next day and quickly became synonymous with the great battle in Pennsylvania, but the performance on July 2, 1863, of Longstreet's First Corps was at least equal to the next day's effort. *Photo courtesy of CRC*

88

JACOB DURRUM
ninth-plate ambrotype

On September 9, 1863, Pvt. Jacob Durrum was with the Star Rifles, officially designated as Company D, 1st Texas Infantry, when the men passed through Richmond, Virginia, to redeploy westward. Durrum had joined the army on May 27, 1861, at Linden, Texas, and is listed on the muster roles as being present throughout the first three years of the war. In September 1863 the 1st Texas was part of two divisions that Longstreet took to reinforce Gen. Braxton Bragg's Army of Tennessee. The over eight-hundred-mile trip was the most complicated strategic movement made by the Confederate armed forces in the war. Longstreet's men were going to north Georgia to add striking power to the unfolding Southern offensive in that area.

On September 17, 1863, Durrum arrived with the rest of the Texas Brigade at Catoosa, Georgia. At sunrise the next day they began moving toward Chickamauga Creek, where the two armies were concentrating. As the brigade neared the creek, enemy opposition increased and the men had to fight their way to the stream. Durrum was seriously wounded during the skirmishing; on September 19, his regiment engaged in bitter fighting around the Viniard House and was actually forced to withdraw.[30] The Battle of Chickamauga eventuaily cost the 1st Texas 170 casualties; Durrum died from his injuries on September 22, 1863. *Photo courtesy of the Jefferson Historical Museum, Jefferson, Texas*

89

WILLIAM R. SMITH
copy print

William R. Smith was twenty-two years old when, on July 27, 1861, he joined the Guadalupe Rangers as a private. The Rangers, which were sometimes referred to as the Knights of Guadalupe County, were one of four companies that trained together at Camp Clark on the San Marcos River before becoming part of the 4th Texas Infantry. Smith's unit became Company D of the 4th Texas. Although he missed many months of service due to illness, Smith did participate in the Battle of Antietam (where he was wounded) and probably saw action at Gettysburg. By the time of the Chickamauga campaign, Smith was the 5th sergeant of his company.

On September 20, 1863, Bragg resumed his pounding attacks against the Union right. Around 11:30 A.M. Longstreet's advancing troops stumbled into a hole in the Union line that developed from a mix-up in orders. The Federal right collapsed as the Texans and others poured through the gap. Before the sun set, the Union army had avoided a catastrophe only because Maj. Gen. George Thomas kept his head and managed to cobble together a force that contained the victorious Confederates. That evening Thomas's men covered the Federal retreat to Chattanooga. Smith was killed during the Battle of Chickamauga, but the date of his death is uncertain. Since the Texas Brigade took most of its casualties on September 19, Smith may have either been dead or mortally wounded before the Southerners secured their greatest victory in the Heartland. *Photo courtesy of CRC; original owned by L. E. Smith*

JACOB LOWN
copy print from J. B. Polley,
A Soldier's Letters to Charming Nellie

Bragg had inflicted slightly more than 16,000 casualties on the Union forces engaged at Chickamauga, but it had cost him over 18,000 men. The Federals were soon under partial siege in their stronghold of Chattanooga, Tennessee. However, the Rebels lacked the resources to destroy them, and recriminations among Bragg and his subordinates practically paralyzed the army. Longstreet had been openly critical of Bragg's performance and was glad when the unpopular commander detached the First Corps to operate in East Tennessee.

Jacob Lown was twenty-two years old when he enlisted at Anderson, Texas, on March 26, 1862, in Company H, 4th Texas Infantry. On June 27, 1862, he was wounded and sent to the rear during the Battle of Gaines' Mill. Lown remained in the hospital until September, when he was furloughed and did not return to the ranks until January 1863. He was soon ill and back in the hospital but returned in time to fight at Gettysburg and at Chickamauga.

Longstreet's move forced the Federals to withdraw to their base at Knoxville; by November 16, 1863, the Rebels were closing in on the city but lacked the strength to completely besiege the defenders. Finally, Longstreet decided to attack a salient known as Fort Sanders. The Texans' only role in the battle was to demonstrate in their sector in order to deter reinforcements from moving to the point of attack. The assault was a miserable failure that cost the Confederates over 800 casualties; Union losses were put at only 100 men. The demonstration cost Lown his freedom and eventually his life: he died as a prisoner of war at Louisville, Kentucky, on January 18, 1864.

EUGENE OSCEOLA PERRY
copy print

It had been over seven long months since the Texans left Virginia; undoubtedly most of the men were glad the harsh winter and frustrating campaigning in East Tennessee were over. It had been a hard time, but now the men were back where they belonged—with the Army of Northern Virginia. One of the soldiers who returned to Virginia in the spring of 1864 was Pvt. Eugene Osceola Perry of Company E, 1st Texas Infantry. The original company, which was locally known as the Marshall Guards, had mustered into the service in June 1861 and left Texas bound for Virginia. At that time, Eugene Perry was a captain at the Kentucky Military Institute and a graduating senior; this image shows him in his cadet uniform. In September 1861 Eugene and three of his brothers joined Company E and served together without serious incident until the Battle of Antietam. Earle and Clinton E. Perry died on that bloody battlefield, while the two remaining brothers were wounded but survived and soon returned to the colors. It is likely that Eugene, who had been periodically sick, missed the earlier battles of Gaines' Mill and Second Bull Run, but he did fight later at Gettysburg. Eugene was wounded a second time at the Battle of Chickamauga when a ball passed through his cartridge box and into his left hip. The caps buried into his leg and, as he wrote his father, "made the wound more painful than it would have been otherwise."[31]

On May 6, 1864, Perry was killed during the Battle of the Wilderness when the Texas Brigade played a crucial role in repairing Lee's shattered line. The final brother, George Perry, survived the war and was one of eleven members of Company E who surrendered at Appomattox. A total of 118 men had served with the Marshall Guards by war's end. *Photo courtesy of CRC*

WILLIAM F. SCHADT
photo copy

Pvt. William F. Schadt was also a member of the 1st Texas Infantry when it went into action on May 6, 1864. He had joined the Lone Star Rifles at Galveston, Texas, on August 1, 1861, when he was nineteen years old. On August 30, 1861, the Rifles were in Virginia and mustered into the service as Company L, 1st Texas. Charles Schadt, who was probably William's brother, had also enlisted in the same company, and was killed in 1862 at Eltham's Landing. William Schadt escaped injury there as well as at Gaines' Mill, Second Bull Run, Antietam, Fredericksburg, and Gettysburg. He was, however, slightly wounded at Chickamauga.

On May 6, 1864, the Texas Brigade was down to around 800 men when it arrived on the battlefield. It and two other depleted brigades rushed forward to try to restore the shattered Confederate right wing, which had been overwhelmed by elements of nine attacking Union brigades. The advancing Rebels had to literally push themselves through the human debris of two shattered Confederate divisions. A Texan who had survived many desperate fights remembered that he had never witnessed such confusion with both moving and stalled wagons, horses, and mules intermingled with a tangled mass of retreating soldiers, "each with his face to the rear."[32] By the time the fearsome Battle of the Wilderness ended the next day, the 1st Texas had lost 121 men. One of the wounded was Pvt. William Schadt, who remained in the general hospital at Danville, Virginia, until late June 1864. *Photo courtesy of the San Jacinto Museum of History, Houston, Texas*

94

D. C. Farmer enlisted in the Bayou City Guards at Houston, Texas, as a 2d lieutenant on July 19, 1861, and was promoted to captain four months later. His unit became Company A, 5th Texas Infantry. Farmer was wounded at Gettysburg, and on September 26, 1863, he was injured in the right leg by a shell fragment during the siege of Chattanooga.

On the morning of May 6, 1864, he was with his men in Virginia as they came forward at the double-quick. They had gone nearly a mile when Brig. Gen. John Gregg halted the soldiers and formed a line of battle. About this time General Lee rode up near the Texans. He spoke with Gregg, telling him that he expected the Texas Brigade to drive the enemy back. Gregg moved forward and ordered the advance. Suddenly, and probably on impulse, Lee rode forward as if he intended to lead the soldiers personally. The men shouted for him to go back, crying that they would not advance until he retired to safety. Lee, who saw how desperate the situation was, refused to move. Immediately about twenty men from the brigade ran forward and began pushing Lee's horse to the rear. One soldier reached out for the bridle; Lee relented and began moving toward the rear. The brigade, in one of its finest performances of the war, drove the Federals back more that five hundred yards and played a decisive role in saving Lee's army from a crushing defeat. Their losses, however, had been terrible, amounting to 400 casualties out of a total of 811 soldiers who went into action. Farmer escaped with only a slight wound to the hip. Shortly afterward, he was detached to Texas on recruiting service and never returned to the regiment.

D. C. FARMER
copy print from J. B. Polley, *A Soldier's Letters to Charming Nellie*

CLINTON MCKANNY WINKLER
copy print

When the Civil War began, Clinton McKanny Winkler helped raise the Navarro Rifles and was captain of the company when it was accepted into the Confederate Service as Company I of the 4th Texas Infantry. Winkler went on to serve faithfully with his regiment, and on July 21, 1863, he was promoted to major. Major Winkler was with the 4th Texas during the Battle of the Wilderness. The two-day struggle was a soldiers' fight, and the combat skills of Lee's infantry had given him a tactical victory. In the past, Lee's old adversary, the Army of the Potomac, would have probably withdrawn, but now it fought under U. S. Grant, who was determined to continue his offensive until the Army of Northern Virginia was destroyed. During the next six weeks, Grant hammered Lee at Spotsylvania, North Anna, Bethesda Church, and Cold Harbor. Winkler's personal correspondence gives some idea of what those horrendous days were like:

May 8th.—Marched to Spottsylvania Court House, advanced under shell and grape on the enemy. 9th.—Strengthened breastworks, skirmishing and sharpshooting. 10th.—Enemy attacked our lines. 12th—Battle of Spottsylvania Court House. 23d—I have survived the bloody days of the 6th and 12th. June 9—The impression is general that Grant cannot get much more fighting our of his hirelings.[33]

Winkler's prediction was wrong, and Grant's "hirelings" eventually drove the Rebels into the trenches that protected Richmond. However, Lee's men did not break. *Photo courtesy of CRC*

In 1861 Tacitus T. Clay was managing his father's land in Washington County, Texas, and serving as mayor of Independence. One of his last official acts as a city official was to chop down the town square "liberty pole" holding the American flag. On August 3, 1861, Clay enlisted as 1st lieutenant of the Texas Aides, which became Company I, 5th Texas Infantry. He was promoted to captain on October 31, 1861, and commanded his company until seriously wounded in the leg and side at Gaines' Mill. Clay was then furloughed to Texas until he was well enough to return to duty in the early summer of 1863. At the Battle of the Wilderness on May 6, 1864, Clay received his second wound.

During the Richmond-Petersburg siege, the Texas Brigade spent most of its time defending the Rebel capital. Grant's attention was usually aimed at cutting the railroad south of Petersburg, but he did launch some diversionary attacks near Richmond, and Lee often responded with limited counterattacks of his own. Either scenario meant more casualties for the Texas Brigade. On September 29, 1864, the Federals captured Fort Harrison, which had protected Confederate positions along the James River. The loss forced Lee to respond. On October 7, 1864, Clay was part of the Rebel counterattack along the Darbytown Road. The failed assault cost the Confederates 1,300 casualties including Clay, who was seriously wounded in the right leg. The surgeon had to remove the limb just above the knee, but Clay wrote his wife that he was doing well, "with a prospect of a speedy recovery...." He added, "this looks like a terrible calamity, but I bear the loss without repining."[34] *Photo courtesy of CRC; original owned by Mrs. R. D. Elliott*

JOHN GREGG
albumen print

It is doubtful if the Texas Brigade numbered more that 450 men in the Darbytown Road fight on October 7, 1864, but it cost them 100 casualties. This was its heaviest loss since the Battle of the Wilderness and would be their largest number of losses in any one incident during the ten-month Richmond-Petersburg siege.[35] Brig. Gen. John Gregg commanded the brigade when it fought at Darbytown Road. Gregg was born on September 28, 1828, in Alabama. He later moved to Fairfield, Texas, where he practiced law and was elected district judge. In 1861 Gregg was a delegate to the secession convention and voted to leave the Union. He then briefly served in the Confederate Congress, but resigned in the summer of 1861 and returned home to organize the 7th Texas Infantry. Gregg was colonel of the regiment when it surrendered with the Fort Donelson garrison on February 16, 1862. On September 27, 1862, Gregg, who had been earlier exchanged, was promoted and given command of a brigade of Tennessee and Texas troops. His first action with the new command was on May 12, 1863, at Raymond, Mississippi, where his lone brigade fought hard against almost two Yankee divisions. Later, Gregg was seriously wounded during the Battle of Chickamauga. He returned to duty at a fortuitous time, because even though his old brigade had been disbanded, Longstreet was fed up with Jerome Robertson and wanted another commander for the Texas Brigade. Replacing Robertson with a hard-fighting Texan would soothe the sensibilities of the men from the Lone Star State, and Gregg fit that description perfectly. He assumed command of the brigade in the winter of 1864. Gregg led his men with skill and daring until he was killed on October 7, 1864, at Darbytown Road. He was the last general who led the Texas Brigade. *Photo courtesy of MOC*

98

WILLIAM A. WATSON
sixth-plate ambrotype

William A. Watson was from Grimes County, Texas, and had enlisted as a private in the Porter Guards in May 1861. The Guards became Company H of the 4th Texas Infantry. Watson was recorded as sick in a Fredericksburg, Virginia, hospital in April 1862, but he recovered in time to fight at Gaines' Mill on June 17, 1862. He may have missed Second Bull Run while on detached duty but did fight at Antietam. On October 15, 1862, Watson was promoted to 5th sergeant and served with his regiment during the campaigns of 1863 and 1864.

Watson was with the 4th Texas on Saturday evening, April 2, 1865, when the brigade received orders to evacuate Richmond. At daylight the next morning, the men boarded box cars and disembarked about noon near Petersburg. The soldiers could see that the Rebel army had abandoned its positions and

that the Federals were moving in a westerly direction. That evening the brigade also began marching westward, bringing up the rear of Lee's retreating army. All that night and the next day they traveled without being attacked. Most of what they had to eat on the march consisted of only a thin gruel of water and corn meal. On April 5th the pursuing Federals overtook the Texas Brigade and the men were engaged in a brief firefight. The brigade continued to withdraw in good order until the morning of April 9, 1865, when the men made their last march. That afternoon some of the brigade's teamsters came from Appomattox Court House to tell the infantry that Lee had decided to surrender.[36] Watson was one of nine men from his company who received their paroles on April 12, 1865, but he had lost his sergeant's stripes and was once again a private. *Photo courtesy of Michael Jones*

Chapter 5

Texans in the Armies
of the Heartland

*I am determined to stand by our
colors to the last.*

—JAMES DOUGLAS

In the fall of 1861, every Confederate theater commander needed troops, but none was more desperate for men than Gen. Albert Sidney Johnston, who was trying to protect a line that ran from Arkansas to the Cumberland Gap in eastern Tennessee. Out west in the Lone Star State good men were available, and more that 1,200 had just joined the army to serve under two illustrious Texans, Benjamin Franklin Terry and Thomas S. Lubbock. Both men had earlier served as volunteer aides to Brig. Gen. James Longstreet during the First Battle of Bull Run, and they were eager to return to Virginia with their own unit, which on September 9, 1861, had mustered into the service as the 8th Texas Cavalry. Several days later the first companies started for Virginia, but Johnston persuaded the War Department to reassign the regiment, which became popularly known as Terry's Texas Rangers, to his command. The leading elements began arriving in Nashville in early October 1861. About the same time, another Texan, John Gregg, who had resigned from

the Confederate Congress to raise a regiment of infantry, was passing through Nashville on his way to Texas to assemble his companies when he received instructions to send for all the men he had available. By early November, Gregg had 749 soldiers under his command; they were designated the 7th Texas Infantry and stationed near Hopkinsville, Kentucky.[1] Terry and Gregg's commands were the first of twenty-two Texas units that would see substantial service with the Rebel armies that struggled to protect the central states of the Confederacy from invasion.

One influential military theorist who first appreciated the strategic importance of the central states to the Confederacy was the British historian John Frederick Charles Fuller. He defined the northern border of this vast strategic Heartland as running southward along the Allegheny Mountains to Chattanooga, Tennessee, where it turned westward, following the Tennessee River to Savannah, Tennessee. The boundary then continued almost due west until it crossed the Mississippi River north of Memphis and terminated at Little Rock, Arkansas. Behind this line lay the Chattanooga-Atlanta corridor. Fuller believed the Confederacy had to maintain control of these two vital cities if it was going to have any chance to survive because the South's two main lateral railroads passed through them. These roads, in turn, linked the strategic western cities with their counterparts in the Carolinas and Virginia.[2] This admittedly weak railroad system bound the Confederacy together and gave it a semblance of political, economic, and military unity. Along its rickety lines flowed the men and materials that the Confederacy needed to survive. The Federals were determined to destroy the unity which rested in the strategic Heartland of the Confederacy. That fact drew the Texas regiments across the Mississippi River, for the South was chronically short of men for the defense of such a vast area.

The first Texans to fight to protect the Heartland were Terry's Texas Rangers, who on December 17, 1861, participated in a brief but bloody skirmish near Woodsonville, Kentucky. During the fight Colonel Terry and seventy-five of his Rangers routed about three hundred of the enemy. Terry and three other men from the regiment died there. However, the Texans who first felt the real power of the Federal army were the men of the 7th Texas Infantry. On February 16, 1862, the regiment and its colonel, John Gregg, were taken prisoner at Fort Donelson on the Cumberland River by Brig. Gen. Ulysses S. Grant; ten days earlier Fort Henry, which protected the Tennessee River, had surrendered. The loss of these two forts smashed Johnston's line, forcing the Rebels to evacuate Nashville and hastily withdraw to the Tennessee-Alabama border.

Less than two months after the retreat, other Texans faced Grant and his soldiers again when the Confederates, after a remarkable recovery, assumed the offensive. On April 6, 1862, Johnston's men surprised the Federals in their camps along the Tennessee River near Shiloh Church. The 2d and 9th Texas Infantry Regiments, along with Terry's Texas Rangers, fought at Shiloh. The 9th Infantry had organized in late 1861. It came east of the Mississippi River in January 1862 to reinforce Johnston, but arrived too late to be of assistance in the defense of Forts Henry and Donelson. The 9th Texas only took 226 men onto the Shiloh battlefield; their losses totaled 14 killed, 42 wounded, and 11 captured. The 2d Texas Infantry had also been organized late in 1861 but did not come east of the river until after the fall of Forts Henry and Donelson. At Shiloh the regiment suffered about 150 casualties, or 33 percent of the soldiers who were with the colors during the battle.[3] Terry's Texas Rangers performed scouting and screening duties at Shiloh and covered the army's retreat for several days. The campaign cost the Rangers 66 casualties and 56 dead horses.[4] Johnston lost his life at Shiloh, and with combined Federal and Confederate casualties that totaled almost 24,000 men, the battle shocked the public and portended an ominous future for Civil War soldiers.

After Shiloh, the Confederates withdrew to their entrenched camp at Corinth, Mississippi, where they were reinforced with any troops that the already over-strained Confederate War Department could spare. Even before the Battle of Shiloh, Federal pressure along the vulnerable river system in the Heartland was forcing Confederate authorities to strip troops from less strategic areas in the Trans-Mississippi states. Among the troops ordered across the river were those commanded by Maj. Gen. Earl Van Dorn, who had recently been badly defeated at Pea Ridge, Arkansas. His solders arrived too late to help Johnston at Shiloh, but they were welcome reinforcements nonetheless. Among the veterans of the Pea Ridge fight were Douglas's Texas Battery and the 3d, 6th, 9th, and 11th Cavalry Regiments. The core of two other Texas regiments that arrived in Mississippi with Van Dorn had also fought at Pea Ridge. The first of these units had originally begun in the fall of 1861 when five companies organized as the 4th Cavalry Battalion. In early 1862, seven more companies were added and the battalion was redesignated the 27th Texas Cavalry. The second unit, the 32d Cavalry Regiment, was organized in May 1862 at Corinth. The genesis of that regiment began in late 1861 when several companies were mustered into the service as the 1st Texas Cavalry Battalion. These seven commands that had fought at Pea Ridge were joined by the 10th, 14th, and 17th Texas Cavalry and the 6th Texas Infantry. These regiments had served mostly in the Lone Star State since being organized in mid-1861. The eleven units that arrived in Corinth in April and May 1862 were the largest group of Texans to move east of the river at one time.[5] And since the Confederacy desperately needed infantry, almost all the cavalry troopers were either already dismounted when they reached Corinth or lost their horses shortly after arriving there.

The Federals failed to capitalize on their victory at Shiloh largely because Maj. Gen. Henry Wager Halleck decided to assume personal command of the more than 100,000 men that were being assembled to advance on Corinth. Halleck had shown great skill as an organizer when he operated from his office in St. Louis, but it soon became apparent that he had no talent for field command. After Shiloh the general first dallied too long and then seemed unable to do more than creep toward Corinth. Meanwhile the new commander of the Confederate forces, Gen. P. G. T. Beauregard, used the time Halleck gave him to bring his army's strength to 80,000 men, but even this force was not large enough to hold Corinth. On the night of May 29, 1862, Beauregard withdrew his army under Halleck's nose and fell back toward Tupelo, Mississippi. Halleck seemed to be at a loss as to what to do next, but eventually decided to divide his army, leaving part of his soldiers under Grant to protect western Tennessee, while sending a second force eastward to operate against the railroad network in the vicinity of Chattanooga. Halleck's decision to divide his forces stalled his own offensive and handed the initiative back to the Confederates.

Within weeks, two of the South's more resourceful cavalrymen, Nathan Bedford Forrest and James Hunt Morgan, were harassing the divided Federal forces. Among Forrest's troopers were Terry's Texas Rangers. The Rangers' brief connection with Forrest ended in September 1862, when the regiment became part of Brig. Gen. Joe Wheeler's command. The 8th (Terry's) Texas Cavalry Regiment went on to become the most famous mounted unit from the Lone Star State as they campaigned under Wheeler in Tennessee, Georgia, and the Carolinas.

At Tupelo, Beauregard, who was disliked by Pres. Jefferson Davis, declared himself ill and took leave from the army. On June 17, 1862, Davis ordered one of his favorites, Gen. Braxton Bragg, to assume command of the troops at Tupelo. In July 1862 Bragg decided that the best way to engage the enemy was to cooperate with Maj. Gen. E. Kirby Smith at Knoxville, Tennessee, in a two-pronged invasion of central Kentucky. Their object was to draw the Federals away from Chattanooga and perhaps win over more Kentuckians to the new Confederacy. Prior to his advance, Bragg sent one division to reinforce Kirby Smith's men. Among these troops were Douglas's Battery and the 10th, 11th, 14th, and 32d Texas Cavalry (dismounted), as well as a regiment of Arkansas sharpshooters (whose colonel, T. H. McCray, commanded the brigade). The 9th Texas Infantry, attached to Brig. Gen. Patrick R. Cleburne's command, also joined Smith's troops. The offensive got off to a good start on August 30, 1862, at Richmond, Kentucky, where Smith's men practically destroyed a largely untested column of 6,500 Union soldiers. McCray's brigade suffered 149 casualties; Douglas's Battery, which was temporarily attached to Cleburne's brigade, had 2 men killed and 4 wounded. Smith's victory at Richmond occurred two days after Bragg had left Chattanooga and moved rapidly northward. The two events forced the Federal army back, but the Rebel leaders were unable to capitalize on their enemy's misfortune, and the initiative slowly shifted away from the Confederates. Bragg's grand Kentucky offensive ended ingloriously on October 8, 1862, when he was defeated at the Battle of Perryville. Confederate casualties totaled almost

3,500 men; the only Texas regiment engaged at Perryville was the 9th Infantry, which had one man killed and none wounded. By November 1862 most of Bragg's army was encamped around Murfreesboro in central Tennessee.

When Bragg decided to invade Kentucky, he left behind almost half his strength under the commands of Van Dorn and Maj. Gen. Sterling Price. They had instructions to both defend central Mississippi and keep Grant from sending men to reinforce Buell. The 3d, 6th, 9th, and 27th Texas Cavalry (dismounted) and the 2d Texas Infantry were among the troops that remained in Mississippi. The 6th and 9th Cavalry Regiments were brigaded together with two Arkansas units and an artillery battery. The 3d and 27th Texas Cavalry served together in a mixed brigade along with Louisiana and Arkansas units. The 2d Texas Infantry was brigaded with Alabama, Arkansas, and Mississippi troops under the command of Brig. Gen. John Creed Moore. As a colonel, Moore had led the 2d Texas at Shiloh. All five Texas units were attached to Price's corps, which was still referred to as the Army of the West.

While the other Texans campaigned with Bragg, Price's men carried out operations against the Federal troops that simultaneously guarded west Tennessee and protected the Memphis and Charleston Railroad which ran eastward to Chattanooga. On September 14, 1862, the Texas units were with Price when he drove a small Union garrison out of Iuka, Mississippi, and gained control of a section of the railroad line. Five days later Price was preparing to withdraw from Iuka to concentrate with Van Dorn for a larger operation when he was attacked by Union infantry. Much of the fighting fell on the second brigade of Brig. Gen. Henry Lewis Little's division, which contained the 3d and 27th Texas Cavalry. Losses among the 3d Cavalry totaled 94 out of an aggregate strength of 388 men; The 27th Cavalry suffered 99 casualties out of a total muster of 460. Little was also killed in the fight. Price's

second division, under Brig. Gen. Dabney Maury, contained the other three Texas regiments, but that command was hardly engaged in a fight that cost the Confederates over 1,700 casualties.

Ten days after the Battle of Iuka, Price and Van Dorn united their forces at Ripley, Mississippi. Van Dorn, who now commanded 22,000 men, wanted to free west Tennessee from Federal control, but he could not do that until the Union garrison at Corinth, Mississippi, was either eliminated or driven away. Van Dorn launched his three divisions against the already alerted Union force on October 3, 1862. The 3d and 27th Texas Cavalry Regiments were part of Little's old division, now commanded by Brig. Gen. Louis Hébert. It attacked on the left. The other three Texas regiments remained with Maury's division and were assigned to attack the Union center. Both divisions were under the command of Price. A third Rebel division, commanded by Maj. Gen. Mansfield Lovell, was assigned to advance on the right. Price's men made good progress during the first day's fight, but they failed to dislodge the Federals from their entrenched positions. On the right, Lovell advanced but seemed hesitant to commit his troops fully. Van Dorn hoped to launch a general attack at dawn the next day, but a command change caused delays and disrupted the advance. On the left, several regiments did break into Corinth, but they were thrown back by Federal counterattacks. In the center, the Confederates took heavy casualties as they vainly tried to overrun Battery Robinett, which controlled part of the Federal line. Around noon Van Dorn began withdrawing; he had lost almost 2,500 in dead and wounded. By the time he reached the safety of Ripley, another 1,700 men were reported missing; many had deserted during the retreat. The five Texas regiments had 285 men either killed or wounded in the Corinth campaign. The largest number of fatalities was in the 6th Texas Cavalry, which lost 55 men. Two hundred forty-eight other Texans were reported missing; the largest number,

118 soldiers, were from the 2d Texas Infantry, one of the regiments that tried to take Battery Robinett.[6]

Shortly after the campaign, the four Texas cavalry regiments were remounted and brigaded under the command of Col. John Whitfield of the 27th Texas Cavalry. Van Dorn, who had commanded horse soldiers prior to the Civil War, gave up his infantry and assumed command of Lt. Gen. John C. Pemberton's cavalry. On December 20, 1863, Whitfield's brigade participated in Van Dorn's celebrated raid on Holly Springs, Mississippi, disrupting Grant's overland campaign to take Vicksburg and forcing him to abandon the advance.

Whitfield, who was fifty-one years old when the war began, was promoted to brigadier general on May 9, 1863, and continued to command the Texans until his health began to fail. He was granted a leave in October 1863, and Col. Lawrence Sullivan "Sul" Ross replaced him. Ross commanded the 6th Texas Cavalry which, since March 1863, had been on detached service. He was promoted to brigadier general to rank from December 21, 1863, and led the Texans throughout the remainder of the war. In 1864 the four regiments served in the Meridian, Atlanta, and Franklin-Nashville campaigns.

After Corinth, Moore's brigade, including the 2d Texas Infantry, was attached to Pemberton's forces guarding Vicksburg. An additional Texas command, Waul's Legion, also joined the 2d Texas there. The legion, organized at Brenahm, Texas, in May 1862, originally consisted of twelve companies of infantry, six companies of cavalry, and one light artillery battery. Several so-called legions had been created by various states, but none functioned as a combined-arms unit for very long. Waul's command was no exception, and only the Legion's infantry went to Vicksburg. The 2d Infantry and Waul's Legion were the only two Texas units to serve in the Vicksburg garrison and were surrendered there on July 4, 1863. Both commands subsequently reorganized and finished their service west of the Mississippi River.

In November 1862 General Bragg officially designated his forces at Murfreesboro, Tennessee, as the Army of Tennessee; unfortunately, it remained under Bragg's command. On December 26, 1862, Maj. Gen. William S. Rosecrans, who commanded the newly organized Union Army of the Cumberland, began moving his 47,000 soldiers toward Murfreesboro. Bragg had deployed his army of 38,000 men a little over a mile northwest of the town with their backs to Stones River. The 9th Texas remained part of Brig. Gen. Preston Smith's brigade; after detached service with Cleburne, the men had returned to Maj. Gen. B. F. Cheatham's division. When the fight at Murfreesboro began on December 31, 1862, Cheatham's division was near the center of the Rebel line. The 10th, 11th, 14th, and 15th Texas Cavalry (dismounted) and Douglas's Texas Battery were now under the command of a fellow Texan, Brig. Gen. Matthew D. Ector. The men were part of Maj. Gen. John Porter McCown's division on the extreme left of the Confederate line. Terry's Texas Rangers, now under the command of Col. Thomas Harrison, were in Brig. Gen. John A. Wharton's brigade. In 1861 Wharton had entered the service as a captain in the Rangers and became colonel of the regiment after both Terry and Lubbock died. During the Battle of Murfreesboro, the brigade performed scouting and screening duties on the left wing of the Rebel army.

Ector's brigade participated in the initial Confederate advance on the left, while Cheatham's division, including the 9th Texas, later attacked near the center of the line. The massive Confederate assault eventually drove the Union right flank back until their line resembled an inverted "V," but the attackers could not dislodge the stubborn Federals. Neither side renewed the battle the next day. On January 2, 1863, a final Confederate attack against the left flank of the Union line was broken up by a massive artillery barrage. No Texas units were involved in that assault. Bragg began withdrawing from the field the next evening; each side had lost about 12,000 men in the indecisive battle. Ector's brigade suffered 343 casualties and the 9th Texas lost 122 men in the fight.

For the next six months, both Bragg and Rosecrans remained idle in Middle Tennessee while Grant was hard at work against the citadel of Vicksburg. An incidental consequence of the campaign against Vicksburg was the capture of Arkansas Post, a Rebel stronghold along the Arkansas River, on January 11, 1863. Among the Confederate units surrendered there were the 15th, 17th, 18th, 24th, and 25th Texas Cavalry Regiments. All five units had been dismounted in the spring and summer of 1862. In addition, the 6th and 10th Texas Infantry were among the more that 5,000 Rebels that the Federal army bagged at Arkansas Post. The soldiers from these seven Texas regiments were exchanged in April 1863 and subsequently reorganized east of the Mississippi River. The exchanged men eventually made their way to Chattanooga to join the Army of Tennessee. There they were attached to Maj. Gen. Patrick Cleburne's veteran infantry. The men were now part of the best combat division in the Army of Tennessee, and the Texas brigade's subsequent performance under Cleburne would more than erase the humiliation of being captured at Arkansas Post.

In late June 1863 Rosecrans finally began moving to maneuver Bragg out of Chattanooga. His plan took the Federal army west and south of the city, but the maneuver caused Rosecrans to spread the Union columns over a forty-mile front. The stratagem forced Bragg out of the city, but it also gave him an opportunity to strike a hard blow at Rosecrans before the latter could concentrate his forces. Furthermore, Bragg had already been reinforced and more troops were on the way. On September 19, 1863, the bloodiest battle fought in the Heartland began several miles south of Chattanooga along Chickamauga Creek.

When the fighting began, Cleburne's division, including the seven Texas regiments that had been exchanged after Arkansas Post, were deployed near the center of the Confederate line. They were commanded by Brig. Gen. James Deshler. Ector's brigade was also present at Chickamauga. In the summer of 1863, the brigade had been detached briefly from the Army of Tennessee and sent to campaign in Mississippi, but it returned to Bragg's command in August. The brigade still retained the 10th, 14th, and 32d Texas Cavalry (dismounted). A fourth regiment, the 11th Texas Cavalry, had been remounted and transferred, but it had been replaced by the 9th Texas Infantry. Ector's reorganized command also contained three non-Texas artillery batteries and was in Maj. Gen. William H. T. Walker's division in the right wing of Bragg's army. The remounted 11th Texas Cavalry joined Terry's Texas Rangers as part of the second cavalry brigade of Wharton's division; both regiments fought in the cavalry operations during the Chickamauga campaign. A third infantry brigade containing the 1st, 4th, and 5th Texas was also present on the battlefield. These soldiers were part of the troops that came from Virginia to reinforce Bragg and were commanded by Brig. Gen. Jerome B. Robertson. Finally, Brig. Gen. John Gregg's brigade, which included the 7th Texas Infantry, was also on the field. The 7th Texas and Robertson's brigade all went into battle near the center of the Rebel line.

In two days of brutal fighting, Bragg's men won a great victory, but they failed to prevent their beaten enemy from reaching the safety of Chattanooga, where the Federals occupied good defensive positions. The Chickamauga campaign had cost the Rebels more than 18,000 casualties; losses among the Texas units totaled at least 1,200 men including Deshler, who died in the battle. It quickly became apparent that Bragg could not capitalize on his victory, as he lacked the men either to attack the Federals or to completely surround them in their mountain retreat. By mid-November 1863 transfers and attrition had reduced Bragg's force to about 40,000 soldiers, while the Federal army had been strengthened to nearly 70,000 men. In front of Chattanooga, the Texas regiments went through yet another realignment. On November 12, 1863, the 7th Texas Infantry was transferred to Deshler's old brigade, now commanded by Brig. Gen. James A. Smith. Douglas's Battery was removed from the brigade and eventually reassigned to Maj. Alfred R. Courtney's artillery battalion in the Second Corps. By late October 1863 Ector's brigade had left the Army of Tennessee and returned to Mississippi as part of Maj. Gen. Samuel French's division. The 8th and 11th Texas Cavalry remained in Wharton's division.

On November 23, 1863, the new Union commander in Chattanooga, U. S. Grant, began his offensive to drive Bragg off of Missionary Ridge. Two days later Grant's men, in a remarkable charge, collapsed the center and then the left of the Confederate line. However, on the right, Cleburne's brigades and a few other units held firm until Bragg's demoralized troops could withdraw. Cleburne's men then covered the retreat. Two days later at Ringgold Gap, his division held back a Union corps until Bragg's army reached the safety of Dalton, Georgia. During most of the fighting, Cleburne's brigade of Texans was under the command of Col. Hiram B. Granbury of the 7th Texas Infantry, replacing Smith who had been seriously wounded early on November 25. Cleburne later received the thanks of the Confederate Congress for his defense of Ringgold Gap and wrote that there were not four better brigade commanders in the army than those in his division.[7] On March 5, 1864, Granbury was promoted to brigadier general and given command of the Texas brigade. Except for a brief two week period in July 1864, Granbury would lead his Texans until he and Cleburne both died during the Battle of Franklin.

On May 7, 1864, the new Federal commander of the western armies, Maj. Gen. William T. Sherman, began advancing toward Atlanta, Georgia. His orders from Grant were to move against the Army of Tennessee "to break it up, and to get into the interior of the enemy's country as far as you can, inflicting all the damage you can against their war resources."[8] Sherman's adversary, Gen. Joseph E. Johnston, who had replaced Bragg after the latter resigned, was determined to prevent Sherman from destroying the Heartland. Granbury's brigade was with Johnston when the Atlanta campaign began, and it saw action at Dug Gap (May 8) and Resaca (May 14–15). On May 17, 1864, Ector's brigade rejoined the Army of Tennessee as part of 15,000 reinforcements that Johnston received. During the next six weeks, elements of the two Texas brigades were engaged at Pickett's Mills (May 27) and Kennesaw Mountain (June 27). In each case the Confederates held their ground but later retreated when Sherman used his superior numbers to threaten the Southerners' flank. Each withdrawal took the Federals closer to Atlanta. On July 17, 1864, Davis, who disliked Johnston personally and was displeased with his Fabian tactics, named Lt. Gen. John Bell Hood to command the Army of Tennessee. The new commander quickly began the offensive that Johnston had carefully avoided. On July 20, 1864, the Texas brigades were on the battlefield but not heavily engaged when two of Hood's corps were repulsed at Peachtree Creek. Two days later, Ector's brigade missed the fight at Bald Hill, but Granbury's men were involved in that failed attack.

After the unsuccessful Southern offensive, Hood settled into the entrenchments around Atlanta. On July 27, 1864, during one of the frequent bombardments, Ector was stuck in the thigh by a piece of shrapnel and subsequently lost his leg. He was replaced by Col. William H. Young of the 9th Texas Infantry. The Federals continued to inflict casualties on the entrenched Rebels, but the fortifications protecting the city were too strong to be carried by assault. Sherman then decided to move against his enemy's last supply line, the Macon and Western Railroad. If that line could be severed, Hood would have to evacuate Atlanta. On August 31, Granbury's brigade was part of the Confederate corps that attacked the Union infantry near Jonesborough along the Macon and Western Railroad. The Rebels were repulsed and the loss of the railroad made Atlanta untenable. Hood began withdrawing his men from the city on the afternoon of September 1, 1864. Shortly after midnight the soldiers of Granbury's brigade heard the first of eighty-one ammunition cars explode as the Confederate cavalry fired them to keep the material from falling into enemy hands. Second Lt. Oliver Bowser of the 18th Texas Cavalry remembered that "many a soldier in the brigade regarded the dismal sounds as the death knell of the Confederacy."[9]

The long campaign had worn down the Army of Tennessee until its infantry numbered only 27,000 effectives. In the next three months Hood would waste these precious veterans in a futile invasion of Middle Tennessee. The genesis of the campaign came from the desperate need of the Confederate government to rid the Heartland of Sherman's army. Hood first hoped to force such a withdrawal by threatening Sherman's long supply lines that ran through north Georgia and central Tennessee. Initially, the strategy appeared to work; Sherman responded by sending some troops to reinforce his supply-line garrisons and taking 40,000 men northward to hunt for Hood. However, the Union commander soon tired of the cat-and-mouse game. Sherman later wrote that "I . . . finally resolved on my future course, which was to leave Hood to be encountered by General [George] Thomas, while I should carry into full effect the long-contemplated project of marching for the seacoast, and thence to operate toward Richmond." He added that he would give Thomas ample means to handle "any and every emergency."[10] Hood's response to Sherman's movement toward the sea was to launch his own invasion ultimately aimed at Nashville, Tennessee. The odds favoring the success of Hood's offensive would have been small even in earlier years when the South still had the

power to conduct limited offensives, but in late 1864 the dying Confederacy lacked all the essentials for such a fantastic scheme.

Hood began his advance on November 21, 1864, and Ross's brigade of Texas cavalry formed part of the screening force as the Army of Tennessee began its last campaign. The brigade had earlier rejoined the army in mid-May 1864 and served throughout the Atlanta campaign; by November the four regiments contained only 686 men.[11] Granbury's Texans as well as Ector's old brigade and Douglas's Battery were with the advancing infantry. Far to the east, Terry's Texas Rangers and the 11th Texas Cavalry were part of Wheeler's horsemen trying to disrupt Sherman's march to the sea.

Hood's offensive looked promising at first, and on the evening November 29 the army had an excellent opportunity to maul elements of two retreating Union corps at Spring Hill, Tennessee. However, the seemingly paralyzed Rebel commanders let the Federal column slip away and withdraw to the fortifications that protected Franklin, Tennessee. Hood, who quickly blamed the fiasco at Spring Hill on one of his corps commanders, arrived in front of Franklin that afternoon. He was tired and exasperated with the performance of his troops. To the astonishment of several senior officers and despite their strong protests, Hood ordered eighteen infantry brigades to attack the fortifications without any support from the army's artillery, which had yet to arrive. Late that afternoon 16,000 soldiers, including the men in the two Texas brigades, participated in one of the war's largest assaults. The charging infantry did manage to break into the Federal fortifications in a few places, but the slaughter was terrible. The dead included Cleburne, Granbury, and three other generals. Five more generals were wounded and another was captured. Fifty-four regimental commanders were casualties. Among the Texas infantry, only one regiment was still commanded by a colonel while at least six units were now led by captains.[12] Hood was left with fewer than 18,000 infantrymen, and the senior leaders within the army were mostly gone. Franklin was the death rattle of the Army of Tennessee, but Hood still insisted on continuing the offensive. In early December 1864 the small force deployed outside Nashville. On December 15, General Thomas, who now had almost 50,000 Union troops in Nashville, attacked and drove back the left wing of Hood's line. The next day his men smashed the Rebel army and sent it reeling back south. In early January the remnants of the once powerful Army of Tennessee reached the safety of Tupelo, Mississippi. On January 13, 1865, Hood asked to be relieved; his request was granted ten days later.

The two Texas infantry brigades never fought together again. Granbury's soldiers were part of 5,000 men that the War Department transferred to the Carolinas. There the soldiers fought once more under Joe Johnston. On April 26, 1865, the 440 men who still remained with the Texas infantry regiments surrendered with Johnston in North Carolina. Terry's Texas Rangers and the 11th Texas Cavalry, after earlier service in Georgia and then the Carolinas, also surrendered there. Confederate authorities sent Ector's men and Douglas's Battery with the troops who reinforced the garrison at Mobile, Alabama. It is doubtful if the combined units still mustered 700 soldiers when they surrendered at Citronelle, Alabama, on May 4, 1865. Ross's Texas brigade returned to Mississippi after the Franklin-Nashville campaign. The men were camped along the Black River when Lt. Gen. Richard Taylor surrendered his department on May 4, 1865. Approximately 550 men were still with the colors.

At least one-third of the Texans who fought for the Confederacy spent most of their time serving in the Heartland. The men who campaigned there were poorly equipped, indifferently supplied, and sometimes led by mediocre army commanders. Despite such handicaps the Heartland soldiers generally fought well; the Texans were no exception. The men in the vast theater that stretched from the Mississippi River to the Alleghenies had done their best against long odds. That was all a soldier could do, and the Texans returned home knowing they had made the enemy pay a huge price to seize the Heartland.

PETER L. KENDALL, WILLIAM A. LYNCH, FELIX G. KENNEDY, THOMAS S. BURNEY, WALTER S. WOOD
tintype

The first Texas regiment to arrive in the Heartland was the 8th Cavalry, and it would become the most famous mounted outfit from the state to serve there. The unit was commonly called Terry's Texas Rangers in honor of its first commander, Col. Benjamin F. Terry, who died leading a charge early in the war. The 8th Texas Cavalry spent most of its time with the Army of Tennessee in Gen. Joe Wheeler's cavalry, but the men also saw some service with Generals Nathan Bedford Forrest and Wade Hampton.

All five soldiers in this image came from Springfield, Texas. They enlisted together at Houston on September 12, 1861, and were originally members of Company C. Privates Peter Kendall, William A. Lynch, Thomas S. Burney, and Walter S. Wood served until the war ended. It is unclear if Pvt. Felix Kennedy was still with the colors when his friends surrendered. Lynch, Wood, and Kennedy were wounded during the war. Kennedy, who received his injury at Stones River, was captured there and later exchanged. Thomas Burney also spent a brief time in captivity. In the summer of 1864 Lynch, Kennedy, and Burney joined Shannon's Scouts (see page 155) but the other two soldiers remained with the Rangers. Only one of the soldiers, Thomas S. Burney, left behind any personal record of his service with the Texas cavalry.

The Rangers became known as hard and ruthless fighters. In 1862 an officer from the regiment wrote that the unit contained "some scoundrels who would disgrace the place over which Lucifer presides. . . ."[13] Such soldiers helped the 8th Texas Cavalry earn its reputation as a good fighting outfit, but they also contributed to the command's ruthless behavior. On February 22, 1865, for example, Union Maj. Gen. Judson Kilpatrick reported that the 8th Texas Cavalry murdered eight of his men after they had surrendered and left their mutilated bodies with notes on their breasts reading "Death to foragers."[14] Unfortunately such brutal incidents intensified as the war hardened its participants and broke down their conventions of civilized behavior. *Photo courtesy of Panhandle-Plains Historical Museum, Canyon, Texas*

WADE HAMPTON BURKE
copy print

Twenty-one-year-old Wade Hampton Burke enlisted in Marshall, Texas, as a private in Capt. W. B. Hill's company of volunteers on October 1, 1861. Hill's men were part of a regiment being raised by Col. John Gregg. Three days after Burke enlisted, Gregg received instructions from Gen. Albert Sidney Johnston to immediately bring the partially recruited regiment east of the Mississippi River. By November 7, 1861, Gregg had nine companies totaling 749 men (including Burke) in Kentucky. A majority of the men were not armed, and those who did have weapons sported a great variety; Burke's company reported having only nineteen double-barreled shotguns and eight rifles that were in good order. Nevertheless, the regiment was accepted into service at Hopkinsville, Kentucky, on November 9, 1861, as the 7th Texas Infantry; Burke's

unit became Company H. That winter measles, typhoid, pneumonia, and other aliments common to newly recruited troops decimated the 7th Texas. Burke was stricken with measles and left behind when the Texans, in late 1861, received orders to join the garrison at Fort Donelson on the Cumberland River. On February 16, 1862, approximately 12,000 Rebels were captured there. The loss of Fort Donelson shattered Johnston's defensive line in Kentucky and Tennessee. The 7th Texas, which now numbered only about 360 men, had 20 soldiers killed defending Fort Donelson. Before they were exchanged in September 1862, another 65 had perished as prisoners of war. Burke never recovered from his illness and died at Hopkinsville, Kentucky, on June 1, 1862.[15] *Photo courtesy of the Jefferson Historical Museum, Jefferson, Texas*

111

DAVID L. KOKERNOT
copy print

Third Sgt. David L. Kokernot of Company I, 2d Texas Infantry, enlisted in the Confederate service on September 16, 1861, at Galveston. Most of the men in the company, which was known as the Wilson Rifles, were from Gonzales County. In early March 1862 Kokernot's regiment received orders to report to Corinth, Mississippi. There, Johnston was gathering reinforcements for an offensive he hoped would counter the recent reverse at Fort Donelson. The regiment arrived in Corinth on April 1. Two days later the Texans marched northward through ankle-deep mud as 40,000 Rebels moved against Grant's forces near Shiloh Church on the Tennessee River. On Sunday, April 6, 1862, the Texans, "with empty stomachs and appetites made voracious by the faint smell of commissaries" from the Federal camps, began advancing. "A terrible noise[,] great smoke, incessant rattling of small arms, [and] infernal confusion," stunned one Texan who remained dazed until he realized that the Federals were reeling back in disorder. A member of Kokernot's company paused to grab a skillet of fried meat from a campfire and eat it on the run while chasing the Federals.[16]

Grant's men were surprised but not yet beaten. Soon their resistance stiffened. That evening, Grant received reinforcements and the battle resumed the next day. In the early minutes of Monday's battle, the 2d Texas was ambushed and fled in disorder. The brief struggle cost them 150 casualties. The men eventually regained their composure and returned to the battle line. However, by 3:00 P.M. the Rebels were withdrawing. Kokernot survived the fight at Shiloh but was discharged for disability on July 29, 1862. *Photo courtesy of ITC; original owned by Miss Clifton McNeel*

SELEN STOUT
copy print from Celia M. Wright,
Sketches from Hopkins County History

The other infantry regiment from the Lone Star State that fought at the Battle of Shiloh was the 9th Texas. The unit mustered into Confederate service on December 1, 1861, for twelve months and went east of the Mississippi River in January 1862. Selen Stout, a farmer from Hopkins County, Texas, mustered into the service at Camp Rusk on November 26, 1861. At that time he was a 3d sergeant in Capt. James A. Lettwich's unit, which became Company F of the 9th Texas Infantry. During the first day of the Battle of Shiloh, the 9th Regiment twice failed to carry an enemy battery by bayonet charge, but when they were given adequate artillery support for their third attempt, the green troops succeeded in taking the position. The men then passed through two Federal camps before they encountered another battery, which inflicted heavy casualties before it too was overrun. By now the soldiers were exhausted and almost out of ammunition; they withdrew for the night. The 9th Texas went back into action the next day, but the reinforced Federal army drove the Rebels back. When the 9th Texas withdrew from the battlefield, its casualties were fourteen killed, forty-two wounded, and eleven missing.[17] Stout was slightly injured during the first day's fighting but managed to withdraw with the 9th Texas.

JAMES K. STREET
carte de visite

James K. Street was born in 1837 and joined the Lamar Rifles of the 9th Texas Infantry as a private on September 26, 1861. Less than three months earlier, Street, who lived in Lamar County and listed himself an artisan, had married Melinda "Minnie" East Pace. In March 1862 he explained to Minnie why he had joined the service:

. . . these are perilous times and unless matters take a change for the better, men who will not volunteer will have to be drafted. Would you have it said of *me*—He refused the call made by his country & had to be *drafted*? Shall toryism be cast in the teeth of *our* offspring? *Never! Never!* Darling I do not dread the hardships thro' which I shall pass during this campaign. I have been used to these all my life. . . . I want to meet with ills and disappointment. It stimulates, It makes me morally courageous. . . .[18]

Street got his first taste of battle at Shiloh, where a Yankee bullet came close enough to tear off the flap of his cartridge box. He also saw two friends receive serious wounds from the enemy.[19]

The searing experience of battle satisfied Street's need for stimulation and replaced it by the more mundane but timeless concern of soldiers about the quality of the leadership that placed them in harm's way. Thus, after his first battle, Street wrote that what the service needed was "less stripes and brass buttons, and more *honest* men to control our army."[20] *Photo courtesy of the Southern Historical Collection, University of North Carolina*

HEZEKIAH CULWELL
copy print

Hezekiah Culwell was born in 1839 in Washington County, Arkansas. Three years later the family moved to Collin County, Texas, where Hezekiah's father, Andrew Jackson Culwell, had acquired 640 acres. On October 21, 1858, nineteen-year-old Hezekiah married sixteen-year-old Missouri Roberts. The couple resided on Andrew Culwell's land, and the young man continued farming until about six months after the war began.

On October 2, 1861, Culwell joined the army as a private in Company G, 11th Texas Cavalry. The men saw action at Chustenahlah, Indian Territory, on December 26, 1862, and at Pea Ridge, Arkansas, on March 7–8, 1862. Culwell was with the 11th Texas when it went to Corinth, Mississippi, to reinforce Johnston's Army of the Mississippi, but the regiment arrived too late to participate in the Shiloh campaign. After a year of fighting, the Confederate army in the Heartland badly needed to replenish its depleted infantry, so several cavalry units, including the 11th Texas, were dismounted and converted to foot soldiers.

Corinth was little more than a pesthole for the Confederate soldiers; of the 80,000 Southerners assembled near the city, by May 1862 at least 18,000 were hospitalized. Culwell fell sick while stationed in Corinth and was taken to Canton, Mississippi, where he died on May 21, 1862. Eight days later the Confederates abandoned Corinth and fell back to Tupelo, Mississippi. *Photo courtesy of Martin Callahan and the owner, Charles Culwell*

115

JOHN CALVIN RUSHING
copy print

At Tupelo Gen. Braxton Bragg rested his army and began planning his own offensive. In cooperation with Maj. Gen. E. Kirby Smith, who had 13,000 troops in East Tennessee, Bragg devised an ambitious scheme to invade Kentucky. As a prelude to the operation Bragg sent a division to reinforce Smith. On August 16, 1862, Smith's command crossed into Kentucky. Twelve days later Bragg began moving northward.

Pvt. John Calvin Rushing of Company A, 10th Texas Cavalry (dismounted), was with the reinforcements that Bragg sent to Smith. Rushing was nineteen years old when he enrolled at Taos, Texas, on October 31, 1861, for twelve months' service in the cavalry. On the morning of August 30, 1862, Rushing's brigade, which also included the 11th, 14th, and 32d Texas Cavalry (dismounted) and McCray's Arkansas Infantry, was near Richmond, Kentucky, when it received orders to

deploy for battle. It was Rushing's first fight since joining the regiment. The brigade helped drive the Federals in confusion from their first position. The entire Rebel line followed the retreating infantry for almost two miles until the Federals rallied and counterattacked. The brigade helped break the attackers' momentum and the enemy fell back again. The engagement at Richmond cost the Federals more than 5,000 men, most of whom were taken prisoner. Confederate losses were put at 600 soldiers with 149 coming from Rushing's brigade.[21] Private Rushing was not hurt; he remained with the 10th Texas until deserting at Morton, Mississippi, on August 23, 1863. The triumph at Richmond was a heartening victory, but Bragg's Kentucky offensive ultimately ended in defeat at Perryville on October 8, 1862. *Photo courtesy of CRC*

116

JOHN J. FELPS
sixth-plate ambrotype

Bragg left 16,000 men in northeast Mississippi under Maj. Gen. Sterling Price with instructions to discourage Union forces in the area from moving to counter the unfolding Kentucky invasion. Price, who had earlier become convinced that the Federals were indeed preparing to reinforce the Union forces opposing Bragg, seized Iuka on September 14, 1862, denying the Union army access to the Memphis and Charleston Railroad. The district commander, Maj. Gen. Ulysses S. Grant, reacted to Price's movement by ordering a two-pronged advance which he hoped would trap the Rebels in Iuka. However, by September 18, Price realized that Grant was not reinforcing anyone. He decided to move westward and link his forces with those of Maj. Gen. Earl Van Dorn. The next day one of Grant's columns struck Price's men as they were withdrawing from Iuka.

Pvt. John J. Felps was a member of Company C, 3d Texas Cavalry (dismounted) when the unit fought at Iuka. Felps had enlisted in Cherokee County, Texas, on June 3, 1861; he traveled 160 miles to get there, and Confederate authorities valued his horse and equipment at $145. By the late summer of 1862, attrition had reduced the regiment to only 388 men, but they had been hardened by drilling and campaigning. The fight at Iuka lasted little more than two and one-half hours, but it cost Price 1,500 casualties. The 3d Texas Cavalry had 22 men killed and another 74 injured; only two Rebel regiments suffered more losses in the battle. Felps was among the wounded that the retreating Confederates were forced to leave behind. He was captured and then exchanged on October 18, 1862. *Photo courtesy of J. Dale West*

117

JAMES HENRY SMITH
copy print

Twenty-two-year-old James Henry Smith mustered into the service as a private in Capt. M. I. Brinson's cavalry company at Camp Reeves, Grayson County, Texas, on November 14, 1861. Brinson's men became Company D of the 9th Texas Cavalry and participated in their first major battle on March 7–8, 1862, at Pea Ridge, Arkansas. During the April 1862 reorganization, the men were dismounted and ordered east of the Mississippi River to Corinth, Mississippi. On May 10, 1862, Smith was elected 2d lieutenant of his company. He was on the battlefield at Iuka on September 19, 1862, but the 9th Cavalry was not seriously engaged.

On October 3, 1862, the 9th Texas was part of Brig. Gen. C. W. Phifer's brigade, which fought in the center of the Rebel line during the Battle of Corinth. The regiment suffered minor casualties as it helped push the Federals from their outer works. The next morning the 9th Texas was one of the lead regiments in the grand assault that Van Dorn hoped would drive the enemy from their final entrenchments. Before the attack began, Smith was promoted to 1st lieutenant on the battlefield. The 9th Texas came "under a fire of grape & canister from artillery and the most terrible fire of small arms conceivable" as it advanced on the left of the road that led to Corinth. In front of them was Battery Robinett, which quickly became the storm center of the most vicious fighting of the battle. Men from the 9th Texas eventually scaled the parapet protecting the battery, but they were driven back. Lieutenant Smith, who was wounded in the Corinth campaign, may well have been injured in that assault. Regimental losses for the battle and subsequent retreat totaled 117 men out of a muster of less than 300 who marched against Corinth.[22] *Photo courtesy of June E. Tuck*

JOHN CREED MOORE
carte de visite

John Creed Moore was born in Tennessee in 1824, and graduated seventeenth in West Point's class of 1849. He resigned from the army in 1855 and was a professor at Shelby College, Kentucky, when the war began. Moore, who had originally entered the service as an officer in the First Louisiana Heavy Artillery, received an appointment as a captain in the Regular Confederate Army on April 15, 1861. He was ordered to Galveston, Texas, to help organize that port city's defenses but almost immediately received permission to raise a regiment of Texas troops. On September 2, 1861, Moore became colonel of the newly organized 2d Texas Infantry. Moore led his men at Shiloh on April 6, 1862, and the next day he assumed temporary control of the brigade when the commander became separated from his regiments. After the battle, Moore's superiors praised his performance and recommended him for promotion. On May 26, 1862, Moore was promoted and given permanent command of the brigade he had led at Shiloh.

On October 4, 1862, Moore's brigade contained five regiments and one artillery battery. The general brought his 1,900 soldiers up on the right of Phifer's brigade, and they were greeted by withering fire from the Federals. Most of Moore's troops were drawn into the fight for Battery Robinett, but some of the men lapped around that obstacle and fought their way into Corinth before being thrown back. The charge cost Moore 1,296 casualties or 68 percent of his brigade. However, since 985 soldiers were listed as missing, Moore's commander noted that he believed many of the "men had straggled off and will return to their commands."[23] *Photo courtesy of the Alabama Department of Archives and History*

REBEL DEAD BEFORE BATTERY ROBINETT
copy print

The dead Confederate in the background and just to the left of the stump in the center of this image is likely Col. William P. Rogers, who commanded the 2d Texas Infantry when it assaulted Battery Robinett. Before the war Rogers had been a prominent attorney in Houston, Texas. He had joined the service as lieutenant colonel of the regiment and became colonel of the 2d Texas Infantry after Moore's promotion to brigadier general.

At Corinth, Rogers was on horseback leading his men when the 2d Texas emerged from the protection of the woods and began advancing toward the battery. The 2d Texas numbered about 340 fighting men. Rogers survived the terrible firing and reached the ditch in front of Battery Robinett. There he dis-

mounted and went forward with the other Rebels scrambling up the parapet. The men managed to seize a section of the line for a few moments but quickly faced an overwhelming counterattack. Rogers, who must have realized the hopelessness of the Confederate position, began waving a handkerchief as he desperately tried to surrender his troops. In the confusion, neither side saw or perhaps understood what Rogers was trying to do, and the colonel was killed by a Federal fusillade.[24] Shortly after the failed attempt on the battery, Van Dorn began withdrawing his beaten army. Over half of the 2,500 Southern casualties had been in Moore's brigade; the 2d Texas lost 166 men.
Photo courtesy of the Library of Congress

WILLIAM BURGESS
ninth-plate ambrotype

Twenty-five-year-old William Burgess enlisted on August 24, 1861, at Hallettsville, Texas, as a private in John W. Whitfield's company of Texas troops. Whitfield took his cavalry to join Brig. Gen. Ben McCulloch in Arkansas, where the command and four other companies were organized as the 4th Texas Cavalry Battalion. Burgess's unit became Company C. The battalion fought at Pea Ridge, but it is likely that Burgess missed the battle because of illness. In April 1862 the battalion was expanded to a regiment and Whitfield became its colonel. The unit, now designated the 27th Texas Cavalry, carried the nickname Whitfield's Legion throughout the war, even though it was not a legion and Whitfield seldom commanded it. Like many cavalry regiments in the spring of 1862, the 27th Texas was dismounted and converted to infantry.

Private Burgess was in the ranks of the 27th Texas when it suffered 97 casualties at Iuka. On October 3, 1863, Burgess was with the regiment as part of Col. Bruce W. Colbert's second brigade when the Confederates tried to drive the Federals out of Corinth, Mississippi. The brigade anchored the left of Van Dorn's line and suffered 283 casualties in the two-day fight. Burgess was not injured, but his regiment lost 3 men killed, 17 wounded, and 75 missing.[25] During the retreat from Corinth the 27th Regiment was engaged at Hatchie Bridge. There, on October 5, 1862, they helped delay the advancing Federals long enough for Van Dorn's beaten and demoralized army to escape capture. *Photo courtesy of Gary Hendershott*

In less than a month the 3d, 6th, 9th, and 27th Texas Cavalry Regiments had fought as infantry at Iuka, Corinth, and Hatchie Bridge; they had lost at least 525 soldiers combined. After the campaign, the four units were remounted and placed under the command of Whitfield.

Pvt. George W. Fulgham, at the age of twenty-one, had joined the Cypress Rangers at Camp Reeves, Texas, on October 14, 1861. The Rangers became Company F, 9th Texas Cavalry. They fought their first engagement at Round Mountain, Indian Territory, on November 19, 1861. Fulgham was reportedly present during that month, but he was in camp sick on March 7–8, 1862, when the company suffered four casualties at Pea Ridge. Fulgham recovered from his illness in June 1862 and subsequently served with the 9th Cavalry when it campaigned in Mississippi. On December 20, 1862, Fulgham was with his regiment when Van Dorn captured the Federal supply depot at Holly Springs, Mississippi, which ended Grant's first advance on Vicksburg. Three days later the 9th Cavalry was in Middleburg, Tennessee, where they charged down the railroad, destroying the track, telegraph station, and winter quarters of the regiment guarding the town. However, Federal troops were posted in a fortified brick house and the 9th Texas was unable to dislodge them. The regiment had nine men wounded and another four, including Fulgham, were missing.[26] Private Fulgham had been taken prisoner; he was sent to Camp Douglas and exchanged in early 1863. That summer he was detached as a butcher and served the rest of the war in that capacity. *Photo courtesy of Warner Wallace*

GEORGE W. FULGHAM
copy print

122

JAMES S. WHITE
carte de visite

After Perryville, Bragg fell back to Murfreesboro in central Tennessee. The day after Christmas 1862, the Federals began advancing toward Bragg, who responded by deploying his men on a four mile line a little northwest of the town along Stones River. Pvt. James S. White of Company K, 10th Texas Cavalry (dismounted), Ector's Texas brigade, was one of 350 men from the regiment who fought at Stones River.

The 10th Texas was accepted into service on October 31, 1861, but White did not enlist until March 18, 1862. At the time, the regiment was in Jacksonport, Arkansas, where the men first were decimated by measles and then received bad news—they were to be dismounted and then sent to Corinth, Mississippi. When the regiment arrived in Corinth, many of the men were still armed only with shotguns. The 10th Texas fought at Richmond, Kentucky, and the soldiers were finally able to rearm themselves from the weapons taken from Federal prisoners.

Before daybreak on December 31, 1862, the 10th Cavalry fell into ranks. For two days the men had been exposed to freezing weather, and that morning also looked cold, wet, and foggy. Around 6:00 A.M. the soldiers began advancing across a muddy field studded with rotten cornstalks. The men overran a Federal battery but not before it fired six rounds of canister into the ranks of the Texans. Within an hour the regiment had suffered about 80 casualties. The combined attack continued to push the Federal right wing back, but the advance was slowing. The last fighting for the 10th Texas began about 1:00 P.M. when they helped extract two Texas regiments that were pinned down by Federal fire. Private White was not injured but his regiment suffered 118 casualties.[27] *Photo courtesy of Dale Snair*

JOHN H. BINGHAM
copy print

John H. Bingham of McKinney, Texas, was twenty-three-years-old when he enlisted as a private in Douglas's Battery at Dallas on July 2, 1861. For the next several months, Bingham was on detached duty with the 3d Texas Cavalry and did not return to the battery until the fall of 1861. In the summer of 1862, Bingham was elected 2d lieutenant and held that rank when he fought at Richmond, Kentucky. During the battle, the battery's 1st lieutenant, James N. Boren, was almost cut in two by a cannon ball; shortly after Richmond, Bingham took the slain 1st lieutenant's place.

On December 31, 1862, Bingham led a section of Douglas's Battery as it supported the advance of Ector's dismounted Texas cavalry regiments. Ector's men moved so fast that the battery lost contact with the infantry. Capt. James Douglas left the guns with Bingham and rode forward to find the front. Douglas was near the Federal battery that had been recently captured by the 10th Texas Cavalry (dismounted) when he realized that the infantry was now well in advance. He hastened back and ordered the battery forward at the gallop. The men, without any infantry support, reached the site of the captured battery and were surprised to see a line of Federal infantry advancing on their right. Without the assistance of friendly riflemen, batteries were very vulnerable. The advancing Federals opened fire before the guns unlimbered, but the artillerymen quickly got the pieces in place and loaded them with canister. Bingham's section helped decimate the enemy ranks. Douglas's Battery, which had two men wounded at Stones River, continued to support the Texas infantry throughout the day.[28] *Photo courtesy of the Smith County Historical Society, Tyler, Texas*

Jeremiah Crook enrolled as a private in Company A, 9th Texas Infantry at Paris, Texas, on September 26, 1861. On May 8, 1862, Crook was elected 2d lieutenant of the company and was with his men when they fought at Stones River. The regiment, which was the only Texas infantry unit on the battlefield other than those in Ector's brigade, was with Maj. Gen. Benjamin F. Cheatham's division near the center of the line. Early in the advance the 9th Texas mistakenly entered an open field, stopped, and began firing at the hidden enemy. The colonel of the regiment, William Hugh Young, was desperately trying to correct the mistake when his horse was shot from under him, adding to the confusion. In only five minutes almost 100 men were either killed or wounded. Young regained control by notifying each company that he intended to "charge and rout" the enemy. He then grabbed the colors and led his men forward. The enemy fled and Young's bravery was noted by his commanding officer.[29] Crook escaped injury at Stones River, but his regiment suffered 122 casualties in the three-day fight. *Photo courtesy of the MOC*

LEONIDAS CARTWRIGHT
copy print

Bragg withdrew his battered army to a new base at Tullahoma, Tennessee, where for the next five months the men rested and refitted. Meanwhile, the Rebel command hoped to disrupt the Federals in central Tennessee with cavalry raids against the Union line of communications. Pvt. Leonidas "Lon" Cartwright was with the 3d Texas Cavalry when his brigade moved out of Mississippi and began slogging northward over the half-thawed winter ground. Cartwright had originally enlisted at Shelby County, Texas, on June 3, 1861; he was from San Augustine, Texas, and only nineteen years old when he joined the army. On February 21, 1863, the regiment reached Columbia, Tennessee. When the weather began clearing, Bragg decided it was time to use his cavalry. Bands of Confederate horseman began raiding Union supply lines, and the Federals responded by reinforcing garrisons and step-

ping up patrols. On March 5, 1863, Cartwright was with the cavalry when the men attacked a Union column of 2,800 soldiers at Thompson's Station, Tennessee. Cartwright and his fellow-privates, Drew S. "Bully" Polk and Hugh Leslie, were together when Company E began advancing in the second assault against a Union skirmish line posted on a hilltop. During the advance, Cartwright saw a Federal taking aim at the unsuspecting Polk; he raised his rifle and snapped off a shot at the skirmisher but the weapon misfired. Before Cartwright could react, a bullet tore through Polk's head, killing him instantly. A split-second later Leslie killed the Federal. Cartwright was heartsick about failing to protect his friend, but he took some satisfaction in knowing that the Union soldier had paid with his life for killing Polk.[30] *Photo courtesy of David D. Jackson*

BEN T. ROBERTS
copy print

Third Sgt. Ben T. Roberts was also with Company E, 3d Texas Cavalry, when it fought at Thompson's Station. Roberts was twenty-three years old when he enlisted as a private at Shelbyville, Texas, on June 3, 1861, and he served continuously with the regiment until being captured during the Battle of Iuka on September 19, 1862. Roberts was exchanged in October 1862 and returned to his regiment in time to participate in Van Dorn's celebrated cavalry raid against the Federal depot at Holly Springs, Mississippi.

At Thompson's Station, the 3d Cavalry made repeated charges against the Federals, who were protected by the scrub cedars and thickets that covered the hill. By the end of the day, the regiment had lost the colors that the men had received earlier from the Choctaw maidens in Indian Territory. They had also suffered 24 casualties. Total losses for the Confederates were 357 men, but the victorious Rebels had wounded or killed 377 Federals and captured 1,151 prisoners. Roberts was one of five sergeants from the 3d Texas Cavalry who was injured at Thompson's Station.[31]
Photo courtesy of David D. Jackson

ARCHILLE FERRIS
copy print

In April 1863 Pvt. Archille Ferris was with the 8th Texas Cavalry when Bragg sent Maj. Gen. Joseph Wheeler after the Tennessee railroads that supplied the Union forces. Ferris had enlisted in Company E at Richmond, Texas, on May 14, 1862, and was with Wheeler's men during the Stones River campaign when they created havoc among the Federals by destroying several hundred wagons and capturing 700 men. On April 10, 1863, Ferris and 500 other men from the 8th Cavalry reached a section of the railroad near Antioch Station, Tennessee. There the raiders spread the track and waited in ambush. Soon a train with the tops of its cars crowded with soldiers approached at full speed. The Texans opened fire about the time the train ran off the track. The cavalry continued to fire into the confused mass until they charged and captured the train. The raid netted about 150 prisoners while another 75–80 Federals were either killed or wounded. The victorious cavalry also freed at least 50 of their own men who had been captured earlier at Lebanon, Tennessee.[32] Ferris was uninjured in the raid and continued to serve with the cavalry until surrendering in 1865. Despite such successes as this one and the affair at Thompson's Station, the Federal commander, Maj. Gen. William Rosecrans refused to loosen his grip on Middle Tennessee. In June 1863 Rosecrans maneuvered Bragg out of his base at Tullahoma and forced him into north Georgia. *Photo courtesy of CAH, Cased Photographs Collection, CN 0604*

JOHN WILSON SWINNEY
copy print

Bragg's cavalry raids were only a sideshow to the campaign against the great citadel at Vicksburg which guarded the Mississippi River. Two Texas units, the 2d Texas Infantry and Waul's Legion, were among the troops that protected the city. Pvt. John Wilson Swinney was eighteen years old when he enlisted in Waul's Legion at Liberty, Texas, on May 19, 1862. The legion was ordered to Mississippi in August, but the men received no weapons until October. On February 17, 1863, they went to Fort Pemberton on the Yazoo River to assist in blocking Grant's attempt to approach Vicksburg via that waterway. On March 11, Waul's men helped stymie Grant's advance. The legion remained on the river until early May, when all but 300 men were ordered back to reinforce the Vicksburg garrison. They were needed there because Grant had placed Vicksburg in peril by getting his army on dry ground below the city. Grant sealed the fate of Vicksburg when he defeated the Rebel field army at Champion's Hill on May 16, 1863, and drove it into the garrison's defenses. However, the trapped army was still dangerous, and three days later Grant failed to carry the city by assault. He attacked again on May 22, and Waul's Legion played an important role in repulsing that attack. When the Vicksburg garrison finally capitulated on July 4, 1863, the legion had suffered a total of 245 casualties.[33] At the time of the surrender, nineteen-year-old Private Swinney was hospitalized with chronic diarrhea; he died in the U.S. Hospital at New Orleans on July 23, 1863. *Photo courtesy of CRC*

RICHARD S. LYLES
copy print

Richard S. Lyles was thirty years old when he enlisted on September 25, 1861, as a private at Taos, Texas, in Capt. Anderson Whetstone's company. The unit eventually became Company H of the 10th Texas Cavalry. On May 6, 1862, Lyles was elected 3d lieutenant of the company which, with the rest of his regiment, had recently been dismounted. Lyles was promoted to 1st lieutenant on September 11, 1862, but missed the Battle of Stones River because he was on detached duty. In early May 1863 Lyles and the 10th Cavalry were part of Ector's Texas brigade when it was sent to Mississippi to participate in the unsuccessful effort to lift the siege of Vicksburg.

In late August 1863 the brigade returned to the Army of Tennessee as part of the reinforcements that Bragg received to stop Rosecrans's advance. On the morning of September 19, 1863, Ector's brigade participated in a series of piecemeal attacks near the remains of Reed's Bridge on Chickamauga Creek. Both sides committed more units to the battle, which now raged over a four-mile front, but the day's results were indecisive. Lyles was seriously wounded on September 19 (and was unable to return to duty until February 14, 1864). When the battle finally ended the next day, 59 men from Ector's brigade were dead, 239 more had been wounded, and another 138 were missing.[34] *Photo courtesy of the T. C. Crenshaw Collection, U.S.A.M.H.I.*

131

ALEXANDER MCDONALD
copy print

Twenty-three-year-old Alexander McDonald mustered into the service on October 23, 1861, as a private in the unit that became Company B, 10th Regiment Texas Infantry. On January 11, 1863, McDonald was with his regiment and was one of approximately 5,000 Rebels who surrendered at Arkansas Post, Arkansas.

McDonald was first sent to Camp Douglas, Illinois, and later delivered to City Point, Virginia, where on April 7, 1863, he was declared exchanged. Among these soldiers from Arkansas Post were portions of seven Texas regiments that eventually made their way to the Army of Tennessee. When the Texans arrived in camp, they were sometimes greeted with soldiers hollering that these were the men "who raised the white flag in

Ark[ansas]." Others jeered, "We don't want you here if you can't see a Yank without holding up your shirt to him. . . ."[35] Only one commander, the Irish-born general Pat Cleburne, was willing to take them, but the taunts would continue until the men proved themselves in battle. That proof came at the Battle of Chickamauga, where the brigade took 1,783 men into combat and lost in the fight 52 killed and 366 wounded.

McDonald, however, was probably not with his fellow Texans when they showed their courage to the soldiers who had jeered them. On June 25, 1863, he had been detached as a teamster and was sick during the Battle of Chickamauga. *Photo courtesy of Don Scoggins*

THOMAS GLIMP AND JOHN DAVID BRANTLEY
copy print

On July 6, 1861, John David Brantley and Thomas Glimp volunteered as privates in the Shiloh Home Guards. Both men were from DeWitt County, Texas. Their unit became part of the 24th Brigade of Texas State Troops, and the commander confidently declared that his men were ready to serve in any part of the state. On February 24, 1862, Brantley left the State Troops to become 2d lieutenant in Company K of the 24th Texas Cavalry. Glimp remained in the Shiloh Home Guards and reenlisted for the remainder of the war on September 26, 1863.

Brantley was captured with the 24th Texas at Arkansas Post on January 11, 1863. He was exchanged and joined Cleburne's division in the Army of Tennessee. Because the ranks of the Texas troops were badly depleted, Bragg decided to consolidate several of the units. The 6th and 10th Infantry and 15th Cavalry were merged into one regiment, as were the 17th, 18th, 24th, and 25th Texas Cavalry. Many of the Texans disliked this reorganization and resented serving east of the Mississippi River. Brantley was unhappy enough to resign his commission on September 16, 1863. However, his request had not been accepted when the Battle of Chickamauga began, so Brantley went into the battle. On the afternoon of September 20, 1863, Brantley's consolidated unit arrived at the crest of a hill where it was ordered to halt. "It was here that the regiment suffered terribly," reported its commander, "losing about 200 in killed and wounded . . . until it was ordered to fall back."[36] Brantley was not hurt during the battle, and his resignation was approved on October 2, 1863. *Photo courtesy of Jean Brantley Tidwell Collection, U.S.A.M.H.I.*

133

NATHAN A. SMITH
ninth-plate ambrotype

When the Civil War began, nineteen-year-old Nathan A. Smith of Marshall, Texas, joined Capt. Sam J. Richardson's company for one year as a private. The men became part of the 2d Texas Cavalry and went to serve on the frontier. When the soldiers' enlistments expired, most of the Texans, including Smith, decided to stay with Richardson, who had wrangled permission to raise an independent company. On April 19, 1862, the men reenlisted in their captain's new company and then went to San Antonio "to pledge their fidelity to each other and their country; by getting on a big spree."[37] Richardson eventually led his cavalry company to Arkansas Post, where on January 11, 1863, most of the men were captured. Smith, who had been elected 2d lieutenant when he reenlisted, and his companions were exchanged and attached to the Army of Tennessee as an independent company of infantry

in Brig. Gen. James Deshler's Texas brigade. Most of Richardson's men, including Smith, were unhappy about being converted to infantry and having to serve across the Mississippi River. On September 20, 1863, Smith was with his men on the Chickamauga battlefield. A member of the company wrote that around 4:00 P.M. the fighting suddenly increased "with ten fold more fierceness than ever" and the "very heavens and earth seemed to vibrate and quake. Then, just as suddenly, there was a death-like stillness and soldiers knew that the enemy had given way."[38] Smith was not injured; in early November, he and a handful of men from the company left the Army of Tennessee and returned to Texas to serve under their old commander, Captain Richardson (who had earlier recrossed the river). *Photo courtesy of J. Dale West*

134

John Alphonso "Fon" Beall moved to Rusk County, Texas, from Georgia in 1851 when he was sixteen years old. In November 1861 Beall joined Company B of the 14th Texas Cavalry. The unit was dismounted in the spring of 1862 and spent almost all of its subsequent career as part of Ector's Texas brigade. Early in 1863, Fon was commissioned a 2d lieutenant and became ordnance officer of the regiment.

After Chickamauga, the Army of Tennessee, for one of the few times in its history, was in possession of a major battlefield, and it yielded large quantities of war material for the Confederates. Among the serviceable items were thirty-six artillery pieces, over 270,000 rounds of ammunition, 8,000 muskets, 250 carbines, and 70 Spencer Rifles. Beall is shown holding one of the Spencer Rifles recovered from the battlefield. It is likely that the rifle belonged to a trooper from Col.

John T. Wilder's mounted infantry brigade, which had acquired such weapons in May 1863. These and other repeating rifles were fearful weapons because of their high rate of accurate fire. Wilder, for example, reported that during the battle his men "kept up a constant fire with our repeating rifles, causing a most fearful destruction in the rebel ranks."[39] Despite the obvious superiority of such weapons, the Union army never purchased repeaters in large numbers, and those that were acquired mostly went to the cavalry. Finds such as the Spencer Rifles were very rare, but they did the Rebels little good since the South lacked the ability to manufacture appropriate cartridges and therefore were dependent on captured supplies. Nevertheless, Beall was proud enough of this particular spoil of war to have his picture made with the famous weapon.
Photo courtesy of George Esker

135

The defeated Federals retreated to Chattanooga, but the Rebels lacked the manpower to dislodge them and recriminations within the high command over the recent campaign paralyzed the Army of Tennessee. Pvt. Edmund "Ed" Bedell served with Lt. Nathan Smith and was among the troops that waited passively as the Federal army regained its strength. Bedell, like Smith, had originally enlisted in Richardson's company for one year and went to the frontier with the 2d Texas Cavalry. On April 19, 1862, he and Smith reenlisted together, and Bedell also was captured at Arkansas Post.

On November 25, 1863, the Texas brigade, with the rest of Cleburne's division, was deployed on Tunnel Hill on the extreme right wing of Bragg's line on Missionary Ridge. That morning the Federals launched a powerful attack against Cleburne. By 10:30 A.M. the pickets were driven in, and thirty minutes later the Federals moved up the steep slopes of Tunnel Hill. At one point some of Cleburne's troops jumped on the breastworks and threw rocks at the advancing Federals. These men were later celebrated in the folklore of the Civil War, but the real power that contained the Federal attack was the disciplined fire of Cleburne's infantry and artillery. Unfortunately, the splendid stand was not being repeated anywhere else, and the Confederate line on the rest of Missionary Ridge collapsed. Cleburne continued to hold his position to protect the shattered left wing of the Rebel army as it retreated. The Texas brigade, along with one Arkansas regiment, bore the brunt of the long day's fight. Bedell was slightly injured but withdrew with the retreating army. Private Bedell, like Smith, protested against serving east of the Mississippi, but he remained with the Army of Tennessee until the end of the war.

JAMES ALEXANDER WESTMORELAND
copy print

James Alexander Westmoreland was eighteen years old when he enlisted on March 15, 1862, at Elysian Fields, Texas, in Capt. Sterling Hendrick's unit, which later became Company E, 17th Texas Cavalry. Westmoreland was captured with the regiment at Arkansas Post. The men were exchanged and became part of the Texas brigade in Cleburne's division. Westmoreland was present at both Chickamauga and Missionary Ridge. The day after the latter battle, the Texas brigade, commanded by Col. Hiram B. Granbury, covered the rear of the retreating Rebel army, which was struggling to reach a safe haven at Dalton, Georgia. As they retreated, Cleburne's men burned large qualities of supplies in the abandoned Rebel depots and fired the railroad bridge that crossed Chickamauga Creek. The next day a column of pursuing Federal infantry was nearing Ringgold Gap, which was occupied by Cleburne. He had to hold the position so Bragg's beaten army could continue to retreat unmolested. The gap was less that one hundred yards wide and Cleburne posted his men on either side of the road and two hundred yards up the slope. The Federals, moving in four columns, were about eighty yards from the gap when they were met by a heavy fire. The Federals recoiled but came forward again. For the next several hours, Cleburne held his ground until the last of the Rebel army's wagon trains were out of harm's way. Westmoreland was not hurt in the fight, but his regiment had eight men killed and another twenty-nine wounded.[40] Cleburne's tenacious defense at Tunnel Hill and Ringgold Gap were bright spots in an otherwise dismal performance by the Army of Tennessee. *Photo courtesy of CRC*

LAWRENCE SULLIVAN ROSS
copy print from the
Confederate Veteran

In early May 1864 Brig. Gen. Lawrence Sullivan "Sul" Ross brought his brigade of Texas cavalry to Georgia to reinforce the Army of Tennessee. When the campaign began that month, the Federals had assembled 100,000 soldiers to march against Atlanta, and the Rebels had managed to find 60,000 men to stop them. The soldiers on both sides were mostly veterans, so the summer of 1864 was going to be a bloody time. Ross, a native of Iowa who had moved to Texas as an infant and later graduated from Wesleyan University in Alabama, was not yet twenty-six years old when the 1864 campaign began. Prior to the war, Ross had a reputation as an Indian fighter, and on September 12, 1861, he had became major of the 6th Texas Cavalry. On May 14, 1862, Ross was promoted to colonel of the temporarily dismounted regiment and led his men with distinction at the Battles of Corinth and Hatchie Bridge. On December 21, 1863, he was appointed brigadier general and assumed permanent command of the Texas cavalry brigade. Ross showed great talent for handling traditional cavalry duties such as screening, scouting, and raiding, but he also trained his men to dismount and fight as hard-hitting infantry. The general commanded 1,009 men when the fight for Atlanta began; around 700 of these would still be in the ranks when the city fell one hundred days later. During that time, his men were in eighty-six confrontations that ranged from skirmishes to pitched battles. His tough-fighting brigade of Texans helped make the ultimate Union victory at Atlanta a costly affair. By the end of the war, Ross was purported to have fought in 135 engagements and to have had five horses shot from under him.[41]

139

WILLIAM DAVID SWANN
copy print

Throughout the war Confederate soldiers were sometimes detached and sent home to recruit new members for their unit. In January 1863 Lt. Julius Sanders returned to his outfit, Douglas's Battery, from such duty. He brought with him several recruits including William David Swann. Private Swann had enrolled at Tyler, Texas, on December 8, 1862, and except for a brief illness during the early summer of 1863, he served continuously with the battery.

On May 13, 1864, Swann was present with the battery at Resaca, Georgia, where the first large engagement in the unfolding campaign against Atlanta began. The three-day fight cost the battery three casualties and fourteen horses. On the evening of May 15, 1864, Johnston began withdrawing from the Resaca line after he learned that the Federals were moving to turn his flank. Resaca set the pattern for the next six weeks as Sherman used part of his superior force to pin Johnston while other columns tried to work around the Rebel flank. In each case the ever alert Johnston pulled his army back to previously prepared defenses and the routine started again. Swann served in the Marietta–Kennesaw Mountain line for most of June and was with the battery during the various battles around the environs of Atlanta. He survived the war and surrendered in May 1865 in Mississippi. *Photo courtesy of the Smith County Historical Society, Tyler, Texas*

140

James C. Bates saw his first action at the Battle of Chustenahlah on December 9, 1861. He later served with the 9th Texas Cavalry at Pea Ridge and fought dismounted at Iuka and Corinth. Late in 1862 the regiment was remounted and participated in Van Dorn's December 20, 1862, raid on Holly Springs, Mississippi. Throughout most of 1863 the 9th Texas campaigned in Tennessee and Mississippi. Bates, who was promoted from captain to major on March 3, 1863, served with the 9th Cavalry until placed on temporary duty in August 1863. He returned to the regiment, which was part of Ross's brigade, in April 1864 and was present when the men went to Georgia. On May 14, 1864, the brigade was ordered to the vicinity of Rome at the juncture of the Etowah and Coosa Rivers. For the next week, Ross's brigade operated around Rome while General Johnston tried to decide if he needed to retreat across the Etowah River. On May 20, 1864, the Rebel infantry finally crossed the stream behind a screen of cavalry. The next day Bates was with the 9th Texas when it attacked elements of two Federal cavalry regiments which were trailing the withdrawing army. The Yankees resisted two charges before retiring from the field. During the skirmish a minié ball smashed Bates's mouth knocking out some teeth, breaking his jaw, and splitting his tongue. Two days later Sherman's Federals crossed the Etowah River. Bates took no nourishment for nine days and then was only able to feed himself after forcing a rubber tube down his throat. It would be months before he returned to duty.[42] *Photo courtesy of CRC*

HENRY ELMS
carte de visite

On May 27, 1864, Private Henry Elms was with Cleburne's division on the right wing of the Rebel line near Pickett's Mills. Elms was born in Independence County, Arkansas, on May 3, 1844, and joined Company F, 6th Texas Infantry, at Victoria, Texas, on November 3, 1861. Except for a brief two-month stint in Mississippi during the summer of 1862, the regiment remained west of the Mississippi River until it was captured at Arkansas Post on January 11, 1863. The men, including Elms, were exchanged about three months later. The 6th Infantry then became part of the Texas brigade in Cleburne's division. In 1863 Elms was present during the Battles of Chickamauga and Missionary Ridge.

At Pickett's Mills, Cleburne's men occupied a rocky wooded ridge that dominated a semicircular depression through which the Federals tried to push an entire corps. The division, including Elms and the 6th Texas, poured a devastating fire into the Union lines and turned back several assaults. Around ten o'clock that evening, Cleburne ordered two brigades, including the men from Texas, to counterattack. Granbury's soldiers "raised a regular Texas Yell, or an Indian Yell or perhaps both together and started forward through the brush. . . ." In the dark, the fire from the weapons illuminated the woods like flashes of lightening, and the Rebels could see the line of blue coats in front. The Texans were quickly on top of the enemy, who withdrew in panic. Federal losses at Pickett's Mills were put at 3,000 men. Cleburne's division of 4,683 soldiers had 85 men killed and 363 wounded.[43] *Photo courtesy of Mrs. Mark Kerr Collection, U.S.A.M.H.I.*

142

JAMES PHILLIP CRAVER
copy print

James Phillip Craver was born on December 22, 1844, in Georgia and later moved to Harrison County, Texas, with his parents. He joined the service on December 20, 1862, as a private in Company D, 15th Texas Cavalry Regiment. At the time, the regiment was at Arkansas Post, so Carver had likely enlisted in response to the call of some officer who was home on recruiting duty. However, there is no indication that Craver had joined the 15th Texas prior to its surrender on January 11, 1863, so his active service began when he joined the Army of Tennessee sometime in the spring of 1863.

In 1864 the 15th Cavalry (dismounted) was part of Granbury's Texas brigade, Cleburne's division; the men saw action at Resaca and then Pickett's Mills before falling back with the Rebel army to a strong series of entrenchments around Kennesaw Mountain.

On June 27, 1864, Craver was in the line when the Federals launched a major assault against Cleburne's and another division. The attack cost the Federals more than 3,000 casualties and was easily repulsed. The Confederates losses were less than 500 men, but one of the wounded was Private Craver. The ball that struck Craver pierced his right lung and carried away part of a rib. Few soldiers who were hit in the lungs survived, and the surgeon, believing that Craver was mortally wounded, placed him among those solders who were likely to die. The next morning someone discovered that Craver was still alive and took him back to the hospital. After many weeks of suffering, he returned to the 15th Texas Cavalry and surrendered with the unit in 1865.[44] *Photo courtesy of Dorothy Cravens Collection, U.S.A.M.H.I.*

On the evening of July 9, 1864, Johnston led his army across the Chattahoochee River, the last natural barrier before Atlanta. The move was more psychologically damaging that tactically harmful, but President Davis was now totally disgusted with Johnston's performance. He removed Johnston on July 17 and replaced him with Lt. Gen. John Bell Hood, who was then serving as a corps commander in the Army of Tennessee. Ironically, Hood had favored Johnston's decision to withdraw across the Chattahoochee River. At the time of the appointment, Hood was still regarded as a fine divisional commander, but he had not yet had time to prove his abilities as the leader of a corps, much less to warrant his being trusted with an entire army. Furthermore, Hood's health was questionable since his left arm had been shattered at Gettysburg and his right leg had been amputated after being wounded at Chickamauga. This image shows how the general's physical condition had deteriorated after those wounds.

In the Army of Northern Virginia, Hood had been beloved by the Texans he led, but in the Heartland the situation was different. There, the Army of Tennessee lacked the winning tradition of Lee's troops, and despite Johnston's troubles with his superiors, he was well-liked by the common soldiers, including the men from the Lone Star State. Notwithstanding Hood's connection to Texas, some of the men from the state were skeptical about his abilities. One Texas officer wrote in his diary that Johnston "had so endeared himself to his soldiers, that no man can take his place." After the fall of Atlanta, that same officer wrote that Hood had "virtually murdered 10,000 men," and added that "the Yank[s] capture the first piece of public property they have seen this summer, for which they must thank Jeff Davis for removing Gen. Johnston and appointing Hood in his place."[45]

Hood's performance as an army commander was dreadful, but neither he nor anyone else could have saved the Confederacy from its fate in that terrible summer of 1864. To the Texans whom he led in Virginia, Hood remained a hero, but those men from the western regiments usually took a different view of the highest ranking Texan in the Confederate army. *Photo courtesy of Gregg Gibbs*

JOHN BELL HOOD
copy print

MALCOLM M. HORNSBY
copy print

Pvt. Malcolm M. Hornsby was with Company B, 18th Texas Cavalry (dismounted), Granbury's brigade, on July 20, 1864, when Hood committed the Army of Tennessee to the first of three major battles. This particular engagement took place in front of the Atlanta entrenchments and along Peachtree Creek. Hornsby was from Bishop County and twenty years old when he mustered into the service at Dallas on March 15, 1862. The 18th Texas and Hornsby were captured at Arkansas Post and, after being exchanged, became part of Cleburne's division in the Army of Tennessee. On July 20, 1864, the men marched and countermarched, but they saw no heavy fighting. That night the men withdrew to the Atlanta line and filed into the trenches that formed a salient near a ridge known as Bald Knob. The next morning they were blasted by massed artillery; one devastating shot killed or wounded at least 17 men in the 18th Cavalry. Soon afterward, they faced probing infantry attacks which, though repulsed, inflicted more casualties on the brigade. Throughout the rest of the day, sporadic artillery and infantry fire continued to harass the brigade; by evening 47 men were dead and 120 more wounded.[46] Hornsby was not injured during the fight, but the next day, July 22, he was captured during Hood's second attempt to break the Federal grip on Atlanta. *Photo courtesy of the Archives Division, TSL*

145

WILLIAM JAMES OLIPHANT
copy print

Pvt. William James Oliphant was with the 6th Texas Infantry of Granbury's brigade when Hood attacked the Federals on July 22, 1864. Oliphant, who was from Austin, had originally mustered into service in Company G on November 14, 1861, at the age of sixteen. The 6th Infantry was captured at Arkansas Post and subsequently attached to the Army of Tennessee after being exchanged. While a prisoner, Oliphant showed his disdain for the Federals by refusing to salute a Union medical officer. The furious doctor reacted by calling the guards and having them take the defiant young Texan to the smallpox ward, where he was forced to work for ten days.[47]

On the night of July 21, 1864, Oliphant and the rest of his corps pulled out of the line and began marching south and then east; their orders were to move around the southern flank of the Union army and attack. The 6th Texas had already lost seventeen men to enemy fire during the day and the long march further sapped the energy of the men. Nevertheless they attacked around 10:00 A.M. the next morning. During the noise and confusion, the 6th Texas and the 15th Texas Cavalry became separated from the rest of the brigade. The soldiers soon found themselves flanked and forced to fall back. The regiments reformed and went back into battle only to be thrown back again. Around 5:00 P.M. the men attacked for the last time. About half the soldiers from the 6th Texas "reached the enemy's works, where they fought with bayonets and clubbed muskets. . . ." However, the enemy was strong and resisted stubbornly. The 6th Texas was forced to fall back again. Regimental losses for the day were five killed, twenty-four wounded, and fifteen missing.[48] Oliphant was captured and finally exchanged near the end of the war. *Photo courtesy of the Austin History Center, Austin Public Library*

William Hugh Young was born on January 1, 1838, in Booneville, Missouri, and moved to Red River County, Texas, as a child. He graduated from the University of Virginia in 1861 and returned to Texas. In September Young raised a company of infantry; the men elected him captain and they became part of the 9th Texas Infantry. Young led his men at Shiloh and became colonel of the 9th Texas when the regiment reorganized after the battle. Young then commanded the 9th Texas at Stones River and Chickamauga; he was wounded in both battles.

Young and the 9th Texas were part of Ector's brigade when it rejoined Johnston in May 1864. During the next two months, the Army of Tennessee was forced back to the environs of Atlanta, and on July 19 the 9th Texas entered the fortifications that protected the city. When Ector was seriously wounded eight days later, Young assumed command of the brigade. By then the men had improved their position by digging a continuous line of rifle pits and constructing two parallel lines of abatis. They later built a large redoubt and added an eight-foot-high palisade to the sector they guarded.[49] Such powerful defenses deterred Sherman from directly attacking Atlanta, but Hood lacked the men to both occupy the entrenchments and protect his supply line to the south. When Sherman's men cut the Macon and Western Railroad, Hood had to abandon the city. Around 9:00 P.M. on September 1, 1864, Young's men pulled out of their well-prepared trenches and left Atlanta. Young was subsequently wounded in the foot by a shell and captured at Allatoona, Georgia. On February 20, 1865, the Confederate Congress approved Young's promotion to brigadier general even though he was still being held as a prisoner of war. *Photo courtesy of the Library of Congress, US Z62-59348*

FELIX HUSTON ROBERTSON
copy print

After the fall of Atlanta, the desperate plight of the Rebel army, combined with Sherman's growing tolerance of violence against civilians to break the spirit of the waning Confederacy, put an even harder edge on an already brutal war. On October 3, 1864, that hardness was apparent in the actions of Felix Huston Robertson of Texas. Robertson, the son of Brig. Gen. Jerome Robertson, resigned in his senior year at West Point and joined the Confederate army as an artillery officer. He commanded batteries at Shiloh, Stones River, and Chickamauga. In January 1864 Robertson took charge of the artillery attached to Maj. Gen. Joseph Wheeler's cavalry corps; by the end of the Atlanta campaign he commanded a cavalry brigade with the unconfirmed rank of brigadier general.

On October 2, 1864, Robertson's men were part of a small force at Saltville in southwest Virginia that, in heavy fighting, repulsed a column of Union cavalry raiders, including the 5th U.S. Colored Cavalry. The withdrawing Federals left about 350 men behind. The next morning Robertson's men moved among the wounded men, methodically killing black soldiers and shooting an occasional white trooper.[50] When Robertson's superior heard about the atrocity, he ordered Robertson's arrest. By then, the Texan and his men had already returned to the safety of Wheeler's lax command. Confederate authorities never condoned such killings and tried to bring Robertson before a court of inquiry, but the confusion within the dying Confederacy frustrated the attempt. After the war one of the perpetrators of the Saltville massacre was hanged by a Federal court, but Robertson was never brought to trial. *Photo courtesy of CRC*

148

ABRAM HARRIS
copy print

In the weeks following the loss of Atlanta, Hood harried Sherman's supply lines in the hope of drawing him out of the city. On October 5, 1864, a division of the Rebel army attacked the Union garrison that protected the railroad line at Allatoona, Georgia. Among these troops was Lt. Col. Abram Harris of the 14th Texas Cavalry (dismounted), Ector's brigade. Harris, who was from Tarrant County, had joined the regiment as a 1st lieutenant in Company H, on February 15, 1862. At the time he was thirty-six years old. The 14th Cavalry was dismounted in the spring of 1862 and transferred to Corinth, Mississippi. Harris was promoted to lieutenant colonel on May 8, 1862, and appears to have been with the regiment not only during the Atlanta campaign but also in the earlier battles at Stones River and Chickamauga.

At Allatoona, Harris was with the 14th Cavalry when it attacked the Federal lines. The men moved forward with a yell and carried the outer works in five minutes, "driving the enemy out of their entrenchments with the butts of our guns and rocks, as we did not have any bayonets. . . ."[51] The Texans then charged through the second line, where the colonel of the regiment was severely wounded; Harris took command. His men took cover in some buildings and for the next two hours sniped at the main fortifications that protected Allatoona, but the Rebels were unable to break in. Attrition had so reduced the 14th Texas Cavalry that it only took eight-seven men into the fight; four were killed and forty-five were wounded. Harris concluded his report by noting that the casualty figure "speaks more for the undaunted bravery and heroism of one and all on that day than any thing I could say."[52] *Photo courtesy of Martin Callahan and Don Scroggins*

BENJAMIN FRANKLIN BATCHELOR
copy print from H. J. H. Rugeley,
Batchelor-Turner Letters, 1861–1864

Benjamin Franklin Batchelor, a New Yorker by birth, was practicing law in Gonzales, Texas, when the Civil War began. On September 12, 1861, Batchelor joined the army as a sergeant in Company C, 8th Texas Cavalry; within a year he was 1st lieutenant of the company. Batchelor's letters to his family are sprinkled with acrid dislike for the "abolition horde" and a strong belief in the value of cavalry operations. On January 25, 1863, he told his father that:

The damage our cavalry inflicts upon them by cutting off supplies & munitions of war is almost incalculable. . . . When the history of this war is written it will be found that the inability of our enemies to overrun the South was attributable as much to the blows inflicted upon them, when least thought of, by our intrepid cavalry, as to the unconquerable violence of our infantry.[53]

During the Atlanta campaign, Hood used his cavalry corps for the activities that Batchelor favored. Such tactics annoyed Sherman, but they failed utterly to thwart him. After Atlanta fell, Hood hoped to use his fast moving cavalry to threaten Sherman's lines of communication and force him to disperse his army. On October 13, 1864, Batchelor was with the 8th Cavalry when it made a feint at the Federals in Rome, Georgia. Batchelor was wounded and captured when his regiment was charged by a overwhelming cavalry force and routed. He died in captivity three days later at Rome, Georgia.

150

HIRAM BRONSON GRANBURY
copy print

Hiram Bronson Granbury led the best-known Texas infantry brigade that served in the Army of Tennessee, but no uniformed image of the general has ever been discovered—a later photographer produced this composite view of the Texan as a brigadier general. When Texas seceded, Granbury, who was serving as chief justice of McLennan County, Texas, organized the Waco Guards, which became Company A of the 7th Texas Infantry. In October 1861 Captain Granbury was elected major of the regiment. The 7th Texas was captured at Fort Donelson on February 16, 1862, but several senior officers praised Granbury's performance. After being exchanged, Granbury was promoted to colonel of the 7th Texas on August 29, 1862. He commanded the regiment in the Vicksburg campaign and led his men during the Battle of Chickamauga. On November 25, 1863, at Missionary Ridge, Granbury first assumed command of a brigade when its commander, Brig. Gen. James A. Smith, was wounded near the end of the fight. The command included the 6th, 7th, and 10th Texas Infantry as well as the 15th, 17th, 18th, 24th, and 25th Texas Cavalry (dismounted). The next day he participated in Cleburne's celebrated defense at Ringgold Gap. Cleburne was most complimentary of Granbury's performance at both Missionary Ridge and Ringgold Gap. On January 2, 1864, Granbury was promoted to brigadier general; he led the brigade until Smith returned to duty in mid-July. Granbury assumed permanent command of the Texans when Smith was wounded again on July 22, 1864. Granbury and his mentor, Patrick Cleburne, both died on November 30, 1864, while leading their infantry at the Battle of Franklin. *Photo courtesy of MOC*

151

CALLOWAY REID
tinted ambrotype

Calloway Reid enlisted as a private in Company F, 7th Texas Infantry, on February 15, 1863; he was a thirty-nine-year-old farmer from Upshur County. Reid joined the regiment while it was campaigning in Mississippi, but he was sick when the 7th Texas later fought at Chickamauga. Reid did return to the ranks in time to serve at Missionary Ridge, Ringgold Gap, and in the Atlanta Campaign.

Hood's invasion started well but began unraveling on November 29, 1864, at Spring Hill, Tennessee, when poor tactical coordination allowed a retreating Union column to escape attack and withdraw to the safety of fortified positions at Franklin. The incident at Spring Hill only increased Hood's illogical belief that his infantry was fearful of attacking the enemy. The next day Hood brought his army before the entrenchments at Franklin; he intended to discipline his men by attacking the Federals in their stronghold.[54] Around 4:00 P.M. he sent eighteen brigades of Confederate infantry forward in an advance that rivaled Pickett's Charge at Gettysburg in both size and violence. Of the almost 27,000 Confederates on the battlefield that day, some 6,500 became casualties. Most of the losses came from the almost suicidal charge ordered by a physically exhausted man who mistakenly believed that his soldiers lacked either the will or the courage to fight. Reid was one of the soldiers who perished in the charge. *Photo courtesy of George Esker*

152

ROBERT BUTLER YOUNG
copy print

In the fall of 1861, Robert B. Young of Meridian, Bosque County, Texas, advertised in a circular that he had authority from the Confederate War Department to raise a regiment of Texas riflemen: "Companies, who desire to participate in the glorious struggle for independence, will send their muster rolls to the undersigned at once."[55] The response was good, and that fall the ten companies that Young helped raise became the 10th Texas Infantry. Young served briefly as major until September 12, 1862, when he was promoted to lieutenant colonel of the regiment. When Young was thirty-three years old, he and the 10th Texas were captured at Arkansas Post on January 11, 1863. Young was exchanged that spring and served with the regiment at Chickamauga, Missionary Ridge, and in the Atlanta campaign. On November 30, 1864, Young was killed while leading his men at Franklin. After Hood finished slaughtering the infantry that he did not think would fight, Young's fellow officer wrote:

And the wails and cries of widows and orphans made at Franklin . . . will heat up the fires of the bottomless pit to burn the soul of Gen. J. B. Hood for Murdering their husbands and fathers at that place that day. It can't be called anything else but cold blooded Murder.[56]

The remains of Young, his brigade commander, Hiram Granbury, and their divisional commander, Patrick Cleburne, were interned alongside each other. The fierce charge at Franklin proved that the Army of Tennessee had the courage to attack against impossible odds, but after the fight there was almost no infantry left to carry on the campaign. *Photo courtesy of Jenece Waid-Hurst*

153

HOWELL POPE HALE AND JAMES MONROE WATSON
copy print

Howell Pope Hale enlisted as a private on September 23, 1861, at Taos, Texas; his friend, Pvt. James M. Watson, enlisted two days later. The men soldiered together in Company G, 10th Texas Cavalry. When the regiment was dismounted in April 1862, Watson and several other men were detached to take the horses back to Texas. Before he returned to the 10th Texas, Watson was temporarily attached to Col. Walter P. Lane's Texas cavalry regiment and served in the Prairie Grove, Arkansas, campaign in December 1862. Near Cane Hill, Lane's men captured thirty-two wagons and 200 prisoners. Watson rejoined his old regiment, which was part of Ector's brigade, in March 1863. Watson and Hale fought together at Chickamauga, where Watson received a severe stomach wound. The injury kept him in the hospital for several months, but

Watson was back with his unit by April 1864. Sometime that summer his friend, Hale, was badly wounded and sent home to Texas. On July 19, 1864, Watson was captured at Rodney, Mississippi, and held until at least October 7.

After being exchanged, Watson was with the few soldiers left in the 10th Texas Cavalry when they fought at Franklin. He was also in the ranks when the Army of Tennessee later tried to lay siege to Nashville, Tennessee. There, on December 15–16, 1864, the Federals smashed what remained of the once powerful Army of Tennessee and sent it reeling southward. Watson was slightly wounded by a piece of shrapnel but managed to withdraw with the beaten army. He finally surrendered at Citronelle, Alabama, on May 4, 1865. *Photo courtesy of Jeneal Riley*

ALEXANDER MAY SHANNON
copy print

While Granbury's and Ector's brigades campaigned in Tennessee, a weak force of Wheeler's Confederate cavalry and some Georgia militia offered token opposition to Sherman's 62,000 veterans as they marched toward the sea. The penchant for Wheeler's undisciplined cavalry to inflict injury on friend and foe alike raised the ire both of the civilians caught in their path and the more responsible Rebel commanders who tried to control the growing violence of their own troops. Some of the more serious offenders were led by Capt. Alexander May Shannon. In the spring of 1861, Shannon raised what became Company C, 8th Texas Cavalry. In October 1862 he was promoted to captain, and in the summer of 1864 Shannon received permission from Hood to organize an irregular force to gather information and punish marauders. Many of the two dozen soldiers who served in the scouts were from Company C and, more specifically, from

Limestone County, Texas. The scouts stayed behind when Hood moved into Tennessee in the fall of 1864. Unfortunately, the men spent less time gathering information than bushwhacking stragglers from Sherman's army. One scout later recalled that "sometimes we would wait until dark and act as the rear guard and grab every fellow that got behind, catch him, or kill him. The next thing after that was to go through his pockets and you would be surprised to see the things we would get from him."[57] Another scout saw a fellow trooper kill a Yankee prisoner simply because he would not be quiet. Years later, overzealous ex-Confederate patriots tried to turn these ruffians into heroes, but the surviving documents indicate that the scouts did little to honorably serve the dying Confederacy.[58] *Photo courtesy of Washington County Historical Society, Fayetteville, Arkansas*

CHRISTOPHER C. WEIR
copy print

In early 1865 the remains of the Army of Tennessee were dispersed to provide meager reinforcements for other commands in the rapidly dwindling Confederacy. Granbury's brigade went to North Carolina to assist in a last ditch effort to delay Sherman's soldiers as they pushed northward. In 1861 twenty-three-year-old Christopher C. Weir had mustered into the service at Houston as a private in Company C, 10th Texas Infantry. Weir was captured with the 10th Texas at Arkansas Post on January 11, 1863, and after being exchanged, fought with the Army of Tennessee at both Chickamauga and Missionary Ridge. Weir then served in both the Atlanta and Franklin-Nashville campaigns. He was with the regiment when it arrived in Raleigh, North Carolina, probably in February 1865. Weir, promoted to sergeant, was wounded in the shoulder while skirmishing against the advancing Federals on March 7. He returned to duty on March 29 after missing the last major action of the Army of Tennessee at Bentonville, North Carolina (March 19–21, 1865). On April 9, 1865, the last reorganization of the Army of Tennessee took place. What remained of the units from Granbury's old brigade were consolidated together into one regiment and designated the First Texas Consolidated Infantry. The new regiment saw its first and only action three days later at Salisbury Point, North Carolina, when it was part of a Rebel force attacked by Union cavalry. Weir was captured there and was not released until he took the oath of allegiance on June 13, 1865. His new regiment surrendered with the rest of the army on April 26, 1865. *Photo courtesy of Larry D. Shields Collection, U.S.A.M.H.I.*

156

FRANCIS ASBURY TAULMAN
copy print

In 1860 Francis "Frank" Asbury Taulman, eighteen years old, left Kentucky for Texas. Taulman settled in Dallas and took a job in which he could learn accounting. On October 2, 1861, he enlisted as a private in the Lamar Cavalry, which was officially Company G, 1st Texas Cavalry Battalion. Taulman fought at Pea Ridge, Arkansas, before his unit was dismounted and sent to Corinth, Mississippi. In May 1862 the battalion was expanded to regimental strength and designated the 32d Cavalry. It remained dismounted and became part of Ector's Texas infantry brigade. Taulman's parents had not wanted their son to move to Texas, and his subsequent support of the Confederacy caused a real rift in the family. He had no contact with his parents for years, but in May 1864 Taulman tried to heal the breach when he wrote the following:

Long years have rolled by since you received tidings from me. . . . The side I have thought proper to choose in this unhappy war, contrary to your expressed wishes, I cannot think would create personal enmity between us; it is a political difference. I was influenced alone by a sense of right and justice. I looked carefully before I leaped, and the result is. . . . I have been a Confederate soldier 3 years. . . . I hope I have not incurred your displeasure, or lessened your love and esteem for me, for choosing the path I am now treading. . . ."[59]

Taulman later served in the Atlanta and Franklin-Nashville campaigns. He also was with Ector's brigade when it left the Army of Tennessee to join the garrison at Mobile, Alabama. On April 9, 1865, he was in Fort Blakely when it surrendered to an overwhelming Union force. Three days later he wrote his father saying, "I have the honor to report that I am now a prisoner of war, basking in the sunshine of numerous Fed. countenances as they silently glide to and fro around the guard line. . . ."[60] The few survivors of Ector's brigade surrendered at Citronelle, Alabama, on May 4, 1865. *Photo courtesy of CAH, John Brown Papers, CN 06048*

Chapter 6

The Forgotten War:
Texans in the Indian Territory,
Arkansas, and Southern Missouri

The only difference by which we recognized that we were in Arkansas was a sign-board with the learned inscription, 'Ark-Saw.' . . . After crossing the imaginary line, three hearty cheers were given for Texas.

—J. P. Blessington

At the beginning of the Civil War, authorities in Richmond were too busy with other issues to think very much about how to conduct operations along the extreme northwestern borders of the fledgling Confederacy. Beyond the obvious fact that Arkansas needed to be protected, the only plan was to secure the support of as many tribes as possible in the Indian Territory and to try to bring slave-holding Missouri into the new Confederacy. However, implementing this strategy, or any plan for that matter, was going to be hard since these border areas were sparsely populated, possessed few materials necessary to fight a war, had only a rudimentary railroad system, and were badly divided in their loyalties. And pressures in other, more important theaters of operations soon forced Richmond first to neglect and then largely to forget about the war across the Mississippi River. One of the few available sources of support outside the region was Texas, and the Lone Star State played a vital role in supporting the war effort in the forgotten border states of the Trans-Mississippi West.

The men in the first Texas regiment to see action in the region mostly came from the eastern counties; they had organized out of fear that radical Unionists in Kansas would sweep through the Indian Territory and invade the Lone Star State. The colonel of the unit, Elkanah Greer, named it the South Kansas–Texas Regiment in anticipation of such an event. However, the regiment was officially accepted into the service as the 3d Texas Cavalry and then sent to Fort Smith, Arkansas, rather than Kansas. Greer was also given permission to raise an artillery battery, which was accepted into service on July 2, 1861, and commanded by Capt. John J. Good. When Good resigned in early 1862, James P. Douglas assumed command, and the unit became known as Douglas's Battery.

In the summer of 1861, the 3d Cavalry and Good's Battery traveled together to Fort Smith only to discover that their fellow Texan and commander of the region, Brig. Gen. Ben McCulloch, had already taken his men northward to rendezvous with Missouri State Guard troops under Sterling Price. The artillerymen remained in Fort Smith to find additional horses and to repair equipment while the cavalrymen made a forced march to join McCulloch and Price. On August 10, 1861, the Confederates won an impressive victory over a smaller Union force at Wilson's Creek, Missouri. However, the victors, having suffered 1,200 casualties while inflicting 1,300 losses, were too exhausted and disorganized to pursue their beaten enemy. The 3d Cavalry had only 6 men killed at Wilson's Creek.[1] In the aftermath of the battle, Price and McCulloch could not agree on a common strategy, and by late September 1861 the Federals had regained the initiative. Meanwhile, the newly raised 6th and 11th Texas Cavalry Regiments and the 4th Texas Cavalry Battalion reinforced McCulloch. Elements of the 3d, 6th, and 11th regiments were ordered into the Indian Territory in the middle of December 1861 to help locate and punish a group of Creeks who were trying to maintain their neutrality but were seen as potential allies of the Federals. On December 26 the mounted Confederates smashed the hapless Indians at Chustenahlah.[2] The Texans then returned to Arkansas, where they were soon joined by the 9th Texas Cavalry and the 1st Texas Cavalry Battalion.

On January 10, 1862, Maj. Gen. Earl Van Dorn assumed command of the recently created Trans-Mississippi District, which included Arkansas, most of Missouri, the Indian Territory, and Louisiana north of the Red River. The appointment seemed reasonable for two reasons: First, it ended the bickering between Price and McCulloch. Second, Van Dorn was an experienced soldier, having graduated from West Point, served in the Mexican War, and spent many years fighting Indians in Texas and elsewhere. During the early months of the Civil War, Van Dorn's brief but successful command of the Department of Texas had favorably impressed the Rebel War Department. A man with such experience, it was believed, should be able to manage the situation in the West. Confederate authorities had high expectations of Van Dorn, and the general had every confidence in his own abilities. The new commander arrived in Little Rock in late January 1862 and quickly developed an ambitious plan to invade Missouri with the ultimate aim of capturing St. Louis. However, 10,000 Federals under Maj. Gen. Samuel Ryan Curtis had recently invaded Northwest Arkansas and had to be eliminated before any offensive could begin.

On March 3, 1862, Van Dorn assumed command of the men that Price and McCulloch had gathered in the Boston Mountains near Fayetteville, Arkansas. At that time all the Texas units were part of McCulloch's division, comprising one cavalry and one infantry brigade. Brig. Gen. James McIntosh commanded the cavalry in the division: the 3d, 6th, 9th, and 11th Texas Regiments plus the 1st Texas Battalion. The infantry brigade, commanded by Col. Louis Hébert, contained the 4th Texas Cavalry Battalion, which had been recently dismounted, while Good's six-gun battery was part of the divisional artillery. Arriving from Indian Territory, Brig. Gen. Albert Pike commanded a mixed force of 2,500 mounted Indians and a squadron of Texas cavalry commanded by Capt. Otis G. Welch. Van Dorn's total force consisted of 16,000 men.

After some preliminary maneuvering, the two armies met in Northwest Arkansas at Pea Ridge on March 7, 1862. Shortly after 12:30 P.M. the Confederate command structure on the right wing, where all the Texas units were deployed, began collapsing when the Federals killed McCulloch. McIntosh then assumed command, only to die shortly afterward. Hébert, third in command, could not be located and was captured by the Federals that evening. Eventually, command of the disorganized division devolved on Colonel Greer of the 3d Texas Cavalry, who managed to hold the rattled troops together. That evening he got most of the units moving toward the still organized left wing under Price. On March 8, only Good's Battery and the 4th Battalion engaged the enemy. Around 10:00 A.M. Van Dorn ordered the beaten Confederates to withdraw. For the next several days, the 3d Texas Cavalry helped cover the beaten army as it withdrew to safety. The exact number of Texans who were casualties at the Battle at Pea Ridge is unknown, but it is doubtful if that number reached one hundred. Despite minimal losses, the winter campaign and a difficult retreat had worn the Texans down; both men and horses were reported as being "in dreadful condition."[3]

From the security of Van Buren, Arkansas, Van Dorn refused to admit he had been beaten by Curtis, writing, "I was not defeated, but only foiled in my intentions."[4] The Rebel commander added that he would take the offensive again at the first opportunity. Before Van Dorn could act on such a rash promise, he received orders to bring his entire command east of the Mississippi River; his men were desperately needed to recover from the blow of Forts Henry and Donelson falling into enemy hands. By late April 1862 most of Van Dorn's troops were in Mississippi, which left the Trans-Mississippi District with practically no organized force to protect it from Union invasion. In Arkansas the political leadership was in an uproar at what appeared to be the calculated abandonment of the state. However, authorities in Richmond had no resources to spare, and Pres. Jefferson Davis merely wrote Van Dorn suggesting that he issue a proclamation to reassure the people of the Trans-Mississippi District. Instead, Van Dorn, acting on his own authority and without Richmond's approval, appointed Maj. Gen. Thomas C. Hindman to command the district. Hindman was an ambitious Arkansas political who had been a leading secessionist in the U.S. Congress. When the war began he decided to try his hand at soldiering. Later events would show that Hindman had little talent as a field commander, but he was a first-rate organizer who had no time for anyone who did not get behind the war effort. Shortly after arriving in Little Rock, he

announced on May 31, 1862, that he had come "to drive out the invader or to perish in the attempt." He added that under the dire circumstances "it is essential that the soldier and citizen each shall do his whole duty."[5] Hindman desperately needed organized troops to protect Arkansas, and one place to get them was Texas. Seventy days later, when Maj. Gen. Theophilus Holmes arrived to assume command of an expanded theater renamed the Trans-Mississippi Department, Hindman proudly noted that he had drawn from the Lone Star State twenty-five regiments and three batteries (which represented slightly less than 50 percent of the entire force he had raised). Hindman did admit that many of the new units were under strength and poorly armed, but they were an army whose very presence helped protect Arkansas from being overrun during the crucial summer of 1862.[6]

Holmes's new command now included not only Missouri, Arkansas, and the Indian Territory, but also all of Louisiana west of the Mississippi River, Texas, and Arizona Territory. On September 28, 1862, Holmes, who soon proved to be a most incompetent theater commander, assigned Hindman to lead the troops into Northwest Arkansas. His new command was officially designated as the First Army Corps, Army of the West. Hindman, like Van Dorn, was captivated with the idea of invading Missouri and decided to launch a winter advance. On December 7, 1862, his men were checked and forced to retreat after a bitter fight at Prairie Grove, Arkansas. The largest number of Texas troops, about 1,400 men, or 12 percent of Hindman's army, was under the command of Brig. Gen. John S. Roane. These were the 20th, 22d, 31st, and 34th Texas Cavalry Regiments (dismounted). The only other unit present on the battlefield was the 1st Texas Cavalry (Partisan Rangers), which contained 444 effectives. The Battle of Prairie Grove cost the Rebels 1,150 casualties, or 9.5 percent of those engaged. Considering the actual number of Texans on the battlefield, their reported losses were surprisingly light, totaling only 2 killed and 10 wounded.[7]

Prairie Grove was the last feeble attempt of the Confederates to seize southwestern Missouri; it was a serious setback, but a bigger disaster was about to occur in the eastern section of Arkansas. The genesis of that defeat rested in Holmes's need to block the lower reaches of the Arkansas River from Union naval incursions. Undoubtedly, the river had to be protected, but time and again the Federals had proven that fixed fortifications along waterways could be taken. That lesson was lost on Holmes, who ordered his men to construct a major fortification at Arkansas Post and then garrisoned it with over 5,000 troops. On January 11, 1863, a combined Union force of 30,000 men and thirteen gunboats overwhelmed the position and captured most of its defenders. Among the surrendered troops were the 4th Texas Field Artillery, the 15th, 17th, 18th, 24th, and 25th Cavalry Regiments (dismounted), plus the 6th and 10th Texas Infantry. Arkansas Post netted the Union the biggest collection of prisoners in the West since the fall of Island Number 10 on April 8, 1862, and it was the largest body of Texans to surrender until the end of the Civil War.

The twin defeats at Prairie Grove and Arkansas Post led to yet another shakeup in the Trans-Mississippi West. On January 30, 1863, Richmond relieved Hindman of his command; six months later he assumed control of a division in the Army of Tennessee. It had become painfully obvious to those same authorities that Holmes could not manage such a large department, so on March 7, 1863, he was replaced by Lt. Gen. Edmund Kirby Smith, who mistakenly left Holmes in command of the District of Arkansas.

During the first half of 1863, Federal operations against Vicksburg drew Union and Confederate resources away from the District of Arkansas and largely dictated military operations there. In mid-April 1863, for example, Smith sent Brig. Gen. John S. Marmaduke with 5,000 cavalry on a raid into southeastern Missouri to try to draw as many Federals as possible away from Vicksburg. Among the troopers was Col. George F. Carter's Texas brigade, which contained the 19th and 21st Cavalry, Maj. Charles L. Morgan's cavalry battalion, and a section of Pratt's Texas artillery. Carter's command, which probably numbered 1,700 cavalrymen, suffered 54 casualties in the unsuccessful attempt to divert Union forces. A few months later, Smith allowed Holmes to attempt to distract the Federals again by attacking Helena, Arkansas. However the belated and unsuccessful assault took place on July 4, 1863, the day that Vicksburg finally fell. No Texas troops were involved in the battle that cost the Rebels more than 1,600 men.

During the summer of 1863, other Texas troops were campaigning in the Indian Territory. On July 17, several units were present at the Battle of Honey Springs, the decisive engagement of the Civil War in Indian Territory. On that day Texans from the 20th and 29th Cavalry, the 5th Partisan Rangers, and the Lee-Humphrey Battery held the center of the line. The Confederate force, which numbered about 6,000 men, suffered slightly more than 600 casualties before they were forced to withdraw. After the battle, Confederate operations in Indian Territory were largely confined to raiding activities to disrupt Union supply lines. Occasionally, the Rebels scored major successes. On September 19, 1864, for example, Col. Richard M. Gano of the Lone Star State, while leading an all-Texas force (including the 1st Cavalry Regiment, Arizona Brigade; the 5th Partisan Regiment; the 29th and 30th Cavalry; two independent cavalry companies; and Howell's Battery), captured 255 wagons at Cabin Creek. Successes like this annoyed Union forces, but the raiders never forced the Federals to relax their ever tightening hold on Indian Territory.

After the fall of Vicksburg, many Union troops were freed for other duties, and several thousand veteran troops came to reinforce the Federal base at Helena. On August 11, 1863, Maj. Gen. Frederick

Steele left Helena with about 12,000 men and began the long-anticipated advance on Little Rock. Guarding the capital city were 8,000 Rebels under Maj. Gen. Sterling Price, who had temporarily assumed command of the district because Holmes was ill. Among the Texas troops available for the city's defense were the 12th, 19th, and 21st Cavalry, as well as Morgan's cavalry battalion and part of Pratt's Battery. Price believed that he lacked the manpower to defend the capital adequately and offered only token opposition as Steele closed on Little Rock. On September 10, 1863, the Federals laid a pontoon bridge across the Arkansas River, the last natural barrier protecting the capital. Pratt's Battery inflicted some damage on the advancing Federals, but the Rebels offered only slight resistance before withdrawing to safety. By the close of the year, Union forces controlled Little Rock and the major towns north of the Arkansas River. The capture of Fort Smith in western Arkansas on September 1, 1863, guaranteed continued Federal dominance in the Indian Territory. The Union could begin the new year with the reasonable belief that the final occupation of Arkansas was about to begin.

In January 1864 the Union commander of the Department of the Gulf, Maj. Gen. Nathaniel Banks, received orders from Washington to begin plans for an advance along the Red River in Louisiana with the ultimate aim of occupying East Texas. Banks's resulting plan directly affected Arkansas, because it called for Steele to bring his men from Little Rock down through the southern part of the state for a rendezvous with Banks near Shreveport, Louisiana. Banks, with about 25,000 soldiers, began advancing on March 13, 1864. Ten days later Steele began moving into southern Arkansas; his first target was Camden. Because the town was located on a navigable river, Steele wanted to use it as a supply base to support the long march to the vicinity of Shreveport.

Meanwhile in Confederate Arkansas Holmes

recognized that he was too infirm to remain in command of the district and asked to be relieved. His superior, Kirby Smith, who had already reduced the old general's authority in October 1863 by removing the Indian Territory from the district, also informed Richmond that Holmes needed to go. On March 16, 1864, Holmes relinquished his command to Sterling Price.

Weeks before the Union campaign began, Smith had already grasped the magnitude of the threat and was planning to use all the infantry he could scrape together to oppose Banks. On March 18, 1864, Price received orders to send his infantry immediately to Louisiana. Kirby Smith's plan to concentrate against Banks made sense because that column posed the greatest danger to his department, but the decision denuded southern Arkansas and left Price with only a few thousand Missouri and Arkansas cavalrymen to oppose Steele's advance. However, Smith did try to help Price by ordering more cavalry to Arkansas. On April 6, 1864, the first of Texas Brig. Gen. Samuel B. Maxey's reinforcements from Indian Territory began arriving. These included Col. Tandy Walker's brigade of mounted Choctaw Indians and Brig. Gen. Richard Gano's Texans. Gano's brigade included Welch's independent cavalry company; the 1st regiment, Arizona Brigade; the 29th and 30th Cavalry; and Krumbhaar's Battery. These reinforcements helped, but Price's forces were still too small to do more than harass Steele. The only serious engagement occurred April 9–12, 1864, at Prairie D'Ane, and Gano's Texans were involved in that fight.

Steele occupied Camden on April 15. The Federals were now low on supplies, and the town had been stripped of all foodstuffs. Two days later, Steele learned that Banks's expedition had failed. In Louisiana, Smith had already ordered three divisions of infantry, including Maj. Gen. John Walker's Texans, to reinforce Price. For the present, Steele was less threatened by the enemy than he was by the need to find food for his men and their horses.

On April 18, 1864, Gano's Texans and elements of

163

four other Rebel brigades practically destroyed a Union forging column at Poison Spring. Total losses among the Confederates were 111 men, 31 of whom came from Gano's units. Federal losses totaled 301 men, including 181 who were killed. Most of the dead, some 117 soldiers, came from the ranks of the 1st Kansas Colored Infantry, many of whom were murdered after they had been wounded and captured. The 29th Texas Cavalry had a particular hatred for the 1st Kansas, because less than a year earlier at the Battle of Honey Springs, Indian Territory, the black infantrymen had routed them. The soldiers from the 29th Texas were not the only ones involved in the killings, but they played a major role in the tragedy at Poison Spring.[8]

By April 20 the Rebel infantry was closing on Camden and Steele's tenuous supply line back to Pine Bluff was in constant jeopardy from marauding Confederate cavalry. On April 25 the Confederates ambushed a returning supply train at Marks' Mill, which cost the Federals 300 wagons and 1,300 casualties, most of whom were captured. When Steele learned of this latest disaster, he made immediate plans to evacuate Camden and retreat by forced march to Little Rock. On April 30 the pursuing Confederate infantry caught Steele near Jenkins' Ferry on the Saline River. Walker's Texas Division had two of its three brigade commanders killed in the fight and suffered 340 casualties. Total casualties for the approximately 10,000 combatants was around 1,700 men, but Steele managed to escape.

Steele's Camden Expedition was the last major campaign in Arkansas, but the murderous irregular fighting continued unabated. Few Texans, however, were involved in the guerrilla war in Arkansas. On September 3, 1864, Maj. Gen. John H. Forney assumed command of Walker's division, which was then occupying camps in the southern part of the state. By late October 1864 the division had crossed into Louisiana and never returned to Arkansas. Only one Texas unit, Hynson's Battery, participated in Price's famous Missouri raid. That adventure began on August 28, 1864, at Camden and ended at Washington, Arkansas, on December 3. Gano's Texans returned to Indian Territory after the Camden Expedition, and the brigade served there until it was broken up in early 1865. When Kirby Smith accepted the surrender terms for the Trans-Mississippi Department on May 26, 1865, most organized resistance in Arkansas, Indian Territory, and southern Missouri had already ended and few, if any, Texas troops remained in the area.

During the war at least forty regular Texas units saw some service in this forgotten war, and many spent their entire career defending the region. Conditions in the Trans-Mississippi were always physically hard, and the men were sometimes engaged in bitter fighting that went largely unnoticed in the rest of the war-torn country. A decade after the war, a soldier from Walker's division wrote that Texas had "given too many . . . regiments and brigades to the late Confederate States service to let their history sink into obscurity. . . ."[9] To the men who served in southern Missouri, Indian Territory, and Arkansas, it could never be the forgotten war.

WILLIAM J. WOMACK
copy print

The majority of Texans who fought in the forgotten war in the Trans-Mississippi West enrolled to serve in the cavalry, but many soon found themselves dismounted and fighting as infantry. By early spring 1862, ten Texas cavalry units totaling 6,100 men were stationed either in Arkansas or Indian Territory. Shortly after the Battle of Pea Ridge in March 1862, most of these soldiers were dismounted and sent east of the Mississippi River. However, by September 1862, eleven new Texas units totaling 8,000 men had arrived as replacements.[10] Most of these men would also eventually be dismounted, but one who retained his horse was Pvt. William T. Womack of Company F, 19th Texas Cavalry.

Womack, at the age of twenty-nine, enlisted at Veal's Station, Parker County, Texas, on March 31, 1862. Early in 1863 his regiment was brigaded with three other cavalry units from Texas. Col. William H.

Parsons's name is popularly associated with that brigade, which spent more time campaigning in Arkansas than any other Texas cavalry command. Sometimes the men operated in detachments of scouts and pickets as they watched Federal activities in the state. Occasionally, they rode together in raids against isolated Union garrisons. Most engagements in which they fought were small affairs, but some, such as the Little Rock campaign in 1863 and the 1864 Red River Expedition in Louisiana, involved thousands of troops. After the war Parsons wrote that the campaigns in the West might seem "small indeed by comparison with the more imposing and dramatic events of the far east," but he knew that his men and others like them deserved more credit than they got for sustaining the war in the Trans-Mississippi West.[11] Womack's service record is incomplete, but he did survive the war with the rank of corporal. *Photo courtesy of CRC*

JOHN DEAN AND HIS WIFE, SUSAN
quarter-plate tintype

On June 17, 1861, Elkanah Greer, a planter and merchant in Marshall, Texas, issued General Orders No. 1 to the South Kansas–Texas Regiment that he commanded. The colonel began by apologizing to the men because the War Department had not yet provided the regiment with the arms, equipage, and transportation that it needed to join Brig. Gen. Ben McCulloch in Arkansas. Greer told his men to remember that "the eyes of our aged parents, wives, children, friends, nay, of the whole country are upon us," and that their actions must "convince the world that we are worthy of the rights and liberties we seek." He ended his order by reminding the company captains that they were "respectfully requested to enforce strict discipline in camp, and keep, as much as possible, their men in the company bounds."[12] One of the young soldiers who doubtless read Greer's first official order was Pvt. John William Dean of Company K. Dean, who was from Smith County and lived near Tyler, had joined the army on June 13, 1861. His regiment, which officially became the 3d Texas Cavalry, was the first outfit from the Lone Star State to see action in what would become the Trans-Mississippi District of Arkansas, Indian Territory, and southern Missouri. Dean remained with Company K throughout the war and ended his career as its captain. He is shown in this 1864 photograph with his wife, Susan. *Photo courtesy of J. Dale West*

ALBERT B. BLOCKER
copy print

In May 1861 the Texas Hunters assembled in Jonesville, Texas, and sixteen-year-old Albert B. Blocker stood proudly in the ranks as the men accepted from the "fair ladies" a silk flag emblazoned with the unit's name against a deer-hunting background. The company was formed in a double line and dressed in full uniforms of cadet gray. Some of the men were armed with new Colt pistols, which had been presented to them by the "patriotic citizens of the neighborhood." After much speech-making, the flag changed hands. That evening the speeches continued while the guests enjoyed a fine barbecue dinner. On June 13, 1861, the Texas Hunters were officially accepted into the Confederate service as Company A, 3d Texas Cavalry. Blocker became the company bugler.

On August 10, 1861, Blocker was with his company when the 3d Texas Cavalry fought its first battle at Wilson's Creek, Missouri. Years later, Blocker wrote that the Texas Hunters, firing their Navy Colt pistols, and four other companies of the 3d Cavalry rode into a line of Union infantry and drove them back.[13] The regiment had six men killed, twenty-three men wounded, and six missing when the battle ended in a Rebel victory. Blocker later participated in the winter 1861 campaign against the Creeks in Indian Territory and fought at Pea Ridge. On June 16, 1862, he was discharged from the service because the recently passed Conscription Act classified him as being too young for military service. *Photo courtesy of Max S. Lale*

JAMES C. BATES
copy print

As a teenager, James C. Bates of Paris, Texas, attended the local schools and then studied for two years at Bethel College, in west Tennessee. Bates was back in Texas when the war began, and on October 14, 1861, enlisted as 3d lieutenant of Company H, 9th Texas Cavalry. He was twenty-three years old.

The new regiment received orders to report to McCulloch in Northwest Arkansas, but while crossing Indian Territory, it was diverted to assist Col. William H. Cooper in subduing recalcitrant Indians. Cooper urgently needed the men as a sizable number of Indians in the region did not support the growing tilt toward the Confederacy. Among the dissidents were more than 7,000 Creeks and a few Seminoles. Their Creek leader, Chief Opothleyahola, owned slaves but wanted to keep his people neutral. Confederate authorities feared that such a large body of uncom-

mitted Indians might encourage Union sentiment in the region. On November 14, 1861, they sent Cooper, with a force of Indians and the 9th Texas Infantry, to deal with the Creeks. The move forced Opothleyahola to withdraw from his camp and move toward the Kansas border. On November 25, 1861, about seventy men from the 9th Texas were forced to retire after attacking a band of retreating Creeks near Round Mountain. On December 9 Cooper attacked the Indians again at Bird's Creek. The Rebels inflicted heavy losses on the Creeks; during the fight, Bates risked his life to rescue a wounded Confederate who was about to fall into the hands of the Indians. Bates went on to fight at Pea Ridge and then served east of the Mississippi River. *Photo courtesy of Mrs. Frederick Finka and DeWayne Lener Collection, U.S.A.M.H.I.*

DOUGLAS JOHN CATER
carte de visite

Douglas John Cater grew up near Mansfield, Louisiana, and graduated from school at Keachie in 1859 when he was eighteen years old. In August he accepted a job teaching music in the high school at Rusk in Cherokee County, Texas. Early in 1860 Cater joined a local militia unit, the Lone Star Defenders, and drilled with the men until he moved to Henderson, Texas. There, in early 1861, Cater joined a company which was first organized for infantry service but finally accepted as cavalry. On June 13, 1861, he mustered into the service as a private in Company B, 3d Texas Cavalry. Although Cater was well educated, he did not want to be an officer because he felt too young to command men. Cater saw his first action at Wilson's Creek on August 10, 1861.

In the winter of 1861, Opothleyahola's Creek braves were proving to be a more difficult adversary than Cooper had anticipated, and he asked for assistance

from Arkansas. Brig. Gen. James McIntosh responded by bringing 1,400 Texans to reinforce Cooper. Among the troops were Pvt. Cater and 350 other men from the 3d Texas Cavalry. The reinforced column finally brought on a decisive engagement and crushed the Creeks at Chustenahlah on the day after Christmas 1861; the 3d Texas fought as infantry in the battle. Just before Cater dismounted, an arrow passed close in front of his face, which he noted "produced a strange sensation in me." The ensuing infantry charge broke part of the Creek line, but Cater later wrote that some of the Indians were "brave and daring and would not leave." During the fight, Cater emptied his shotgun and pistol at one "big feather cap fellow" but could not say if he actually killed the man.[14] The Confederate dead totaled 15 men, including 5 from the 3d Texas Cavalry. *Photo courtesy of the Library of Congress, LCMS-15387-2*

169

BEN MCCULLOCH
ambrotype

Ben McCulloch was the personification of the tough Texas frontiersman who often appeared in contemporary popular writings. As a young man he left Tennessee to follow David Crockett to Texas, but a case of measles saved McCulloch from dying with him at the Alamo. McCulloch subsequently fought at the decisive victory at San Jacinto and later joined the Texas Rangers, in which he gained a statewide reputation as a talented Indian fighter. In the Mexican War he performed ably as Zachary Taylor's chief scout, and Samuel Reid's *The Scouting Expeditions of McCulloch's Texas Rangers* popularized those adventures and brought the Texan before a national audience. By 1861 the fifty-year-old McCulloch was widely known and well-respected as a scout, soldier, and Indian fighter. Shortly after Texas seceded, McCulloch was commissioned a colonel in the Texas army and received more favorable attention when, on February 16, 1861, he

accepted the surrender of the Federal garrison at San Antonio. On May 14, 1861, McCulloch was promoted to brigadier general and eventually assumed command of Confederate forces in Northwest Arkansas. He won a major victory at Wilson's Creek, Missouri, on August 10, but constant bickering with the commander of the Missouri State Guard, Sterling Price, prevented the two from exploiting their success. Richmond's solution was to appoint Maj. Gen. Earl Van Dorn to command both forces.

On March 7, 1861, McCulloch led a division of Texans, Arkansans, and Louisianians at Pea Ridge. Around 12:30 P.M. the general, who preferred his black velvet coat to a uniform, was riding through thick underbrush looking for the enemy line when he was shot and killed. *Photo courtesy of CAH, John Henry Brown Papers, CN 05947*

JOHN HENRY BROWN
copy print

John Henry Brown was seventeen years old in 1837 when he moved from Missouri to Texas. He was undoubtedly acquainted with Ben McCulloch by August 12, 1840, when the two men served together in the force that administered a stinging defeat to the Comanches at the Battle of Plum Creek. For the next twenty-two years, he and McCulloch remained friends; they occasionally saw action together fighting Indians or Mexican raiders. By the time of the Civil War, Brown was an established Texas journalist who had also served in the state legislature and been twice elected mayor of Galveston. In 1861 Brown joined McCulloch's staff with the rank of major and was on the field at Pea Ridge when his friend was slain. Sometime, probably on the evening of March 7, 1862, Brown retrieved the body from the battlefield. The next day he headed toward Texas with McCulloch's remains. On March 16, 1862, Brown wrote his wife to tell her of McCulloch's death. He also complained that the feud between McCulloch and Price seemed to be continuing even after the latter's death. "The vile Missourians who have fled to Texas breathing vile slanders upon him [McCulloch]," he wrote, "should be scourged through the land." Brown added that "floods of tears daily, hourly, force their way from my wearied eyes as I dwell upon his fall." Late on the evening of April 9, 1862, he delivered the general's remains to the State Capitol in Austin. The body was received by the governor and Ben McCulloch's older brother, Henry.[15] *Photo courtesy of CAH. John Henry Brown Papers, CN 06053*

171

JOHN CRIST
copy print

Pvt. John Crist of Company G, 6th Texas Cavalry, also served under McCulloch at the Battle of Pea Ridge. He had earlier enlisted at Dallas on September 7, 1861. Crist was twenty years old and brought with him a horse, one double-barrel shotgun, and a six shooter; the Confederacy valued his animal and weapons at $120.00. The 6th Cavalry joined McCulloch's command on October 20, 1861. Crist was reported as sick in camp in November and December, but he returned to duty in January 1862.

During the Civil War infantry and its supporting artillery dominated the battlefield, while cavalry was used primarily for scouting, raiding, and screening activities. The colorful and often overly-romanticized cavalry charges of past eras were rare, but sometimes isolated circumstances allowed the mounted arm to recreate its historic mission of breaking an enemy line by the shock of a mounted charge. On March 7, 1862, elements of the McCulloch's cavalry brigade, led by the 6th Texas, did participate in a spectacular charge at Pea Ridge. There, in the open ground around Foster's farm near Leetown, 3,000 screaming Confederate cavalrymen waving an assortment of shotguns, rifles, pistols, swords, and knives galloped across a wheat field toward the enemy. The men crashed into a Federal battery, driving the cannoneers and supporting cavalry back in confusion. The Battle of Pea Ridge cost the 6th Texas 19 casualties, most of whom were lost during the charge at Foster's farm.[16] Crist survived the battle only to die of illness at Granada, Mississippi, on July 22, 1862. *Photo courtesy of CAH, Joseph E. Taulman Collection, CN 06050*

172

ALF DAVIS
copy print

Twenty-six-year-old Alf Davis enlisted as the 2d lieu-tenant in Capt. John J. Good's battery at Dallas, Texas, on June 13, 1861. After the battery received its comple-ment of six guns, which earlier had been captured at San Antonio, Good took his battery to reinforce McCulloch. He arrived in Fort Smith, Arkansas, on July 28 but had to stop to obtain more horses and to repair equipment. The delay caused the battery to miss the Battle of Wilson's Creek. A few days later Good's men joined McCulloch and wintered in Northwest Arkansas. The artillerymen enjoyed the abundant food from the fertile farmland and were pleased to see the "handsome women" in the area. A fellow soldier noted that Davis "and some others of the company lose no good chance to give the Arkansas beauties proper attention."[17]

At Pea Ridge, Davis commanded Good's center section of two 12-pounders when it went into action near Leetown on March 7, 1862. Davis's men helped support the infantry attack that led to the deaths of first McCulloch and then McIntosh. When the attack fell apart, Good's battery was among the troops that withdrew to join the rest of Van Dorn's army near Elkhorn Tavern. The next day Davis's section partici-pated in an unequal artillery duel that caused the majority of the seventeen casualties that the battery suffered at Pea Ridge.[18] Davis was not hurt when Van Dorn withdrew his beaten army; he remained with his section until May 1862, when Confederate regulations reduced all batteries to four guns. Davis later served briefly in Captain Nelson's Independent Company of Georgia Cavalry and finally became a sergeant major in the 27th Texas Cavalry. *Photo courtesy of the Smith County Historical Society, Tyler Texas*

173

JOHN S. PICKLE
copy print

The defeat at Pea Ridge was a serious setback for Confederate ambitions in the Trans-Mississippi District, and any chance of recovering the initiative vanished when Van Dorn's army went to Mississippi. When the new commander of the district, Maj. Gen. Thomas C. Hindman, arrived in Little Rock in late May 1862, he found almost no soldiers available to block the unfolding invasion by the victors of Pea Ridge. Hindman desperately needed troops, and under his immediate control were several thousand soldiers in Indian Territory. On May 31, 1862, he ordered all available white infantry to march immediately to Little Rock. One of the men who fell under Hindman's orders was Pvt. John S. Pickle of Company B, 18th Texas Cavalry. Pickle, of Bishop County, Texas, was twenty-four years old when he joined the army on March 15, 1862.

Pickle's regiment, commanded by Col. Nicholas H. Darnell, was barely in the service before it was dismounted and sent to Indian Territory. The 18th Cavalry reported to Brig. Gen. Albert Pike, a prickly general who recently had performed poorly at Pea Ridge and was always bitterly outspoken against real and imagined enemies. On July 3, 1862, Pike named the 18th Texas as one of two commands that regularly reported lies about his performance, and told Hindman that "Darnell's regiment was such a nuisance that I gladly sent it off to lie *ad libitum.*" As for Texans generally, Pike remarked that "two things are constantly rung in my ears—leave to go home and money—until I am worn out."[19] Pickle and his regiment arrived in Arkansas in time to fight at Hill's Plantation on July 7, 1862. *Photo courtesy of Austin History Center, Austin Public Library #PICB 07051*

J. C. Camp
sixth-plate tintypes

Texas had thousands of men in various states of readiness, and Hindman relied directly and heavily on the Lone Star State for manpower. One of those reinforcements was Pvt. James C. Camp of Grayson County who, on February 22, 1862, had joined the unit that became Company G, 16th Texas Cavalry. Camp's regiment arrived in Arkansas that summer and fought its first engagement on Arkansas soil at Hill's Plantation on July 7. By mid-July the immediate threat to Arkansas had subsided due to a combination of Confederate pressure and acute food shortages. The Union army withdrew to Helena, Arkansas, on the Mississippi River.

However, Hindman's forces were still very weak and he continued to draw support from Texas. A soldier from Camp's division wrote that most of the 25,000 men gathered near Clarendon on the White River in the winter of 1862–1863 were from Texas and Arkansas. The majority were dressed in home-spun clothing and many were armed only with old flintlock muskets. Few tents had been issued, so both officers and men tried to protect themselves when possible by huddling in blankets beside fires, but the wet, cold weather made the camps miserable. That winter, disease swept through the division.[20] Despite the lack of military equipment and the poor physical condition of the men, the army's very existence helped deter the Federals in Helena from resuming the offensive. The image on the left shows Camp in homespun clothing and was likely taken around the time he joined the army. In the photo on the right, probably from a later date, Camp is clothed in a more standard attire. *Photo courtesy of J. Dale West*

175

ROBERT McDONALD FOWLER
copy print

Robert McDonald Fowler was born in Alabama in 1842 and probably migrated to Texas after 1860. On June 27, 1862, he mustered into the service as a private in Company B, 34th Texas Cavalry. Fowler brought his personal weapons with him and enlisted for three years. The regiment, under the command of Col. Almerine M. Alexander, had organized at Fort Washita, Indian Territory, on April 17, 1862, and was sometimes referred to as the 2d Partisan Rangers Regiment.

On September 28, 1862, Major General Hindman assumed command of the Confederate troops in Northwest Arkansas, Indian Territory, and Missouri. At the time, Fowler's unit was one of three Texas cavalry regiments operating in southwestern Missouri. Two days later the 34th Texas, which then numbered 367 men, fought in an engagement at Newtonia, Missouri. The regiment had 9 men wounded in the Confederate victory. However, the Rebels lacked the strength to exploit such local victories and were forced to fall back. Hindman's scheme to conquer southwest Missouri ended with his defeat at the Battle of Prairie Grove, Arkansas, on December 7, 1862. The 2d Partisan Rangers was one of four regiments from Texas that fought at the battle. Fowler's regiment had 491 men present but suffered only 2 wounded in a nasty battle that cost the Rebel army 1,100 casualties. *Photo courtesy of CRC*

WILLIAM B. PRESTON
copy print from W. W. Heartsill,
*Fourteen Hundred and 91 Days in
the Confederate Army*

William B. Preston was a twenty-eight-year-old farmer when he enlisted in Capt. Samuel J. Richardson's newly organized company of independent cavalry on May 10, 1862. Most of the men had earlier served together under Col. John S. Ford in the 2d Texas Cavalry, but Preston was not among that group. On November 30, 1862, Richardson's company arrived at Arkansas Post. A member wrote that "our tents are beautifully pitched along the bank of the [Arkansas] river, and makes quite a hansome display for only one Company." During December and the first days of 1863, Private Preston performed routine guard duties, scouts, and reconnaissance missions. On January 9, 1863, one of Richardson's scouts arrived in camp with an important dispatch for the garrison commander, Big. Gen. Thomas J. Churchill. The report contained the disturbing news that a large fleet was steaming toward the post. The next day, fire from the Federal gunboats forced the Rebel infantry back from their secondary defense. On January 11, the Union troops assaulted the main line anchored by Fort Hindman; Preston was in the trenches during the attack. Churchill, who was faced with overwhelming odds, still put up a spirited defense before he surrendered. Richardson's men, fighting as dismounted cavalry, threw their arms into a muddy bayou. The soldiers briefly contemplated returning to their horses and escaping, but when they neared the mounts the men saw that the horses had already been seized by Federal cavalry.[21] Preston was with the approximately 5,000 men who were shipped north to Federal prison camps to await exchange. He died on April 13, 1863, as an exchanged prisoner at Petersburg, Virginia.

BENJAMIN W. WATSON
copy print

The capture of Arkansas Post on January 11, 1863, was a sideshow of the Vicksburg campaign, but like the earlier fall of Forts Henry and Donelson, it showed how developments east of the river often controlled Confederate operations in the Trans-Mississippi states. In the first six months of 1863, the fate of thousands of soldiers west of the river was inextricably linked to Vicksburg. For example, in the spring of 1863 the Federals in southern Missouri appeared weak because thousands of troops from the area had been sent to operate against Vicksburg. Consequently, Brig. Gen. John S. Marmaduke, who commanded a division of cavalry in northeastern Arkansas, received permission to lead 5,000 troopers into southeastern Missouri. Confederate authorities hoped that the raid would force the Union to divert troops away from Vicksburg and back to Missouri. Lt. Col. Benjamin W. Watson commanded the 19th Texas Cavalry when the raid began on April 17, 1863. Watson was born in Virginia in 1828 and moved to Texas as a teenager. At the outbreak of the Civil War, he was a cotton farmer and slave owner in Ellis County, Texas. In March 1862 Watson raised a company of mounted men from the vicinity of Chambers Creek that became Company C of the 19th Texas Cavalry. Marmaduke's raid ended on May 2, 1863; it accomplished little, but Watson's commander did compliment the young lieutenant colonel for his "gallantry and energy."[22] The 19th Texas had barely returned to Arkansas when it received orders to move to northern Louisiana, where Rebel infantry faced a growing Union presence directly related to the Vicksburg campaign. The reliable Watson was with his men that summer when they campaigned against the enemy in north Louisiana. *Photo courtesy of CRC*

BENJAMIN C. RAIN
copy print

Benjamin Cornelius Rain was thirty years old when he joined the Confederate army at Marshall, Texas, on February 24, 1862, as a lieutenant in Company A, 14th Texas Infantry. In October 1862 Rain became a commissary officer and held similar positions until he was paroled at Marshall, Texas, on July 10, 1865. Rain's regiment spent most of its service as part of Maj. Gen. John G. Walker's Texas Division, which at its maximum size of fifteen regiments and three artillery batteries, was the largest single unit of Texas troops in the Civil War. Many of the regiments initially served together in Arkansas during the summer of 1862. Elements of the division fought their first major engagement at Milliken's Bend, Louisiana, on June 7, 1863. By then Walker's Texans were known for their ability to move rapidly and in good order. A member of Rain's brigade recorded what that pace was like in January 1863, when he ruefully noted that even though it was bitterly cold, "in commemoration of the new year we marched twelve miles." By January 20, 1863, the brigade had been on the move for a total of eight days and had traveled through almost 100 miles of snowy countryside.[23] That spring, the demands on the division increased as the Confederacy tried to distract Grant from Vicksburg. On April 25, 1863, Rain's regiment left Pine Bluff, Arkansas, and covered the approximately fifty miles to Monticello in four days. An officer noted that "our march was [a] dry and fatiguing one, but the men proved more accustomed to the fatigue than was anticipated." Rain, however, may not have held up as well, since he was left sick in Monticello during July and August 1863.[24] Still, the Texans stamina and their speedy marches earned them the sobriquet of "Walker's Greyhounds." *Photo courtesy of Mary Boone*

179

Egbert Munroe Heath and Horatio Gates Bruce
copy print

180

Horatio Gates Bruce of Johnson County, Texas, raised a company of cavalry and was elected captain of the unit when it was accepted by the Confederacy as Company H, 20th Texas Cavalry, on March 15, 1862. At the time of enlistment he was a twenty-nine-year-old farmer with a wife and three children. Although Bruce was never promoted to major, in this image he is wearing a single collar-star showing that rank. His companion fits the description of Bruce's friend Egbert Munroe Heath, who also was from Johnson County. Heath, who was elected Tax Assessor of Johnston County in 1859, was thirty-one years old when he joined Company H as a private. He was immediately promoted to 1st lieutenant of the company. Sometime in 1862 the regiment was dismounted, and by the end of the year the men were stationed in the Indian Territory.

On July 17, 1863, Bruce and Heath were with the 20th Cavalry in the center of the line at the Battle of Honey Springs. The Union commander, Maj. Gen. James G. Blunt, reported that "the fighting was unremitting and terrific for two hours, when the center of the rebel lines, where they had massed their heaviest force, became broken, and they commenced a retreat."[25] The decisive victory gave the Federals control of about two-thirds of the Indian Territory and reduced the war there to a vicious guerrilla action. Bruce and Heath were captured in the engagement, which cost the Confederates 181 casualties. When the two officers applied for exchange in October 1863, both wrote on their application forms that they were disloyal and did not wish to see the authority of the U.S. government restored. Neither man was exchanged and they remained prisoners until the war ended.

Photo courtesy of Anne Bailey; original owned by Bruce's descendants in Cleburne, Texas

The last major campaign in what had become the District of Arkansas began on March 23, 1864, when Maj. Gen. Frederick Steele left Little Rock to support the Red River Expedition. Banks's advance along the river forced Maj. Gen. Edmund Kirby Smith to concentrate all his infantry to stop him. The only available reinforcements for Arkansas were less than two thousand cavalrymen in Indian Territory. Second Sgt. Aaron Seymour of Company D, 30th Texas Cavalry, was one of the men who came to harass Steele's invasion of southern Arkansas. Seymour was from Georgetown, Texas, and had joined the service as a corporal on July 18, 1862. His term of enlistment was for three years. The 30th Cavalry, which was also known as the 1st Texas Partisan Rangers, had spent most of its career either in the District of Texas, New Mexico, and Arizona or in Indian Territory. It saw its first action in Arkansas in a series of skirmishes that took place between April 9 and 12, 1864, near Prairie D'Ane. Mounted units such as the 30th Texas had no chance of stopping infantry; Steele pushed them aside and occupied Camden, Arkansas, on April 15, 1864. Three days later, though, the 30th Texas helped defeat a large Union forging column at Poison Spring. The engagement helped convince Steele that he would have to withdraw from Camden, but unfortunately, the Rebel victory was marred by the murder of several dozen captured black soldiers. Seymour survived the war and returned to his farm in Texas. *Photo courtesy of CRC, Frank W. Latham, Jr., Collection*

THOMAS NEVILLE WAUL
copy print

As soon as the threat from Banks subsided, Kirby Smith led three divisions, including Walker's Texans, northward to strike at Steele. Brig. Gen. Thomas Neville Waul commanded one of the three Texas brigades in Walker's division. Under Waul were the 12th, 18th, and 22d Infantry, the 13th Cavalry (dismounted), and Capt. Horace Halderman's four-gun battery.

In 1861 Waul was farming and practicing law in Gonzales County, Texas. He served briefly as a representative to the Provisional Congress of the Confederacy, and was one of three Texans who signed the new constitution. On May 7, 1862, Waul became colonel of the legion which bore his name. The mixed command originally contained twelve infantry and six cavalry companies plus an artillery battery. In October 1862 Waul took his infantry across the Mississippi River; he and most of the command were captured when Vicksburg capitulated on July 4, 1863. Waul was later exchanged and promoted to brigadier general on September 19. In February 1864 he assumed command of the brigade that he led into Arkansas.

On April 30 the pursing Confederate infantry caught Steele's retreating column near Jenkins' Ferry, Arkansas, on the Saline River. By the time the Texans reached the battlefield, Smith's other two divisions had already been whipped. Waul's men passed several of the beaten Confederate brigades as they moved forward to take their turn in the fight. Waul's brigade was soon pinned down by a murderous crossfire and the general's arm was broken by a minié ball. On the right, However, Waul could hear the a rising volume of small arms fire and knew that the rest of the Greyhounds were beginning their attack.[26] *Photo courtesy of the Library of Congress*

HORACE RANDAL AND HIS WIFE,
JULIA S. BASSETT
quarter-plate tintype copied
from Tomlinson ambrotype

Horace Randal was born in Tennessee in 1833 and came to Texas with his parents in 1839. The family settled near San Augustine. Randal graduated from West Point in 1854, ranking next to last in a class of forty-six—among his classmates were Custis Lee, Oliver Howard, John Pegram, J. E. B. Stuart, Stephen Lee, and William Dorsey Pender, all of whom became famous Civil War generals. After graduation, Randal served mostly in western posts and saw some hard service fighting the Apaches. While on the frontier his wife, Julia, died in 1860. On February 27, 1861, he resigned from the United States Army. Randal first refused a commission in the Confederate army and went to Virginia, where he became an aide de camp on Maj. Gen. Gustavus W. Smith's staff. Early in 1862 Lieutenant Randal returned to Texas, raised the 28th Texas Cavalry, and became colonel of the regiment. In the summer of 1862, his men were dismounted and attached to Walker's Texas Division. Kirby Smith was so impressed with Randal's service during the 1864 Red River Campaign that he promoted him to brigadier general, but the appointment was never confirmed by the Confederate government.

Randal commanded the Texans that Waul heard coming up on his right at Jenkins' Ferry on April 30, 1864. His brigade contained the 11th and 14th Infantry, the 28th Cavalry (dismounted), the 6th Cavalry Battalion (dismounted), and Capt. James Daniel's four-gun battery. Until he was mortally wounded, Randal seemed to be everywhere as he urged his men to attack the enemy.[27] Randal died on May 2, 1864. Brig. Gen. William Scurry, who led Walker's third Texas infantry brigade at Jenkins' Ferry, was also mortally wounded during the bloody repulse.
Photo courtesy of the Henry E. Huntington Library and Art Gallery

RICHARD MONTGOMERY GANO
copy print

The Battle of Jenkins' Ferry was the last major action in Arkansas, and the war degenerated into a brutal guerrilla fight. By late 1864 almost no Texas troops remained there, but several Texas cavalry regiments did continue to operate in Indian Territory. The most active units were under the command of Col. Richard Montgomery Gano. When the Civil War began, Gano, who was a Kentuckian by birth and a medical doctor by training, was operating a ranch in Tarrant County, Texas. Gano first organized two companies of Texas cavalry to serve as scouts for Gen. Albert Sidney Johnston. The squadron became the core of the 7th Kentucky Cavalry. Gano was appointed colonel of the regiment and saw service in Col. John H. Morgan's famous mounted brigade. In 1863 he returned to Texas and eventually assumed command of a brigade of cavalry in Indian Territory. Gano took his men to

Arkansas in 1864, but he missed much of the campaign after being shot in the arm during a skirmish. For the remainder of 1864, Gano's Texas cavalry, often operating in conjunction with the Confederate Indians, continued harassing the Union army. His Texans and their Indian allies scored an impressive tactical victory on September 19, 1864, by overwhelming a Federal escort and capturing 255 wagons at Cabin Creek. Gano later reported that during the raid his men were gone fourteen days, marched 400 miles, killed 97 men, captured 111 prisoners, burned 6,000 tons of hay, and destroyed $1,500,000 in military property. His losses were 6 killed and 48 wounded.[28] On March 18, 1865, Gano was finally promoted to brigadier general, but by then the war in the western border regions was essentially over. *Photo courtesy of MOC*

Chapter 7

Defending the Coastline

We knew we had terrible work before us,
a desperate and hazardous undertaking.
But Texans never flinch from any duty.
—J. W. LOCKHART

Few Texans believed that the Yankees posed an immediate threat to Texas itself. They realized, however, that the state's six hundred miles of coastline running from Sabine Pass along the Louisiana border to Brazos Santiago and Mexico presented their enemy with an opportune target should they desire to move. Several major ports were vulnerable back doors through which the Federals could move against the state, and the defense of such an extended area would be difficult. Northern leaders recognized the possibility of exploiting this situation, although their focus on operations elsewhere prevented any major campaigns from being launched in the first years of the war. Nonetheless, the United States Navy and Army steadily probed Texan defenses from the very beginning of the war.

The Federals quickly established a presence along the state's coast. In July 1861 the USS *South Carolina* arrived off of Galveston and began a naval blockade. It soon was joined by other ships that began aggressive patrols along the coast line. In addition to seizing blockade runners and harassing coastal shipping, the fleet engaged in occasional actions against coastal installations through raids and bombardments. Until the autumn of 1862, however, the Federals launched no serious effort in this direction and the blockading fleet offshore seldom amounted to more than seven ships.

In the meantime, Confederate authorities had been steadily at work developing defensive positions along the coastline. The work had begun under Brig. Gen. Earl Van Dorn, the first commander of the Texas District, and various projects continued under Brig. Gen. Paul O. Hébert. The defensive line was anchored in the east by a small fort at Sabine Pass—although as late as the summer of 1862 it mounted only two 32-pounder and two 18-pounder guns. Further down the coast at Galveston, permanent fortifications were placed at Fort Point and Pelican Spit at the entry to Galveston Harbor and at Virginia Point, where the railroad bridge connected Galveston to the mainland. At Saluria on the northern end of Matagorda Island a work, Fort Esperanza, was established to control Cavallo Pass and its direct access to Indianola and major roads to Austin and San

Antonio. Further to the south, guns were placed on St. Joseph's and Mustang Islands to control Aransas Pass, pathway to Corpus Christi (which offered a superb base for any intended operations toward San Antonio or western Texas). Hébert recognized early that he had neither adequate manpower nor sufficient artillery to properly defend these fortifications and concluded that there was little real chance of holding the coast from a determined Federal offensive.

Early in 1862 the Federals conducted more serious probes of Texas defenses. In April a Union warship attacked the defenses at San Luis Pass, the entry into West Bay at the southern end of Galveston Island. In that attack the Federals seized the *Columbia* with a load of cotton. The following July a landing force actually attacked the Confederate position at Velasco. Further to the south, operations in the vicinity of Aransas Pass, one of the major passageways through the barrier islands into the protected bays off of the coast of southern Texas, began in February and intensified through the summer.

Control of Aransas Pass posed a particularly serious threat. From there, the United States Navy could close off the port of Corpus Christi and other smaller ports in the vicinity, any of which could provide a potential base from which a force might march on San Antonio. Command of Aransas Pass also allowed the navy to pass into Matagorda Bay, where it could operate against Indianola and Lavaca and intercept shipping along the waterway behind the barrier islands. The nemesis of Confederates at Aransas Pass was Lt. John W. Kittredge, who staged numerous raids in the area from his bark, USS *Arthur,* seizing supplies and intercepting shipping. In June, Kittredge was reinforced by the USS *Corypheus,* a shallow draft yacht that allowed him to operate with greater ease inside the barrier islands. After his capture of the *Reindeer* and *Belle Italia* and their conversion into gunboats in June, he had a fleet that was strong enough to stop all coastal commerce and to raid plantations and towns along

the coast. Confederate naval and land forces were totally inadequate to stop Kittredge's forays.

In July, Kittredge determined to take Corpus Christi. Although he had only one hundred men at his disposal, Kittredge had been informed that he could count on Unionist support within the city for his action. The seizure of Corpus Christi would have been a blow to any Confederate effort to hold on to the entire region south of San Antonio and a threat to the border trade. The city's provost marshal ordered cotton into the interior and had three schooners sunk in the ship channel to thwart Kittredge's approach. The 8th Texas Infantry, commanded by Maj. Alfred M. Hobby, was sent to bolster the city's defenses.

Reinforced by the gunboat USS *Sachem* on July 29, Kittredge began his operations against Corpus Christi. On August 12 he finished raising the scuttled schooners, and the next day his smaller vessels passed into Corpus Christi Bay. Kittredge, meeting Major Hobby on the city's wharf, demanded entry into the city to inspect Federal property. If Hobby did not accede, Kittredge threatened to take the city by force. Hobby refused to allow Kittredge to land, but secured a forty-eight-hour truce to allow civilians to evacuate the city.

Kittredge opened fire on the Confederate shore batteries on August 16. Hobby had only three cannon to resist the Federal naval force that was armed with ten guns, including a Parrott rifle with a range of four miles. Hobby had managed, however, to place his guns at the water's edge, where they were well protected by sand embankments, and his men were able to level a damaging fire against Kittredge's ships. At the end of the day the Federals drew off to repair damage. They did not renew the attack until August 18, when naval fire against Hobby's battery was combined with a land assault of thirty men. Hobby himself led a counterattack against the landing party and drove the Federals back to their ship. This ended efforts at taking Corpus Christi.

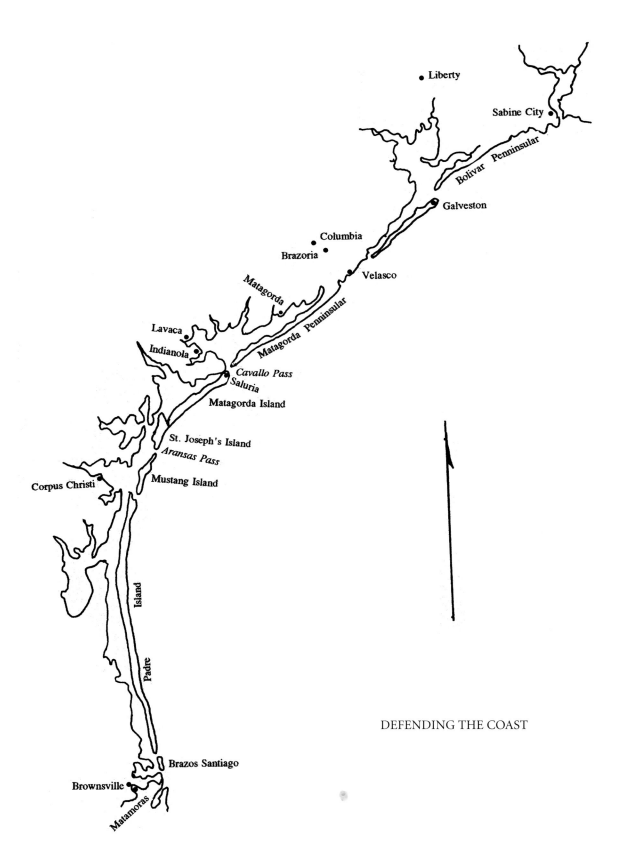

Liberty

Sabine City

Bolivar Penninsular

Galveston

Columbia

Brazoria

Velasco

Matagorda

Matagorda Penninsular

Lavaca

Indianola

Cavallo Pass

Saluria

Matagorda Island

St. Joseph's Island

Aransas Pass

Corpus Christi

Mustang Island

Padre Island

Brazos Santiago

Brownsville

Matamoras

DEFENDING THE COAST

189

Kittredge continued to operate in the vicinity of Corpus Christi until he walked into a trap at Flour Bluff on September 14. Captured and imprisoned at San Antonio until paroled, Kittredge would be transferred to the blockading squadron off of the Georgia coast after his release. The departure of Kittredge provided little respite, however. The Federal blockading force remained on station off of Aransas Pass and continued raiding into the coastal waterways, essentially denying their use to Confederate commerce.

Kittredge's harassment of the lower coast was not the only threat posed by the blockaders in 1862. On September 23, three ships appeared off of Sabine City, and their overwhelming firepower forced the Confederate defenders to evacuate their positions. The Federal presence effectively blocked shipping out of the Sabine and Neches Rivers, and Federal ships began operating in Sabine Lake, stopping coastal shipping in that area.

Even worse, early in October, Cmdre. William B. Renshaw led the Federal gunboats *Clifton, Harriet Lane, Owasco,* and *Westfield* into Galveston Harbor and demanded that city's surrender. Earlier that spring the Confederate commander at Galveston had concluded that the city could not be defended in the event of a strong Federal attack. Given four days to evacuate civilians from the town, Col. J. J. Cook and Col. Xavier B. DeBray removed all of the military equipment that they could carry. In fact, they were able to take even more time since Renshaw did not have a force to occupy the city: Federal troops did not actually arrive until December 24, when three companies of the 42d Massachusetts Infantry were put ashore. Until more troops could be brought in, the Federal force took a position on Kuhn's Wharf on the eastern side of the city's waterfront and fortified. Gunboats remained in the harbor to provide support if needed.

The capture of Galveston, coupled with successful Federal operations farther down the coast, had shaken the faith of many Texans in the ability of the Confederacy to defend their state from Federal attack. General Hébert's defensive posture had created considerable concern and by the autumn of 1862 discontent was widespread. Hébert, however, was only in command awaiting his replacement. In May a new Trans-Mississippi Department had been created and Maj. Gen. John B. Magruder assigned to head it. The new commander did not arrive until November 29.

John Magruder was not content to remain on the defensive. As soon as he arrived, Magruder began to make plans to end the Federal threat along the Texas coast, beginning with the recapture of Galveston. Magruder found that the Federals had left the railroad bridge to the island intact. He devised an attack that would combine the use of infantry and artillery brought in over the bridge to assault the position on Kuhn's Wharf along with whatever naval force he could put together to strike the gunboats.

At Houston, Magruder gathered a small naval force under Leon Smith. This fleet consisted of one river steamer, a mail packet, and two smaller coastal steamers that were protected with cotton bales. The vessels were unable to carry heavy weapons, but Magruder's plan was to load them with boarders and sharpshooters, volunteers from the infantry and cavalry regiments encamped around Galveston and Houston. The steamer CSS *Bayou City* was to take a compliment of 150 men from the 5th Texas Mounted Rifles under Col. Tom Green, while the packet CSS *Neptune* took on 100 men from the 7th Texas Mounted Rifles led by Col. Arthur Bagby. Other volunteers went aboard the steamers CSS *John F. Carr* and CSS *Lucy Gwin*.

Magruder's land force consisted of those from the 5th and 7th Cavalry not accepted for service as "horse marines," plus men from the 2d and 26th Cavalry, 20th Texas Infantry, and 21st Infantry Battalion. Various field artillery batteries also were gathered, providing fifteen pieces. The 1st Texas Heavy Artillery manned the six heavier guns they brought up, including an 8-inch Dahlgren that was mounted on a railroad flatcar and hauled in on the causeway.

On the night of December 31, Magruder's troops began their movement over the railroad bridge into the city. His men were in place around 4:00 A.M. the next morning, at which time Magruder himself fired the gun that signaled the attack. From the beginning, the land assault went poorly. The naval force supporting the 42d Massachusetts heavily out-gunned the Confederates, and Rebel positions along the wharf were raked by solid shot, grape, and canister. By day break, Magruder decided to pull his men back from their exposed positions and farther into the city, and the attack appeared to stall. At that moment, Smith's small armada sailed into the harbor and began their attack.

The Union ships at Galveston should have destroyed Smith's vessels easily, but the Federals never were able to concentrate an effective response. The Confederates drove quickly down on the closest ship, the USS *Harriet Lane,* an old revenue cutter named after Pres. James Buchanan's niece. The first Confederate ship to reach the *Harriet Lane,* Henry S. Lubbock's *Bayou City,* was quickly disabled and forced to pull off. The second attacking ship, the CSS *Neptune,* was sunk by fire from the cutter. The battle appeared to be going badly for the Confederates when the *Bayou City* went in on the *Harriet Lane* again, this time striking it near its paddle wheel and sending over boarders who secured the ship's surrender after the death of its captain and executive officer.

The Federals were still much stronger than the Confederates, but the Union commanders for some reason decided not to continue the fight.

Commodore Renshaw, whose USS *Westfield* had gone aground, determined to destroy his own ship and send the rest of the fleet out to sea. Renshaw succeeded in blowing up the *Westfield,* although he along with two of his officers and ten of his men were killed when the explosive charge went off prematurely. The rest of the fleet successfully crossed the bar out of the harbor, leaving the 42d Massachusetts to surrender. The fighting had not been particularly successful in terms of following the Confederate battle plan, but the results were all that Magruder could have desired. Galveston was back in Confederate hands and denied to the Federals as a possible base from which they could maintain their blockade or raid into the state's interior. The arrival of the USS *Brooklyn* on January 7, 1863, however, ended the brief respite from blockade as the Federal fleet went back on station off the coast.

Magruder followed up the action at Galveston with an equally aggressive effort at Sabine Pass. The blockading squadron there had cut off most movement in the area by moving into the outlet of Sabine Lake. Approximately 300 men, composed of volunteers from Pyron's 2d Texas Cavalry, Spaight's Infantry Battalion, and the 1st Heavy Artillery, were placed on the CSS *Josiah H. Bell* and the CSS *Uncle Ben.* This Confederate force moved down the Sabine River on January 18 and three days later drove the USS *Morning Light* and USS *Velocity* from the lake and captured them.

Magruder's action at Sabine Pass did not relieve the blockade, since more vessels quickly moved in, but the attack did succeed in pushing the Federals farther back from the coast. At least for the moment, Texas received a reprieve.

GETULIUS KELLERSBERGER
copy print

The task of building Texas's coastal defenses fell to the small number of civil engineers present when the war began. From the very beginning, Maj. Getulius Kellersberger played a major role in this effort. Kellersberger, a native of Switzerland, had moved to the United States in 1849, and his family settled in Houston with relatives while he worked in the American West and in Mexico. When the war broke out, he left his job surveying a railroad through the Isthmus of Tehuantepec and traveled to Houston. Kellersberger joined the staff of Gen. Paul Hébert in the autumn of 1861, and immediately went to work building a major fortification to protect the railroad bridge between Galveston and the mainland at Virginia Point. The emplacements were impressive, with a twelve-foot wall running seventy yards on either side of the railroad. The engineer then worked to place and improve existing coastal batteries. From the beginning, however, Kellersberger and the other engineers realized that their fortifications posed little threat to Federal forces, since the district had few guns to mount in them. When built, the Virginia Point works had only three 24-pounder guns and one 8-inch howitzer. *Photo courtesy of ITC*

192

HENRY C. HART
ambrotype

Among the first positions threatened by the Federals was San Luis Pass at the southern end of Galveston Island. The 13th Texas Infantry, with Pvt. Henry C. Hart in its ranks, represented the sole defenders, and they had little with which to respond to Federal activities. When an enemy ship attacked the Pass in April 1862, only forty men were on San Luis Island. The rest of the regiment was encamped sixteen miles away at Velasco; the first contingent of reinforcements to arrive was not even armed. Hart was typical of the men of the regiment, having joined only two months before for a twelve-month tour because he was unable to make any money farming. With only field artillery to counter naval guns, the regiment provided little opposition to Federal coastal operations. *Photo courtesy of Museum of the Big Bend*

USS *CONSTITUTION* AND USS *SANTEE*, 1863
copy print

Even at critical points, Confederate forces did not have the resources to stop the naval raiders. On May 15 the old frigate USS *Santee*, which had joined the blockading squadron, approached Galveston's shore batteries and engaged them. Two days later *Santee* returned and its captain, Henry Eagle, demanded the surrender of the city. There was little that military officials could do. They certainly did not have the guns to fight the *Santee*, and they prepared to spike their guns and evacuate the island. Eagle did not have a landing force large enough to actually occupy the island, and after having given the community's inhabitants a fright, he sailed off. Even this important city, however, was clearly available for the taking. *Photo courtesy of U.S. Naval Historical Center*

WILLIAM J. GOODMAN
ambrotype

The 13th Texas Infantry was engaged again in a more serious encounter with the enemy three months later at Velasco, where on July 4, a Federal steamer landed men to burn a cotton-laden schooner. Soldiers from the regiment attempted to protect the vessel but were driven back with a heavy barrage of round shot and shell; the schooner was lost. Maj. William J. Goodman from Tyler was the regiment's surgeon at this time. Son of a prominent doctor and nephew of a Smith County planter, the twenty-nine-year-old Goodman had been educated at South Carolina College and at the Medical College at Charleston. Goodman had little business in this incident, for despite the fire of the Federals only a few of the men of the regiment were wounded and none were killed. On August 11 a two-masted steamer crossed the bar and shelled the regiment's position. Col. Joseph Bates's report reflected the frustration of the Texans. "I am confident that if we had even a single piece of heavy ordnance she could have been disabled." He was convinced that the aggressive actions by his enemies were due "in part from a knowledge (how acquired I know not) of our defenseless position."[1] Bates and his regiment were charged with defending this vital coastal position with only one 18-pounder cannon. *Photo courtesy of Smith County Historical Society*

GEORGE WASHINGTON BETHARDS
ambrotype

In the autumn of 1862, Federal forces along the coast proved even bolder with a foray into the bays behind Matagorda Island and an attack on the town of Lavaca. Pvt. George W. Bethards of Company A, 4th Artillery Battalion, was one of the town's defenders. Twenty-six years old, this Kentuckian had moved to Texas in the 1850s. He joined his unit in the summer of 1861, and it had been sent to Lavaca, where they had struggled to build two batteries while fighting off disease. On October 31, 1862, two Federal gunboats cast anchor off the town and demanded its surrender. The Confederate commander refused, and after a two-and-one-half hour truce for civilians to leave town, the two ships opened fire and tried to move close into shore.

The land batteries returned fire with enough effect to force the Federals to withdraw beyond the range of the Confederate guns and begin a long-distant bombardment of the town and Confederate emplacements. The assault continued the next day before the ships sailed away. The Confederate defenders, unable to fire back, received some 252 rounds of shot and shell in the attack. Gen. Hamilton Bee believed their "patriotism and courage" had forced the enemy to retire. The bombardment of Lavaca, which Bee called "the most atrocious of all the acts which have so marked their [the Federal's] conduct in this war,"[2] showed again the ability of the Yankees to move unimpeded along the Texas coast. *Photo courtesy of Alvin Y. Bethard*

ALFRED M. HOBBY
copy print

After a year in which Union naval forces had moved at will along the Texas coast, the Federals suffered their first defeat and Texas had one of its first local heroes when Maj. Alfred M. Hobby's command successfully turned back a Federal landing force at Corpus Christi on August 16–18, 1862. Hobby, a native Georgian who had opened a store at St. Mary's in Refugio County in 1857, had been an ardent secessionist. In 1861 he resigned his seat in the state legislature and helped raise the 8th Texas Infantry. In July 1862 he and 350 men of his unit had arrived at Corpus Christi to help protect the city. When the Federals attacked on August 16, Hobby personally directed the battery that responded, inflicting damage on the fleet. On August 18, when a party of Marines supported by artillery landed to flank the battery, Hobby led 25 men in a counterattack. In the face of gunboat fire, Hobby and his men advanced rapidly, stopping to fire when in rifle range. The Marines withdrew, saved when Hobby ordered his cavalry, which he feared would be shredded by grape and canister from the gunboats, to stop their charge. The day was won, however. Hobby and his men had saved Corpus Christi. *Photo courtesy of CRC*

XAVIER DEBRAY (CENTER) AND STAFF
albumen print
P. H. Rose, Galveston

Conditions worsened appreciably in October when Cmdre. William Renshaw and a small Federal fleet sailed into Galveston Harbor and demanded the surrender of that crucial port. The military commander there was Xavier DeBray, a native of France who had received military training at St. Cyr before moving to Texas in 1848. DeBray had been a military aide to Governor Clark at the beginning of the war, then served for a brief time as major of the 2d Texas Infantry, finally becoming colonel of the 26th Texas Cavalry. In the autumn of 1862, he was commander of the Eastern District of Texas and responsible for the defenses of Galveston. When a Federal fleet entered the harbor in October, he realized that little could be done to oppose them. On October 5 he reported: "Galveston cannot be defended, and a fight in the city would be a useless braggadocio against forty guns, or about, at 1 mile from the wharf. The place shall not be surrendered, but slowly evacuated. . . . I shall by all means prevent a landing and protect the railroad."[3] He ordered Col. J. J. Cook "to avoid making within the city a resistance, which would bring about the destruction of the property of our citizens without resulting in any good to the country."[4] Without a shot being fired, Galveston fell. *Photo courtesy of Gary Hendershott*

199

JOHN BANKHEAD MAGRUDER
carte de visite

The arrival of Gen. John Bankhead Magruder to replace Paul Hébert in late 1862 brought a commander determined to reassert Confederate control in Texas. He found the state's harbors closed and the Rio Grande frontier virtually abandoned and "resolved to regain the harbors if possible and to occupy the valley of the Rio Grande in force."[5] His energy led Col. John S. "Rip" Ford to consider his presence "equal to the addition of 50,000 men to the forces of Texas."[6] Among his first goals was reoccupying Galveston. The city had fallen on October 8, 1862, but the Federals had not immediately garrisoned their prize. If Magruder could drive the Federal fleet out of the harbor, the city would be restored to Confederate control. His plan of operation was simple: He proposed to move artillery into the city over the railroad causeway that the Federals had not cut, then attack the fleet in conjunction with a hastily assembled naval force of cottonclad river steamers armed with cannon and sharpshooters selected from cavalry veterans of the New Mexico campaign. Magruder was forced to push his plans forward even faster when the Federals landed a detachment of the 42d Massachusetts Infantry in the city on December 25. Further reinforcements would make the reoccupation of the city impossible. *Photo courtesy of Gregg Gibbs*

200

JOHN ROBERT BAYLOR
albumen print

Magruder quickly assembled all of the artillery that he could gather and planned his attack for the morning of January 1, 1863. On the evening of December 31, Magruder ordered his six siege guns and fourteen field pieces over the railroad bridge and into the city. They opposed five Federal steamships—*Harriet Lane, Westfield, Owasco, Clifton,* and *Sachem*— in all mounting thirty guns, plus a number of smaller armed transports and warships. Magruder's regiments,

according to one of the soldiers, had been "divided and subdivided until we lost our identity."[7] Infantry and cavalry all helped to manhandle the guns into the city. Everyone pitched in. Gov. John R. Baylor, who was visiting but not connected with a command, labored as a private and would be cited by Magruder for his gallant conduct, "with his coat off working to place [the guns] in position during the night."[8] *Photo courtesy of LLMVC*

202

HARRY BETTYS
copy print

When the battle began, despite the assistance of many volunteers, most of the guns were served by the men of the 1st Texas Heavy Artillery. Harry Bettys of Company E was typical of the artillerymen. Bettys had enrolled at Fort Stockton on May 1, 1861, in Capt. Edward Von Harten's artillery company, which became part of the 1st Artillery the following April. Exactly where Bettys was the morning of the battle at Galveston is unknown, but the guns his company worked had been placed along the city's waterfront in a line extending from its western-most wharf to Fort Point at the eastern end of the island. Magruder signaled the beginning of the battle by firing a cannon. Bettys and the other artillerymen quickly came under heavy naval gunfire, and a delay in the appearance of Magruder's navy allowed the Federals to devote all their attention to the shore. Firing grape and canister, the naval guns swept the shoreline, dealing out destruction among the Confederate gun crews. *Photo courtesy of Roger Hurt Collection, U.S.A.M.H.I.*

Strand No 1 looking N.E. 1861

KUHN'S WHARF
copy print

When the artillery opened fire on the ships in the harbor, a storming party attacked the 42d Massachusetts, which was positioned upon Kuhn's Wharf to the east of the city's main business district. The wharf had been selected because Federal naval officers believed it could be easily defended from their ships. In addition, an attacking force would have to cross a shallow but broad expanse of water to get to the wharf and then use ladders to get on it. The men of the 42d Massachusetts had been busy reinforcing their position. They threw up a series of breastworks to resist rifle-fire, ripping up the two- and two-and-one-half-inch planking in front of the wharf. These boards were laid on top of one another breast high and two deep, creating a shield thirty inches thick. An entrance port was protected by a cotton bale. Magruder's men would not take the wharf easily.
Photo courtesy of Rosenberg Library

205

Col. Isaac Burrell, commander of the 42d Massachusetts, had only three companies landed prior to the Confederate attack. With the naval commander, he had identified the wharf as the best defensive position. His men now faced a charge determined to drive them into the bay, and Burrell walked among his men, reassuring them and exhorting them not to forget their home state. It was later remembered that Burrell "walked the wharf during the entire time the action continued, with shot and shell flying around in unpleasant proximity. While risking his own life in this manner, in order to be able to observe all that was taking place, he kept his men under shelter as much as possible. They rose to their feet from behind the breastwork only when ready to fire on the enemy."[9] Although untested in battle, the men fought well in the face of a massive artillery and small arms assault. *Photo courtesy of MOLLUS, Mass., U.S.A.M.H.I.*

Sgt. Alexander Coker was a member of Company K of the 2d Cavalry. Coker had joined the unit from Live Oak County in 1862. His company formed part of Colonel Cook's five-hundred-man storming party, along with companies from the 20th Texas Infantry Regiment and the 21st Battalion. The men were expected to wade the shallow waters between the shore and the wharf, carrying scaling ladders they would then have to climb to get to the enemy. J. W. Lockhart of the 20th Texas wrote to his wife: "We knew we had terrible work before us, a desperate and hazardous undertaking. But Texans never flinch from any duty."[10]

The assault troops found the water deeper than expected and their ladders too short to reach the wharf. Coker and the other men were exposed "to a fire of grape and canister and shell from the ships as well as of the musketry from the land forces" as they struggled to accomplish what proved to be an impossible task.[11] Suffering severely in the punishing fire, Cook withdrew his men under the cover of artillery fire. The 42d Massachusetts had successfully resisted this effort to take their position. *Photo courtesy of Martin Callahan*

TWENTIETH STREET AT THE WHARF
copy print

The collapse of the infantry assault on Kuhn's Wharf was accompanied by a growing desperation among the Confederate artillerymen along the waterfront. The artillery moved into battlelines along streets parallel to the waterfront and then advanced toward the gunboats by streets that ran to the wharves. Twentieth Street was one of these avenues. At this position, in front of the city's tallest brick building, several batteries were placed. The scene is typical of the landscape along the wharf. The guns had no natural protection, and their crews did not have enough time or materials at hand to throw up any earthworks. When the infantry gave up its attack, the naval guns were able to devote full attention to the artillery. *Photo courtesy of Rosenberg Library*

SIDNEY SHERMAN JR.
copy print

From their location only three hundred yards offshore, the gunboats leveled a deadly fire on the Confederate gunners. At a gun only a block west of the batteries at Twentieth Street, Lt. Sidney Sherman Jr., son of Gen. Sidney Sherman (who had fought at San Jacinto and been considered a hero of the Republic), worked along with other men from Company A, 1st Texas Heavy Artillery. The younger Sherman had already given evidence that he might live up to his father's reputation. His commander considered him "a young man of steady habits and of great physical and moral courage" who had "given evidence of his superior qualifications as a soldier having been on the Rio Grande Expedition."[12] Along the Rio Grande the enemy had surrendered without a fight, but at Galveston the Federals clearly had the upper hand. A round of grape fired at Sherman's gun brought down the young lieutenant with a wound to the abdomen. He was carried to the city hospital, but nothing could be done. The promising young lieutenant soon died. *Photo courtesy of San Jacinto Museum of History*

209

W. A. Hogan
carte de visite

W. A. Hogan was another member of Cook's artillery who had been dispersed among the gun crews on the wharf. Hogan had enlisted in the Rough and Ready Guards in Harris County in the summer of 1861, then in September he transferred to Company D, 1st Texas Heavy Artillery, and was elected lieutenant. Until January 1, 1863, they had seen no combat action; for these untried artillerymen, the situation that morning must have appeared bleak. A participant reported on the situation along the waterfront: "To fight Gunboats carrying the heaviest metal with light field artillery was a severe test for raw troops—Veterans *might* have stood it for a short time. But for a raw recruit to see a green bucket-full of grape thrown at him for a single dose was trying to the nerves—very."[13] Under such conditions, many of the men began to run, and Magruder feared he might lose his guns. *Photo courtesy of Martin Callahan*

GEORGE MAGRUDER
albumen print
Louis de Planque Gallery,
Houston

With many among the gun crews dead or wounded and others having fled their pieces, General Magruder ordered Gen. William Scurry to retrieve the abandoned guns and to bring all of the artillery back into the interior of the city. There, it would be protected and used to hold Galveston, even if the Federal fleet could not be driven off. Scurry was in command of the reserve force, but he now asked for additional volunteers to carry out his mission. The general's nephew, Lt. George Magruder, who had served with his uncle on the Virginia Peninsular and was now one of his aides, volunteered for the perilous task. Magruder and the other volunteers, "without guns or weapons of any kind," followed Scurry "down at a full run in the face of the Enemy's fire to rescue the guns which had been deserted." The situation was desperate, and the same correspondent observed that at "this moment every man's countenance looked as long as a hoe handle."[14] *Photo courtesy of LLMVC*

211

LEON SMITH
albumen print

At the very minute that General Magruder was prepared to abandon the attack and fortify the city, his small flotilla of gunboats appeared in the harbor. Their captain was Leon Smith, who had moved troops to the Rio Grande on his steamboats in 1861 and who had been developing a Confederate fleet at Sabine Pass. Magruder assigned Smith the rank of major to ensure his authority over the army boarding parties placed on his ships. Smith's force consisted of the cottonclads CSS *Bayou City,* a riverboat armed with a rifled gun; CSS *Neptune,* armed with two howitzers; and CSS *John F. Carr* and CSS *Lucy Gwin,* each carrying boarding parties. The *Bayou City* headed directly toward the USS *Harriet Lane,* the closest ship in the Federal fleet. Disabled when her boarding planks fell into her paddle wheels, the *Bayou City* veered off and the *Neptune* followed in. After ramming the *Harriet Lane,* however, Federal fire drove the *Neptune* off, where she sank in shallow water off the wharf. In the meantime, the *Bayou City* cleared away her damage and returned to the attack, this time driving into the side of the *Harriet Lane.* Confederate soldiers and sailors, led by Smith, quickly boarded the *Harriet Lane,* where a wild melée broke out. *Photo courtesy of CRC*

JONATHAN M. WAINWRIGHT
copy print

Captain of the USS *Harriet Lane* was Cmdr. Jonathan M. Wainwright. With 130 veteran sailors and marines aboard, the *Harriet Lane* should have easily thrown back Smith's boarders. From the beginning, however, the fight went badly for the Federals. Smith rushed aboard and found Wainwright and demanded that the officer surrender. When Wainwright refused, Smith shot him through the head with his pistol. The ship's executive officer, Lt. Cmdr. Edward Lea of Texas—the son of Confederate Maj. Albert M. Lea—also fell mortally wounded in the first rush aboard. Leaderless, the Federals aboard the *Harriet Lane* quickly surrendered. *Photo courtesy of the U.S. Naval Historical Center*

WILLIAM B. RENSHAW
carte de visite

Following an attempt to recapture the *Harriet Lane* by the USS *Owasco,* the Federal fleet disengaged, its officers uncertain what should be done. When Capt. Henry S. Lubbock of the CSS *Bayou City* demanded that the Federal fleet surrender, he secured instead a three-hour-truce. In that time the uncertainty of the Federals was made clear. Concern that the *Bayou City* was an ironclad convinced the ships' captains to abandon the harbor. Cmdre. William B. Renshaw, aboard the USS *Westfield,* was unable to leave, however, because his ship had grounded on Pelican Spit. As the other ships steamed for the harbor entrance, Renshaw decided to blow up his own vessel. When the initial charge failed to explode, he returned and was killed, along with twelve other members of his crew, after another charge exploded and destroyed the ship. The flight from the harbor was condemned by Union officials, as well as by Confederates who charged that the fleet had taken advantage of a flag of truce to flee. *Photo courtesy of U.S.A.M.H.I.*

USS *BROOKLYN*
copy print

The recapture of Galveston was only the first Confederate naval victory in Texas that month. Magruder used infantry and artillery aboard cotton-clads to break the blockade at Sabine Pass, where on January 21, 1863, the nine-gun warship USS *Morning Light* was captured and the three-gun USS *Velocity* driven off its station. The combined victories were cause for much celebration among Texans. However, while the Federals never attempted to recapture Galveston, the relief of the blockade was only temporary. Adm. David G. Farragut quickly sent additional warships to the Texas coast. Despite the loss of *Harriet Lane, Westfield,* and *Morning Light,* the blockade was renewed. Among the new arrivals was the old ship-of-the-line USS *Brooklyn.* Magruder had provided relief from the tightening snare of the Union naval blockade, but it would be only a brief respite. *Photo courtesy of U.S. Naval Historical Center*

Chapter 8

Enemies Within

I witnessed a sight yesterday which I never wish to see again in a civilized and enlightened country.

—THOMAS C. SMITH

From the very beginning, political and military leaders in Texas were aware that an invading Yankee enemy was not the only potential threat to the state. Texans had been fighting a war for decades with the Native American population on the state's northern and western frontiers. In addition, the people of the state remained divided over the issue of secession, and strong sentiments against the new Confederacy existed in various parts of the state. Dealing with both Indians and a variety of dissidents —usually lumped together as Unionists by Confederate loyalists—ultimately consumed much of the state's resources and a considerable amount of the government's attention.

The vulnerability of the Texas frontier had been one of the reasons why Governor Houston had always opposed secession. Even with a sizable Federal force on the Texas frontier, settlements had not been well protected from Indian raids. In 1859 and 1860, Comanches and Kiowas had staged serious raids on the northwestern settlements. In the far west, Apaches proved a constant danger. With the withdrawal of the U.S. Army, it appeared likely that such raids would increase.

During the secession crisis the Texas Committee of Public Safety tried to fill the void in frontier protection by dividing the region into three military districts and assigning commanders to raise companies to man the various posts. John S. "Rip" Ford was assigned the line from Brownsville to a point beyond Laredo and Fort McIntosh; Ben McCulloch took over the defense of the line from the Rio Grande to Fort Chadbourne (near modern Colorado City); Ben's brother Henry was assigned the area from Fort Chadbourne to the Red River. This military subdivision of the frontier was retained by Texas and the Confederacy throughout the war.

In February the legislature provided for the organization of Ranger companies drawn from and stationed in the counties along the frontier. However, authorities believed that a regular army presence was needed in the area. Texas officials wanted the Confederate government to commit at least one regiment to frontier defense, but Richmond, facing more immediate dangers, initially left this responsibility to the state. In April 1861 the legislature authorized the formation of the 1st Texas Mounted Rifles, commanded by Col. Henry E. McCulloch. The 1st Texas was to serve as the nucleus of a frontier force supplemented by local militia companies. The Confederacy accepted the regiment into service.

As soon as his unit was organized, McCulloch began to occupy and patrol the four-hundred-mile line assigned to him. He established his headquarters at Camp Colorado in Coleman County. With such a limited force, McCulloch initiated a system of scouting operations from the frontier posts. These regular patrols would discover the presence of any Indian raiding parties. With these early warnings, a larger force could be dispatched from the post garrisons to intercept the raiders.

By December 1861 the Texas Legislature was faced with new demands from the frontier for protection. McCulloch, whose assignment now extended to much of the District of Texas, wanted to pull his own regiment to the coast when Federal threats there increased. McCulloch's men, after almost a year of constant patrols, also wanted to leave. As a result, the legislature authorized a new unit. Known as the Frontier Regiment, it was to consist of ten companies raised primarily from the frontier counties themselves. The terms of enlistment were for twelve months, and recruits had to bring their own weapons, horses, and equipment. The Confederacy was to pay for this regiment, but under the Texas law the state would maintain control over the unit. The conflict of authority inherent in such a measure provoked opposition from the Confederate government and created a controversy that lasted for two years.

Despite these difficulties, the Frontier Regiment began organizing in January 1862. Col. James M. Norris was named its commander by the governor. The following April, as the 1st Mounted Rifles left the frontier posts, the newly organized companies replaced them. They occupied a line of posts each approximately twenty-five miles apart and garrisoned with about twenty-five men. Every two days, five-man patrols covered the ground between their post and the one to the south. Primarily because Indian activity along the frontier was limited at the time, it appeared to be a success. Although the regiment engaged in frequent clashes with Indian bands, these incursions were little more than nuisances. During its first six months on duty, the Frontier Regiment killed twenty-one Indians and recovered some two hundred stolen horses.

In February 1863 the Frontier Regiment was reorganized into the Mounted Regiment of Texas State Troops, commanded by James E. McCord, as a first step to turning it over to Confederate authorities. Continued disputes between Austin and Richmond delayed the transfer, however. In the meantime, McCord brought a new aggressiveness to frontier operations. In May he ordered the patrol system discontinued and began company-strength scouts into the areas west of the frontier line on three to four week expeditions. Under McCord, fighting on the frontier increased, with companies actively pursuing Indian bands and forcing fights.

McCord's policies were fortuitous but still inadequate for an impending storm of raids. Through the spring of 1863, Indians mounted increasingly aggressive forays against the frontier settlements, possibly encouraged by Unionists and deserters who had begun to cluster in the region. The situation became serious enough that five companies of DeMorse's 29th Texas Cavalry and parts of James Bourland's Border Regiment were placed at Gainesville in Cooke County. However, the Confederacy never had the manpower to deal with all of its problems, and Federal activity in the Indian Territory that summer diverted attention and resources away from the western areas. As a result, when Indians staged major raids in Wise and Parker Counties during August 1863, Texas forces in the region failed to stop them. Raiders entered the western counties almost undetected and essentially unopposed.

In October and December 1863 some of the

largest Indian raids of the war took place. Their increased size and frequency were encouraged in part by the establishment of better relations between the United States government and Kiowa and Comanche bands. With the Federals purchasing horses and cattle from these Indians, the latter became bolder in their attacks. Thousands of head of stock were taken from the settlements and sold to Yankee agents. The largest of these incursions began on December 21, 1863, when a party of 300 Comanches rode into Montague County for two days of pillaging. The Comanches left about twenty Texans killed and wounded, and returned with several women and hundreds of horses and cows. The settlers were never warned that the Indians were in the vicinity.

Outrage at these raids forced Gen. John Bankhead Magruder to consider new measures on the Indian frontier. In August he assigned Henry E. McCulloch to carry out that task. Back on the frontier after a two-year absence, McCulloch assumed command in the midst of the autumn raids and found settlers abandoning their homes and seeking security farther in the interior. Unfortunately for the settlers, McCulloch's soldiers were more often used to find deserters and those who tried to avoid conscription rather than to provide protection against Indian attack. Through the end of the war, this practice seriously interfered with Confederate efforts at defending the frontier. Ultimately, McCulloch did not have the resources to carry out his mission; the situation further deteriorated as the Federal threat along the Gulf Coast and the Rio Grande worsened.

By the winter of 1863–1864, General Magruder was much more worried about activities of the Union Army than the Indians. The Frontier Regiment seemed a much-needed resource for defending the state from Federal invasion, and Magruder was ready to remove it from the frontier. In a final reorganization of the frontier command, the state legislature in December 1863 authorized the creation of local companies for Indian defense, to be paid for by the Confederate government. This potentially freed up the Frontier Regiment for service elsewhere, relieved the state from paying for frontier defense, and provided a modicum of protection.

The local companies hardly filled the need for frontier defense, and during the remaining years of the war Indians continued to raid along the entire frontier line. The best known of these, the Elm Creek Raid, took place in Young County on October 13, 1864. This raid apparently was intended to obtain horses by Comanches who were engaged in renewed warfare with Union troops farther north. The Indians burned eleven homes and drove off large numbers of livestock. Twelve soldiers and settlers were killed in the attack, and seven women and children were taken by the Indians.

Large raids were not typical. Generally, small bands of Indians struck isolated ranches and farms, carrying off the livestock and other booty and killing the inhabitants. Defense forces were occasionally able to catch up with them, but these engagements merely hurried the Indian withdrawal. The only major fighting took place on January 8, 1865, when 380 Texans attacked an Indian camp of some 1,000 warriors at Dove Creek on the South Concho River. The Indians were a migrating party of Kickapoo moving from Indian Territory to Mexico, and neither raiders nor potential enemies. Better armed and outnumbering their attackers, the Indians drove off the Texans in a major defeat for the frontier force, which lost twenty-six men killed and twenty-three others wounded.

Ultimately, Confederate Texas never successfully responded to the Indian threat on its frontier. The Indians, on the other hand, never intended to do more than take property and livestock that they could use for either trade or sustenance. As a result of this failure, frontier settlement was generally abandoned as both property and lives were lost. In the end, however, the war marked only a temporary setback to expansion. The Indians never drove all of the settlers from the frontier, and Texans would continue populating the frontier regions of their state after the war.

More troublesome for Texans, because it produced an even more dangerous opponent as well as postwar social consequences, was the development of armed opposition to the Confederate war effort among the state's own citizens. While the reasons for this internal dissent were multiple, hundreds of Texans had not supported secession in the spring of 1861, and they were not supportive of the Confederacy. A number of prominent political leaders continued resolute in their opposition. Pockets of extensive dissent were particularly strong in the northeastern part of the state and within the German communities scattered throughout the state. Most of these dissidents remained passive, showing their opposition through their failure to support the Confederacy or the war effort. Confederate fear of these Unionists, however, produced serious trouble for many of the more outspoken ones, although there was an initial willingness to let them remain within the state if they caused no trouble.

The first Confederate Conscription Act in the spring of 1862 played a major role in changing the nature of internal dissent. That law, requiring service of all eligible men between the ages of eighteen and thirty-five, made it impossible for those who opposed the Confederacy to remain uninvolved: they either had to submit to the general will and fight for the Confederacy or face imprisonment or persecution. Many chose active opposition to the Confederacy. Wide-spread resistance to conscription made it impossible for the more outspoken Unionist politicians to remain in the state, as they were blamed for fomenting dissent. Confederate authorities acted quickly and brutally to suppress the opposition.

An outbreak of internal resistance began in 1862 in two different sections of the state. Shortly after the imposition of conscription, state authorities received information from around Texas that many Germans were organizing and arming to resist the law. Hundreds of Germans in Austin County were reportedly preparing for an armed conflict over conscription. Word from Fredericksburg warned of a "Loyal Union League" with the public purpose of fighting Indians but an actual goal of opposing Confederate authority in the area.

Confederate officials considered the situation in the Hill Country, where many counties had large German majorities, to be the most threatening. In May 1862 Capt. James Duff was sent to Gillespe County—the heart of German communities in the Hill Country—to arrest any who resisted Confederate authority. Duff's men took prisoners and destroyed homes in their search for opponents of the Confederacy. When they turned their attention to hunting out those who had fled into the countryside, discovery often led to lynchings rather than a formal trial.

In August a band of sixty-eight men from the Fredericksburg and Comfort areas decided to leave for Mexico rather than submit to Confederate authority. This group was led by Frederick Tegener and included many prominent community members, including the sons of Edward Degener, a prominent German leader who helped the men obtain supplies and arms. Before they made it to the Rio Grande, however, a company of two hundred Confederate troopers surprised the Germans on August 10. Only twelve of the Unionists escaped, the rest either died in the fighting or were shot by the victorious Confederates. This episode ultimately became known as the Nueces Massacre.[1]

Authorities believed that the action on the Nueces had suppressed dissent in the area, but it actually escalated the opposition. Protests in German communities against the Nueces Massacre and conscription continued. Of greater concern, more Germans left their Texas settlements for Mexico, where they became actively engaged in activities against the Confederacy.

The Germans were not the only problem. That

autumn, authorities discovered what they believed was another conspiracy against the Confederate government in the "Peace Party," an organization formed within the Red River counties north of Dallas. In the vote for secession in 1861, seven of these counties had voted against secession. Collin, Cooke, Denton, and Wise Counties were the center of particularly strong Unionist sentiments. In September of 1862 Confederate authorities found evidence that some of the Unionists had formed an organization that was stockpiling arms. Frontier troops were used to round up these men. Although they claimed to be gathering weapons to be used in the event of a Federal invasion from Indian Territory, they were tried, found guilty, and executed. More than forty men were hanged in what became known as the "Great Hanging at Gainesville."

These extreme measures quieted the immediate situation, but failed to stifle dissent. As a result of these attacks, many prominent Unionists abandoned Texas and began open efforts at overthrowing the Confederate regime; Andrew J. Hamilton of Austin was one of the most prominent. Some went so far as to help the Union cause militarily. On the Mexican border, Unionist leaders such as Edmund J. Davis worked to take the offensive and secured authorization to raise a regiment of Texas refugees. Davis succeeded in recruiting what became the core for the 1st Texas Cavalry (U.S.).

In Texas itself, the opponents of the war and the Confederacy appear to have simply gone underground. Their hostility reemerged as Confederate authorities found it increasingly difficult during the last years of the war to maintain control over all parts of the state. In April 1864, for example, a new conspiracy to aid a possible Union invasion was uncovered in northern Texas. This involved members of the Frontier military organization itself and had to be suppressed with arrests and trials.

Creating as much trouble as Indians and politi-cal dissidents was a third source of problems for military authorities—the growing concentration of both deserters and men avoiding conscription along the frontier, particularly in the northern counties bordering the Red River. Their numbers possibly reached into the thousands, and their presence created a reign of lawlessness wherever they gathered. As one historian has suggested, both Generals Smith and Magruder saw this problem as the greatest difficulty faced by Gen. Henry McCulloch.[2]

From 1863 until the end of the war, frontier military units devoted as much time to this situation as to fighting Indians. However, neither peaceful nor more ruthless measures solved the problem. McCulloch sent his aides into the northern counties, trying to reason with those who had left their units to return. Pushed for stronger action by Kirby Smith and Magruder, McCulloch finally committed troops to resolve the issue, including the men of William Clarke Quantrill (who had entered northeastern Texas in the early autumn of 1863 following his sack of Lawrence, Kansas). Quantrill's raiders were involved in several engagements with these border groups but failed to break them up. The area remained a haven for those who had enough of war.

Indians, dissidents, and lawless bands of deserters and draft dodgers on the frontier did not change the course of the war in the state, but they could not be ignored. Subsequently, these problems required both the Texas and Confederate governments to divert resources to deal with them. In a state and nation with little surplus to spare, coping with internal enemies further weakened the war effort. In the end, Texas remained a community at war with itself until the very end, and these problems remained largely unresolved even in the postwar years.

HENRY EUSTACE McCULLOCH
quarter-plate ambrotype

From the beginning of the war, Texas officials were forced to deal with a variety of internal enemies. The removal of the United States Army from the frontier opened that region to Indian raids. Unionist sentiment, particularly strong in western counties, posed another potential threat. By the second year of the war, the appearance of large numbers of armed men (some Unionists but primarily draft dodgers and deserters) on the state's border with the Indian Territory was an additional problem. Henry E. McCulloch would be the individual whose various commands would have the greatest responsibility for suppressing these enemies. The U.S. Marshal for the Eastern District of Texas in 1861, McCulloch was assigned to take charge of all Federal posts from Camp Colorado to the Red River and subsequently organized the 1st Texas Mounted Rifles to serve on the frontier. By 1863 he was a brigadier general commanding the Northern Sub-District of Texas, and his men were engaged in blocking Indian raids and trying to control dissidents. Both would be thankless and ultimately fruitless tasks. *Photo courtesy of Milo Mims*

SANTANTA
copy print

One of the most pressing and potentially dangerous problems confronted by Texans was on the frontier. For a decade prior to the outbreak of the Civil War, United States Army troops and Texas Rangers had been fighting a war with the Indians. When Federal soldiers abandoned their posts and thousands of Texans left the state with Confederate units, the frontier was open and vulnerable. Texas authorities attempted to secure treaties with the most important frontier Indian tribes. Santanta, a Kiowa, was one of the chiefs who met with Col. Henry McCulloch in the summer of 1861. McCulloch hoped to obtain a treaty of peace, but the chiefs indicated that they preferred to raid the Texas farms and ranches. Kiowa and Comanche bands quickly took advantage of the reduced white military presence, attacking isolated ranches and farms from which they took livestock, particularly horses, as well as women and children. In 1863 Santanta led one of these raids. His band attacked a farm near Menard, Texas, and then fled to Kansas, where he tried to sell one of his captives. Santanta returned repeatedly to Texas after this action and presented a continuing threat that state and Confederate authorities were forced to address.
Photo courtesy of National Archives

DeWitt Clinton Thomas
copy print from *Confederate Veteran*

In March 1861 Henry McCulloch began organizing the first regiment authorized by the Confederate government to guard the frontier between the Rio Grande and Red River from Indian raids, the 1st Texas Mounted Rifles. He sought volunteers between eighteen and forty-five years of age who could ride and shoot well. He also expected them to be of good moral character and excluded gamblers and drunkards from the regiment. Each volunteer was expected to bring his own horse and equipment, including a six-shot revolver and a rifle or shotgun.

DeWitt C. Thomas had moved to Texas from Mississippi in 1844, settling in Burleson County. While his father farmed and raised cattle, the young Thomas was a clerk in a drygoods store when the war broke out. He joined McCulloch's regiment in April 1861. The regiment never numbered more than about four hundred men, clearly not enough to cover the vast frontier. Companies were garrisoned along a line from Camp Jackson on the Red River to Fort McKavett in San Saba County. Benton and the other men engaged in a tiring series of weekly scouts around their posts and to detached camps looking for signs of Indian invaders. They found few raiders, however, and many of the men looked forward to the end of their twelve-month enlistment so they could join the fight against the Yankees in the East. Thomas left the frontier service in April 1862 and joined the cavalry battalion of Waul's Texas Legion.

224

GEORGE W. GAITHER
copy print from W. W. Heartsill,
*Fourteen Hundred and 91 Days
in the Confederate Army*

The southwestern portion of the frontier was occupied by men from John S. "Rip" Ford's 2d Texas Mounted Rifles. The unit's primary responsibility was the defense of the Rio Grande border, but detachments also were assigned the job of protecting communications to El Paso and looking for Indians. Company F (the W. P. Lane Rangers) was one such unit. While the rest of the regiment rode to join General Sibley's campaign into New Mexico, Company F was ordered to Fort Lancaster on the Pecos River in Crockett County to help guard the frontier against raiding Indians. George W. Gaither was one of the men with the unit. Gaither was working as a carpenter at Marshall when the war broke out and had joined the Lane Rangers. The twenty-two-year-old Alabama native probably hoped to fight Yankees, but found himself riding frontier patrol instead. Like the men of the 1st Mounted Rifles, the Lane Rangers broke up into small squads to keep watch over a vast area southeastward to Camp Wood on the upper Frio River in Edwards County then northward to Fort McKavett in present-day Menard County. Their job, in the words of another member of Gaither's company, was to look for the "Pest of the Frontier."[3] While they found signs of Indian movements, Gaither's company never confronted one of the raiding bands they sought.

W. J. D. ALEXANDER
albumen print

When the term of enlistment for the 1st Mounted Rifles expired, Texas officials hastened to raise a new force to fill the gap on the frontier. The state authorized the Frontier Regiment for twelve-months service in April 1862, then for another twelve months in February 1863. In February 1864 the Confederacy took over frontier defense again with the organization of a third frontier regiment, numbered the 46th Texas Cavalry. At various times this unit was commanded by Col. James N. Norris, Col. James McCord, and Lt. Col. James B. Barry. Under Norris the regiment had been ineffective as a deterrent against Indian raiding, but in February 1863 its tactics were revised by McCord. Maj. W. J. D. Alexander came to the regiment during this reorganization. The major was assigned command of four companies operating from Camp Colorado to the Rio Grande, while Lt. Col. James "Buck" Barry commanded units working north to the Red River. Abandoning passive patrols, Alexander and Barry instituted aggressive reconnaissances. These sweeps produced dozens of skirmishes with small Indian bands, but ultimately were unable to stop the attacks upon frontier settlements. *Photo courtesy of Don Beardslee*

226

DAVID J. WAMPLER
copy print

David J. Wampler of Weatherford served in McCord's Regiment under "Buck" Barry protecting the line between Camp Colorado and the Red River. Wampler enrolled at Fort Belknap in January 1863. The thirty-one year old was elected 3d corporal of Company G. That summer, with Confederate authorities preoccupied with the military situation elsewhere, Indian raids became more numerous and aggressive. Beginning with a raid by seven Indians in Parker County on August 1, 1863, in which two children were taken, and continuing with attacks near Decatur, Fort Worth, and Weatherford, the resources of the Frontier Regiment were strained. In October members of Company G followed raiders who had killed four settlers in Montague County. In a typical encounter, the cavalrymen caught up with the fleeing Indians. In the ensuing skirmish one of the cavalrymen was killed and the Indians made good their escape. *Photo courtesy of CRC*

227

GEORGE W. WATSON
copy print

Some reinforcement for the Frontier Regiment was received in the spring of 1863 when the Texas Border Cavalry Regiment of Col. James Bourland was placed along the border with the Indian Territory. Companies stationed along the western end of this line supplemented the Frontier Regiment in dealing with Indian raids. The Border Regiment was comprised largely of companies that drew from local communities for their men. George W. Watson had moved to the Peatown community in modern Gregg County with his family in the 1850s. Only sixteen years old when the war broke out, he did not join the army until 1863, and then was left behind by his regiment when he contracted measles. As a result, he wound up joining Bourland's regiment and serving in Cooke and Montague Counties. Chasing Indians and later Unionists and Confederate deserters, one of the most important roles played by the regiment came in October 1864, when it was thrown after Kiowa and Comanche raiders who had staged one of the largest raids of the war on settlements at Elm Creek. A band of some five hundred warriors seeking horses struck settlements in Young County at noon on October 13. Scattered about the countryside, the men of the Border Cavalry were unable to effectively counter the raid, although Bourland sent his companies after the Indians as they withdrew. *Photo courtesy of Janeal Riley*

JAMES W. THROCKMORTON
albumen print
William DeRyee

As a consequence of the Elm Creek Raid, Confederate policy toward the Indians shifted to aggressive campaigning. In November 1864 Gen. James W. Throckmorton was named to head the First Frontier District and established his headquarters at Decatur. Throckmorton planned an expedition against the Indians that began on February 1, 1865. Though lasting only ten days, Throckmorton stated that the campaign had taught "the Indians that even in mid winter, we intend to hunt them to their retreats."[4] Subsequently, Throckmorton organized local "minute" companies into a permanent force, ready for action. He, thus, created a third defensive force between the Frontier Regiment to the southwest and the Border Cavalry to the east. The approaching end of the war, however, meant that his efforts would never be seriously tested.
Photo courtesy of Archives Division, TSL

JACK J. CURETON
ninth-plate ambrotype

Jack Cureton had originally enlisted in J. M. Norris's Frontier Regiment in March 186, as captain of Company B. A quarrel with the regiment's lieutenant colonel, Alfred J. Obenchain, had led to charges against Cureton and Obenchain's murder by two of Cureton's friends. The captain was never charged, however, and he left the regiment at the end of his twelve-month enlistment. In 1864 Cureton commanded Company A (from Stephens County) in Maj. William Quayle's Frontier Organization and may have followed the Elm Creek raiders.

On January 8, 1865, Cureton participated in the last major Indian encounter in Texas during the war—the engagement at Dove Creek. When a party of some one thousand Kickapoo entered the state the previous month, soldiers began pursuing them; Cureton's command joined that pursuit about December 31, 1864. On the morning of January 8, a force of some 380 men reached the Kickapoo camp on Dove Creek and attacked what turned out to be a formidable Indian force armed with Enfield rifles as well as bows and arrows. Cureton and the other militia units were not nearly as well equipped. A member of the Frontier Regiment described the "flop-eared militia" as being "armed with all kinds of firearms, shot-guns, squirrel rifles, some muskets and pistols."[5] Taking a loss of 26 killed and 23 wounded, the Texan troops were forced to retreat. The Indians, who were peaceably heading for Mexico in the first place, continued the march to their destination. *Photo courtesy of Gregg Gibbs*

230

MANUEL YTURRI II
carte de visite

In response to Unionist agitation among the German population of the Hill Country during the spring of 1862, Confederate authorities sent troops to reestablish order. The problem had been precipitated primarily by the imposition of conscription by the Confederate government. Many Germans had fled their native land to avoid service in German armies, and they were unwilling to serve forcibly the Confederacy. The troops sent were drawn from units stationed throughout Texas and were under the command of Capt. James Duff. Lt. Manuel Yturri, son of a prominent San Antonio family and a graduate of St. Joseph's College in Bardstown, Kentucky, accompanied the force. He was pleased to have been detailed to Duff's company, at least when it arrived in the Hill Country on May 30. The men marched into Fredericksburg, county seat of Gillespie County, where Captain Duff ordered the inhabitants gathered for a public announcement. Duff read the declaration of martial law in English and a Mr. Slessinger did the same in German. In a letter to his wife, Yturri reported that Duff then assigned men to the roads in and out of town, sealing it to all persons without a pass. The occupation of Fredericksburg quietly began a summer in which Unionists would be bloodied into submission. *Photo courtesy of Yturri Family and Martin Callahan*

ROBERT HAMILTON WILLIAMS
copy print

In response to the declaration of martial law and the arrival of Confederate troops, sixty German unionists gathered near Kerrville on August 1, 1862, planning to ride to the Rio Grande, cross into Mexico, and then go to New Orleans to join the Union Army. Joining five other men, the party was on the Nueces River, only a day's ride from safety, by the evening of August 9. That evening a Confederate force under Lt. C. D. McRae caught up with the refugees. R. H. Williams, a young Englishman who had come to the United States in the 1850s, was a member of this Confederate command.

In camp the Confederates wondered whether or not the Germans would fight, and Williams was convinced that if they decided to fight the battle would be desperate. McRae ordered his attack during the night, and the subsequent fighting was every bit as terrible as Williams had predicted. Initially the Germans stood their ground, returning a deadly fire. Williams was with a group that fired from the edge of the refugee camp, until "four of our party had dropped, one with a bullet through his head, and the other severely wounded."[6] *Photo courtesy of CRC*

232

ADOLPH ZOELLER (STANDING)
carte de visite
A. D. Lytle, Baton Rouge, Louisiana

The Germans ultimately were overwhelmed, and the survivors began to withdraw in small parties. They left nineteen of their group dead, and nine others were quickly captured. Adolph Zoeller, a twenty-six-year-old German immigrant who had joined his brother in Kendall County about 1857, had been a member of the refugee party. He was one of the men who managed to escape, fortunately, since the Confederates took no prisoners. The nine men captured were shot immedi-ately in the head. The Confederates left the German dead unburied and pursued those who had managed to escape. In the following days, McRae's force captured nine more men in the brush and executed them; eight other Germans were killed in an ambush at the Rio Grande. Zoeller, however, was one of the few who escaped into Mexico, where he would ultimately join the Union Army. *Photo courtesy of Emmie Braubach Mauermann Estate and ITC*

JOHN G. DROMGOOLE
ninth-plate tintype

The Nueces Massacre was only the beginning, as Confederate authorities and civilian patriots unleashed a fury against the Unionists in central Texas. Companies of the 32d/36th Texas Cavalry were sent into the area to help round up Unionists and maintain order, although the largely German Company F was not used. Company G of that regiment was deployed and remained in the Hill Country until December. Twenty-four-year-old John G. Dromgoole of Clinton had joined Company G, composed of an equal mix of "Germans" and "Americans," at San Antonio the previous May and found himself fighting his neighbors rather than the Yankees. Company G carried out extensive patrols in the area, and the diary kept by Sgt. Thomas C. Smith of Company G offered witness to the reign of terror that held sway. "The creeks in this vicinity are said to be full of dead men," he wrote. "I witnessed a sight yesterday which I never wish to see again in a civilized and enlightened country. In a water hole in Spring Creek (about two miles from camp) there are four human bodies lying on top of the water, thrown in and left to rot, and that too after they were hanged by the neck and dead."[7] Confederate authorities had reacted with overwhelming force to suppress the German uprising. *Photo courtesy of Martin Callahan*

234

JOHN L. DONELSON
ambrotype

Capt. John Donelson was in command of a battalion of the 2d Texas Cavalry and was in the provost marshal's office at Fredericksburg enforcing martial law. A Tennessean who had come to Texas before the war, Donelson had joined his unit at Fort Brown in 1861. The business of hunting down Unionists was a nasty one. In a letter to Gen. Hamilton Bee in September 1862, Donelson concluded that his and Captain Duff's actions had ensured that the German population would remain peaceable. Nevertheless, he did encourage disarming the population and leaving a company of fifty men to "hold these counties in subjection" and help seize and sell Unionists' property. Despite his confidence, however, Donelson recognized that dissent had not been fully eradicated. "Some twenty or thirty Unionists are still concealed in the cedar brakes near this place," he wrote. "It is difficult to capture them, as their friends & hiding places are numerous."[8] Despite the killings, the area had not been pacified completely. *Photo courtesy of Kenneth C. Thompson Jr.*

JOHN L. HAYNES
albumen print
William DeRyee

The suppression of Unionist sentiment among the Germans in central Texas had serious implications for Unionists throughout the state. The result was a widespread exodus of prominent political leaders identified with the Union cause. John L. Haynes was a resident of Starr County before the war and had served in the state legislature. Through the secession crisis he had been an outspoken opponent of secession. When war broke out, he remained quietly at his home until Confederate authorities began their efforts to suppress Unionist dissent. In the autumn of 1862, Haynes joined hundreds of others who fled the state to Mexico, where they joined a large number of German-Texas refugees. Many moved on later to form large colonies of expatriate Texans at New Orleans and Washington, D.C. These men became a strong lobby pushing the Federal government to send a military force to return the state to the Union. *Photo courtesy of Archives Division, TSL*

THEODORE VAN BUREN
COUPLAND
carte de visite
A. D. Lytle, Baton Rouge

Many of the refugees would continue to be a thorn in the side of the Confederacy. At New Orleans many joined the Union army with the intention of returning to Texas and fighting their persecutors. Theodore Coupland was typical of the well-connected refugees who fled the state in the autumn of 1862. The twenty-six year old was the grand nephew of Rep. Andrew J. Hamilton and of Morgan C. Hamilton, one of the richest landowners in the state. He had come to Texas from Alabama before the war and settled at Austin, where he had been elected deputy sheriff. When his uncle Jack Hamilton fled the state in October, Coupland joined him and wound up at New Orleans with other refugees. On November 6, he joined the 1st Texas Cavalry (U.S.) that was being recruited there by another refugee, Edmund J. Davis. *Photo courtesy of Emmie Braubach Mauermann Estate and ITC*

MARTIN D. HART
albumen print
William DeRyee

238

While the Mexican border provided an avenue of escape for many Unionists in central Texas, the Indian Territory or Missouri was the goal of those in the northern and eastern parts of the state. Martin D. Hart, a wealthy landowner from Hunt County and a former member of the Texas legislature, had opposed secession in 1861 and had signed the Unionist "Address to the People of the State." In 1862 Hart left home for northwestern Arkansas, apparently carrying a Confederate commission. Instead of joining the Texas troops in that state, however, Hart organized a company that he offered for Union service behind Confederate lines. When he was captured on January 18, 1863, Confederate authorities court martialed him for desertion and treason and hanged him on January 23, 1863. Hart proved to be only one of many Texans of suspected loyalty who began to congregate along the northern border of the state at this time. *Photo courtesy of Archives Division, TSL*

ELIJAH STERLING
CLACK ROBERTSON
albumen print

In the autumn of 1863, the problem in the state's northern counties had become so bad that General McCulloch was forced to try to do something about it. Unionists, draft dodgers, and deserters had congregated in the area by the hundreds. E. S. C. Robertson, son of a prominent Texas pioneer, had been an attorney, Texas Ranger, militia officer, and officeholder prior to the war, and in 1861 had served in the Secession Convention from Bell County. In 1862 he was named a volunteer aide-de-camp to McCulloch and was sent to Cooke, Denton, Grayson, and Tarrant Counties in an effort to bring back the large number of deserters who had gathered there. While he reported that many of the men he encountered said they would return to the army, Robertson considered the situation potentially dangerous. He found bands, perhaps as many as a thousand men, in armed camps in the area. Despite pressure by Gen. E. Kirby Smith to take more drastic measures, McCulloch and Robertson continued to negotiate—usually unsuccessfully—to bring these men back into the army without a fight. *Photo courtesy of MOC*

WILLIAM CLARKE QUANTRILL
copy print

A more radical approach to forcing the large bands of men out of northern Texas was taken when McCulloch decided to utilize William Clarke Quantrill and his men. Quantrill had left Kansas following the sack of Lawrence and encamped about fifteen miles from Sherman, Texas, in mid-October 1863. McCulloch welcomed Quantrill as potential help in his efforts at rounding up deserters, although he was concerned about his ability to control the guerrilla leader. E. S. C. Robertson was not impressed and described Quantrill at his meeting with McCulloch that October. Robertson wrote: "Well he is nothing but a man—about five feet ten inches high—spare made—weighs about 150—has fair hair, blue eyes—red complexion. No mark of greatness about him that may not be found [in] many another Man of no worth at all."[9] Quantrill tried to use force against the men along the border, but ultimately his methods proved no more capable of bringing an end to the problem in northeastern Texas than McCulloch had been with his more humane approach. The Red River region became an area where no law ruled, offering a potential danger to Confederate Texas throughout the rest of the war. That situation persisted into the postwar era. *Photo courtesy of Texas Department of Public Safety, Ranger File*

Chapter 9

The Texas Homefront

Their budding prosperity has been completely checked by the war.
—A. J. L. FREMANTLE

Texas was spared the destruction of invading armies that was visited upon many of her sister states in the Confederacy. Through the war the activities of the Union Army in Texas were restricted to a short occupation of Galveston and a more persistent presence along the coast from Corpus Christi to Brazos Santiago. Nonetheless, the war early on affected the economy and people of the state. Fortunes were expended outfitting the units sent to fight for the Confederacy and business everywhere languished. The Federal naval blockade quickly produced shortages of many goods and forced Texans to try to produce critical items on their own.

Col. A. J. L. Fremantle, traveling across the state in the spring of 1863, addressed the problems that had beset the towns in particular when he noted: "their budding prosperity has been completely checked by the war." At San Antonio, Fremantle found trade at a standstill and necessities selling at what he called "famine prices." Coffee, he noted, was selling at seven dollars per pound.[1]

Coastal cities were particularly hard hit, and none more than Galveston. When Fremantle arrived at what had been the state's principal port before the war, he found it "desolate, blockaded, and under military law." Houses were empty, the wharves deserted. The entrance to the harbor was "blocked up with piles, torpedoes, and other obstacles."[2] H. C. Medford, a cavalryman at Galveston, noted in his diary that small children from the city came to the military camps and "beg for something to eat; and take away every scrap that we throw away."[3]

Among the towns along the coast, Brownsville was the one clear exception to the economic troubles suffered elsewhere. Here a thriving trade in many items essential to the state and to the Confederacy began moving through Brownsville to the Mexican town of Matamoras and its port of Bagdad. Prior to increased Union activity in southern Texas in 1864, the trade had become enormous, with hundreds of vessels along the coast at times during 1863. At least one Federal official concluded that trade through Bagdad made the nearby town of Matamoras "to the Rebellion west of the Mississippi what New York is to the United States—its great commercial and financial center."[4]

In the countryside conditions were not appreciably better than in the towns. Even the crossroads villages seemed deserted "except for women and very old men," and Fremantle found "their aspect was most melancholy."[5] Indeed, there was little to be positive about. Shortages of food, clothing, and other supplies plagued every area. Families that had ceased home manufacturing in favor of store-bought textiles were forced to learn the old skills once again. After writing a letter using homemade ink and using homemade blacking on her shoes, Kate Stone, a Louisiana refugee who had moved to Tyler, observed: "Truly we are learning many things."[6]

Ultimately, the Texas and Confederate governments were unable to secure critical supplies for the military effort. This problem forced both to initiate the development of facilities that could produce desperately needed ordnance, munitions, and equipment. Gov. Francis R. Lubbock and the State Military Board were responsible for the earliest attempts at creating such war-related industries.

Lubbock, who defeated Edward Clark in the election of 1861, immediately recognized the problems being created by the Federal blockade and took active measures to overcome shortages. At first he promoted self-sufficiency, encouraging Texans to fill their needs at home through domestic manufacturing. To make his point, Lubbock was inaugurated while wearing a homespun suit. In the end, however, he supported the state's creation or at least sponsorship of enterprises. In April 1862 he encouraged the legislature to create a military board empowered to take whatever measures were necessary to supply Confederate forces.

Among the best known operations of the Board was its attempt to raise money through the shipment of cotton to Mexico. Cotton was purchased with state bonds and then transported to Mexico, where it was sold for gold or used to purchase weapons and supplies. In the first year of this cotton business, the state sold about five thousand bales of cotton in Mexico, but the state's cotton marketing never realized the amount of funds hoped for initially. Many planters with the means preferred to ship their cotton directly to Mexico themselves, receiving gold rather than state bonds. After 1863 the state also faced competition from the Confederate Cotton Bureau, authorized by Gen. E. Kirby Smith to carry out the same sort of operation on behalf of the Confederacy.

In addition to its efforts at importing arms and ammunition, the Board encouraged the development of industries within Texas that could manufacture at least some of the army's supplies domestically. At the Texas State Penitentiary they established a textile mill that produced wool and cotton cloth. Government contracts encouraged the work of businesses such as the Clothing Manufacturers Company and the Southern Hattery at Marshall, the Hussey and Logan Manufacturing Company at Daingerfield, and the Confederate States Hat Factory at Gilmer. Ultimately, small shops that produced canteens, shoes, cartridge boxes, belts, saddles, harnesses, and a wide variety of other goods were located in towns throughout the state.

The manufacture of ammunition and weapons, however, was the Board's primary goal. Among its first experiments was the operation of a percussion-cap factory in the old state land office building at Austin. Powder works were built at Marshall, Waxahachie, and in Burnet County. Ambitious plans to manufacture weapons also were developed. In 1862 the Military Board contracted with J. C. Short of Tyler to produce .577 caliber Mississippi Rifles. Short, along with William S. N. Biscoe and George Yarbrough, formed Short, Biscoe, and Company and built an armory south of Tyler, where they hoped to fill their contract for 5,000 rifles. Dance, Brothers, and Park tried to manufacture pistols based on the Colt pattern of revolver at Old Columbia. Other gun factories included that of Whitescarver and Campbell near Rusk and Billups and Hassel at Plentitude in Anderson County. Smaller facilities operated throughout the state.

Efforts by the Military Board produced considerable equipment, but its ordnance endeavors were not as successful. The state had difficulty providing the materials necessary to manufacture the weapons, and the contractors had trouble finding skilled workers. At times help was drafted from among the soldiers garrisoned near the factories. By the end of its first year of operation, the Short and Biscoe facility at Tyler had delivered only one rifle.

In the autumn of 1863, the Confederate government began to take over many of these facilities. The fall of Little Rock to Federal troops forced the Confederacy to pull many of its manufacturing facilities into either southwestern Arkansas or Texas. In October 1863 the Confederacy bought the Short and Biscoe factory and brought in equipment from Little Rock and Arkadelphia, Arkansas. Col. G. H. Hill took charge and the plant began to manufacture Enfield and Austrian model rifles. Hill also expanded operations of the Tyler facility to include the production of a variety of military equipment.

Among the other problems that the state and Confederate governments were forced to solve—especially as the war came closer to Texas—was the development of prison camps. Confederate successes in the Trans-Mississippi brought with them prisoners who had to be accommodated. Prisoners taken when Magruder recaptured Galveston were kept initially in warehouses at Houston, then moved to the state penitentiary at Huntsville. Disputes over whether or not the military authorities could send prisoners to the state prison, however, ultimately led to the creation of a military prison at Camp Groce in Hempstead County in the summer of 1863. Camp Groce originally had been created as a training camp for Confederate troops in 1861 but had been abandoned because of its unhealthy location. It was no better as a prison camp and the first captives there suffered seriously from sickness.

Eventually Camp Groce was abandoned and its prisoners transferred to a larger facility at Tyler—Camp Ford, another former conscript camp. In July 1863 Camp Ford was turned into a prisoner-of-war camp to hold captured soldiers originally interned near Shreveport. The first barracks at the camp were built of logs by the prisoners themselves, and a stockade was not built until November 1863 after prisoners threatened an escape.

For much of its existence, the camp was commanded by Col. R. T. P. Allen. Allen had few troops at his disposal to maintain control over the inmates. At the time of the thwarted outbreak in 1863, Allen had only seventy militia to guard over five hundred Federal prisoners. These men were usually assisted, however, by one of the companies of the 2d Texas Mounted Rifles that was stationed at Tyler during the last years of the war.

At least in the beginning, conditions were better at Camp Ford than at Camp Groce. Federal officers maintained an effective internal police of the inmates and control over sanitation as long as the population of the prison remained relatively small. This made possible a camp life of much better quality than at other prisons. Inmates planted gardens, engaged in craftworks, and even manufactured such things as eating utensils, crockery, and straw hats for sale in the camp. A subscription among them raised one hundred and ten dollars to purchase a violin, played by Capt. William H. May of the 23d Connecticut, and with the accompaniment of a banjo, a flute, and a fife, furnished the music for prison dances. Prisoners even hand printed a newspaper, *The Old Flag*, published by Captain May.

As with other Southern prison camps, though, the number of captives at Camp Ford quickly over-reached the ability of local authorities to provide adequate shelter, food, and clothing. In the spring of 1864, the addition of some 3,000 prisoners taken in the Red River campaign expanded the inmate population to 4,725 men. There was considerable suffering (until prisoner exchanges began in October), and many of the same charges concerning ill-treatment later made about conditions at Andersonville Prison in Georgia were raised concerning treatment at Camp Ford. Conditions never deteriorated as dramatically as that: of some 6,000 prisoners who went through Camp Ford, only 286 died. This suggests that at least in terms of material conditions, things were never as bad there as they were in Georgia.

In the end, although few Texas civilians encountered Federal soldiers during the war, the conflict did have an impact on the day-to-day life of those who remained at home. Economic hardships, a new role for government, and the presence of Yankee prisoners were everyday reminders that Texans were a people at war.

Galveston had been the chief port of Texas in 1861 and was one of the state's most prosperous cities. This view shows the main business district, looking from the eastern edge to the west and Galveston Island's causeway to the mainland. The street in this image is the Strand, the location of most of the major business. The wharves on the right served the shipping that had filled the port in antebellum days. When the war broke out and the Union navy imposed its blockade, Galveston's economy declined sharply. Even though blockade runners continued to use the port throughout the war, business never recovered and many of the city's merchants moved to Houston to engage in the growing Mexican trade. A short occupation by Union forces further disrupted life in Galveston. The state's second largest city, with a population of 7,347 in 1860, was practically abandoned afterward, an impression borne out by one estimate that no more than 180 families remained by 1863. Like much of Texas, the plight of Galveston during the war showed that even without the presence of Union invading forces, the conflict exacted a price from the people at home. *Photo courtesy of The Rosenberg Library, Galveston*

From 20th Strand Looking West. 1861

GALVESTON
copy print

ELIZABETH STREET, BROWNSVILLE
carte de visite

Brownsville was one of the few places that prospered during the war. As soon as the blockade was established, much of the trade of the southwest was diverted to the mouth of the Rio Grande at Brazos Santiago and through the Mexican port of Bagdad. When blockaders appeared in that region, trade began to move through Brownsville, then to Bagdad by way

of Matamoras. Fortunes were made in the border trade, and thousands came to the area to participate in the economic boom. The population, which had been 2,734 people before the war, may have increased some ten times during the war years. A variety of goods moved through the town. Weapons, powder, percussion caps, blankets, clothing, shoes, medical supplies, and even food filled the holds of ships that put in at Bagdad, items that were then carried on mules and carts to the border and on into the interior of Texas. By 1863 Gen. E. Kirby Smith observed that Brownsville was the only entry through which he could obtain the goods he needed to keep his army supplied.[7] *Photo courtesy of ITC*

FRANCIS R. LUBBOCK
albumen print
William DeRyee

Francis R. Lubbock was a South Carolinian who had moved to Texas in 1836, where he was a successful merchant and rancher. He also had a distinguished political career, including service as comptroller of the Republic of Texas. Lubbock had been lieutenant governor in 1857 but had lost a bid for reelection in 1859. He then represented his state at the Democratic national convention in 1860, and in 1861 he became governor. Lubbock was a strident Confederate, supporting conscription, helping to develop a state foundry and percussion-cap factory, and working to secure trade with Mexico. He continuously tried to increase domestic production to support the war effort. *Photo courtesy of Archives Division, TSL*

250

GUY M. AND LAURA BRYAN
copy print

Guy M. Bryan had been a prominent secessionist politician, attorney, and rancher at Galveston prior to the war. Although he repeatedly requested an appointment to the field, his political talents denied him that wish, and he usually found himself serving as a liaison between civil and military authorities or attached to a headquarters staff. In 1862 he was engaged in efforts to raise money to support the state government as a member of the Cotton Bureau. The bureau would carry a planter's cotton to Mexico, where it was sold. Half of the profits went directly to the planter, while the state took the rest and issued bonds in that amount to the planter. This gave the state access to desperately needed specie. Ultimately, the Bureau was so successful that the Confederate government, which was trying the same means to raise money, ordered Texas to shut down the operation. *Photo courtesy of CAH, Prints and Photographs Collection, CN 08134*

RICHARD L. SPRINGG
carte de visite
Keddy's Photographic Gallery,
Baton Rouge

With a small manufacturing base and access to overseas sources restricted by the Federal naval blockade, Confederate Texas was forced to develop local industries to manufacture weapons, ammunition, and other military supplies. Funds raised by Guy Bryan and the state government supported efforts across the state to produce essential goods. In Burnet County, Lt. Richard L. Springg worked to develop niter from guano deposits found in a local cavern. Springg, a native of Maryland and a nineteen-year-old veteran of the 2d Virginia Infantry, had joined the Confederate Nitre and Mining Bureau in 1862 and was sent to Texas to help develop sources of potassium nitrate, an essential ingredient for gunpowder. The works at what is now known as Longhorn Cavern provided an ample supply of the mineral for local gunpowder manufacturing. *Photo courtesy of Dale Snair*

CARL CORETH
carte de visite
C. D. Fredericks & Company

Elsewhere, local shops took the place of larger factories in the manufacturing of weapons. Pvt. Carl Coreth of the 32d/36th Texas Cavalry found himself involved in that effort in the summer of 1862. Coreth, the twenty-five-year-old son of a Tyrolian army officer who had moved to New Braunfels in 1846, was sent along with other members of his largely ethnic German company to the farm of Ernest Kapp near Sisterdale to manufacture six-shooters, while other members of his unit suppressed German Unionists in the Hill Country. The work at Sisterdale was supervised by Alfred Kapp, who had worked for the Colt company at Hartford, Connecticut, before the war, and he now attempted to manufacture similar pistols for the Confederacy. The soldiers cast metal parts, bored barrels and cylinders, and then assembled their six-shooters. Coreth improved their lathe in a way that saved the workers time and improved the strength of the weapon. Such small shops, in the absence of larger factories, helped balance out the Northern superiority in weapons.
Photo courtesy of Minetta Altgelt Goyne

JAMES C. SHORT
daguerreotype

At Tyler, state authorities developed even larger works to make guns. James C. Short was a gunsmith at Tyler before the war, making and repairing single- and double-barreled rifles, shotguns, and pistols. His shop also made knives. In 1861 his advertisements in local newspapers promised that his rifles could kill abolitionists at four hundred yards and his knives would disgust any Yankee. In 1862 the State Military Board asked Short to make Mississippi Rifles for state troops. In partnership with William S. N. Biscoe and George Yarborough, Short contracted to build five thousand rifles by January 1864. Plagued by shortages of gun barrels, the company had produced only five hundred rifles by September 1863. That October, following the capture of the Little Rock Arsenal, Confederate authorities purchased the Tyler works and moved equipment there from Little Rock. A large blacksmith shop provided support for the rifle factory, forging gun locks, plus a variety of screws and nails. The Ordnance Department manufactured some fifteen thousand cartridges per week in buildings rented from merchants on the town square. Other facilities made saddles, bridles, and harnesses, as well as cartridge belts, cap pouches, and straps. Tinners produced canteens, dishes, and belt hooks. By the winter of 1863–1864, these facilities made eastern Texas a point of considerable interest for U.S. Army commanders and made an invasion of Texas aimed at these works an important strategic consideration. *Photo courtesy of Dr. Larry L. Smith*

DANIEL EDWARD
CAMERON MCPHAIL
copy print

Another major ordnance plant was created by authorities at Marshall. Many soldiers ultimately were assigned to work in these facilities. Pvt. Daniel E. C. McPhail, a North Carolinian, had enlisted in Capt. A. C. Allen's Company (C), 19th Texas Infantry, at Jefferson in February 1862. Although suffering from sickness, he served in Arkansas and in Louisiana in 1862 and 1863. Possibly incapacitated by his illness, he was sent to the Marshall Arsenal in March 1864, and he remained there for the rest of the war. *Photo courtesy of Gary Canada*

255

Henry Clay Wood
quarter-plate ambrotype

Another soldier sent to Marshall was Pvt. Henry Clay Wood. Wood, a Missisippian had moved to Texas in 1858 with his family and settled in Hopkins County. At the age of seventeen, he had enlisted in S. A. Minter's Company (K), 19th Texas Infantry, on May 10, 1862. He had this image made on June 24, 1862, while in training at Camp Waterhouse (named for the regiment's colonel) near Jefferson, Texas. Wood's unit saw extensive service with Walker's Texas Division during the Red River Campaign of 1864, although Wood, who had suffered frequently from sickness, was detailed to the Marksville Hospital in Louisiana in January 1864. In January 1865, however, Wood's company was detached and assigned to the Marshall Arsenal as a guard. They remained there until the Federals reached Marshall and took over the arsenal in mid-June 1865. *Photo courtesy of Gary Canada*

256

State Prison, Huntsville
carte de visite
F. B. Bailey, Navasota

Huntsville and the state penitentiary there became
another major center for producing goods to supply
the armies. As a part of Governor Lubbock's initiative,
state officials located a textile mill at the prison. The
brick buildings provided perfect facilities for the
factory, and the prisoners constituted the labor force.
Photo courtesy of U.S.A.M.H.I.

ROBERT T. P. ALLEN
copy print

After the capture of a significant number of Federals at Galveston in January 1863, other resources had to be dedicated to the construction of prison camps within the state. One of the largest permanent camps was Camp Ford, located near Tyler. In the spring of 1864, its commander was Col. Robert T. P. Allen. Allen, a West Pointer from Maryland who had come to Texas in 1857 and established Bastrop Military Institute, had briefly commanded the 4th Texas Infantry until driven from camp by his men, who considered him a martinet. He had gone on to help raise the 17th Infantry, which he commanded until being placed in charge of Camp Ford in the autumn of 1863. Although Federal prisoners protested conditions at Camp Ford, at least one of their guards thought they were not harsh enough and believed Allen too considerate. In March the guard observed: "I saw Col. R. T. P. Allen, the Commandant of the post, go into the stockade and carry with him, dried peaches, eggs, butter &c. as a prsent to Yankee officers; this is quite different from the treatment that our officers received at Camp Chase; I think it would do Col. Allen good to stay a few months in Ft. Delaware."[8] *Photo courtesy of CRC*

WILLIAM H. MAY
carte de visite
McPherson & Oliver, New Orleans

Capt. William May of the 23d Connecticut Infantry was among the first prisoners sent to Camp Ford when he was transferred from Shreveport to join prisoners captured at Galveston and Sabine Pass. May had been captured on June 20, 1863, at Terre Bonne, Louisiana. The captain was one of the more industrious of the prisoners and hand printed a camp newspaper, *The Old Flag,* which included camp news, fiction, and poetry. The edition of March 15, 1864, even included a poem to the wife of camp commander R. T. P. Allen:

So, Lady! while the heart with mother's love
    and sisters pity cheers the captives lot.
Truth keeps her record in the courts above,
    And thou art not forgot.[9]

He managed to bring three copies of the paper with him when he was exchanged in the summer of 1864. May was a skilled musician as well as an entrepreneur. A subscription among Camp Ford's inmates secured a violin for him, which he subsequently played at camp entertainments and "dances." *Photo courtesy of J. Dale West*

260

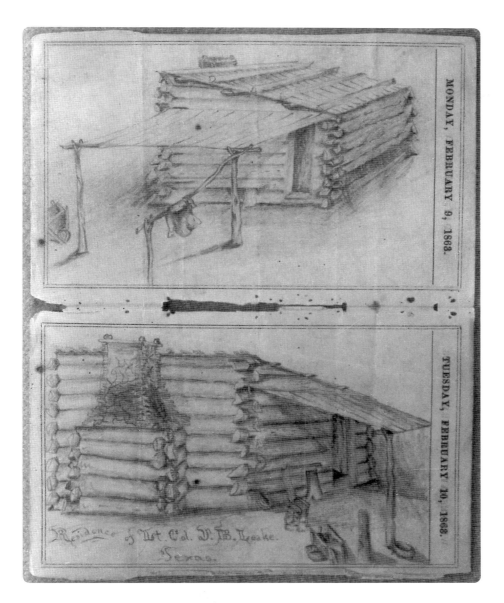

Joseph B. Leake and His Cabin
cartes de visite

Lt. Col. Joseph B. Leake of the 20th Iowa Infantry probably arrived at Tyler about the same time as Captain May, although he was not captured until September 19, 1863, in an engagement at Sterling Farm, Louisiana. Leake kept a diary during his stay at Camp Ford and drew pictures of his cabin, illustrating the living conditions there. Leake's unit was involved in a planned escape in November 1863 in which a soldier of the 26th Indiana was shot by guards and another was wounded. At the time, the prisoners greatly outnumbered their guards, and a bloody encounter was brewing in which the prisoners threatened to break out and sack Tyler. Colonel Leake was one of those who urged the men to reconsider. Leake was exchanged with the rest of the 19th Iowa in July 1864, and this picture shows him at New Orleans soon thereafter, wearing a hat manufactured at Camp Ford. *Photos courtesy of Roger Davis*

261

Chapter 10

Yankee Invasion

We hope to God, this section of Country is not to be abandoned without a struggle. . . . We have certainly done our part towards the Government, and look to it for a share of protection in common with the East.

—RICHARD KING

In November 1863 Richard King, a prominent rancher and entrepreneur from southern Texas, reacted to the landing of Federal troops nearby with a letter to the office of Gen. John Magruder at Houston. King asked for two to three thousand cavalry, which he thought would be enough to thwart any force the enemy might bring into action in the area. If he could not have that, then King wanted five hundred "good determined Texans" to save the country from destruction. King was not convinced, however, that Magruder was willing to commit any men, and he pleaded: "We hope to God, this section of Country is not to be abandoned without a struggle or at least giving the people notice that it is to be entirely abandoned." King clearly was concerned with the commitment of Confederate authorities, writing: "We have cer-tainly done our part towards the Government, and look to it for a share of protection in common with the East."[1] After feints elsewhere along the coast, the Yankees finally had brought the war to Texas.

The lull in Federal activities that followed the successful Confederate actions at Galveston and Sabine Pass in January 1863 had lasted through the summer. In late summer, however, Maj. Gen. Nathaniel P. Banks turned his attention to Texas once again. This time his plans called for a major expedition against Southern forces in the state. Confederates would be on the defensive once again, and this time it would be to save the state from the Federal invaders.

That autumn, action was renewed all along the coast. The U.S. Navy increased the intensity of its probes along the southern coast, but the major threat was an invasion of the upper coast ordered by General Banks. Banks's plan was for a move against Sabine Pass, an invasion aimed at providing a base from which a large force could move over-land to the rear of Houston, taking that city and then Galveston. The task was assigned to Maj. Gen. William B. Franklin and his XIX Army Corps.

Franklin arrived at Sabine City on September 8, 1863, with some five thousand troops. Five gunboats

263

accompanied the force to dispose of Confederate Fort Griffin at Sabine Pass. Only forty-seven men from Company F, 1st Heavy Artillery, defended that small mud fort, which mounted only six guns: two 32-pounder smoothbores, two 24-pounder smoothbores, and two 32-pounder howitzers. The men, commanded by Lt. Richard W. "Dick" Dowling, were well drilled at their guns, however. With unusually accurate fire, Dowling's men disabled two Federal gunboats, the *Sachem* and *Clifton,* and disabled a third. Unable to force the Pass, Franklin ordered the twenty transports with his men back to New Orleans.

The Battle of Sabine Pass would be a major victory for Texas Confederates. The Federal armies, however, had massive resources and, after all, at Sabine Pass it had merely sailed away. Little had been lost, Banks simply determined to move again. For all of Magruder's efforts, he was unable to lift the Federal blockade or to prevent the ready operation of Federal fleets along the Texas coast. At the time of the victory at Sabine Pass, Magruder was already considering pulling troops back to defend Texas between the Brazos and Sabine Rivers at all cost. That meant the possible abandonment of the Rio Grande region, which was the very focus of Banks's next campaign.

The immediate impact of the Federal defeat at Sabine Pass was the frustration of Federal hopes for an easy capture of Houston from the land. Banks turned to other plans, but the Federal general was not through with Texas. His continued interest in planting the national flag on Texas soil had clear political motives, and pressure from authorities in Washington played a major role in his actions. Pres. Abraham Lincoln for one wanted action that would encourage Unionists within the state. In addition, a campaign in Texas also extended the promise of cutting off the important trade between the Southern states and Mexico that thrived in the Rio Grande country. After first considering a march through Louisiana into eastern Texas, Banks concluded that his best option was to occupy the Rio Grande area and move up the coast, closing the passes through the barrier islands to the mainland, reoccupying Galveston, and then moving against the strategic city of Houston. Gen. John Magruder had only a small force to respond to an invasion of the size contemplated by Banks.

On November 2, forty-five hundred Union soldiers commanded by Gen. Napoleon J. T. Dana landed at Brazos Santiago, the island at the mouth of the Rio Grande. Confederate defenders in the area were totally inadequate to stop such a force and abandoned the island the next day. Gen. Hamilton Bee, with fewer than two hundred men, evacuated Brownsville on November 3, burning cotton and government stores when he left. Three days later the 94th Illinois marched unopposed into the town.

District commander John Magruder realized that he did not have an adequate force to resist a full-scale Federal invasion. All of his infantry were in the vicinity of Houston and Galveston, with the 8th and 20th Texas at Galveston, the 2d Regiment near Cedar Lake, and the 3d and 13th Texas at Velasco. Most of his cavalry was also in this area, with only Duff's 33d Texas and Baird's Regiment close to the invading force. He had local militia companies, but staff officers believed many of these could not be relied on.

The inadequacy of Confederate coastal fortifications worsened the situation. Except at Sabine Pass and Galveston, nowhere along the coast did the defenders have enough artillery to prevent the Federals from landing if supported by naval gunfire, nor did the Southerners have garrisons large enough to stop an attack by land. At Aransas Pass the Confederate works contained only three cannon, and all of these were positioned to defend against a naval attack rather than an infantry assault. Fort Esperanza, commanding access to Matagorda Bay, was more formidable. Its twelve-foot-high earthwork walls mounted eight 24-pounders and one

128-pounder columbiad, but again the guns were all aimed at the sea. While they presented a serious obstacle to any effort at passing the barrier islands by the sea, these guns and inadequate garrisons offered less than minimal protection against a land force.

Confederates offered only token resistance when they saw that Banks had landed an overwhelming force, and they pulled back into the interior. Col. Santos Benavides, commanding a small cavalry regiment, remained on the Rio Grande at Laredo some one hundred fifty miles upriver. General Bee fell back with his command to Corpus Christi. Magruder promised support, but from the beginning the general was prepared to abandon much of Texas in order to protect the strategically important region between the Brazos and Sabine Rivers, and he made his plans to that end. Most of his units remained along the coast in Matagorda and Brazoria Counties.

The situation for the Confederates was complicated further by their inability to determine exactly what the Federal invasion force was doing. At Corpus Christi, Bee reported that they were moving by sea up the coast to the east of the barrier islands, which were providing an effective screen behind which to operate. As a result, the small garrison on Mustang Island was surprised on November 16 when fifteen hundred Federals landed near Port Aransas and Bee failed to provide reinforcements. Union infantry supported by gunboats successfully seized the Confederate fortifications at Aransas Pass the next day. Additional troops were landed across the Pass on St. Joseph's Island, sealing entry into Corpus Christi Bay.

By November 27 the Federals had pushed up Matagorda Island and were ready to engage Confederate forces at Fort Esperanza. Skirmishing that day drove Confederate defenders back into the fort, and the next day Federal field artillery began to shell the position. The bombardment began November 29, and that evening the Confederate commander, realizing the hopelessness of the situation, ordered his guns spiked and the magazines burned. The Federals entered the fort in time to save three of the magazines from exploding, but their failure to take an island in the rear of the fort allowed most of the garrison to escape. With the capture of Fort Esperanza, the Federals also garrisoned DeCrow's Point across Cavallo Pass on the tip of the Matagorda Penninsular and sealed off entry into Matagorda Bay. Controlling the latter, Banks believed he could land an army anytime he chose and have easy access to the interior. His forces began probing up the Matagorda Penninsular from DeCrow's Point, scouting out Confederate strength.

While the main body of Banks's men moved up the coast, on November 21 Col. Edmund J. Davis of the 1st Texas Cavalry (US) headed another expedition up the Rio Grande. With part of his force aboard the steamboat USS *Mustang* and the rest marching overland, this force was to move at Davis's discretion toward Rio Grande City. The goal was to recruit men for Davis's loyal cavalry regiment, and Philip Braubach went into the interior to bring whatever loyalists he could out of the state. At the same time, Braubach would seize whatever Confederate property he could lay hands on. Davis's force occupied Rio Grande City and successfully cut off all border trade between the coast and that point, then began to scout further upriver.

At Brownsville, efforts at securing the political goals of the Texas campaign also were implemented. On December 1, Andrew J. Hamilton arrived at that town to assume the office of provisional governor; Hamilton had secured the appointment from President Lincoln.

Although Magruder received urgent requests for help from the border, the general perceived the more serious Federal thrust to be that along the coast. While Davis had cut off trade across the lower Rio Grande, cotton continued to flow across the border at Laredo and Eagle Pass. The capture of

Houston or Galveston would be more damaging to the cause, and Magruder established a defensive line on Caney Creek, approximately twenty miles to the west of Velasco and the mouth of the Brazos River. At this point any Federal force moving up the Matagorda Penninsular or from a landing site along Matagorda Bay could be challenged. Two cavalry regiments, the 2d (Pyron's) and 32/36 (Wood's) Texas, were assigned to these defenses. While the defenders encountered occasional Federal scouts and raiders, the attack that Magruder had feared never came.

Banks's campaign in Texas quickly achieved its early goals, but then the general's fear that his force was inadequate to challenge Magruder on the mainland without naval support brought the operation to a halt. Banks dithered while trying to find reinforcements to support his Texas operations, but the pressing need for men in other Union armies meant that he could secure no troops other than those already within his Louisiana command. By mid-December he had put everything on hold while he planned an invasion of Texas along the Brazos River. Eventually that campaign gave way to one aimed at eastern Texas along the Red River through Louisiana.

While Banks diverted his attention elsewhere, Magruder consolidated what forces he could gather near San Antonio and began a campaign against Banks's army. The man Magruder sent to drive the Federals from southern Texas was John S. "Rip" Ford. Ford gathered his men at San Antonio as a part of what was called the "Cavalry of the West." By March, Ford had put together a column of about 1,300 men and began his movement southward. Their first day's march found them at Camp San Fernando, where the Atascosa flowed into the Frio and Nueces Rivers. In March, Ford's cavalry began to encounter Federal outposts and to drive them back. One of the major skirmishes took place at Los Patricios on March 13.

As Ford probed into southern Texas, Federal activities virtually had ceased. Banks withdrew almost one-fourth of his men for the Red River Campaign, leaving 3,400 men along the Texas coast and in the Rio Grande area. The one expedition undertaken by the Federals was led by Col. Edmund J. Davis against Laredo. The seizure of that town would provide a further barrier to the Confederacy's trade with Mexico. Davis's force of cavalry, followed by infantry and artillery, initially encountered only token opposition and quickly pushed upriver to Ringgold Barracks. On March 12 the Confederates were forced to abandon Fort McIntosh near Laredo. By March 19 the expedition had reached Laredo and prepared to attack.

Ford left the fate of Laredo up to the town's garrison, commanded by Santo Benavides. Fortunately for the Confederacy, Benavides led a successful defense and the Federal column retreated. Ford's main force began operations along the Nueces, while he considered how to carry out his mission. Uncertain at first, he finally decided to take on the main Federal force. In April he ordered the Cavalry of the West toward Ringgold Barracks, which they reached on April 17. There they found that Banks had left only a shell of a force, which when confronted moved back toward Brownsville. The Confederate column moved slowly, with Ford uncertain of Federal strength. By July they had pushed the Federals back into Brownsville, and on July 20 the Federals abandoned that city without a fight.

The Federals, never really defeated but unwilling to risk a general engagement, simply pulled back to Brazos Island. For much of the rest of the war, fighting involved little more than skirmishes between these troops and the Confederate force that occupied the mainland. In fact, the greater threat faced during this time was that of Juan Cortina, a Mexican bandit and general who was leading a force against the French and in the process staging occasional raids into Texas. In September 1864, however, Cortina was defeated at Matamoras, ending the threat from Mexico.

WILLIAM B. FRANKLIN
carte de visite

In the autumn of 1863, Federal forces began operations designed to occupy Texas. Politics and diplomacy lay behind these plans, with Pres. Abraham Lincoln hoping to encourage Texas Unionists and the State Department wanting to discourage French adventurers from Mexico. Gen. Nathaniel Banks prepared the campaign's initial strategy, planning an attack to the west of Sabine Pass that would put Union forces on the Texas and New Orleans Railroad from which they could move on Houston and Galveston. Maj. Gen. William B. Franklin, commander of Banks's XIX Corps, was given command of the invasion force. Twenty-two transports accompanied by gunboats left New Orleans on September 4. Franklin planned to attack Fort Griffin and land his troops on September 7. When the first division missed the Pass, Franklin's plans were changed: He had lost the chance to surprise Confederate forces at Fort Griffin and was uncertain as to the strength of the garrison. Instead of landing the troops on the Gulf shore, he determined to reduce the fort first. His hesitation showed that his lack of information concerning Confederate forces in the area had infused him with an almost paralytic caution. The new plan was put into operation on September 8. *Photo courtesy of U.S.A.M.H.I.*

267

WILLIS E. CRAIG
carte de visite
A. P. Hart, Elmira, New York

As a part of Franklin's new strategy, the gunboats would attack Fort Griffin while an assault force would land on the west bank of the river about one-half mile below the fort. Capt. Willis E. Craig of Company H, 161st New York Infantry, was placed in command of four companies of his regiment and assigned to the storming party while other companies of his regiment were assigned as sharpshooters on the gunboats *Arizona, Clifton, Granite City,* and *Sachem.* Craig took his own men to the steamer *General Banks,* where they joined four companies of the 75th New York and two of the 165th New York (Zouaves) for the intended assault. The men crowded the decks as the naval commander, Lt. Frederick Crocker, maneuvered his four gunboats over the bar, followed by their own ship and six others. *Sachem* and *Arizona* moved upstream along the eastern channel at about 3:30 P.M. and began firing at Fort Griffin. The battle had begun. *Photo courtesy of MOLLUS, Mass., U.S.A.M.H.I.*

268

RICHARD W. DOWLING
carte de visite

Franklin clearly had overestimated the strength of his opponent, although the men of the Davis Guards—Company F, 1st Texas Heavy Artillery—who served the six guns of Fort Griffin ultimately proved formidable enough. In command of the company, composed largely of dockworkers and common laborers from Houston, was Lt. Richard W. "Dick" Dowling, an Irish-born saloon keeper from the city. The gun crews had placed stakes in the channel to help them determine distance, and when USS *Sachem* came into range Dowling ordered his men to open fire. The gunboat was hit several times, ran onto a mud bank, and was put out of action when a shot pierced her boiler. Many of her crew and the sharpshooters placed aboard her were scalded by the boiling water. Turning on the USS *Clifton*, Dowling's gunners soon put her out of commission as well with a shot that cut her steering cables. In the aftermath, the captain of the USS *Granite City* pulled back across the bar, leaving the transports to move on their own, while the USS *Arizona*, temporarily aground, ultimately was able to retire as well. The storming parties on the transports never made it ashore. *Photo courtesy of LLMVC*

269

GEORGE H. BAILEY
copy print from *Confederate Veteran*

Aboard the Federal gunboats the situation was desperate. An infantryman aboard the USS *Clifton* recalled that "her bulwarks were not more than eight inches solid oak covered with a plating of one half inch steel" and that "every shot sent sections of those bulwarks flying across the deck like kindling wood."[2] Under such an assault both gunboats surrendered. Dr. George H. Bailey, a resident of Fort Bend County before the war and the post surgeon at Beaumont, had rushed to Sabine Pass when the Federal attack had begun to help serve the guns and to offer his medical assistance. Bailey accompanied Dowling to the *Clifton*, where the latter received the sword of Lieutenant Crocker. Bailey then went to the USS *Sachem*, where he treated the scalded men by covering them with flour. The Sabine Pass expedition had come to an end in disaster for the Federals. A force of some five thousand men had been turned back by a fort garrisoned with fewer than fifty men.

NAPOLEON J. T. DANA
albumen print

West Point graduate Napoleon Dana had been assigned to Banks's command while recuperating from a serious wound received at Sharpsburg. Dana was selected to command the Rio Grande expedition, but after seizing Brownsville the general was left in command of that post. There he entered into complex diplomatic contact with Mexican authorities, worked to facilitate the return of loyal Texans to the area, and sought to ensure logistical support for the Federal invading column. *Photo courtesy of U.S.A.M.H.I.*

HAMILTON P. BEE
copy print

Commander of Confederate forces at Brownsville was Hamilton Bee, a forty-one-year-old antebellum resident of Laredo. Bee, brother of Gen. Bernard E. Bee Jr., was a veteran of the Mexican War and had been commissioned as general of militia at the beginning of the Civil War. In 1862 he was appointed brigadier general in the Confederate Army.

Bee quickly recognized that his command was totally inadequate to resist Banks's large invasion force. Brownsville was a center for the large border trade with Mexico, and with its warehouses full of cotton and munitions, the general determined that his best course of action was to save as much of these materials as he could. He sent fully loaded trains north and west, thus saving much of these essential supplies from capture. Bee pulled his cavalry back to the vicinity of Corpus Christi to await Banks's further intentions.

Photo courtesy of Mansfield State Commemorative Area, Louisiana Office of State Parks

ISAAC DYER
carte de visite

The Confederates did not have long to wait for the Federals to move from their base at Brownsville. Col. Isaac Dyer of the 15th Maine had been an apothecary from Skowhegan before joining his regiment in 1861. On November 16, 1863, his unit was aboard the steamers USS *Matamoras* and USS *Planter* moving up the Gulf from Port Isabel to close off Texas ports. That evening his troops landed in the dark through heavy surf on Mustang Island. With wet shoes and clothing, they marched overnight some eighteen miles to come up behind the Confederate battery at Aransas Pass. A skirmish line was all that was needed to force the defenders back. The rapid approach of the Federals had surprised the Confederates. Facing a superior force and having only nine officers and eighty-nine men from the 8th Texas Infantry and the 3d Texas State Militia, the Confederate commander surrendered unconditionally. Gen. T. E. G. Ransom named Dyer commander of the post. Corpus Christi was cut off now from the sea and the Federals had begun their move up the coastline. *Photo courtesy of U.S.A.M.H.I.*

PHILIP C. BITTER
carte de visite

Banks's shift from eastern Texas to the Rio Grande area apparently surprised General Magruder. Following the battle at Sabine Pass, the Confederate commander had started concentrating troops in the vicinity of Beaumont. Philip Bitter was with Company F, 36th Texas Cavalry, which moved from Victoria to eastern Texas in late September. After Banks's army began its advance from Brownsville, Bitter's unit was rushed southward once again. Bitter was elected lieutenant while the regiment was on the move, and the campaign showed that all was not well within this Texas regiment. One of his opponents, unhappy at the defeat, was not pleased with the regiment's officers. He wrote of the new lieutenant: "Bitter is an arch-boor, and to that degree he fits very well into our officer class."[3] The regiment was ordered to reinforce Fort Esperanza on the northern end of Matagorda Island and marched rapidly to Houston, Columbia, and then through biting cold weather to Matagorda, where they arrived on November 30. That evening they prepared to board steamboats for Saluria. *Photo courtesy of Martin Callahan*

274

FREDERICK SPEED
carte de visite

The Texans arrived too late. From Aransas Pass the Federals had moved on to Matagorda Island. Frederick Speed was adjutant of the 13th Maine, originally enlisting as a 2d lieutenant in Company A from his hometown of Gorham. His unit, the 15th Maine, and the 34th Iowa were brigaded together when the Federals advanced from Aransas Pass toward Fort Esperanza. On November 22 the regiment crossed to St. Joseph Island and pushed rapidly forward. The next day the brigade brushed aside a guard at Cedar Bayou and crossed to Matagorda Island. By the evening of November 26, they were within ten miles of their objective. The next morning they drove in Confederate pickets, but a "norther" so severe that Federal gunboats could not give supporting fire (and produced suffering in Philip Bitter's regiment) forced a delay in an attack. The next day Speed's unit helped place guns to lay siege to the fort. The badly outnumbered Confederates, however, abandoned their position without a fight on Sunday evening, November 30. *Photo courtesy of U.S.A.M.H.I.*

E. P. TURNER
carte de visite
A. G. Wedge

General Magruder rushed troops to the top of the Matagorda Penninsular, for after the fall of Fort Esperanza the Federals had established a position across Cavallo Pass on the foot of the peninsula. This gave the Union army a position from which it could advance against Galveston and Houston with gunboat support. Capt. E. P. Turner of Magruder's staff was sent to direct the concentration of Confederate forces on the San Bernard River, the logical place to stop any enemy movement in force. On December 28, one hundred men of the 13th Maine Infantry landed about seven miles from the head of the peninsula—a force the Confederates believed much larger and required an immediate reaction. Turner was convinced that the Federals would move on the beach against the works being constructed at either the mouth of the San Bernard River or along Caney Creek and ordered the few troops available to protect these positions. Turner then hastened to join the men of Col. A. Buchel's 1st Texas Cavalry, which had set off immediately to repel the invaders. *Photo courtesy of LLMVC*

276

JACOB DURST
copy print

Jacob Durst was with Company E of the 1st Texas Cavalry. This twenty-two-year-old rancher and farmer was a native of Bettenhausen, Germany, who came to Texas in 1846 and settled first in Fredericksburg. He moved to Mason County in 1859. Unlike many other Germans, he supported the Confederate cause at the beginning, joining the militia in the spring of 1861 and then a regular unit that became a part of the 1st Cavalry in June 1862.

Buchel moved his horsemen down the peninsula at a trot and gallop. As they approached the Federal force, cannon aboard the gunboat USS *Granite City* began to fire at the troopers with shell, shot, and spherical case. Much of the Confederate force began to fall behind as a result of this shelling and the fatigue of the hard-driven horses. Nevertheless, Buchel still had a far larger force with him when the Confederates ran the Federals down on a beach at about 9:00 P.M. on the evening of December 29. The invaders had quickly thrown up a barricade built with driftwood, and through the evening the Confederate cavalry tested the position. *Photo courtesy of Martha Durst*

FRANCIS S. HESSELTINE
carte de visite

Commander of the detachment of the 13th Maine that Buchel had encountered was Lt. Col. Francis Hesseltine. Hesseltine had left Waterville College in 1861 to join the 3d Maine and had served with gallantry at Bull Run. In August 1862, however, he joined the newly formed 13th Maine as lieutenant colonel, and in November and December 1863 he commanded that regiment on Matagorda Island in the successful attack on Fort Esperanza. Although he probably overestimated Buchel's force as badly as Buchel had the Federals, Hesseltine believed that his one hundred men were about to be gobbled up by some eight hundred to one thousand men. On the evening of December 29, his gunboats were forced back by a heavy sea, and he confronted a potential disaster. He determined that "rather than the rebels should meet the first encouragement of this campaign, that they [his men] would die there, with as many of their foes lying about them."[4] Hesseltine kept his front to the enemy and ultimately had his soldiers throw up a barricade of drift branches, logs, and stumps. The Confederates were reluctant to ride headlong into even a company of infantry, and the Yankees successfully held out for two days until their gunboats could find and remove them from the peninsula. For his role in the action, Hesseltine received a Congressional Medal of Honor. *Photo courtesy of U.S.A.M.H.I.*

THOMAS JEFFERSON WEST
copy print

The successes of the Yankees as they moved up the coast and the fall of Fort Esperanza spread gloom among Confederate forces as they waited for what they believed would be the inevitable attack up the Matagorda Penninsular against Houston. Responding to every rumored threat, Confederate regiments marched and countermarched between Houston and Victoria, which did little to improve their outlook. Pvt. Thomas J. West of the 36th Texas Cavalry (shown wearing the rawhide jacket of an Indian he had killed before the war) was among the troops concentrated in the area. The twenty-nine-year-old rancher from Seguin had run cattle along the coast before the war. At San Antonio in March 1862, he enlisted in the army for three years or until the end of the war. With the Yankees moving at will, the end seemed to be coming sooner than had been expected, and morale in West's unit and others was low. Another member of his regiment wrote at the time: "There does not seem to be much confidence in the western troops here. . . . Confidence in this war has sunken very much, even among the Americans. I talked with several and they were all in accord with one another that they would rather have mules than Negroes and Confederate money."[5] Southern commanders were unsure just how reliable such men were. *Photo courtesy of Martin Callahan*

Capt. Lewis Maverick was with the 36th Texas Cavalry in the spring of 1864, working with other officers to keep Magruder's army in the field. General discontent ultimately led to massive desertions in January and February. Militia units and whole companies of regiments in the Confederate army left camp and headed home, either to protect their loved ones or to abandon a war they believed was lost. Maverick certainly had not lost heart. The son of Sam Maverick, Lewis possibly was the first Anglo-American child born in San Antonio. In 1861 he left the University of North Carolina to join the 1st North Carolina. After serving his six-month enlistment, he returned to San Antonio and raised a company of cavalry. The army he joined had yet to experience either heavy combat or success. Now, rather than fighting the enemy, Maverick's men were trying to keep their own men in the ranks. A member of the regiment wrote from Caney Creek in February that the 36th Cavalry had only enough men left to constitute two companies. "There is absolute demoralization."[6] Maverick's company was busy chasing down and arresting deserters. *Photo courtesy of CAH*

Banks apparently never seriously intended to confront Magruder's troops below Houston, and by December his movement up the coast had come to an end. At Brownsville, however, efforts moved forward to install a loyal Union government and to recruit troops from Texas to hold the territory that had been taken from the Confederacy. A Unionist civil government was put in place on December 1, when Andrew J. Hamilton arrived at Brownsville holding President Lincoln's appointment as brigadier general and military governor of the state. Hamilton was a prominent Texas politician before the war, serving as attorney general of the state, a member of the legislature, and a Congressman. He had refused to swear an oath of allegiance to the Confederacy but had remained at Austin until the Confederate government began its suppression of Unionists in August 1862. Hamilton had fled to Mexico, then gone to Washington, D.C., where he lobbied for an invasion of his home state. Although Hamilton ran into opposition from General Dana, among his first actions was the establishment of a federal court through which the property of loyal Confederates could be legally seized. *Photo courtesy of Martin Callahan*

ANDREW J. HAMILTON
carte de visite

John L. Haynes also found himself back in Texas. Commissioned colonel on November 5, he was authorized to raise a second Union cavalry regiment among the Texans. Promising bounties for enlistment, the number of recruits initially was large. The army promised those who joined that their service would be solely in Texas. By the end of December, the 2d Texas Cavalry (U.S.) consisted of approximately three hundred men. Recruiting slowed down, however, when the U.S. Army proved slow in providing equipment necessary for the regiment to begin its training. Failures to deliver bounties and payrolls also damped enthusiasm. *Photo courtesy of Emmie Braubach Mauermann Estate and ITC*

JOHN L. HAYNES
carte de visite
E. Jacobs, New Orleans

MALEK A. SOUTHWORTH
carte de visite

The men who joined Haynes's 2d Texas came from a wide variety of backgrounds and appear to have been somewhat different from the large number of Anglo and German Unionists who had formed the core of the 1st Texas. Dr. Malek A. Southworth, surgeon for the regiment, reflected the growing disillusionment among many Confederates with the course of the war. Southworth had enlisted at the beginning of the war with the 2d Texas Cavalry, but his experiences in New Mexico apparently had convinced him he was fighting for the wrong cause. He was at Brownsville when Banks arrived, and on November 5 the thirty-four-year-old physician enlisted in the 2d Texas. *Photo courtesy of Emmie Braubach Mauermann and ITC*

In addition to ex-Confederates such as Southworth, the 2d Texas enlisted a large numbers of Mexicans. Confederates believed that many of these recruits were Mexican citizens who were attracted by the bounty the Union army was offering, but clearly many were Americans. Sgt. Patricio Perez of Company A had been a herdsman in the Brownsville area before the war. He enlisted at Brownsville on December 15 and was used as a scout for Union units moving out of the city into the frontier areas. *Photo courtesy of Delia Alaniz*

LINO HINOJOSA AND
UNKNOWN BROTHER-IN-LAW
copy print

Another Texas herdsman who joined the 2d Texas was Lino Hinojosa. He had been born in Camargo, Mexico, in 1836, but had moved to the United States before the war and in 1860 was married in Rio Grande City. Like Perez, Hinojosa enrolled in the regiment at Brownsville on December 15 with his wife's brother, shown on the right in this picture. *Photo courtesy of Hidalgo County Historical Museum*

While Colonels Davis and Haynes recruited their regiments from men around Brownsville, Philip Braubach was on a more dangerous mission. Braubach had been a farmer and stage driver near San Antonio before the war. In 1862 he was a deputy sheriff in Bexar County when arrested and imprisoned on charges of recruiting a company of pro-Union Germans for frontier service. Before being jailed, however, Braubach escaped and fled to Mexico. In the fall of 1863, Braubach was sent behind Confederate lines into central Texas for the purpose of encouraging and aiding other Unionists. The extent of his success is unknown, but he did return to Union lines, where the men he helped escape became part of his "Refugee Ranger's Company" and joined the 1st Texas Cavalry (U.S.) in May 1864. *Photo courtesy of Emmie Braubach Mauermann Estate and ITC*

PHILIP BRAUBACH
carte de visite
Washburn, New Orleans

MATTHEW NOLAN
carte de visite
Louis de Planque, Matamoras

In the spring of 1864, General Banks began to withdraw troops from the Texas expedition for a new campaign along the Red River aimed at Shreveport and the Confederate manufacturing centers in eastern Texas. However, he maintained garrisons at the major passes along the coast and in the Rio Grande Valley, even initiating a campaign to cut off the border trade further by taking Laredo. General Magruder sent John S. "Rip" Ford and the "Cavalry of the West" to defend Laredo and reopen the border. With only a small force under his command, Maj. Mat Nolan, a veteran of the U.S. Army who had settled in Corpus Christi, was in the vanguard of Ford's cavalry and among the first to strike Federal positions. On March 13, 1864, his troops attacked a body of eighty Federal cavalry under Cecilio Balerio at Los Patricios, about fifty miles to the southwest of Banquet. In a sharp engagement, he lost three of his sixty-two men killed and six others wounded, but drove off Balerio's command. Four days later his men attacked a Federal raiding party that was trying to carry cotton from where it had been stored to the south on Oso Creek to Corpus Christi. Nolan's arrival provided the first successful counterattacks by the Confederates since the Federal expedition had begun the previous autumn. *Photo courtesy of CAH, John Henry Brown Papers, CN 06056*

EDMUND J. DAVIS
copy print

While Nolan pushed southward from the Corpus Christi area, Col. Edmund J. Davis of the 1st Texas Cavalry (U.S.) commanded an expedition intended to take Laredo. Davis, a leading citizen of southern Texas before the war, had joined the Union army when he fled the state in the autumn of 1862 and had been commissioned to raise a loyal cavalry regiment. He had barely escaped being hanged when captured the previous summer when Gen. Hamilton Bee had intervened on his behalf. Now, his success would have been strategically significant, forcing the Confederate trade with Mexico even farther to the west. On March 19 with some two hundred men he attacked Laredo. Davis found the town defended by only seventy-two soldiers, but they had raised barricades in the town plaza and assumed a defensive position in the houses along the Union approach. Davis ordered his men into the town on foot, sending out skirmishers in advance. They moved forward twice and each time were repulsed by vigorous Confederate fire. That evening Davis encamped to await infantry and artillery reinforcements. *Photo courtesy of U.S.A.M.H.I.*

SANTOS BENAVIDES
copy print

The Confederate commander at Laredo was Josè de los Santos Benavides. The native of Laredo had been mayor of the town in 1856 and county judge in 1859. He had gained military experience against the Indians prior to the Civil War, had been commissioned colonel of his own regiment by the Confederacy, and was a capable foe. Benavides had prepared the small Confederate forces in the town very well.

When the Federals advanced his men gave "the Texas yell, commenced firing on them, and compelled them to retreat."[7] The fight lasted for some four hours, and Benavides did not lose any of his well-placed men. In the meantime, the colonel called for reinforcements from his own regiment, camped twenty-five miles north of town, and from the garrison at Eagle Pass. When his own men arrived at 2:00 A.M., they were greeted with trumpet calls and the ringing of church bells. Apparently, Davis was convinced that Benavides had received much heavier reinforcements than he actually did, for the next morning scouts from Laredo found the Federal encampment abandoned. The Yankees had "left in a stampede, throwing away some jackets and other things"—including five horses.[8]
Photo courtesy of Hidalgo County Historical Museum, Ursuline Academy Collection

290

CRISTOBAL BENAVIDES
albumen print

By June, Ford's force had pushed the Federals back practically into Brownsville. On June 25, Colonel Ford and two hundred fifty of his men engaged about one hundred Federals at Las Rucias Ranch, about twenty-four miles outside of Brownsville on the road to Rio Grande City. The Federals, two companies of the 1st Texas Cavalry, were well positioned in the ranch houses, but heavily outnumbered. Capt. Cristobal Benavides, brother of Santos Benavides and a rancher in southern Texas before the war, commanded one of the companies of Ford's cavalry sent forward to determine the enemy's strength. Benavides and the rest of Ford's skirmishers charged, but encountered a heavy fire in which Benavides's horse was shot out from under him. Ultimately by outflanking the enemy, the Confederates were able to push them from the position, killing twenty, wounding ten or twelve more, and capturing thirty-six. The Federal position at Brownsville, however, was too strong to attack and Ford withdrew to Edinburgh. In the end, Brownsville was regained without a fight, although the Federals withdrew to Brazos Island, where they would remain for the rest of the war. *Photo courtesy of Martin Callahan*

Chapter 11

Texans and the Struggle for West Louisiana

Nothing remains in about three fourths of the town but the bare chimneys and fallen walls of the houses which stand as . . . testimony of the meanness and barbarity of Banks['s] brutal Army.

—George W. Ingram

For the first three years of the Civil War, the only parts of Louisiana seen by most Texas soldiers were the roads and river ports that led to other places in the Confederacy. At the same time, Union strategists looked at Louisiana in the context of their larger plan to seize control of the Lower Mississippi River Valley. Until the issue along the river was settled, Union military leaders in the West had neither the inclination nor the resources to conduct a serious campaign to drive the Rebels out of west Louisiana and then invade east Texas.

In early 1863 the first Texas regiments began seeing sustained action in west Louisiana as the Federals tried to break the Rebel hold over the Lower Mississippi River. The 4th, 5th, and 7th Texas Cavalry, for example, were actively involved against Maj. Gen. Nathaniel Banks's limited offensive along Bayou Teche to disrupt the supply line to the Rebel garrison at Port Hudson. Banks, however, showed little interest in pursuing the campaign even though he defeated the Confederates at Fort Bisland (April 12–13) and Irish Bend (April 14). When the sieges of Vicksburg and Port Hudson finally began, more Texans were drawn into Louisiana as the Confederacy tried to reverse the impending disaster. Texans fought at Milliken's Bend (June 7), Brashear City (June 23), and Donaldsonville (June 28), but none of these engagements brought any relief to the river garrisons.

The capture of Vicksburg, Mississippi, by Maj. Gen. Ulysses Grant on July 4, 1863, and the surrender of Port Hudson, Louisiana, to Banks four days later finally cleared the Mississippi River. The victorious Federals then had to decide where to deploy the considerable number of forces that had been tied down in the campaign to free the Mississippi River. Meanwhile, the Texans continue to harass the Federals in engagements such as Cox's Plantation (July 12–13), Stirling's Plantation (September 29), and Vidalia (February 7, 1864).

In Washington both President Lincoln and his chief military advisor, Maj. Gen. Henry Wager Halleck, were interested in organizing a force to clear west Louisiana and then occupy east Texas.

The reasons that the two men favored such a plan had less to do with military matters than with several pressing political, diplomatic, and economic issues. First and most importantly, there was the lure of obtaining vast supplies of cotton in west Louisiana and east Texas to supply the mills in New England. Second, the occupation of Texas was popular among the older generation of antislavery leaders who persisted in believing that the annexation of the Lone Star State in 1845 was the ultimate example of the cupidity of the slave holders. Finally, many in Washington were irritated by the continued contraband trade across the Rio Grande River and were alarmed about the French presence in Mexico. In contrast, the two ranking military officers in the West, Banks and Grant, saw limited military advantage in pursuing such a campaign; instead they believed that a concentrated move toward the seaport of Mobile, Alabama, would do far more damage to the Confederacy.

The issue of the western campaign was finally decided in late July 1863, when Halleck informed Banks that Grant had been ordered to send one corps to Louisiana to assist in a campaign against Texas. Halleck wrote that "it is important that we immediately occupy some point or points in Texas." Halleck leaned toward following a route that ran up the Red River to Shreveport, Louisiana, but he informed Banks that, "whether the movement should be made by land or water is not decided."[1] Banks, who had a taste of campaigning on the Red River prior to the siege of Port Hudson, thought that the terrain was very difficult and particularly disliked that approach to Texas. For the remainder of 1863, Banks made several half-hearted attempts to invade Texas by routes other than along the Red River, but all failed to make a decisive lodgment. With each failure Halleck grew more insistent that Banks implement the Red River strategy, writing on January 11, 1864, "the best military opinions of the generals in the West seem to favor operations on Red River, providing the state of

water will enable the gun-boats to co-operate."[2] By the end of January 1864, Banks knew he was going to have to make the campaign. Banks could count on having about 27,000 men for the advance, while a supporting column of 10,000 soldiers under the command of Maj. Gen. Frederick Steele in Little Rock, Arkansas, were under orders to rendezvous with Banks near Shreveport. Rear Admiral David D. Porter, with a total of sixty transports and gunboats assigned to the Red River, would assist Banks. By March 26, 1864, Banks's forces supported by Porter's fleet were assembled at Alexandria and prepared to advance on Shreveport.

Banks's opposite number, Lt. Gen. Edmund Kirby Smith, had been watching the Union developments for months; he was busily pulling together all the infantry he could spare and sending it to Maj. Gen. Richard Taylor, who had tactical control of Louisiana. Even before Banks began advancing, Taylor already had seventeen regiments and one battalion of Texans in Louisiana. Thirteen of these units were in the three Texas brigades of Maj. Gen. John Walker's division. French-born Brig. Gen. Camille de Polignac commanded a fourth brigade with five Texas regiments. All these commands were either infantry or dismounted cavalry. In addition, Walker's division contained three batteries of Texas artillery. Since the campaign began in early March 1864, Taylor's men had been harassing the Federals, but they were not yet strong enough to pose any real threat.

At Alexandria, low water made it difficult to get larger gunboats past the town and forced Banks to delay his advance. On April 3, 1864, the river finally contained enough water for the big boats to move forward to Grand Ecore. The leading elements of the Federal forces were closing on Shreveport, but Banks knew that in ten days he had to return one of his corps east of the Mississippi River. The certain withdrawal of these 10,000 men would wreck the Red River campaign, and Banks now decided to temporarily abandon his river route and travel overland thirty-eight miles to Pleasant Hill. It was a risky move, since he would temporarily be without the support of Porter's powerful guns, but it was the quickest way to get to Shreveport. Banks reached Pleasant Hill on the afternoon of April 7, 1864; he was only thirty-six miles from his objective, and Federal cavalry was patrolling several miles in advance.[3]

Smith had used the time that Banks's slow advance had given him to continue bringing troops into Louisiana. Now Taylor had about 14,000 men under his immediate command, and at least 8,000 were within striking distance of Banks's force at Pleasant Hill. Among the reinforcements that came from Texas were six brigades totaling twenty regiments and two battalions of troops. This gathering of Texas soldiers for the 1864 Red River campaign was the largest contingent of men from the Lone Star State assembled for battle during the Civil War.

Early on the afternoon of April 7, 1864, Banks's advancing cavalry encountered the first serious resistance since leaving Alexandria, when they were attacked by a brigade of Texas cavalry. The Rebels inflicted a little more than fifty casualties in the action at Wilson's Farm before Federal reinforcements forced them to withdraw. The sudden presence of Confederate cavalry in force worried Banks, and he sent forward a brigade of infantry to support his own cavalry. On the morning of April 8, 1864, the reinforced Union column was working its way through the thick woods near Mansfield when they were attacked by Rebel skirmishers. When the Federals reached Sabine Crossroads, the forest suddenly gave way to an open field about eight hundred yards deep and twelve hundred yards long. Taylor had deployed his men in a line of woods that abutted the field which the Federals had to cross if they were to continue the advance.

The bulk of the soldiers waiting in the woods were from the Lone Star State. Brig. Gen. Patrick Major's division of two Texas cavalry brigades formed the left wing of Taylor's line. Col. Arthur P.

Bagby commanded one of those brigades, which contained the 4th, 5th, and 7th Cavalry Regiments and the 13th Cavalry Battalion. Col. Walter P. Lane led the other brigade, which included the 1st and 2d Partisan Rangers, as well as the 2d and 3d Regiments, Arizona Brigade. Both Bagby and Lane's brigades were deployed as infantry. Brig. Gen. Alfred Mouton's infantry division, which included Polignac's Texas brigade, was near the center of Taylor's line. Polignac's command contained the 15th Infantry, the 17th Consolidated Cavalry (dismounted), as well as the 22d, 31st, and 34th Texas Cavalry (dismounted). Walker's all-Texas division of three brigades was assigned to the right of the line. Brig. Gen. John Waul's brigade included the 8th (also known as the 12th Infantry—two Texas infantry regiments had been designated the 8th by Confederate authorities), 18th, and 22d Infantry Regiments and the 13th Cavalry (dismounted). Col. Horace Randal led the second Texas brigade, which contained the 11th and 14th Infantry, the 28th Cavalry Regiment (dismounted), and the 6th Texas Cavalry Battalion (dismounted). The third brigade, commanded by Brig. Gen. William Scurry, contained the 3d, 16th, 17th, and 19th Infantry plus the 16th Texas Cavalry (dismounted). On the far right of the Rebel lines, Brig. Gen. Hamilton Bee's division of Texas cavalry protected the right flank of Walker's line of infantry. Bee's first brigade, commanded by Col. Xavier DeBray, contained the 23d, 26th, and 36th Cavalry. Col. Augustus C. Buchel, with the 1st and 35th Regiments and Terrell's Cavalry, led Bee's second brigade of Texans. Supporting Taylor's line were the Texas batteries of Capts. Horace Halderman, James M. Daniels, T. D. Nettles, M. V. McMahon, and William Edgar.[4]

In the early afternoon Union cavalry pushed into the field but withdrew to a low hill in the clearing when they encountered Confederate infantry near the opposite wood line. In the late afternoon Federal reinforcements arrived; Banks now had two infantry brigades deployed with his cavalry.

His total force did not exceed 5,000 men, while Taylor had about 8,000 soldiers on the field. Taylor's patience was at an end, and at around 4:00 P.M. he sent Mouton's division forward. The advancing infantry recoiled under a withering fire which killed Mouton. Polignac then assumed command and led his men forward again, but the Union line continued to hold. Taylor ordered the two wings of the army forward to support Polignac. The Federal line, now faced with encirclement, began to give way in disorder before the hard-pressing Confederates. When the charging Rebels collapsed a second line of 1,300 men about one-half mile to the rear of the initial position, the Union retreat degenerated into a rout. The panicky soldiers were soon intermingled with Banks's supply trains, heightening the confusion. A third Federal line of 5,000 soldiers finally stopped the charging Confederates, who had themselves become disorganized by the very swiftness of their pursuit. Federal losses were put at 2,500 men; Banks also lost twenty guns and approximately two hundred fifty wagons.[5]

Banks's first reaction to the humiliating defeat was to stand and fight, but after holding a counsel of war, he was persuaded to withdraw toward Pleasant Hill to link up with 10,000 fresh troops under the command of Maj. Gen. A. J. Smith. While Banks retreated, Taylor galloped back to Mansfield to hurry forward two fresh infantry divisions under the tactical command of Brig. Gen. Thomas J. Churchill. He then returned to join the Rebel cavalry as it followed Banks toward Pleasant Hill. Along the line of retreat Taylor saw all the debris of a broken army and mistakenly assumed that the Federals were still panicked. Early on the morning of April 9, 1864, Taylor's cavalry found the Federal infantry drawing up for battle near Pleasant Hill. Banks had 18,000 men to oppose Taylor's reinforced army of about 12,500. The bulk of the infantry that had fought at Mansfield arrived that morning, but the new soldiers under Churchill

did not reach Pleasant Hill until early that afternoon; they had marched almost fifty miles in two days. Taylor had to let these exhausted men rest, so he could not begin his attack immediately. Around 3:00 P.M. Taylor began deploying his men.

During the Battle of Pleasant Hill, Major's Division, again fighting as infantry, occupied the left of Taylor's line. Nearby were the remaining mounted Texas cavalry brigades under the command of Maj. Gen. Thomas Green. Walker's Texas Division was in the center of the line while Churchill's two divisions were on the right. Mouton's old division, which had just suffered 700 casualties and was still commanded by Polignac, was near Walker's men. Taylor got his attack under way about 4:30 P.M. when Churchill's men began advancing; soon Walker was also moving forward. At first the attack went well, and Walker's men, supported by Polignac's weary soldiers, actually broke through near the center of Banks's line. Meanwhile, Churchill's attacking infantry drove the Federals back in disorder. However, as Churchill's men began swinging toward Pleasant Hill, they were suddenly struck on the right flank by a powerful line of concealed infantry. The attack drove Churchill's soldiers back toward Walker's men. Close on their heels was the advancing Federal infantry. Walker's advance ended as his men swung around to meet the new threat. The hard-fighting Texans blunted the Union counterattack, but Taylor's army became badly disorganized and was in no condition to continue fighting. Taylor ordered his men to withdraw as darkness began to cover the field. In two days Taylor had led his men to one dramatic victory and then watched them go down in defeat on the next battlefield. His losses in the two battles were 2,500 men, of whom 1,274 of the casualties came from Texas units.[6]

Despite the setback at Pleasant Hill, Taylor still had a better opportunity than Banks to resume the offensive. The two battles had already cost the Federal commander 3,600 men and wrecked a large portion of his supply train. Furthermore, the dangerously low water level in the Red River threatened both Banks's line of communications and the ability of Porter's gunboats to support the infantry. Finally, the deadline to send Smith's corps east of the Mississippi River was almost at hand. Banks, faced with these stark realities, decided that the prudent action would be to retreat. Around midnight he ordered his army to withdraw.

Two hours before Banks gave his order, Taylor was aroused from his resting place near Pleasant Hill by General Smith, who had just come from Shreveport. Smith, fearing that Banks still might somehow use the Red River to seize Shreveport and worrying about the activities of Steele's supporting column of Federals in southern Arkansas, was reluctant to continue the pursuit. Taylor strongly objected, later writing that, "we had but to strike vigorously to capture or destroy both [Banks and Porter]."[7] Smith was unmoved and ordered Churchill's and Walker's men to Arkansas. Taylor was left with only Polignac's weakened division and the Texas cavalry. The force was too small to do anything but pester Banks's withdrawing forces.

For the next several weeks, the biggest problem the Federals faced was protecting their men from Confederate raiders and snipers as they extracted the fleet from low water. On April 12, 1864, some of the Texas cavalry aggressively attacked part of the fleet near Blair's Landing. In the exchange, Taylor's able cavalry commander, Brig. Gen. Thomas Green of Texas, was killed. Eleven days later Taylor tried to use Bee's Texans to block Banks's retreat at Cane River Crossing; they inflicted two hundred casualties on the Federals but failed to hold the position. The way was then open to Alexandria, which Banks began occupying on April 25, 1864. Within two days Porter's fleet was concentrated there also, but the water levels were now so low that the boats could not get below the rapids. Taylor continued to use his Texas cavalry and Polignac's infantry to harass the Federals, who could not leave Alexandria until

a dam had been constructed to raise the water level enough to allow the fleet to escape. By May 13, 1864, the last of Porter's vessels were over the rapids and the retreat resumed. Taylor's men continued to press Banks's army; the last action of the campaign occurred on May 18, 1864, at Yellow Bayou when the Federal rear guard lashed back at the Rebels.

Banks's army and Porter's fleet were safe, but between them they had lost nine boats, fifty-seven guns, and 8,000 men. The statistics were impressive, but Smith's decision to send most of his infantry after Steele in Arkansas denied Taylor the troops he might have used to entirely destroy Banks and Porter. To make matters worse, the Arkansas strategy, which Taylor accurately described as a wild-goose chase, failed to trap Steele. Taylor believed that the sacrifices his men made at Mansfield and Pleasant Hill were wasted. A month after the campaign, he asked to be relieved of duty, believing that nothing in the department could be accomplished as long as Smith remained in command.

Taylor was later promoted to lieutenant general and commanded the Department of Alabama, Mississippi, and East Louisiana when the war ended. Smith remained in command of his department, but showed little inclination to mount any offensive operations. A. J. Smith and his Federals returned to Mississippi, where their military wanderings gave them the sobriquet of the "lost tribes of Israel." Shortly after Red River, Banks was relieved of command and many of his troops were sent to fight in Virginia. Most of the remaining Texas troops withdrew into the Lone Star State, where they remained until the war ended.[8] The sacrifices of the Texans had helped turn back the greatest threat ever made by the Union to occupy large sections of their state.

In Texas, the victors of the Red River campaign settled down to a holding action as Union forces in the southern part of the state drew back to fortified positions along the coast. Federal forces held portions of the Texas coastline until the end of the war, and it was there that the last engagement of the great conflict was fought outside of Brownsville. On May 11, 1865, three hundred Federals from companies of the 62d U.S. Colored Infantry and the 2d Texas Cavalry (U.S.), knowing of the war's end in the East, advanced from Brazos Santiago onto the mainland and headed toward Brownsville. The next day, on the road near Palmito Ranch, they encountered a company of George H. Gidding's Texas Cavalry Battalion. While many Confederates had already given up, these soldiers appeared determined to fight. The Federals fell back and were reinforced during the night by two hundred men from the 34th Indiana Infantry.

On May 13 the Federals, led by Col. Theodore H. Barrett, opened the affair with an attack on the outnumbered Confederate cavalry. The Rebels were pushed back, but they fought with such tenacity that by mid-afternoon the Federal attackers were exhausted. At that time three hundred Confederates from Ford's 2d Cavalry, Benavides' Cavalry Regiment, Gidding's Battalion, and O. G. Jones's field battery arrived to be thrown into the fight by Colonel Ford to wrest victory from the hands of the Federals.

Colonel Barrett was surprised by the renewed attack and by the appearance of artillery and decided to withdraw. The retreat, however, almost turned into a rout until part of the 34th Indiana and the 62d Colored rallied to form a rear guard; their stand made the escape of the rest of the column possible. Nonetheless, Ford continued to push the Federals back to the coast, where they were reinforced from Brazos Santiago. The action was a short one, but Barrett's force lost 145 men and officers killed, wounded, or captured.

Palmito Ranch was merely a last gasp for the Confederate cause, however. As news arrived of the certainty of Lee's and Johnson's surrenders in the East, many soldiers left their units to go home. The army simply disbanded. Nonetheless, when Federal authorities demanded that General Smith surrender the Trans-Mississippi in early May, he refused and called a conference at Marshall for the governors of Arkansas, Texas, and Missouri to plan a resistance. With hopes only of negotiating better terms, the men who attended decided to concentrate the remaining Confederate forces near Houston to hold out as long as possible.

Any faith that resistance could continue, however, was destroyed by events at Houston. On May 14 over four hundred soldiers in that city threatened to desert, and only the intervention of their officers, who promised that the war would soon end, kept them from leaving. Throughout the Trans-Mississippi Department reports indicated that most of the men would no longer fight. When Gen. Smith ordered the evacuation of Galveston on May 21, 1865, the army virtually disappeared and stopped at Houston only long enough to plunder what government stores they could find.

General Smith had no options open. On May 30 he informed Federal authorities that Texas was open for their occupation. Confederate authorities continued to talk with General Canby at New Orleans for recognition of existing state governments as de facto governments until they could be replaced in an orderly manner, but Canby had no authority to negotiate on these matters. Finally, Gen. Edmund J. Davis was sent to Galveston to receive Smith's surrender. Whether the choice of Davis was intentional is unknown, but in a scene few Confederates would have expected four years before, the Confederate commander surrendered his armies to this Texan who had left his state to help maintain the Union.

JAMES REILY
copy print

Sizable numbers of Texans were first drawn into Louisiana in the spring of 1863, when General Banks pushed a strong force into Bayou Teche. His object was to gain control of the Red River in order to cut off western Louisiana as a supply source for the Rebel garrison that guarded Port Hudson, Louisiana, on the Mississippi River. Four Texas units participated in the Bayou Teche campaign, including the 4th Texas Cavalry commanded by Col. James Reily.

Reily was born in Ohio, studied law in Kentucky, and then moved to Texas in the late 1830s. He eventually settled in Houston. In the Texas Republic, he was a representative from Harris County and then minister to the United States. In 1856 Pres. James Buchanan appointed Reily minister to Russia. As a soldier, Reily served as captain in the militia, fought in several Indian campaigns, and commanded a regiment of Texas troops in the Mexican War. On September 21, 1861, Reily entered active service as colonel of the 4th Texas Cavalry Regiment.

The first major engagement in the Bayou Teche campaign began on April 13, 1863, at Fort Bisland. Reily's men began the day in reserve but were soon detached to watch a second Union force whose intentions were unknown. Around 9:00 P.M. Taylor received news from Reily that these Federals had landed near Irish Bend and were moving to cut off the Rebels at Fort Bisland. On April 14 the 4th Texas and several other regiments helped hold the Federals until Taylor could extract his main force from Fort Bisland, but Reily was mortally wounded in the engagement. Banks broke off pursuit of the Rebels when he reached Alexandria and returned to the more direct approach of reducing Port Hudson by either assault or siege.
Photo courtesy of the Library of Congress

EDWARD McMILLIAN ELLIS
copy print

Edward McMillian Ellis enlisted in the Confederate army at Camp Terry on April 1, 1862, as a private in Company A, 17th Texas Infantry. He was with Brig. Gen. Henry McCulloch's brigade of Walker's Texas Division on June 7, 1863, when it attacked the garrison of primarily black soldiers at Milliken's Bend, Louisiana. That engagement occurred because of the irresistible urge of Confederate authorities to assist the beleaguered garrison at Vicksburg by attacking west of the Mississippi River. Confederate authorities hoped that a strike at Milliken's Bend might somehow distract Grant from Vicksburg, which had been under siege since May 18, 1863. McCulloch's men had to fight their way through formidable hedges and then assault the field fortifications that protected the levee where the garrison was camped. Before daylight the brigade came under fire as it picked its way through the hedges. At first light the enemy "opened a terrible fire of musketry," as the Texans moved forward. The Federals fell back to the field fortifications and "made a stubborn fight" before retreating to the levee. There, the black soldiers, with the help of four Union gunboats, repulsed the attack. McCulloch's brigade suffered 185 casualties, of whom 94 came from the 17th Texas Infantry. Ellis was seriously wounded and given medical leave on July 1, 1863. Milliken's Bend was one of the first engagements where black soldiers had a chance to prove themselves. Despite their good showing, most Rebel leaders belittled the performance of black soldiers. However, some men in the ranks knew the truth. "When our troops gained the bloody field," wrote Pvt. J. B. Blessington of the 16th Texas Infantry, "they could see how desperately they had fought for its possession."[9] *Photo courtesy of Hazel Wetzel Collection, U.S.A.M.H.I.*

ROBERT EMMETT CARRINGTON
sixth-plate ambrotype
Grey Walsh

Sometimes the overall superiority of Union numbers in Louisiana meant nothing if the Confederates could move swiftly and attack an isolated Federal post. On June 23, 1863, 1st Lt. Robert Emmett Carrington's outfit, the 2d Cavalry, Arizona Brigade, was one of several Texas regiments that contributed men to a surprise attack against the Federal garrison at Brashear City, Louisiana. Carrington, who was born in Columbus, Mississippi, on September 18, 1845, had originally enlisted in Company G, 6th Texas Infantry, in 1861. He apparently transferred to the 16th Infantry before his old regiment was captured at Port Hudson. Carrington then transferred to the 2d Cavalry, Arizona Brigade, on February 13, 1863, being appointed 1st lieutenant and adjutant.

The successful attack at Brashear City netted the Rebels 1,200 men and eleven heavy guns. Confederate losses were put at two killed and eighteen wounded.[10] It is not likely that Carrington participated in the attack since less than 350 volunteers from four different units conducted the assault. *Photo courtesy of CAH, Leonidas Davis Carrington Papers, CN 03971*

FRANCIS J. MULLEN
AND ALONZO RIDLEY
carte de visite

Lt. Francis "Frank" J. Mullen and Maj. Alonzo Ridley were among the men in Col. James Patrick Major's brigade of cavalry reinforcements that arrived in Louisiana in late May 1863. Ridley was a member of the 3d Cavalry Regiment, Arizona Brigade. Ridley's friend, Frank Mullen, was an assistant quartermaster in the 2d Cavalry Regiment, Arizona Brigade. On June 22, 1863, the two regiments were part of the forces that took the offensive along the Bayou Teche in another attempt to distract the Federals from the sieges of Vicksburg and Port Hudson. The next day the Rebels captured Brashear City, but the offensive ended on June 28, 1863, when the Confederates failed to capture Fort Butler at Donaldsonville, Louisiana. Confederate losses were put at 260, including Major Ridley, who was captured. He was later confined in the police jail at New Orleans and finally sent to Fort Columbus in New York Harbor. Ridley was not exchanged until March 1, 1865. Mullen does not appear to have been a casualty at either Brashear City or Fort Butler. *Photo courtesy of LLMVC*

302

GEORGE GUESS
carte de visite

After the fall of Port Hudson, Banks reluctantly turned his attention west of the Mississippi River. Lt. Col. George Guess of the 31st Texas Cavalry was one of the soldiers who parried the Union forces trying to extend their influence in western Louisiana.

In February 1861 Guess, who was a thirty-two-year-old widower living in Dallas, joined the Good-Douglas artillery but soon left that unit for cavalry service. On May 14, 1862, he became lieutenant colonel of the 31st Texas Cavalry. That year his unit participated in battles at Newtonia, Missouri (September 30, 1862), and Prairie Grove, Arkansas (December 7, 1862). On September 29, 1863, Guess was part of two brigades that surprised several regiments of Federal infantry and cavalry at Stirling's Plantation near Morganza, Louisiana. The fight took place in a drizzling rain, and most of the action fell on Col. Joseph Speight's Texas brigade, which included Guess's regiment. A soldier who was in the brigade wrote that bullets sung around his head like angry bumblebees while the "mud was about knee deep and as slick as a muskadime [*sic*] hull. . . ."[11] The Rebels suffered 121 casualties in the two-hour battle, but they captured more than 450 infantrymen. However, most of the Federal cavalry escaped, taking with them Lieutenant Colonel Guess as a prisoner. Guess was confined in New Orleans; he was at first given wide latitude as a prisoner of war, including the right to cross between the lines. Federal authorities later accused him of "speculating in cotton, the profits to be shared between himself and others within the enemy's lines."[12] Guess was not paroled until June 10, 1865. *Photo courtesy of LLMVC*

SIMEON JASPER CREWS
quarter-plate ambrotype

Pvt. Simeon Jasper Crews joined Company F, 7th Texas Cavalry, on September 1, 1863, in New Salem, Texas. At that time the regiment was operating in Louisiana, where the men already had seen action at Ford Bisland (April 13), Brashear City (June 23), Donaldsonville (June 28), and Cox's Plantation (July 12–13). The 7th Texas was again engaged at Stirling's Plantation on September 29, 1863, and since Crews's service record indicates he was present that month, it is likely that he saw his first fighting there. After Stirling's Plantation the 7th Texas Cavalry moved southward to watch the Union garrison in New Iberia on the Bayou Teche. At daybreak on November 20, 1863, a column of Federal cavalry from the town surprised Camp Pratt, an outpost manned by part of the 7th Cavalry. In the brief skirmish 2 soldiers were wounded and 113 enlisted men were captured. Crews was one of the prisoners taken at Camp Pratt. Private Crews and most of the other enlisted men who were captured at Camp Pratt were exchanged before the end of November 1863. Crews went on to serve with the 7th Texas Cavalry during the 1864 Red River campaign; his regiment lost almost 90 men in the final Union effort to end the war in Louisiana and carry the conflict into east Texas.
Photo courtesy of Gregg Gibbs

ANDERSON AUGUSTUS KING
copy print

By the beginning of 1864, the conflict in Louisiana had degenerated into a war of bitter skirmishes as small groups of Rebels harassed the Federal garrisons that maintained control of the rivers. For the individual soldiers these fights could be as deadly as any battle fought in the great theaters of actions.

Pvt. Anderson A. King had left his wife at Melrose, Texas, in 1861 when he joined the army. In January 1863 he escaped being captured with the 17th Cavalry at Arkansas Post; the consolidated unit in which he now served consisted primarily of men from his old regiment plus the remnants of six other Texas units that had not been taken at Arkansas Post.

On February 7, 1864, King and his regiment were engaged against a Federal post at Vidalia, Louisiana. Advancing in line of battle, they ran into three hundred men of the 2d Mississippi Heavy Artillery, African Descent. The Confederate line faltered after it met one well-aimed volley; a second equally well-aimed volley sent the Rebels fleeing in disorder.[13] The Confederates left behind one dead soldier and carried away several wounded, including King, who died on February 16, 1864.

By the end of the Civil War, Texans had fought in hundreds of actions and skirmishes like those of Brashear City, Fort Bisland, Stirling's Plantation, Camp Pratt, and Vidalia as the Confederacy struggled to protect western Louisiana. That long defense faced its greatest test in the spring of 1864 when the Union finally made a major effort to seize the Red River territory. *Photo courtesy of David Smith*

JONATHAN THOMAS KNIGHT
copy print

Cpl. Jonathan Thomas Knight was born in Alabama on December 4, 1840, and moved with his family to Texas during the next decade. When the Civil War began, he was married and living in Winnsboro, Wood County, Texas. On May 10, 1862, Knight enlisted in the Rebel army; his outfit became Company H, 22d Texas Infantry. During the winter of 1864, Knight and his company became part of the garrison at Fort DeRussey, Louisiana, which the Rebels had constructed to block any Union fleet that might try to ascend the Red River above Natchitoches. In a letter to his wife, Knight described the position as having a breastwork of "timbers, dirt and iron large enough to plant ten cannons, . . ." and a main fort about one-quarter mile behind with positions for four more artillery pieces when they arrived. Knight added that his company drilled daily on the guns and that the men liked garrison duty much better than life in the

infantry. "As for myself," he mused, "they will not insult me if they keep us in the fort as long as the war lasts. . . ." Corporal Knight, however, hoped that the bitter conflict would not go on much longer, but he had little doubt that there would be a fight at Fort DeRussey very soon. When the time came, he believed that his company would stay "until the Feds drive us away, which I think will be very hard to do for the place is well fortified."[14] Knight wrote his letter on March 10, 1864, as the leading elements of Banks's army were closing on Fort DeRussey. Just four days later, a powerful combined infantry and gunboat attack overwhelmed the garrison in less than an hour. Knight and about three hundred soldiers were captured and sent to New Orleans. The first engagement of the long awaited Red River campaign had ended in an easy Federal victory. *Photo courtesy of Gary Canada*

CAMILLE ARMAND POLIGNAC
carte de visite

Camille Armand Jules Marie, Prince de Polignac, commanded a brigade of Texas troops in the 1864 Red River campaign. The French aristocrat was born in France in 1832, and entered the French army after graduating from college. Polignac served as a lieutenant in the Crimean War but resigned his commission in 1859 to pursue a career in science. Prior to the Civil War, Polignac had become acquainted with a future general of the Confederacy, P. G. T. Beauregard, and in 1861 he volunteered for service on Beauregard's staff. Polignac entered the Confederate army as a lieutenant colonel and served on various staffs until he was promoted to brigadier general on January 10, 1863. Two months later he was ordered to the Trans-Mississippi Department to assume command of a brigade of Texans. At first some of the men from the Lone Star State were not pleased to be under the control of what appeared to them to be a French dandy whose name did not roll easily off the Texas tongue. Some of the men took to calling him "Polecat," which seemed to ease tensions a bit. Taylor responded to the unrest by reminding the men that they were soldiers, but he did agree to remove Polignac if the men were still unhappy after he commanded them in battle.[15] In early 1864 Polignac led a raid into eastern Louisiana which raised the men's confidence, but the real test came during the Red River campaign, when the Frenchman and his Texans fought at Mansfield and Pleasant Hill. In two days his five regiments lost slightly more than 210 men, which was the highest level of brigade casualties of any Texas unit engaged in the campaign. Polignac emerged from the campaign with the reputation of a hard fighting commander whom the men could trust. *Photo courtesy of the Alabama Department of Archives and History*

JOSEPH R. GARZA
sixth-plate tinted ambrotype

Joseph R. Garza (José Maria Jesus Andres Rafael de la Garza) first joined the 6th Texas Infantry as 2d lieutenant of Company K. He mustered into the service at San Antonio, Texas, on March 31, 1862. Late that year his regiment was sent to Arkansas Post. On December 9, 1862, Garza wrote his brother that pneumonia had been raging through his brigade for about a month, and they were burying from three to fifteen men a day.[16] Most of the 6th Regiment was subsequently captured when Arkansas Post fell on January 11, 1863, but Garza was not among the prisoners. The remnants of at least seven Texas units that escaped capture were organized into the 17th Consolidated Texas Cavalry (dismounted). Garza was assigned to duty in the regiment as 1st lieutenant in Capt. John J. McCown's company on June 28,

1863. During the 1864 Red River campaign, the 17th Consolidated Cavalry was attached to Polignac's brigade and was present at Mansfield on April 8, 1864. Around 4:00 P.M. Taylor ordered one division to attack the Union line. Garza was in command of his company when the division moved forward. The 17th Texas was met by several volleys that staggered the advance. Shortly afterward the divisional commander, Brig. Gen. Alfred Mouton, was mortally wounded as was the colonel of the 17th Texas Consolidated. Polignac then assumed command of the division and pressed the attack. Sometime in the battle Garza was struck above one knee by a shell fragment and died soon afterward. *Photo courtesy of Martin Callahan*

308

JOHN SAMUEL BRYAN
albumen print

John Samuel Bryan was twenty-seven years old when he enlisted in the service at McKinney, Texas, on February 17, 1862. Private Bryan became a soldier in Company B, 16th Texas Cavalry. In April 1862 the unit was dismounted and subsequently served in Walker's Texas Division throughout the rest of the war. The night before the Battle of Mansfield, Bryan, who was now a 1st sergeant, wrote his wife begging her to send a note, because for soldiers "it is but little pleasure that we see and there is nothing more pleasant . . . than to get a friendly letter."[17] On April 8, 1864, Bryan was with his company as Walker's men moved forward against the Union left; their line extended far beyond the Federal infantry, and the Union cavalry assigned to guard that flank was easily swept aside. The division pressed on against the enemy's front and vulnerable flank. One soldier looked around to see the regimental flags "floating in the breeze" as each unit ran forward trying to be the first group to scale the fence in front of the Union infantry. "In this fearful charge, there was not flinching nor murmuring," wrote the Texan, "but the subdued talk of soldiers, the gritting of teeth for revenge, as they saw their comrades falling around them." At last the men reached the fence and a "loud and prolonged Texas yell" rose as the enemy gave way. Sergeant Bryan never got a chance to mail the letter he had earlier written to his wife, because he was seriously wounded during the battle and died on April 16, 1864. *Photo courtesy of the Mansfield State Commemorative Area, Louisiana Office of State Parks*

Chauncey Berkeley Shepard joined the army at San Antonio, Texas, on September 4, 1861, as a private in Colonel Green's 5th Texas Mounted Rifles. He was immediately transferred to the regimental staff as a sergeant major. By the time of the Battle of Mansfield, Shepard was a captain and A.D.C. for his old commander, who was now a brigadier general and chief of Taylor's cavalry. The attacks by Mouton and Walker had shattered the Union line. As the Federals fled, the Confederate tide rolled after them in a wild chase. The beaten men streamed through another line about one-half mile to the rear and then became entangled in part of the Union supply train, which only heightened the panic. Taylor's men pounced on the helpless trains and continued to press the retreating enemy. However, the Rebels, believing they were pursuing a totally beaten enemy, were themselves shaken when they were suddenly attacked by elements of a division of fresh Union troops under the command of Brig. Gen. William Emory. In a fierce half-hour fight, Emory broke the momentum of the disorganized Rebel advance. Shepard died during the battle, and since the cavalry was not heavily engaged in the initial attack, it is likely that he was killed in the pursuit that ended with Emory's fierce defense. *Photo courtesy of the Mansfield State Commemorative Area, Louisiana Office of State Parks*

OSCAR AUGUSTUS DURRUM
copy print

Lt. Oscar Augustus Durrum was one of hundreds of Rebels who was wounded in the Confederate victory at Mansfield. Durrum had originally joined the 3d Texas Cavalry as a 1st lieutenant at Jefferson, Texas, on June 8, 1861. He was twenty-two years old at the time of his enlistment. Durrum's service record does not indicate if he was present when the regiment fought at Wilson's Creek and Pea Ridge. On May 20, 1862, Lieutenant Durrum was discharged from the service and it is unclear what he did until early 1864. However, when it became apparent that Banks's invasion posed a real threat, Durrum rejoined the colors. It is probable that at the Battle of Mansfield he was serving as a volunteer aide de camp to Col. Richard Waterhouse, who was also from Jefferson, Texas. At the time of the Red River campaign, Waterhouse commanded the 19th Texas Infantry in Walker's division. After the battle, Durrum sent the following message to his father:

I am now lying at the above named place [College Hospital, Mansfield] with my leg pierced through about 2 inches above the knee, and I am inclined to think the bone is much shattered. If you can procure a hack, please come after me. . . . If it will trouble you very much you need not come for I will be on soon in a few days. We have had a decisive victory, but our loss is heavy. I cannot give you any particulars now.[18]

Gus Durrum died on April 11, 1864, without ever seeing his father. He was buried in a common grave on the Mansfield battleground. *Photo courtesy of the Jefferson Historical Museum, Jefferson, Texas*

311

JACOB HENNRICH
copy print

Banks continued his retreat on the evening of April 8, 1864, and by morning he had rendezvoused with elements of A. J. Smith's corps near Pleasant Hill. About that time Taylor began bringing his infantry forward. Cpl. Jacob Hennrich of Company H, 17th Texas Infantry, was in the ranks as Taylor's soldiers trudged toward the Union line at Pleasant Hill. Hennrich emigrated to America from Germany in the early 1850s and became a naturalized citizen on February 16, 1857. Jacob married the next year and was farming in Colorado County, Texas, when the war began. On July 1, 1862, Hennrich enlisted in the army at Camp Terry, which was outside of Austin near the Colorado River. He was enrolled as Jacob Henry.

At Pleasant Hill, Taylor wanted to attack immediately, but a brief look at his infantry convinced the general that his men were too exhausted to attack.

Taylor ordered them to rest for a few hours. Around 4:30 P.M. his assault finally got underway. On the Confederate right, the Missourians and Arkansans under Brig. Gen. Thomas J. Churchill made good progress as they probed Banks's left. Hennrich's regiment, which was part of Brig. Gen. William Reed Scurry's brigade of Walker's Texas Division, moved to attack the Union center when the men heard the sound coming from Churchill's advance; Hennrich and the other men in Scurry's brigade were deployed adjacent to Churchill's troops. The Texans were soon engaged in a heavy firefight, but they were pushing the enemy back. The attack had gotten off to a good start. Hennrich was later captured in the battle and subsequently exchanged. He stayed with the 17th Infantry until the end of the war and was paroled at Columbus, Texas, on June 27, 1865. *Photo courtesy of Donaly Brice*

312

GEORGE S. MCWHORTER
copy print

George S. McWhorter enlisted as a private in Lt. Col. George T. Madison's 3d Cavalry Battalion, Arizona Brigade, on May 3, 1862. In early February 1863, enough companies were added to expand the battalion to a regiment. Since that time the 3d Cavalry, Arizona Brigade, had served most of the war in Louisiana, seeing action at Donaldsonville, Cox's Plantation, and Bayou Bourbeau (November 3, 1863).

At Mansfield the regiment was temporarily dismounted and fought as infantry. The next day, at Pleasant Hill, the regiment was still on foot; the men were part of two brigades of dismounted cavalry which had orders to get around the right flank of Banks's army. The dismounted Texans drove the Federals back and briefly threatened their rear. About that time Taylor thought victory was assured, but Churchill's troops suddenly gave way, and the whole Confederate line was in danger. McWhorter's regiment suffered a combined total of thirty-two casualties in the battles of Mansfield and Pleasant Hill. McWhorter was unhurt, and he surrendered when the war ended. *Photo courtesy of Frank Jasek Collection, U.S.A.M.H.I.*

313

WILLIAM L. CRAWFORD
carte de visite
Bell & Souby photographers,
Jefferson, Texas

In 1843, four-year-old William L. Crawford was brought to Texas by his family. As a young man he attended McKenzie College and studied law in Jefferson, Texas. William was twenty-one when, in the summer of 1861, he enlisted in a ninety-day company known as the Jefferson Guards. The Guards were never in action. In early 1862 Crawford left the unit and raised a company of infantry, which on March 31, 1862, mustered into the service as Company A, 19th Texas Infantry. Captain Crawford first led his company in a major action when it fought at Milliken's Bend on June 7, 1863.

At Pleasant Hill, Churchill's collapsing line was driven back toward Brig. Gen. William Scurry's brigade of Walker's division. Walker met the crisis by ordering Scurry to change his front and reinforce Churchill's men. The soldiers quickly threw down their blankets and knapsacks and moved across a field toward the enemy. They were met by a hail of close artillery fire, and from a nearby wood line the Federals "poured a stream of lead" into the advancing infantry.[19] Crawford was one of the soldiers in Scurry's brigade who was now fighting against four-to-one odds. Unless they were reinforced quickly, the Texans were going to be overrun by the attacking Federals. *Photo courtesy of Gary Canada*

314

JOHN T. STARK
copy print

The crisis on the Confederate right left Taylor with no choice but to order the remaining two brigades of Walker's division to suspend their successful advances and turn to rescue the embattled soldiers of Churchill and Scurry's commands. Capt. John T. Stark of Company H, 13th Cavalry (dismounted), Waul's brigade, had led his men in battle at Mansfield, and he was at Pleasant Hill when his company moved forward to support Scurry. Stark, at the age of forty, had enlisted in the army at Burkeville, Texas, as a 1st sergeant on February 14, 1862, and was elected 1st lieutenant of his company on May 24, 1862. The two Texas brigades coming to support Scurry were led by Brig. Gen. Thomas Waul and Col. Horace Randal; they furiously attacked the Federals. "Leading their fine brigades with skill and energy," wrote Taylor, "these officers forced back the Federals and relieved Scurry."[20] The counterattack by the two Texas brigades stabilized the front and allowed Taylor to withdraw his army. The battles of Mansfield and Pleasant Hill cost the Confederates about 2,600 casualties; approximately half were from the Texas units. Waul's brigade suffered a total of 176 casualties in the battles of Mansfield and Pleasant Hill. Stark's regiment reported 28 wounded in the campaign. Captain Stark was not among these losses, but he was later discharged from the service for illness on November 11, 1864. *Photo courtesy of Mansfield State Commemorative Area, Louisiana Office of State Parks*

TOM GREEN
copy print

Pleasant Hill was a bloody defeat for Taylor, but Banks was determined to continue his withdrawal anyway. Taylor wanted to resume the offensive, but he could not because Smith had foolishly detached most of the infantry to chase the Federals out of southern Arkansas. Without adequate infantry Taylor could only annoy Banks and hope the Federal commander would make an error that would lead to his ruin. Fortunately, Taylor had several tough Texas cavalry brigades with experienced leaders who might force Banks to make a mistake. One of these men was Brig. Gen. Tom Green, who had begun his service with the Confederacy as colonel of the 5th Texas Cavalry. He subsequently took part in Sibley's 1862 New Mexico campaign and then played a crucial role in the recapture of Galveston, Texas, on January 1, 1863. In the spring of 1863, Green took the 5th Texas to Louisiana, where Taylor praised him for his service in the Bayou

Teche campaign. He described Green as an upright and modest soldier who rejoiced in combat. "His men adored him," Taylor wrote, "and would follow wherever he lead; but they did not fear him, for though he scolded at them in action, he was too kind-hearted to punish breaches of discipline."[21] Green was Taylor's most aggressive cavalry commander, and with a little luck he might force Banks into a costly mistake. Taylor believed that the best way to damage the Federals was to take advantage of the falling water level on the Red River to harass the fleet that supported the Federal army. On April 12, 1862, he sent his best cavalry leader, Tom Green, to attack part of the fleet near Blair's Landing. When Green arrived, several vessels were laboring in the shallow water and one big monitor was already aground. *Photo courtesy of MOLLUS , Mass., U.S.A.M.H.I.*

USS *Osage*
copy print

The grounded boat that Green saw was the USS *Osage.* The vessel represented a new class of heavily armored monitors that were specifically designed to operate on the Mississippi River and its tributaries. At 523 tons, the boat was large enough to face any adversary but drew less than four feet of water, allowing it to operate efficiently on the sandbar-ridden western rivers. The two horizontal high-pressure steam engines could push the *Osage* in calm waters at twelve miles per hour. Her main battery was a single forward rotating turret with two 11-inch smoothbore guns which were protected by six-inch iron plates. The *Osage* and her sistership, USS *Neosho,* were the only two monitors that were built with stern wheels.

When Green saw the *Osage,* he immediately ordered three field pieces and his dismounted cavalry to begin firing at the stranded monitor and the trans- ports she was protecting. The commander of the *Osage,* Lt. Com. Thomas O. Selfridge, already had seen three vessels sink under him during the war, and he was not ready to take even the remotest chance on that happening again, even though the powerful *Osage* was never in any real danger from the puny efforts that Green's men could make. The *Osage's* heavy guns immediately returned fire. During the exchange Selfridge saw a mounted officer who appeared to be in command, and he ordered the guns to fire on him.[22] One shell took off Green's head. Without Green, the men fell back. The crew of the *Osage* dislodged their vessel, and the flotilla continued down river. Neither side suffered many casualties, but as Taylor noted, the loss of Green was "an irreparable one."[23] *Photo courtesy of the U.S. Naval Historical Center*

JAMES PATRICK MAJOR
carte de visite

James Patrick Major was born in Missouri in 1836 and graduated from West Point twenty years later. In the spring of 1857, Major joined the 2d U.S. Cavalry in Texas and eventually married the sister of Thomas Green. During the early years of the Civil War, Major served on the staff of Maj. Gen. Earl Van Dorn. On May 19, 1863, Major received command of a brigade of Texas cavalry and was promoted on July 21 to brigadier general. Major often served with his brother-in-law, and the two men earned a reputation as excellent leaders of cavalry. Taylor respected the skills of both men and came to understand the peculiar temperament of the Texas cavalry. After the war, Taylor described the troopers and their behavior as follows:

The men, hardy frontiersmen, excellent riders, and skilled riflemen, were fearless and self-reliant, but discharged their duty as they liked and when they liked. On a march they wandered about at will, as they did about camp, and could be kept together only when a fight was impending. When their arms were injured by service or neglect, they threw them away, expecting to be supplied with others. Yet, with these faults, they were admirable fighters, and in the end I became so much attached to them as to be incapable of punishing them.[24]

Major was with Green when he was killed at Blair's Landing, and in the ensuing weeks of the campaign he continued to harass the Federals as they withdrew along the Red River. On May 1, 1864, Major attacked and captured the steamer USS *Emma* about twenty-five miles below Alexandria. Two days later he struck again, capturing the USS *City Belle* and 276 soldiers from the 120th Ohio Infantry. Major and the other mounted Texas raiders made life miserable and dangerous for the retreating Federals, but they lacked the power to trap Banks. *Photo courtesy of the Alabama Department of Archives and History*

PETER CAVANAUGH WOODS
copy print

The best opportunity for Taylor to inflict substantial damage on the withdrawing Federal army came on April 23, 1864, at Monett's Ferry on the Cane River. Taylor knew that Banks would have to cross the river at that point to continue the retreat to Alexandria, and he had already given orders to the cavalry division under Brig. Gen. Hamilton P. Bee to occupy the bluffs that dominated the river crossing at Monett's Ferry. Bee's men were in place before the leading elements of Banks forces arrived on April 23, 1864. Another division of Texans under Maj. Gen. John Wharton followed closely on the retreating Federals' heels. Taylor hoped to pin the enemy between these two forces.

Col. Peter Woods commanded the 36th Texas Cavalry Regiment, which was part of the 2,000 man force that occupied Monett's Bluff on April 23, 1864.[25] Woods was born in Tennessee in 1820 and graduated from the Louisville Medical Institute in 1842. When the Civil War began, Woods was practicing medicine and farming in Hays County, Texas. On March 22, 1862, Captain Woods arrived in San Antonio with eighty men ready for service. When ten companies were assembled, the 36th Texas Cavalry was accepted into the service and Woods elected colonel. Most of the men came from within fifty miles of San Antonio. The 36th Cavalry remained in Texas until March 1864, when it was ordered to reinforce Taylor.

Woods's men performed well at Monett's Ferry, but Bee, who had little battlefield experience, mistook a Federal feint for a serious attack on his flank and withdrew his small force. With Bee's blocking force gone, Banks crossed the river and continued toward Alexandria. *Photo courtesy of ITC, Wilton Woods Collection*

The final engagement in the Red River campaign occurred on May 18, 1864, when the rear guard of the Federal army struck back at its dogged antagonists at Yellow Bayou. By then the vanguard of Banks's army had reached the safety of Simsport, Louisiana. Second Lt. John W. Harris was with 36th Texas Cavalry when it fought at Yellow Bayou. At the age of twenty-seven, Harris had mustered into Company B on March 22, 1862, as a 2d sergeant. On July 4, 1862, he was elected 2d lieutenant of the company.

At Yellow Bayou the Texas cavalry dismounted and fought alongside the Confederate infantry. Their force totaled about 5,000 soldiers and roughly equaled the number of Federals who participated in the engagement. The bottom lands were covered with dense undergrowth, and a blazing sun bore down on the men. A soldier from the 36th Texas wrote that when they moved into the brush, it was so thick that the men had trouble seeing each other. Soon the firing lit the undergrowth with a smoldering flame, and the thick pall near the ground made it impossible to see more than a few feet. Once, the soldier wrote, "the Yankees seemed to be all around us and we could hear the firing on each side of us, kind of getting in behind us. . . ." The indecisive fight at Yellow Bayou added several hundred more casualties to a list that now approached 8,000 for the defeated Federals and half that number for their victorious adversaries. Sixty-five of those casualties came from the ranks of the 36th Texas, but Harris was not among them. In the days following the campaign, the men got a chance to wash the clothes they had worn continuously for thirty days and to repair their equipment in preparation for the next campaign.[26] *Photo courtesy of Martin Callahan*

JOHN WESLEY HARRIS
copy print

320

JOHN A. WHARTON
albumen print

Kirby Smith's army had driven the Federals out of Louisiana and thus protected Texas, which then became a military backwater as the Confederacy struggled to survive the hammer blows delivered against it east of the Mississippi River. Under such conditions of neglect, the military preparedness of the army deteriorated, and in some cases personal grievances that might otherwise have been ignored were settled. One such case involved Gen. John Wharton, who had been a prominent attorney and planter in Brazoria County before the war and by 1860 owned some 135 slaves. He had been a successful commander of the 8th Texas Cavalry and subsequently received promotions to brigadier and then major general. In February 1864 he was transferred to the Trans-Mississippi Department of Louisiana in time for the Red River campaign. During the spring of 1865, Wharton became embroiled in a conflict with Col. George W. Baylor concerning military organization in the department. In an encounter at General Magruder's headquarters at Houston on April 6, 1865, Wharton apparently slapped Baylor and called him a liar. Such an insult could not be ignored, and the results in this instance were fatal. *Photo courtesy of the Alabama Department of Archives and History*

GEORGE WYTHE BAYLOR
copy print

George Baylor would not, even in the best of times, have ignored Wharton's insult. The brother of John Baylor and an aide to Gen. Albert Sidney Johnston at Shiloh, George had returned to Texas, where he became the colonel of the 2d Cavalry, Arizona Brigade. The exact nature of Wharton's dispute with him is unknown, but Baylor immediately drew his pistol and shot Wharton. Even though Wharton was unarmed, a subsequent inquiry held Baylor unaccountable for his actions. *Photo courtesy of LLMVC*

JOHN ELLIS CHAFFIN
ninth-plate ambrotype

While their officers feuded, morale among Confederate enlisted men in Texas reached new lows, and the surrender of the major Confederate armies east of the Mississippi River caused most to conclude that the war was over. John E. Chaffin, owner of a farm along the Navasota River in Limestone County, had joined Hubbard's 22d Infantry in September 1862. Except for some action in the Red River campaign, the regiment had seen little active service, and in the spring of 1865 was at Hempstead, where Confederate military and political leaders tried to keep the men in the ranks. A member of Chaffin's regiment observed a meeting where the "brass buttons from Houston" urged the soldiers to "fight on, boys." The soldier noted, however, "If they would leave the say-so to the citizens, they would say 'Go home.'"[27] Even if any of the leaders had any intention of continuing to fight, it was clear that the majority of the men had given up. *Photo courtesy of the CAH, Joseph E. Taulman Collection, CN06052*

OFFICERS OF BENAVIDES'S CAVALRY (REFUGIO BENAVIDES, ATANCIO VIDAURRI, CRISTOBAL BENAVIDES, AND JOHN Z. LEYENDECKER)
copy print

Despite the fact that most soldiers had accepted the end of the war, lives would still be lost before the conflict finally ended in Texas. In what would be the last engagement on Texas soil—if not in the entire South—a Federal force of some five hundred men engaged a smaller Confederate force on the road to Brownsville at Palmito Ranch on May 12–13, 1865. The Federals appeared to have the advantage until reinforcements of cavalry and artillery arrived. Benavides's Cavalry, including the officers shown here, were among the new troops on the field, and the Confederate command formed a line of battle in front of the Federals and at the same time pushed forward to reach the right flank of the enemy. The Union troops expected a charge, but the Confederate cavalry was content to maneuver for a more favorable position while their artillery fired upon the enemy. The Confederate tactic placed the Federals in a vulnerable position. *Photo courtesy of ITC*

JOHN J. WILLIAMS
carte de visite

Faced with the possibility of being cut off completely, the commander of the Federals, Col. Theodore H. Barrett of the 62d U.S. Colored Infantry, ordered a retreat. At that point the Confederate cavalry pressed forward, but forty-eight skirmishers from the 34th Indiana Veteran Volunteer Infantry slowed them down until they themselves were cut off and forced to surrender. Skirmishers from the 62d U.S. Colored then moved out to delay the Confederate pursuit, and the main body of Federals managed to escape back to Brazos Santiago. Thirty Federals were killed or wounded in this final battle of the war that served no real purpose. John J. Williams of the 34th Indiana had fought with the skirmishers who helped delay the Confederates long enough for the Federal force to escape. Williams, however, was killed in the action, one of the last men to die in the war. *Photo courtesy of MOLLUS, Mass., U.S.A.M.H.I.*

USS *Fort Jackson*
copy print

Even though the Confederate cavalry had been successful in the Rio Grande Valley that May, the Confederate cause had died almost everywhere else. Gen. Edmund J. Davis, sent by Gen. E. R. S. Canby to Galveston to secure the surrender of Gen. E. Kirby Smith, reported that Smith told him that "a complete disorganization of the rebel forces through the department commenced about the 20th of May."[28] On June 2, Gen. Smith and Maj. Gen. John B. Magruder at Galveston boarded the USS *Fort Jackson*, a steamer that had been appropriated for military use, where General Davis presented them with the terms of surrender. The document was signed, and Federal forces with the fleet immediately occupied the customs house and the fortifications around the harbor and raised the Stars and Stripes once again. The fighting had now come to an end. *Photo courtesy of* Review of Reviews *Collection, U.S.A.M.H.I.*

FLETCHER S. STOCKDALE
copy print

The civil officer in Texas who performed the last official acts of the Confederate state government was Lt. Gov. Fletcher S. Stockdale, who assumed office when Gov. Pendleton Murrah fled the state to Mexico. Stockdale, an attorney and railroad promoter from Calhoun County, had been a prominent member of the Texas Secession Convention and had been on the committee that drew up the ordinance of secession. During the war he had been first an aide to Governor Lubbock and then elected lieutenant governor in 1863.

In 1865 it was left to this secessionist leader to turn the reigns of state government over to his Unionist successor. That July, Stockdale received Gov. Andrew J. Hamilton at Austin and welcomed this Texas refugee into town. In the final act of the Confederate state government, he officially turned over the keys to the state buildings in August 1865. The war had finally come to an end. *Photo courtesy of CAH, John Henry Brown Papers, CN06054*

327

Chapter 12

After the War

It is sometimes said that our cause is lost. Some causes are never lost.

—GEORGE CLARK

When the war was over, the Texans who returned to their homes faced an unpredictable future. The agricultural economy was in total disarray. Slaves, who had provided the chief source of labor on cotton farms, were now free as a result of the war. Sources of credit and markets were also uncertain. The political future seemed even more uncertain. No one knew for sure what would happen, and at least some Confederate military and political leaders fled to Mexico to avoid retribution from the victorious Yankees.

In the end, rebuilding the state's economy proved the easiest problem to solve. The task was made easier by the immigration of thousands of families from elsewhere in the South. In a survey of members of the United Confederate Veterans made in 1894, the editors of the *Confederate Veteran* found that only 2,448 had served from Texas out of 6,222 who reported. The large-scale movement to Texas caused the editors to declare: "Confederates Inherit Texas."[1]

Bad weather and insect pests dealt Texas farmers setbacks during the period of Reconstruction, but the recovery was delayed only a short time. By 1873, with a crop of over 500,000 bales of cotton, Texas farmers had surpassed the 431,000 bales grown in 1859. The economic future of Texas also was brightened by the development of a thriving livestock industry. Within a decade following the war, much of the economic destabilization produced by the conflict was clearly in the past.

Conflict over political reconstruction was more troublesome, although even this lasted only a relatively short time, with Texas restored to the Union by 1870. The political problem faced by Texans was that, in many ways, the war did not end for them in the summer of 1865. Under the policies of Pres. Andrew Johnson, political reconstruction from the beginning was returned to the hands of local voters. As a result, in Texas the struggle between Confederates and Federals continued into the postwar years. Texas Unionists had been prominent before the war, and many had fought with the Federal army. Now these same men believed they had the right to lead the state's government and shape the state's future. For a year, until the elections of 1866, the Unionists controlled state and local government under the leadership of provisional governor Andrew J. Hamilton.

The old Confederate leaders, however, quickly returned to political power. They controlled the Constitutional Convention of 1866 and were largely responsible for the election of James W. Throckmorton, a former Unionist who found he could not cooperate with Hamilton, as governor in 1866. Throckmorton took power at the same time that a legislature dominated by former Confederates arrived in Austin. For a year they held sway, using office to protect their political and economic interests from the Unionist assault. Their legacy was a concerted effort to destroy the political power of Unionists and passage of labor legislation that tried to put the freedmen back under the control of the state's planters.

Throckmorton's governorship would have marked the permanent return to power of the former Confederates, except that Congress intervened, required a new constitutional convention for the state, and changed politics by adding the freedmen to the state's voting population. All of this gave the Unionists another chance for political power. In the Constitutional Convention of 1868–1869 and in the election of 1869, Unionists allied with the newly enfranchised African-American voters and regained power. From the spring of 1869 to January 1874 Gov. Edmund J. Davis and the Unionists who had joined the Republican Party ruled with a program that promised economic development, education, law and order, and the protection of the freedmen's civil rights.

By 1873, however, the Davis program had proven too unpopular because of its racial policies and costs, making it possible for the Democratic Party to mobilize a majority against it. When Richard Coke took office in 1874, the political conflict came to an end. Coke and a long series of former Confederate leaders would govern the state in succession for most of the rest of the nineteenth century. The Civil War had settled the issue of disunion but had raised questions of who would rule at home.

By 1874 the answer to that question had been settled. The state government was controlled by individuals representing much the same interests as had governed in 1861.

At the same time the old leadership had recaptured power, the state witnessed a new interest in the war itself, encouraged by the emergence of veterans' organizations among ex-Confederates. These groups had many purposes, but typically they were designed to honor the Confederate dead, to preserve the memory of the war, and sometimes to provide assistance for comrades who were unable to help themselves. In some cases these groups were simply local associations that decorated the graves of Rebel soldiers on Confederate Memorial Day. Larger groups such as the Parson's Brigade Association and the Hood's Brigade Association made their appearance by the 1880s.

Throughout the 1880s these groups became even more active in ritual activities that memorialized the Confederacy. Some oversaw the proper internment of the Confederate dead on battlefields across the South. A common work across the state was the raising of monuments to these soldiers. At first these monuments were in cemeteries, but with their return to political power of former Confederates, these efforts became more public. Few town squares in the older parts of the state lacked a Confederate statue, and major monuments were erected on the state capitol grounds.

The political clout of veterans was particularly effective in the legislature, where they actively and effectively pushed for laws and programs that aided war veterans. In 1881 they secured legislation granting 1,280 acres of land to disabled veterans and widows. In 1884 an association was organized at Austin specifically for the purpose of establishing a facility in the capital city for indigent veterans physically unable to support themselves. Raising money from throughout the state, they purchased 15 acres with a two-story house in western Austin.

After 1889 many local veteran memorial associations and organizations began to constitute themselves as local camps in the nationally organized United Confederate Veterans (UCV). Within the UCV they continued to play an important role in assisting veterans and honoring the memory of those who had died for the Confederacy. In addition, in 1891 the UCV began a successful lobbying efforts to have the State of Texas take over operations of the Confederate Home in Austin, and in 1895 the veterans supported a constitutional amendment that allowed general revenues to be appropriated for its maintenance. In 1896 the Home had 180 residents, a total of 377 veterans since it opened.[2]

In addition to its support for needy veterans, the UCV increasingly became a vehicle through which the story of the Confederacy's side of the war was created and passed on to the community. Their activities regarding history texts in the public schools were particularly vigorous. In 1900 veterans meeting at Bonham protested an encyclopedia that was being used in the schools because it referred to Jefferson Davis as the leader of a rebellion and it gave a full column to Gen. Ulysses S. Grant while only a half column to Gen. Joseph Johnson. In 1904 Texas veterans protested an arithmetic book that asked students to calculate the age of Grant in days at the time of Vicksburg's surrender. Protests against university texts used in 1913 centered on the fact that they "disregard the true courtesy due our people."[3] Ultimately, UCV camps in Texas secured a textbook law that required books used in the public schools to be nonpartisan.

In the 1890s, as the veterans aged, new organizations emerged that were connected with the UCV. In 1894 the United Daughters of the Confederacy (UDC) emerged nationally, and Texas women participated in the first convention at Nashville, Tennessee. Two years later they were joined by the Sons of Confederate Veterans. In 1902 the state gave the UDC a room in the capitol to use as a museum for Confederate relics. The Daughters were also responsible for the organization of a Confederate Women's Home for widows and wives of honorably discharged Confederate soldiers that opened at Austin in 1908. In later years, members of both the UDC and the SCV continued activities honoring the memory of those who had served the Confederacy. Their task, in the words of a veteran in 1908, was "to take up the work" as those who actually had participated disappeared.[4]

For the veterans themselves, however, as the distance in time from the war passed, the UCV increasingly provided a center for social activities. Annual reunions brought veterans together. The hardships and bad times were forgotten, and a more romantic memory of a "Lost Cause" emerged. The annual reunion of the Joe Johnston Camp No. 24, organized at Mexia in 1888, reflected this trend. The Johnston Camp provided a center around which the community came to celebrate the past. Each summer it held a three-day reunion at which presentations and concerts attracted thousands. The veterans, a reporter noted, "are entertained by each other, recounting the heroic deeds that were done by themselves and comrades during the lurid '60's. Of this they never seem to tire."[5]

In the end, the veterans created their own story of the Civil War, which ultimately became the basis for reconciliation with the rest of the nation. For Texans, the story of Unionists and Texans in the Union army was largely forgotten. Instead, a story of gallant men fighting for a Lost Cause, men with whom anyone would like to identify, provided the means by which Confederate history was melded with that of the nation. In 1894, George Clark, political associate of Redeemer governor Richard Coke, told veterans at their reunion in Waco:

We stand today with our brethren of the whole country, marshaled now under a different flag, and we will be as true to this as we were to that. . . . It is sometimes said that our cause is lost. Some causes are never lost. . . . Tell me not that the cause is lost where hosts of Americans are marshaling in defense of these rights [state and property rights], and that flag, the flag of the old Confederates, typifies the fight."[6]

Clearly, Confederate Texas had rejoined the Union.

ANDREW J. HAMILTON
carte de visite

Jack Hamilton left Texas when the Union army abandoned the mainland in 1864 and returned to Washington. There he continued to be a spokesman for the Union cause in Texas, and at the end of the war Pres. Andrew Johnson named him provisional governor of the state in his reconstruction proclamation of June 17, 1865. Hamilton arrived at Galveston on July 21 and announced that the process of reconstruction would be fair. However, he also indicated that a new order had arrived and those who had pushed for secession would have to accept that they no longer controlled the state. The new governor announced plans for the registration of Texas voters and the calling of a new constitutional convention that would pave the way for the state's readmission into the Union. Hamilton hoped that antebellum Unionists would be able to secure control of the state, but from the beginning of the registration process, he became convinced that the old leadership would stop at nothing to regain power and grew concerned with the ability of the Unionists to persevere. *Photo courtesy of U.S.A.M.H.I.*

332

MONUMENT TO MARTYRED UNIONISTS
carte de visite

The Unionists who returned to Texas in 1865 were not as forgiving of Texas secessionists as the president, who required nothing more for the vast majority of Confederates to regain their civil rights than an oath of loyalty. Many of the men of the 1st and 2d Texas Cavalry (U.S.) had been driven from the state as traitors and returned as angry victors. In central Texas the families of the men murdered on the Nueces gathered the bones of their loved ones, which had been left unburied, and on August 10, 1865, interred them at Comfort under a monument that read "Treue der Union"—True to the Union. Certainly, they were not willing to forget their treatment by Confederate Texans during the war. Under the president's policy, however, too many of their enemies were readmitted to suffrage, and the Unionists, dispersed and ravaged by the war, were not strong enough to resist. Worse, they were divided among themselves over the proper course to pursue. When James W. Throckmorton, a conservative Unionist, ran for governor in the June 1866 elections with Democratic support, Hamilton and the others who had sought to change the political order within the state were doomed. *Photo courtesy of U.S.A.M.H.I.*

JAMES W. THROCKMORTON
albumen print

Throckmorton was an unquestionable Unionist in 1861, but he had supported the Confederate state government during the war, even accepting a commission in the army. In 1865 he had been concerned with the radical tendencies that he believed he saw in Hamilton, particularly the provisional governor's insistence that the freedmen be protected in their new rights. Hamilton had been convinced that the North would demand state legislation protecting the freedmen in their liberty, but Throckmorton and most Texans failed to understand how important this was to many Northerners. When Throckmorton took office with a conservative legislature composed largely of ex-Confederates, the state actually pursued policies known as the "Black Codes" that were designed to restrict the liberties of the freedmen. Such laws passed across the state contributed to a variety of forces that brought Congress into the task of Reconstruction. Throckmorton's government was declared provisional, and Texas was placed under the authority of a military district whose administrators were charged with protecting the freedmen while preparing for a new constitutional convention in which the freedmen would help elect delegates. Ultimately, in 1867 Throckmorton would be removed from office by military authorities as an impediment to Reconstruction. Under the Congressional plan, the Unionists were given one more opportunity to seize power within the state. *Photo courtesy of Library of Congress*

EDMUND J. DAVIS
albumen print

When E. J. Davis returned from the war, he had quickly become involved in Unionist politics. When state Republicans organized in 1867, the former general became a major leader of the new party and served as president of the Constitutional Convention of 1868. In 1869 he ran as the Radical Republican candidate for governor against A. J. Hamilton and won. Between 1870 and 1874, Davis's government pursued policies designed to build a new majority in Texas: offering aid to railroads, encouraging industries, establishing a public school system, and trying to restore law and order through the use of the newly created state police and the state militia. In the face of economic problems among the state's farmers, however, the programs were seen as too costly. Davis's willingness to allow the freedmen to share in the state's new programs also raised the ire of racists. The resulting political combination was overwhelming, and in 1873 Davis was defeated for reelection by Democrat Richard Coke. The defeat of Davis brought an end to any possibility that Unionists would control the state and brought back into power representatives of the men who had ruled in 1861. *Photo courtesy of U.S.A.M.H.I.*

CONFEDERATE MONUMENT AT DALLAS
albumen print

During the 1880s and 1890s, Texas veterans of the Confederate army took on new prominence within the state. As part of the national reconciliation that took place during the late nineteenth century, the service of Confederate soldiers was increasingly memorialized in Texas and throughout the South. The Confederate monument at Dallas was planned by the United Daughters of the Confederacy and dedicated on April 29, 1897. In a typical ceremony attended by the daughter of Jefferson Davis, the wife of Stonewall Jackson, and a niece of P. G. T. Beauregard, speakers (including former Confederate Postmaster General John H. Reagan) eulogized the Confederate soldier and his leaders. The monument featured life-sized statutes of President Davis, Robert E. Lee, Stonewall Jackson, and Joseph Johnston. A reporter for the *Confederate Veteran* described the main shaft: "The uniform of the Confederate soldier was gray, and the towering column must be of gray granite; thus it would be a reminder of the unwavering lines of grayclad soldiers who, under the stars and bars, ever stood as a stone wall ready to repel every attack of the foe."[7] Such ceremonies across the state integrated the Confederate soldier into the pantheon of national heroes. *Photo courtesy of U.S.A.M.H.I.*

JOHN H. REAGAN CAMP, UCV
albumen print
F. B. Bailey

Another reflection of the growing celebration of the Confederate past was the spread of chapters of the United Confederate Veterans across Texas. In 1902 veterans at Palestine were invited to join the UCV "to perpetuate the reminiscences of the past; to extend the cordial grasp of a brother soldier; to aid you if in need; to attend you if sick, and when the last tattoo shall have sounded, to follow your body to the grave, and unfurl the flag you followed."[8] The camp at Palestine had this picture made during their annual meeting on October 6, 1902, and their guest of honor—top row center in this image—was the camp's namesake, John H. Reagan, Postmaster General of the Confederacy. *Photo courtesy of Martin Callahan*

338

W. T. Gass
cabinet card

Sharing memories increasingly became the preoccupation of the veterans. W. T. Gass, color sergeant of the 11th Texas Battery, had this photograph of himself made in 1906 with the battalion flag that he had kept at the end of the war, and he apparently sent the image to surviving members of the unit. Gass's battery had been raised at Bonham in December 1861 and served primarily in the Indian Territory. It did not receive its flag until 1864, however, when the women of Bonham secured material from Mexico and made this banner. It accompanied the unit into battle first at Cabin Creek, Indian Territory, and then in three subsequent engagements. Gass was wounded once, and the flag was struck fourteen times. The personal note to a friend written on the back—"How would you like to be a stride another 'old gray' and have a 'sawley' exploded under you"—reflected how time had replaced many of the horrors of war with nostalgic memories. *Photo courtesy of Tommy Knox*

Appendix

Adair, Isaac

Isaac Adair was wounded and captured by the Federals on the battlefield at Glorieta Pass. He was taken to Santa Fe, where he died on April 9, 1862.

Alexander, W. J. D.

W. J. D. Alexander signed his parole on August 18, 1865, and returned to his home in Smith County.

Allen, Robert T. P.

Following the war, Robert Allen returned to Kentucky where he served as superintendent of the Kentucky Military Institute. He drowned on July 9, 1888, while swimming in the Kissimmee River in Florida.

Bagby, Arthur Pendleton

Arthur Bagby practiced law and edited the *Advocate* at Victoria after the war. He later moved to Halletsville, where he died on February 21, 1921.

Bailey, George H.

Dr. George Bailey settled in Austin County after the war. He continued to suffer from lung problems that had begun when he served in Kentucky. In 1873 he moved to San Diego, California, but returned to Texas in 1882. Seven years later he went back to California and lived for a time at Anaheim. In 1900 Bailey moved to Phoenix, Arizona, but at time of his death on August 4, 1909, he had returned to Anaheim.

Batchelor, Benjamin Franklin

Benjamin Batchelor was mortally wounded at Rome, Georgia, on October 13, 1864. He died three days later.

Bates, James C.

James Bates's mouth injury permanently affected his speech pattern. However, he did return to his regiment and was paroled at Citronelle, Alabama, on May 4, 1865. After the war Bates graduated from the medical department of the University of Virginia and took further training at Bellvue Hospital in New York City. Bates began practicing medicine in Paris, Texas, in 1869 and soon married Miss Motie Johnson, who was the daughter of a local doctor. Between 1880 and 1887 he resided in Palo Pinto County, but health problems forced him to abandon the practice of medicine and return to Paris. He died there on August 11, 1891, leaving a wife and seven children.

Baylor, George Wythe

Little is known about George Wythe Baylor's life after the war until he joined the Texas Rangers in 1879. While in their service he helped destroy Victorio's Apache band. Baylor left the Rangers in 1885 and later represented El Paso County in the Texas legislature. He also served as clerk of the district and circuit courts. Baylor died in San Antonio on March 17, 1916, and was buried in the Confederate cemetery there.

Baylor, John Robert

John Robert Baylor settled at San Antonio after the war. He was a candidate for the Democratic gubernatorial nomination in 1873 but was beaten by Richard Coke. In 1878 Baylor moved to a ranch on the Nueces River at Montell. He died there on February 6, 1894.

Beall, John Alphonso

In October 1863, John Beall was named acting ordnance officer of Ector's brigade and later held a similar position in Maj. Gen. Samuel French's division. Beall was a captain when he surrendered on May 5, 1865, at Citronelle, Alabama. He returned to Smith County, Texas, and in 1865 married Sarah Elizabeth Butts. The marriage produced two children before Sarah died. In 1870 Beall married her cousin, Roxanna Butts. This marriage produced fourteen children. In 1873 Beall moved his mercantile store from Jamestown to Overton, Texas. Beall became a successful merchant and lived until October 28, 1922. His was buried in Overton.

Bedell, Edmund Thomas

Sometime after the Battle of Chattanooga, Edmund Bedell joined a Tennessee scouting company. He returned to Harrison County some time after the war. He died there on December 29, 1915.

Bee, Hamilton P.

Hamilton Bee fled to Mexico following the war and remained there until 1876, when he returned to San Antonio. He died there on October 3, 1897.

Benavides, Cristobal

After the war Cristobal Benavides married the daughter of Gen. Hamilton P. Bee. He resumed ranching in Webb County. When he died on September 2, 1904, he was one of the wealthiest men in the county.

Benavides, Refugio

Refugio Benavides returned to Laredo after the war. In 1873 he was elected mayor of that town and was reelected in 1875. In 1874 he raised a ranger company to operate against the Kickapoo Indians and border bandits, and that company staged at least one raid into Mexico. Benavides died on June 29, 1899, suffering from chronic diarrhea, and was buried in Laredo's Old Catholic Cemetery.

Benavides, Santos

Santos Benavides remained in Laredo, continuing his business as a merchant and a rancher. He was actively involved in Democratic party politics. He also engaged in efforts to overthrow the regime of Porfirio Diaz in Mexico. He died on November 9, 1891.

Benton, Benjamin E.

Benjamin E. Benton was married during the war to an Arkansas girl. Following the conflict he settled in Jefferson County, where he was an active civic leader and prominent member of the J. Ed. Murray Camp, UCV. Benton died on June 18, 1914, and was buried in his gray uniform.

Bethards, George Washington

George Washington Bethards later transferred to the 8th Texas Infantry, then Waller's Cavalry Battalion. He was captured, however, while serving as a fireman on the CSS *William H. Webb* when it was taken in April 1865. Following the war he settled in Catahoula Parish, Louisiana, where he worked as a carpenter and a farm laborer. He later operated a hotel at White Sulphur Springs in LaSalle Parish. He died on June 18, 1902.

Bettys, Harry

Harry Bettys's battery was broken up in December 1863 because of a mutiny among its members. Bettys apparently left Texas, and by the spring of 1865 he had joined the Union army at New Orleans.

Bingham, John H.

John H. Bingham is listed as being on detached duty in Texas when his unit, Douglas's Battery, surrendered in May 1865. After the war Bingham ran a newspaper, the *McKinney Enquirer,* in McKinney, Texas. Bingham was alive as late as 1904, but the authors found no other information.

Bitter, Philip C.

The authors found nothing more about Philip C. Bitter.

Blocker, Albert B.

This native Texan returned to Jonesville in Harrison County, where he worked a farm. He was married and in 1869 the couple had a son, William.

Boozer, Hugh Dickson

Hugh Boozer returned to Texas after the war and married Judith O. Gresham on October 2, 1865. He died at Round Mountain, Blanco County, Texas, on April 30, 1907.

Brantley, John David

John Brantley left the service shortly after Chickamauga and returned to Texas. After the war Brantley lived in De Witt County, Texas, until sometime in the 1880s. Brantley eventually resettled in Mason County and raised livestock. He died there on October 13, 1907.

Braubach, Philip

Philip Braubach was discharged from the army in 1865 and returned to Texas. He and his wife, Louise, acquired a two-hundred-fifty-acre farm near San Antonio, where they and their four children raised cattle, cotton, corn, and sugar cane. He began receiving a government pension of eight dollars per month in 1884. Braubach died of bowel cancer in 1888. At his death Braubach left an insurance policy that his wife used to pay off the mortgage on their land. She continued to receive a pension until her own death in 1937.

Brown, John Henry

John Henry Brown later served on Brig. Gen. Henry E. McCulloch's staff, but poor health forced him to resign from the army. However, Brown remained in the Texas militia and participated in the last engagement of the war on May 13, 1865, at Palmito Ranch. He then emigrated to Mexico but returned to Texas in 1871, settling in Dallas. He was active in Democratic politics, serving in the state legislature and in the Constitutional Convention of 1875. In later life Brown began to publish books on Texas history, including his own autobiography. His most important historical works were *Indian Wars and Pioneers of Texas* and *The History of Texas from 1865 to 1892.* Brown died in Dallas on May 31, 1895.

Bruce, Horatio Gates

Horatio Bruce returned to Johnson County. He served in the Texas House of Representatives in the 1874–1875 session and died in Dallas on January 11, 1882.

Bryan, Guy M.

Guy M. Bryan spent most of his life after the war at Galveston. He served three terms in the state legislature and was speaker of the Fourteenth Legislature, marking the end of Reconstruction. He helped form the Texas Veterans Association in 1873 and served as its president from 1892 until his death at Galveston on June 4, 1901. He was also a charter member of the Texas State Historical Association.

Bryan, John Samuel

John Bryan was wounded at the Battle of Mansfield and died on April 16, 1864.

Burgess, William

Pvt. William Burgess was still with the 27th Texas Cavalry as late as June 1864, but no further military record for him exists.

Burke, Wade Hampton

Wade Burke died of measles at Hopkinsville, Kentucky, on June 1, 1862.

Burney, Thomas S.

Thomas S. Burney returned to Limestone County, Texas, where he farmed for most of his life. On October 6, 1879, he married Mary Wimbish; the marriage produced eight children. On September 15, 1905, his pension was approved by the State of Texas. Burney told of his war experiences in a series of letters written to his sister between 1910 and 1911. The letters are a frank account of the activities of both the 8th Cavalry and Shannon's Scouts. Those letters were serialized in the *Groesbeck Journal.*

Burrell, Isaac S.

Isaac S. Burrell was released from prison in 1864, but his health was seriously affected by the conditions he had experienced. For the rest of his life, Burrell suffered from what his doctors called miasma and a bad heart. He was unable to work and depended on the help of neighbors and friends to survive. His friends supported his request for a government pension, observing that his imprisonment had made him a "ruined man." He died in 1895.

Camp, J. C.

J. C. Camp returned to his home at Denison in Grayson County after the war. He applied for a Texas pension in 1902. Eventually moving to Collin County, he died there on February 17, 1925.

Carrington, Robert Emmett

Robert Carrington's regiment participated in the 1864 Red River campaign and surrendered at Houston, Texas, on June 2, 1865. Carrington returned to Austin and married on May 23, 1867. He lived in the city for the rest of his life and died there on February 25, 1900.

Carson, Christopher "Kit"

Following the battle at Val Verde, "Kit" Carson was placed in command of a force that fought the Navajo and forced them onto reservations. He served in the U.S. Army after the war until 1867, when he resigned to become Indian agent for the Colorado Territory. He died May 23, 1868, at Fort Lyons, Colorado.

Cartwright, Leonidas

Leonides Cartwright served in the Atlanta campaign and was detached as a scout to operate against Sherman's rear as the Federals moved through the Carolinas. In December 1868 he married Ludie Ingram. Cartwright farmed until 1870, when he assumed control of his late father's estate. He ran the family land business until 1894, when he bought a ranch in Cooke County, Texas. In 1895 Cartwright moved to Terrell, Texas. He died there on February 25, 1922. Cartwright was survived by four sons and five daughters.

Cater, Douglas John

Douglas Cater fought at Pea Ridge before transferring to the 19th Louisiana Infantry in June 1862. He later participated in the Battles of Chickamauga and Missionary Ridge, as well as in the Atlanta and the Franklin/Nashville campaigns. Cater lived in Texas after the war and died in San Antonio in 1931 at the age of ninety. He kept extensive pocket diaries of his war experiences, which were published posthumously under the title *As It Was.*

Chaffin, John Ellis

After the war John Chaffin returned to his plantation on the Navasota River in Limestone County. He died in 1870 and was buried near modern Mount Calm, Texas.

Chivington, John M.

Colonel Chivington was commander of the District of Colorado after the New Mexico campaign. On November 29, 1864, he commanded Federal troops in what became known as the Sand Creek Massacre. After the war he first moved freight in Nebraska but then relocated to California and later to Ohio. In 1883 Chivington moved back to Colorado and worked for a newspaper in Denver. Through the rest of his life, Chivington's role at Sand Creek overshadowed his important action at Glorieta. He died of cancer on October 4, 1894.

Clark, Edward

Edward Clark, after his defeat in the 1861 election, was commissioned colonel of the 14th Infantry, Walker's Texas Division. He was wounded at Pleasant Hill during the Red River campaign. After the war Clark left Texas for Mexico, but soon returned. He died at Marshall on May 4, 1880.

Clay, Tacitus T.

Tacitus T. Clay resigned from the service on January 9, 1865, and returned to Texas and his home at Independence. He died on June 14, 1868, probably as a result of his wartime wounds.

Coker, Alexander

Alexander Coker left the army in 1864 after being elected sheriff of Live Oak County. After the war he lived in Oakville with his wife, Sarah. Coker served

as district clerk from 1866 to 1870, sheriff and county tax collector from 1876 to 1888, and county treasurer from 1891 to 1899. He was active in the John Donaldson Chapter of the UCV and was its commander in 1894. Coker died on September 19, 1898.

Collings, Wesley

Wesley Collings farmed in Llano County after the war. He did not marry until 1884. Collings died on January 29, 1891.

Cooke, Hugh

After his initial service, Hugh Cooke reentered the army in April 1864, joining Waller's Battalion. He served until the end of the war and fought at Yellow Bayou. Cooke returned to Hempstead County and married in 1870. He died on December 16, 1909.

Coreth, Carl

Carl Coreth suffered repeated illnesses while in the army. On January 13, 1865, he died at San Augustine of "congestion of the brain."

Coupland, Theodore Van Buren

Theodore Coupland rose to the rank of captain in the 1st Texas Cavalry (U.S.) before he transferred with the same rank to the 2d Texas Cavalry (U.S.). In the autumn of 1864, he became a member of the staff of Gen. Edmund J. Davis. Following the war Coupland married the daughter of a New Orleans shipowner (who was also the niece of the Louisiana governor). He lived in New Orleans until 1883, holding appointments as collector of customs and deputy clerk of the United States circuit court. In 1883 Coupland returned to Texas and settled in Williamson County on land he inherited from Morgan Hamilton. He died January 3, 1890.

Craig, Willis E.

Following his service in Texas, Willis Craig was stationed temporarily at Key West, Florida, where he was injured when accidentally shot in the leg.

As a result of this injury, plus periodic bouts with rheumatism, "back bone fever," and dizziness contracted during the war, he was unable to do manual labor. He was employed for a time, however, as a roundhouse foreman in Buffalo, New York. Married twice, Craig had no children. He died in 1912.

Craver, James Phillip

James Craver surrendered with the 15th Texas Cavalry in North Carolina and returned home. He was a member of the W. P. Lane Camp of the UCV. Craver died at his home in Tarleton, Texas on June 25, 1906.

Crawford, William L.

William L. Crawford ended his military career as lieutenant colonel of the 19th Texas Infantry. He returned to Jefferson, Texas, and was admitted to the bar in 1866. In 1880 Crawford moved to Dallas and opened a law practice with his brother. Crawford was a member of the 1875 Texas Constitutional Convention and was elected to the Texas House of Representatives, where he served only one term, in 1890. In later years Crawford was active in Confederate veteran activities in the Dallas area. He was married twice and had four children. Crawford died on February 17, 1920, and was buried in Oakland Cemetery in Dallas.

Crews, Simeon Jasper

Simeon Crews survived the war and returned to Texas, where he spent most of his life farming in Cherokee County. He died on May 30, 1919, and was buried in Georgia.

Crist, John

John Crist was transferred with his regiment to Mississippi in the spring of 1862. He became ill during the defense of Corinth and died at Granada on July 22, 1862.

Crook, Jeremiah

Lieutenant Crook served with the 9th Texas Infantry until sometime in the spring of 1864, when he was listed as being on detached duty at Henderson, Texas. He was dropped from the rolls of the 9th Texas on May 18, 1864. Crook died at Paris, Texas, on March 15, 1909. At the time of his death, he was a member of the Albert Sidney Johnston Camp, UCV.

Culwell, Hezekiah

Hezekiah Culwell died in Canton, Mississippi, on May 21, 1862. He was buried in the Confederate section of the Canton Cemetery.

Cureton, Jack J.

In 1870 Jack Cureton worked as a guard for an immigrant train to California. From 1876 to 1880 he was sheriff of Bosque County. He died May 12, 1881.

Currie, Edward

Edward Currie returned to Crockett following the war. He died there on February 27, 1886.

Curtright, Cornelius R.

Cornelius Curtright apparently left the 1st Texas Infantry in late 1863 or early 1864 and returned to Texas, where he joined another unit that fought in the Indian Territory. After the war little is known of his life, although he retruned to Cass County. In November 1923 he died at Queen City, Texas.

Dana, Napoleon J. T.

Napolean Dana was a railroad executive following the war and also served as deputy commissioner of pensions from 1895 to 1897. He died at Portsmouth, New Hampshire, on July 15, 1905.

Davis, Alf

Alf Davis returned to Texas after the war. In 1878 he was living in Tyler and listed as the original incorporator of the East Texas Fair Association. He apparently returned to his family's plantation in Putnam County, Georgia, and was living there in 1893. He had been one of five brothers originally from Eatonton who had served in the Confederate army. When his brother Clark died in 1921, Alf and the other three siblings were already dead.

Davis, Edmund J.

Edmund J. Davis stayed in Austin and practiced law after leaving the governorship in 1874. He remained active in Republican politics and steadfastly opposed policies designed to reconcile his national party with the white South. He died on February 7, 1883.

Dean, John

John Dean was paroled at Talladega, Alabama, on May 15, 1865, and returned to Texas. He died at Fort Bend on December 4, 1874. His wife, Susan, later moved to Mississippi.

DeBray, Xavier

Xavier DeBray lived in Houston immediately after the war. He later resumed his old job as translator in the General Land Office and moved back to Austin. He died there on January 6, 1895.

Donelson, John L.

John L. Donelson rejoined his regiment in October 1862 and was elected major on October 8. In January 1863 Donelson learned that he had tuberculosis. He resigned the following January as a result of the disease. He apparently died that spring and was buried at San Antonio.

Douthet, Evan Van Devander

Evan Douthet returned to Palestine, where he died on June 24, 1918.

Dowling, Richard W.

"Dick" Dowling ultimately was promoted to the rank of major, but spent most of the rest of the war as a recruiter. After the war ended he returned to Houston and resumed the operation of his saloon and liquor business. His fame gave him new opportunities, and he invested in everything from steamboats to oil and gas leases. Dowling died on September 23, 1867, in the yellow fever epidemic that hit the Gulf coast.

Dromgoole, John G.

John Dromgoole signed his parole on August 10, 1865, and returned to his wife, Minerva, in Guadalupe County. He continued raising livestock until his death on January 13, 1886. Dromgoole and his wife had ten children.

Duncan, Thomas

Severely wounded by a cannon ball at Albuquerque on April 8, 1862, Thomas Duncan saw no further combat during the Civil War. In 1866 he returned to service as the lieutenant colonel of the 5th Cavalry in the Department of the Platte. He retired in January 1873, however, because of continuing medical problems. He died in Washington, D.C., on January 7, 1887.

Duncan, William B.

Apparently, William Duncan contracted some sort of debilitating illness during the war. He did survive the conflict and returned to his plantation, but his service-connected health problem continued. Duncan died from his illness in 1867, leaving behind a wife and six children.

Duponte, Durant

Originally from Virginia, Durant Duponte came to Texas on the staff of General Magruder. Sent to Cuba to procure arms during the war, he never returned to Texas.

Durrum, Jacob

Jacob Durrum died on September 22, 1863, from the injury he received four days earlier at the beginning of the Battle of Chickamauga.

Durrum, Oscar Augustus

Oscar Durrum was wounded at the Battle of Mansfield and died on April 11, 1864.

Durst, Jacob

Returning to Mason County, Jacob Durst farmed and ranched, and he was also engaged as a road overseer and a school trustee. Durst was active in the Fort Mason Camp of the UCV. He died on November 17, 1920.

Dyer, Isaac

Isaac Dyer, originally from Yorkshire, England, settled in Wisconsin after the war. He suffered constantly from diarrhea, piles, and a weak heart when he was discharged in 1864 and continued to suffer from a variety of medical problems for the rest of his life. He died some time after 1917.

Ellis, Edward McMillian

Edward Ellis was still on furlough in the fall of 1863. He probably never returned to his unit since as late as April 1865 he is still listed as absent without leave. Ellis lived in Texas after the war and died in Brown County on March 24, 1908.

Elms, Henry

After the war Henry Elms lived in Nacogdoches, Texas, where on July 14, 1868, he married Frances "Fannie" Craig. The Elms had five children. The family later moved to Oklahoma, where Henry died on September 5, 1912. He was buried in the Frances Cemetery at Humphreys, Oklahoma.

Erath, Edwin P.

Following his return home, Edwin Erath enlisted in a cavalry regiment that was sent to Louisiana. He died of a fever contracted there, sometime after the Battle of Yellow Bayou.

Farmer, D. C.

After the war D. C. Farmer returned to Houston, where he practiced law and apparently married his wife, Mattie. In 1878 the couple had a son, Robert Lee Farmer.

Felder, Miers E.

The authors found nothing more about Miers E. Felder.

Felder, Rufus King

Rufus Felder surrendered at Appomattox and returned to Texas. He died on September 6, 1922, in Washington County, Texas.

Felps, John J.

John Felps surrendered with the 3d Texas Cavalry in Mississippi in May 1865. Shortly after returning to Texas, he married Amanda Ruth Kendrick and they had eight children. Felps died at his home near Jacksonville, Texas, on September 1, 1909. At the time of his death, he was commander of the J. I. A. Barker Camp, UCV.

Fentress, Thomas H.

Thomas H. Fentress died at Albuquerque on April 8, 1862, from the wounds that he received at Glorieta.

Ferris, Archille

Private Ferris surrendered and was paroled at Demopolis, Alabama, on June 13, 1865. He may have returned to his family home at Richmond in Fort Bend County.

Fowler, Robert McDonald

Robert Fowler probably saw action during the Red River campaign and remained with the 34th Cavalry until September 20, 1864, when he was admitted to the general hospital in Shreveport, Louisiana, with *Febris Remittens;* McDonald's illness was probably malaria. He is last listed on a regimental return from April 1865 as being on furlough. In 1870 Fowler was living with his mother and farming in Grayson County. He married the next year. In 1880 Fowler, his wife, Jane, and two daughters were residents of Burlington, Texas; the next year a third daughter was born. Fowler died February 9, 1899, and was buried in the Spanish Fort Old Cemetery.

Franklin, William B.

William B. Franklin was wounded at Mansfield on April 8, 1864. He resigned his command because of ill health twenty-three days later. He was captured on a train by Confederate raiders in July 1864 but managed to escape. After the war he was a vice president of the Colt Arms Company at Hartford, Connecticut. He died in that city on March 8, 1903.

Fulgham, G. W.

The last entry in the compiled service records for Private Fulgham is in July 1863, when he was detailed as a butcher.

Gaither, George W.

The authors found nothing more about George W. Gaither.

Gano, Richard Montgomery

Richard Gano was promoted to brigadier general on March 17, 1865, and surrendered with Kirby Smith. He returned to Texas and became a minister in the Christian Church, which he served for forty-five years. He died in Dallas on March 27, 1913.

Garza, Joseph R.

Lieutenant Garza was killed at the Battle of Mansfield on April 8, 1864.

Gass, W. T.

When the war ended, W. T. Gass returned to Bonham, Texas, where he married Nannie Givan. The couple had two children. Gass spent much of his life as a newspaperman, working at various times for publications in Fannin, Grayson, and Hopkins Counties. After Nannie died, Gass married Maud McDade in 1883, and they had six children. The flag shown with Gass was given to the 11th Texas Battery in 1864, and it remained in his possession long after the war ended. Gass died in Bonham, Texas, on May 15, 1914.

Gaston, Robert H.

Robert Gaston was killed at the Battle of Antietam on September 17, 1862.

Gaston, William H.

William Gaston rose to the rank of captain of Company H, 1st Texas Infantry, and was engaged in most of that unit's battles. His brother, Robert, was killed at Sharpsburg, after which William returned to Texas and served as an aide-de-camp at Galveston for Col. A. T. Rainey. He returned to Anderson County after the war, married, and started a family. He later moved to Dallas, where he became a prominent banker and civic leader. He died on January 24, 1927.

Giles, Valerius Cincinnatus

Valerius Giles survived the Battle of Gettysburg and later fought at Chickamauga. Shortly after the latter battle, he was captured and sent to Camp Morton, Indiana. In late 1864 he escaped and returned to Texas. Giles was married in 1873 and lived in Austin. In later years Giles wrote several articles about his service in Hood's brigade and tried to keep track of his old comrades. Giles planned to compile his writings into a memoir, but the work was uncompleted when he died on January 31, 1915, at the age of seventy-three. Mary Lesswell compiled and edited Giles writings, which in 1961 were published under the title *Rags and Hope.*

Glimp, Thomas

Thomas Glimp never appears to have served in any unit except the Shiloh Home Guards. In the 1880s he and his friend John David Brantley left De Witt County, Texas, and eventually settled in Mason County. Apparently, both men were trying to avoid some unspecified trouble associated with a local feud between the Sutton and Taylor families. Glimp later moved to Burnet County and died there on November 4, 1907.

Goodman, William J.

William J. Goodman spent the rest of the war as surgeon for Luckett's brigade and then for Slaughter's division. He was paroled at Marshall, Texas, July 31, 1865, and returned to Tyler. He resumed his medical practice that autumn. He married in 1867, raised a family, and became a prominent rancher and businessman as well as physician. He was an active member in the UCV. Goodman died on August 21, 1921.

Granbury, Hiram Bronson

General Granbury was killed November 30, 1864, in the Battle of Franklin. Buried initially near the battlefield, his remains were moved in 1893 to Granbury, Hood County, Texas.

Green, Tom

Tom Green was killed at Blair's Landing on April 12, 1864.

Gregg, John

John Gregg was killed while leading his brigade at Darbytown Road on October 7, 1864.

Guess, George

George Guess returned to his law practice in Austin after the war. He was elected mayor to fill an unexpired term. On July 18, 1868, Guess was aboard a steamer returning from a trip to Memphis, Tennessee, when he died from sunstroke.

Hale, Howell Pope

On April 6, 1865, Howell Hale married Sue Morgan. The two had at least one daughter and lived in Rusk County. Hale died there on February 28, 1886. His wife began drawing a pension in 1909 and lived until September 9, 1930.

Hamilton, Andrew J.

Following his service as provisional governor, Andrew J. Hamilton actively campaigned for congressional intervention in Reconstruction and for the enfranchisement of African Americans. He was appointed bankruptcy judge at New Orleans in 1867, but then returned to Texas, where he was a delegate in the Constitutional Convention of 1868–1869. He ran unsuccessfully for governor as a moderate Republican against Edmund J. Davis in 1869 and subsequently worked against the Davis administration. He died at Austin of tuberculosis on April 11, 1875.

Harris, Abram

While Lieutenant Colonel Harris was stationed in Georgia, he met Sallie L. Logan and married her on August 22, 1863. Harris surrendered with the 14th Texas Cavalry in Alabama in May 1865. He and his wife then settled in Tarrant County, where he was a business man and civic leader. He was still living in Fort Worth in 1903.

Harris, John Wesley

After the war John Wesley Harris returned to Guadalupe County, Texas, where he farmed and raised cattle. In 1917, Harris, who was then eighty-three, wrote that his first wife and all their children were dead, but he had five girls by his second wife.

Hart, Henry C.

After the war Henry Hart returned to Grimes County where he farmed near Bedias. He was married in 1871. Hart died at his home on November 20, 1893.

Hart, Martin D.

Martin Hart was executed January 23, 1863.

Haynes, John L.

Following the war John L. Haynes returned to Texas with his unit to be mustered out, and he went back to his home in Starr County. Haynes became active in Republican politics and was appointed collector of customs at Galveston from 1869 to 1870 and then at Brownsville from 1872 to 1884. He was also an active member of the Grand Army of the Republic. He died at Laredo on April 2, 1888.

Heartsill, William W.

William Heartsill was at his home in Marshall after the war, operating a business and promoting railroads, when he began to collect the images for his war history. He apparently was active in politics and is supposed to have been a founder of the local Ku Klux Klan. In his later years he was active in veterans organizations. He died July 28, 1916. His volume, *Fourteen Hundred and 91 Days in the Confederate Army*, is now one of the rarest imprints produced by a Confederate veteran.

Heath, Egbert Munroe

Egbert Heath returned to Johnson County, where he farmed and served as sheriff from 1865 until 1869. By 1881 Heath was also practicing law, and in that year he helped start the Johnson County Bank. Heath was still alive in 1893.

Henderson, John Beverly

John Beverly Henderson does not appear on any regimental muster role after June 1862 and apparently returned to Texas. He lived near Linden in Cass County for the rest of his life. He died on August 8, 1928, and was buried at Red Hill Cemetery north of Linden.

Henderson, John Nathaniel

At the war's end, John N. Henderson returned to Baylor to finish his study of law. In 1867 he was admitted to the bar and opened an office at Millican. Politically, he was a Democrat and held numerous state offices—district attorney for Bryan in 1874; state senator in 1880; district judge in 1888 and 1890; and associate justice on the Texas Court of Criminal Appeals in 1894. He died on December 22, 1909.

Hennrich, Jacob

Jacob Hennrich returned to Colorado County after the war and was listed in the 1870 Census as a grocer. Thirteen years later Hennrich was in the saloon business in Ellinger, Texas. Hennrich died on April 2, 1885; his wife, Friederika, died on November 9, 1913.

Hesseltine, Francis S.

Francis Hesseltine returned to Portland, Maine, where he studied law. He practiced law for a time at Savannah, Georgia, and was a register of bankruptcy there until 1870, when he moved to Boston. He was still practicing law there with his son in 1898.

Hinojosa, Lino

Lino Hinojosa returned to Rio Grande City after the war and operated a ranch in Hidalgo County. He died in February 1900.

Hobby, Alfred M.

Settling at Galveston after the war, Alfred Hobby engaged in the mercantile business and also pursued various literary interests, including a biography of David G. Burnet. He died on February 5, 1881, at Silver City, New Mexico.

Hogan, W. A.

The authors found nothing more about W. A. Hogan.

Hood, John Bell

In January 1865 General Hood, at his own request, was relieved from command of the remnants of the Army of Tennessee. In the postwar years Hood, whose health had been shattered by his wounds, spent much of his time in New Orleans. There he worked in the insurance business and sometimes found employment as a cotton factor. Hood died on August 30, 1879, when yellow fever struck the Crescent City; his wife, Mary Hennen, and a daughter also perished in the epidemic. Hood's memoirs, *Advance and Retreat,* were published posthumously. Most later historians would largely ignore his splendid career as a divisional commander and concentrate on attacking his admittedly terrible performance as leader of the Army of Tennessee.

Hornsby, Malcolm M.

Malcolm Hornsby was not released from prison until near the end of the Civil War. Hornsby returned to his wife and his farm along the Colorado River in Travis County. The couple had five children between 1862 and 1870. She died in 1887 and Malcolm died on September 28, 1892. He was buried in the Hornsby Bend Cemetery.

Houston, Sam

Sam Houston moved to Huntsville after stepping down as governor. Houston's son, Sam Jr., entered the Confederate army, and the old governor offered public support for the state's military forces. He died of pneumonia following a short illness on July 26, 1863.

Hubbard Richard B.

After the war Richard B. Hubbard resumed the practice of law, as well as speculation in real estate and investment in railroads. He was elected lieutenant governor in 1873 and 1876 and in 1876 assumed the governorship when Richard Coke became a United States senator. He was named minister to Japan by Pres. Grover Cleveland in 1885. He died at Tyler on July 12, 1901.

Hughes, Thomas P.

Although he had opposed secession, Thomas Hughes served as a private in Company A, Morgan's Cavalry Battalion, a unit that served primarily in the Trans-Mississippi. He returned to Georgetown after the war. In 1872 he was elected district attorney of his local judicial district. He continued to practice law and also acquired extensive landholdings in Williamson County. He died at Georgetown on December 31, 1899.

Jemison, Elbert S.

Elbert S. Jemison resigned from the army on August 19, 1864, due to a disability from his wound. The authors found no additional information.

Johnson, Joshua G.

Returning to his home near Mount Vernon in Titus County following the convention, Joshua Johnson remained at home through the war and refused to support the Confederate government. At the war's end he was named Titus County judge by Gov. Andrew J. Hamilton. He served in the Constitutional Convention of 1866 and was also a delegate to the Constitutional Convention of 1875. Johnson practiced law, farmed, and preached as a Baptist minister. He died at his home from pneumonia on February 15, 1877.

Johnson, William H.

Following the secession convention, William Johnson helped recruit the 22d Texas Cavalry and was its lieutenant colonel. After the war he returned to Paris and resumed his law practice. Although he ran for several political offices during the postwar years, he was never successful. He died at Paris on November 13, 1891.

Kellersberger, Getulius

Fleeing to Mexico with many other staff officers, Getulius Kellersberger worked for a time as an engineer for the Vera Cruz-Mexico Railroad. In 1867 he and his family returned to Texas, settling for a time at Cypress Mill in Blanco County. After the death of his wife, Kellersberger returned to his native Switzerland and died there in 1900.

Kendall, Peter

Peter Kendall returned to Texas, and spent much of his life in the town of Mexia. He married a twenty-five-year-old woman on October 9, 1884. Kendall died in Rusk, Texas, on November 9, 1919. His wife began drawing a pension on November 26, 1928.

Kennedy, Felix G.

Felix G. Kennedy returned to Limestone County and died there on May 21, 1887.

Kennedy, Thomas

After the war Thomas Kennedy returned to Anderson County, where he married and raised a family. He died on June 30, 1905.

King, Anderson Augustus

Anderson King died in Louisiana on February 16, 1864, probably from wounds received in the skirmish at Vidalia.

Knight, Jonathan Thomas

Jonathan Knight was exchanged after being captured at Fort DeRussey and returned to his regiment in October 1864. He was with the 22d Texas Infantry when it disbanded at the end of the war. Knight lived in Winnsboro, Texas, until the 1880s, when he moved his family to Commerce. There, Knight was a farmer and merchant. He died on March 29, 1907, and was buried in the Rosemound Cemetery.

Kokernot, David L.

After his discharge on July 29, 1862, David L. Kokernot briefly served in a home guard unit, but generally remained at his home in Gonzales supervising his family's extensive ranching interests. When he died on December 10, 1892, he was buried in the family cemetery in southwestern Gonzales County.

Langley, Thomas Horace

Thomas Langley surrendered at Appomattox and returned to Texas, where he married on April 29, 1885. Langley died at Marshall, Texas, on March 4, 1914.

Langley, William L.

William Langley was killed at Gettysburg on July 2, 1863.

Leake, Joseph B.

Although Joseph B. Leake filed for a pension following the war, no more specific information could be found on him.

Leyendecker, John Z.

Returning to Laredo after the war, John Leyendecker married the sister of his diseased first wife, both siblings of Santos Benavides. This couple had ten children. Leyendecker was active in city politics and closely associated with the political faction of Benavides. In the general election of 1866, he was elected county treasurer. He also served for a time during Reconstruction as the city's postmaster. In 1872 Leyendecker played a role in the overthrow of the Republican county government when he was elected county treasurer as a Democrat. In the 1880s he was elected city secretary as an independent candidate.

Lindsey, F. L.

F. L. Lindsey was discharged from the service on May 24, 1865, and returned to farming in Smith County. In August 1909 the sixty-four-year-old veteran was still a farmer, but citing poor health he applied for a pension. Lindsey's application languished for over two years as Texas bureaucrats tried to establish if, in fact, he had actually served in the Rebel army. Lindsey eventually procured two sworn statements from his old comrades-in-arms that verified the claim, and he received his first pension check in December 1911. He died of heart disease on October 14, 1924, in Hughes Springs, Cass County, Texas.

Lown, Jacob

Jacob Lown died in prison on January 18, 1864.

Lubbock, Francis R.

Governor Lubbock did not run for office in 1863 and became a member of the staff of John B. Magruder. He organized troop-transport and supply trains in the Red River campaign. In August 1864 he went to Richmond, where he became an aide to Jefferson Davis and a specialist in Trans-Mississippi activities. After an eight month imprisonment at Fort Delaware, he returned to Texas and engaged in business at Houston and Galveston. He died at Austin on June 22, 1905.

Lyles, Richard S.

Richard S. Lyles recovered from his wound at Chickamauga and returned to duty on February 21, 1864. On August 3, 1864, he was promoted to captain. Lyles was wounded again at Allatoona (October 5, 1864) and died on March 3, 1865, but it is not clear if his death was the result of that wound.

Lynch, William A.

The authors found nothing more about William A. Lynch.

McCulloch, Ben

General McCulloch was killed on March 7, 1862, during the Battle of Pea Ridge.

McCulloch Henry Eustace

After the war Henry McCulloch returned to Seguin, where he resumed his business interests. He was also active in Democratic politics. In 1873 he was sergeant-at-arms in the famous Coke-Davis dispute. In 1876 he was named superintendent of the Deaf and Dumb Asylum. McCulloch died at Seguin on March 12, 1895.

McDonald, Alexander

Alexander McDonald returned to Texas after the war and married Sarah Ann Elizabeth Laswell on October 17, 1867. The couple had five children. McDonald died at Iredell, Bosque County, on October 31, 1879. An obituary in a local paper stated that the wound McDonald received during the war never healed properly and caused the illness that killed him. His widow received a Confederate pension in 1909. She died in 1931 and was buried with Alexander in the Old Iredell Cemetery.

McPhail, Daniel Edward Cameron

Paroled on June 26, 1865, Daniel McPhail returned home. Possibly suffering from diseases contracted during the war, he died on October 8, 1866, and was buried near Tarleton.

McWhorter, George S.

George S. McWhorter surrendered at the end of the war.

Magruder, George

George Magruder died on September 2, 1870.

Magruder, John Bankhead

General Magruder went to Mexico after the war and served in the army of Maximilian. He returned to Houston when Maximilian was overthrown. He died in that city on February 19, 1871.

Major, John Patrick

John Patrick Major fled to France after the war, but he soon returned to the South. He farmed in Texas and Louisiana until his death at Austin on May 7, 1877. Major was buried in Donaldsonville, Louisiana.

Marshall, John

Colonel Marshall was killed at Gaines' Mill on June 27, 1862.

Maverick, Lewis

Lewis Maverick subsequently was wounded at Blair's Landing. He was sick at Goliad through most of the rest of the war. Afterward he returned to his home in San Antonio and married. He died, however, in June 1866 from heart disease.

Maverick, Samuel A.

Samuel Maverick was chief justice of Bexar County and mayor of San Antonio during the war. Following the war he received a pardon as a Unionist, but opposed the Reconstruction policies of Andrew J. Hamilton and other Unionists who came to power at this time. He died on September 2, 1870.

May, William H.

The authors found nothing more about William H. May.

Milburn, Williamson

Shortly after he returned to Smith County in 1862, Williamson Milburn was killed in a fight over a dog.

Moore, John Creed

John Moore was captured with the Vicksburg garrison. After being exchanged he fought at Chattanooga and later assisted in the defense of Mobile, Alabama. Moore resigned his commission on February 3, 1864. He probably returned to Galveston and was there when the war ended. Moore later taught school and lived in Mexia and then Dallas. During the postwar years he published widely in magazines and journals. Moore died at Osage, Texas, on December 31, 1910, at the age of eighty-seven.

Mullen, Francis J.

The authors found nothing more about Francis J. Mullen.

Nolan, Matthew

The authors found nothing more about Matthew Nolan.

Oliphant, William James

After having been captured twice and suffering from seven or eight wounds, William Oliphant returned to Austin after the war, then briefly studied photography with well-known Civil War photographer Alexander Gardner. In 1868 he opened a studio in Austin and took pictures until 1881. At that time, possibly because of troubles from his wounds, he retired as a photographer and held numerous city offices. He died on November 11, 1930, and was buried in Austin's Oakwood Cemetery.

Oliver, Absalom Carter

Absalom Carter survived the war and surrendered with Lee's army at Appomattox. He returned to Cass County at the war's end and resumed the practice of medicine. He was elected to the state House of Representatives in 1880, 1896, and 1898. In 1913 he was elected to the state Senate. He was superintendent of the Texas Confederate Home from 1913 to 1916. He died at his home in Douglassville, Cass County, on March 4, 1929.

Oliver, Henry

Henry Oliver died from pneumonia at Fredericksburg, Virginia, in 1862.

Oliver, John

John Oliver died from pneumonia at Fredericksburg, Virginia, in 1862.

Oliver, Thomas Frances

The authors found nothing more about Thomas Oliver.

Oliver, William

William Oliver died in 1863 from wounds received during the Battle of Chickamauga.

Perez, Patricio

Patricio Perez was discharged in 1865 and returned to Hidalgo County, Texas. He apparently suffered from severe rheumatism as a result of his service with the 1st Texas in Louisiana and was unable to perform manual labor. He and his wife, Martina Salinas, reared six children. She died in 1904 and Patricio followed in 1908. At the time of his death, Perez's children requested government assistance to bury their father.

Perry, Eugene Osceola

Eugene Perry was killed during the Battle of the Wilderness on May 6, 1864.

Pickle, John S.

John S. Pickle was married in December 1862 and survived the war. He returned to Bastrop, where he worked as a cabinet marker and wood carver. At a later date he moved to Austin. He died there on July 3, 1884, and was buried at Oakwood Cemetery.

Pinckney, John

John Pinckney surrendered at Appomattox and returned to Texas. In 1875 he was admitted to the bar and practiced law in Hempstead. Pinckney served in the U.S. Congress from 1901 until being assassinated in Hempstead, Texas, in 1905 by an anti-prohibitionist.

Pinckney, Richard

At the end of the war, Richard Pinckney worked for the Houston and Texas Central Railroad, which was extending its line into Calvert in Robertson County. He later returned to his family home near Hempstead and married Emily Speed in 1875. He farmed, served briefly as postmaster and city marshal, and also periodically worked for the railroad. He died at Houston on January 19, 1921.

Polignac, Camille Armand de

On June 13, 1864, General Polignac was promoted to major general. Polignac remained in command of the Texas-Louisiana division until near the end of the war, when he was sent to France to urge Napoleon III to intervene on behalf of the Confederacy; Polignac had not yet reached France when the war ended. He remained in France and later led a division in the Franco-Prussian War (1870–1871). When Polignac died in Paris on November 15, 1913, he was the last surviving major general from the Confederacy. He is buried in Frankfort-on-Main, Germany.

Preston, William B.

William B. Preston died as an exchanged prisoner at Petersburg, Virginia, on April 13, 1863.

Quantrill, William Clarke

In 1865 Quantrill led a final expedition of his men into Kentucky. The group was surprised and Quantrill was shot. He died at Louisville on June 6, 1865.

Rain, Benjamin C.

Benjamin C. Rain returned to Texas after the war, and on March 4, 1867, married Frances "Fannie" Eley. Rain died on February 11, 1893, and was buried in the Webb Cemetery near Elysian Fields, Texas.

Randal, Horace

On April 30, 1864, Horace Randal was mortally wounded while leading his brigade at the Battle of Jenkins' Ferry, Arkansas. He died on May 2.

Reid, Calloway

Private Reid died in the charge at Franklin on November 30, 1864.

Reily, James

Colonel Reily was killed at Irish Bend, Louisiana, on April 14, 1863.

Renshaw, William B.

William B. Renshaw was killed at the Battle of Galveston on January 1, 1863.

Ridley, Alonzo

Alonzo Ridley had originally come to Texas from California in 1861, riding with Albert Sidney Johnston. Prior to the war he had been sheriff of Los Angeles County, California. Little is known about him in later years, although in 1877 he lived near Phoenix, Arizona.

Roberdeau, James Daniel

James Roberdeau returned to Texas after the war. He engaged in business in Galveston until 1878 and then spent eight years working in the general land office. Roberdeau died in Austin, Texas, on May 18, 1910. He left a wife and six grown sons. At the time of his death, only four members of his old company were still alive, and two were too feeble to attend the funeral.

Roberts, Ben T.

Ben T. Roberts recovered from the wound he received at Thompson's Station and remained with the 3d Cavalry until the war's end. He then returned to his farm a few miles east of San Augustine. On January 10, 1869, he married Anne Wigglesworth, and the couple had seven children. In 1870 Roberts moved into San Augustine, from where he directed expanding farming operations, eventually acquiring major landholdings throughout eastern Texas. He died at San Augustine on November 6, 1887.

Roberts, Benjamin S.

Later in the war Benjamin Roberts commanded a division of the XIX Corps in Louisiana and was Chief of Cavalry in the Department of the Gulf. In 1865 he was named commander of the cavalry division in the District of Western Tennessee. After the war he was lieutenant colonel of the 3d Cavalry. In 1868 he became professor of military science at Yale and filled that post until he resigned in 1870. He

subsequently was engaged in efforts at manufacturing the Roberts breechloading rifle, although the weapon was never successful. He died in Washington, D.C., on January 29, 1875.

Roberts, Oran M.

Through the rest of the war Oran Roberts helped raise the 11th Infantry but returned to the law and served as a justice on the Texas Supreme Court. He renewed his political activity following the war, serving in the Constitutional Convention of 1866. He was appointed to the state supreme court again in 1874, and Roberts then was elected governor in 1878 and 1880. He spent his later years as a professor of law at the University of Texas. He died at Austin on May 19, 1898.

Robertson, Elijah Sterling Clack

Elijah Robertson returned to Salado, practiced law, engaged in Democratic politics, and participated in educational efforts. He died there on October 8, 1879.

Robertson, Felix Huston

Felix Robertson saw little active service after the Saltville affair, although he was sent to negotiate the surrender of Macon, Georgia. The Confederate Congress ultimately rejected his nomination to brigadier general. Robertson eventually settled in Waco, Texas, where after studying law, he began his practice. He died on April 20, 1928, and was buried in Waco.

Robertson, Jerome Bonaparte

Jerome Robertson ended his military career serving in Texas. He returned to his home in Independence and practiced medicine until 1874, when he was appointed superintendent of the Texas Bureau of Immigration. Robertson left the position after five years and moved to Waco, where he became heavily involved in railroading. He died in Waco on January 7, 1891, and was buried there.

Ross, Lawrence Sullivan

"Sul" Ross returned to Texas after the war and began farming in the Brazos Valley. Ross's political career began in 1873, when he was elected sheriff of McLennan County. He was a member of the 1875 constitutional convention and then served two terms in the state senate. He was governor from 1887 until 1891. When Ross left the governor's office, he became president of the Agricultural and Mechanical College of Texas (now Texas A&M) and held that position until he died on January 3, 1898. Ross was buried in Waco.

Rounsavall, William David

William Rounsavall resigned from the service on September 13, 1862, and returned to Texas, where he was married the next year. He died on Christmas Day, 1895.

Runnels, Hardin R.

Hardin Runnels remained in Bowie County after the war and was a member of the Constitutional Convention of 1866. An unreconstructed Rebel, he was one of the first vice presidents of the Texas Historical Society. Runnels died on December 25, 1873.

Rushing, John Calvin

John Rushing settled in Van Zandt County at the end of the war. He died there on March 11, 1915.

Santanta

Continuing his raiding during and after the war, Santanta was arrested and imprisoned following an attack upon a government wagon train in 1871. Sentenced to die by a Texas jury, he was released in 1873 by Gov. Edmund J. Davis, who was pressured by the Federal government to make the gesture in return for the Kiowa's ending their raiding. The raiding did not stop, however, and in 1874 Santanta was arrested again and returned to the Texas state penitentiary at Huntsville. He died there on October 11, 1878, when he jumped to his death from a window in the prison hospital.

Schadt, William F.

William F. Schadt was taken prisoner at Bermuda Hundred on October 7, 1864, and declared exchanged on February 18, 1865. When the war ended he was on furlough at Sumter, South Carolina. He did not returned to Galveston until March 1866, and in that city established himself as a prosperous businessman. He was still alive in 1899.

Scurry, William Read

William Scurry bled to death after being wounded at the Battle of Jenkins' Ferry on April 30, 1864.

Seymour, Aaron

Aaron Seymour survived the war and returned to his farm in Williamson County near Georgetown. He and his wife, Martha, had a daughter in 1866, then another daughter in 1869 whom they named America.

Shannon, Alexander May

Alexander Shannon surrendered in North Carolina in 1865. He was purported to have held the rank of colonel, but there is no evidence of such promotion in his service records. After the war Shannon returned to his ranch along the San Antonio River but soon moved on to New Orleans. In 1869 he joined Gen. John Bell Hood in the insurance business and subsequently moved to Galveston to take charge of the Texas division of the company. In the 1880s Shannon was in the construction business building jetties along the Texas coast. In 1890 he became general manager of the Galveston and Western Railway, and three years later he was appointed postmaster of Galveston. In 1872 he married Clara Viola Scott and had seven children with her. Shannon died in Galveston on October 28, 1906.

Shepard, Chauncey Berkeley

Captain Shepard was killed at the Battle of Mansfield on April 8, 1864.

Sherman, Sidney, Jr.

Badly wounded at Galveston, Sidney Sherman died on the day of the battle.

Short, James C.

The authors found nothing more about James C. Short.

Shufford, A. P.

A. P. Shufford was a member of the Constitutional Convention of 1866, but nothing more has been found about his career or life afterward.

Slough, John Potts

John Slough returned to the practice of law in New Mexico. In 1866 he became First District judge on the territorial Supreme Court and chief justice. He was murdered in the office of the Fonda Hotel on December 15, 1867, by Capt. William L. Ryerson, a member of the New Mexico state legislature from Donna Ana.

Smith, James Henry

James Smith is listed as surrendering with his unit at Citronella, Alabama, in May 1865. He returned to Hopkins County and lived there until his death on January 4, 1899. He was buried in Sulphur Bluff Cemetery.

Smith, John Porter

John Porter Smith returned to the 5th Texas and remained in the ranks until early 1863, when he was detailed as a teamster. He was still with the regiment as late as December 1864 but is not listed among the surrendered at Appomattox Court House. Smith died on April 18, 1919.

Smith, Leon

The authors found nothing more about Leon Smith.

Smith, Nathan A.

Lieutenant Smith left the Army of Tennessee and served west of the Mississippi River until the war ended.

Smith, William R.

William Smith was mortally wounded in the Battle of Chickamauga and died on September 19, 1863.

Southworth, Malek A.

The authors found nothing more about Malek A. Southworth.

Speed, Frederick

The authors found nothing more about Frederick Speed.

Springg, Richard L.

Following the war Richard L. Springg settled in Cincinnati, Ohio, where he worked as the representative of a thread manufacturer. He died on November 30, 1918.

Stark, John T.

On November 11, 1864, John Stark, because of health reasons, was detailed as an enrolling officer in Hardin County, Texas. After the war he practiced law and ran a store in Newton, Texas. In 1873 he moved to Orange, Texas, where he served as county judge. Stark died there on September 21, 1893.

Steele, William

William Steele was a merchant at San Antonio after the war. In January 1874 he was named adjutant general of Texas and held that position until January 1879. He died January 12, 1885, at San Antonio.

Stockdale, Fletcher S.

Fletcher Stockdale returned to Calhoun County at the war's end. He was president of the Indianola

Railroad. In 1873 he moved to Cuero, where he practiced law and developed land. He returned to politics, serving in the Texas Senate in 1868 and the Constitutional Convention of 1875. He remained active in Democratic party politics into the 1880s. He died on February 4, 1890.

Stout, Selen

Selen Stout was discharged for disability on May 11, 1862. He returned to his home in Hopkins County and died there on July 19, 1897.

Street, James K.

In the fall of 1863, James K. Street transferred to the 14th Texas Cavalry and on November 25 became chaplain of the regiment. He was captured at Deer Creek, Mississippi, on January 14, 1864, and may have spent the remainder of the war in prison. After the war he settled at Waco with his wife, Melinda East Pace, and remained in that city until his death on October 11, 1914.

Swann, David William

Private Swann surrendered at Artesia, Mississippi, in May 1865 and returned to his home in Smith County Texas. He served as a representative in the Thirty-Seventh Legislature (1921–1922). Smith was granted a pension on January 21, 1931, and lived until March 6, 1935. He was eighty-five years old at the time of his death, having lived in Smith County for seventy-four years.

Swinney, John Wilson

John Swinney died in the U.S. Hospital at New Orleans on July 23, 1863.

Tappan, Samuel F.

Samuel F. Tappan commanded various posts in Colorado after the Battle of Glorieta Pass. In 1864 he was head of a board of inquiry that examined the role of John Chivington at Sand Creek, sitting on that board despite the objections of Chivington.

He subsequently held many positions with the government in dealing with the Indians. He later moved to Washington, D.C., where he died on January 6, 1913.

Taulman, Frances Asbury

After the war Francis Taulman returned to Brazos County, Texas, and was married in 1866. The Taulmans had three children. Taulman lived in Bryan until 1881, when he moved to the newly incorporated city of Hubbard, Texas. In 1881 he opened a store there, and the next year he formed the *Hubbard City News*. Taulman was the first mayor of Hubbard and served three consecutive terms. He was active in the Odd Fellows, the local UCV camp, and the Hubbard City Literary Society. Taulman died in Hubbard on December 4, 1910.

Thomas, DeWitt Clinton

DeWitt Clinton Thomas later joined Waul's Legion. About three hundred men, including Thomas, were stationed at Yazoo City when Vicksburg was isolated by Grant, and consequently they escaped capture. However, Thomas, was subsequently taken prisoner on September 23, 1863, and was not released until the war ended. He later returned to Burleson County, where he was elected sheriff. He moved to Lampasas in 1871 and worked in a general store. He was county clerk from 1875 to 1885 and county judge from 1885 until 1889. In 1871 Thomas married Jennie Hewlett. Thomas was still living in 1896.

Throckmorton, James W.

After his term as governor ended when he was removed from office in 1867, James Throckmorton continued to be active in Democratic politics. He was also an active railroad promoter and worked as an attorney for the Texas and Pacific Railroad. He was elected to Congress in 1874 and 1876, then returned again in 1882, 1884, and 1886. Throckmorton died as a result of complications from a fall during a business trip at his home in McKinney on April 21, 1894.

Turner, E. P.

E. P. Turner settled in Dallas after the war and became a passenger agent and land developer for the Texas and Pacific Railroad. He also was active in the UCV. He was still alive in 1903.

Turner, Ike

Ike Turner was killed on April 14, 1863, during the siege of Suffolk.

Vidaurri, Atancio

Antancio Vidaurri returned to Laredo and Webb County, where he engaged in extensive sheep raising operations. In November 1872 he was elected a city alderman in the Democratic triumph over a Reconstruction Republican administration. He later became associated with the Democratic machine of Raymond Martin and ran successfully for mayor of Laredo in 1876.

Wainwright, Jonathan M.

Jonathan Wainwright was killed in the Battle of Galveston.

Wampler, David J.

David J. Wampler went back to Weatherford after the war. He died September 20, 1897, in an accident involving a Texas and Pacific train.

Watson, Benjamin W.

Benjamin Watson helped defend Little Rock in the fall of 1863 and then served in the Red River campaign. He surrendered at the end of the war and returned to his farm in Ellis County. Watson died in Waxahachie, Texas, on September 16, 1873, at the age of forty-five. He was buried in the family cemetery near Italy, Texas.

Watson, George W.

George W. Watson farmed and ranched at Peatown after the war and was married in 1869. In 1874 his family moved to Bowie, then in 1901 settled in Kiowa County, Oklahoma, where he farmed. He died on February 21, 1920, just thirty-two days after the death of his wife of forty-six years.

Watson, James Monroe

James Watson returned to Texas, and on December 24, 1867, he married Myra Whittington. The Watsons reared eight children on their farm in Rusk County. James Watson died there in July 1914. His two brothers, Alvin and John, both died during the war.

Watson, William A.

William A. Watson returned to Texas after surrendering at Appomattox. He died in Limestone Count on January 11, 1908. Private Watson's obituary in the 1908 issue of the *Confederate Veteran* stated that he was in twenty great battles, being wounded at Gaines' Mill, the Wilderness, and Cold Harbor.

Waul, Thomas Neville

After the war Thomas Waul first returned to his farm in Gonzales County and later moved to Galveston. He practiced law there until 1893, when he retired to a farm near Greenville, Texas. Waul died on July 28, 1903, at the age of ninety-one. He was buried in Fort Worth.

Weir, Christopher C.

Christopher C. Weir returned to Texas after the war. He died on March 14, 1921, in Jack County and was buried in the Graves Cemetery.

West, Thomas Jefferson

Thomas West returned to Seguin and his ranch. He subsequently married and then moved his family to McMullen County. He died on September 9, 1874, after having been injured in an accident in a cattle pen.

Westmoreland, James Alexander

Private Westmoreland was paroled at Greensboro, North Carolina, on May 1, 1865. After the war he farmed in Harrison County, Texas. Even though Westmoreland was in good health, he began receiving a pension on January 11, 1918. He was then seventy-four. Westmoreland died on April 12, 1932.

Wharton, John A.

On April 6, 1865, Col. George W. Baylor killed John A. Wharton in a quarrel over unspecified "military matters."

Williams, Lemuel H.

Following the convention, Lemuel H. Williams returned to Lamar County. He joined the Confederate army.

White, James S.

James S. White was paroled at Meridian, Mississippi, on May 9, 1865.

Wilkinson, Albert G.

Albert Wilkinson returned to Burleson County and his farm. He apparently married in 1861 and by 1870 had three children, his first born in 1864. He was active in the UCV, belonging to Washington Camp No. 239 in Brenham, and attended the Houston reunion of 1895. In 1885 he was diagnosed as having cancer but survived until February 10, 1899, when he died in Deanville, Texas.

Williams, John

After Val Verde, John Williams was appointed sergeant. The pastel drawing of him was made in April 1862 by a Mexican artist in Santa Fe. When Sibley abandoned Santa Fe, Williams was left behind in the hospital, captured, and imprisoned at Camp Douglas. After rejoining his unit in September 1862, he was present in battles at Galveston, Bayou Lafouche, Karencok, Mansfield,

and Yellow Bayou. After the war he returned to Cameron and grew cotton in Milam and surrounding counties. Williams was married twice and had five children with his second wife. He was an active Mason. During the war Williams had sworn that he would never cut his hair if the South was defeated, and he never did—afterward he was called "Long John" by those who knew him. He died in 1901 and was buried near Rockdale.

Williams, John J.

John J. Williams was killed at Palmito Ranch on May 13, 1865. He is usually recognized as the last soldier to die in the Civil War. His wife remarried shortly after the war's end. His son later received a federal pension.

Williams, R. H.

R. H. Williams continued to travel and work in the southwest after the war. In 1907 a relative published the memoirs of his life to 1868, *With the Border Ruffians: Memories of the Far West*. What happened to Williams after the years covered in his autobiography, however, is not known.

Winkler, Clinton McKanny

Clinton Winkler surrendered at Appomattox and returned to Texas, where he resumed both his law practice and political career. In 1872 he was elected to the state legislature. Four years later the people elected Winkler to the Court of Appeals, on which he served until his death on May 13, 1882. Winkler was buried in Corsicana and was later honored by having a county in west Texas named after him.

Womack, William J.

William J. Womack returned to Parker County after the war and remained there until shortly after the death of his second wife in 1875. He then moved to Jack County, where he married two more times. In the 1880s Womack was active in the Farmers Alliance and organized chapters in several counties. He probably died between 1895 and 1900.

Wood, Henry Clay

Henry Clay Wood went back to Hopkins County, where he lived until March 4, 1916. During his life he worked as a farmer, a merchant, and a school teacher and was named postmaster. He married twice and had thirteen children. Wood was buried in the Como Cemetery in Hopkins County.

Wood, Walter S.

Walter S. Wood apparently returned to Texas after the war.

Woods, Peter Cavanaugh

Peter Woods disbanded his regiment on May 21, 1865. He farmed and practiced medicine after the war. Woods died in San Marcos, Texas, on January 27, 1898.

Wright, George W.

Although he had opposed secession, George W. Wright became provost marshal in Lamar County. Following the war he lived near Paris and occasionally participated in the activities of the state Democratic Party. He died at Paris on August 2, 1877.

Yturri, Manuel, II

Manuel Yturri II returned to San Antonio following the war.

Young, Robert Butler

Lieutenant Colonel Young died at the Battle of Franklin on November 30, 1864.

Young, William Hugh

William Young became a prominent attorney and real estate developer in San Antonio. He died on November 28, 1901, and was buried in the Confederate Cemetery.

Zoeller, Adolph

Adolph Zoeller made it to New Orleans, where he joined Company C, 1st Texas Cavalry, serving as lieutenant and later captain. He returned to Texas during Banks's Rio Grande campaign. After the war he operated a ranch and speculated in land around Boerne. He died at Boerne on September 18, 1909.

Notes

Chapter 1

1. *Austin Texas State Gazette,* November 23, 1861.

2. David Haynes, *Catching Shadows: A Directory of 19th-Century Texas Photographers* (Austin: Texas State Historical Association, 1993), viii, 26; David Haynes, "Photography," *The New Handbook of Texas* (Austin: Texas State Historical Association, 1996), 5:187.

3. *Tri-Weekly Galveston News,* September 24, 1861.

4. *Tyler Reporter,* April 11, 1861.

5. *Clarksville Northern Standard,* January 19, 1861.

6. *San Antonio Weekly Alamo Express,* April 6, 1861.

7. *San Antonio Herald,* May 21, 1865.

8. *Tyler Reporter,* April 11, 1861.

9. *San Antonio Herald,* May 21, 1859.

10. *Austin Southern Standard,* May 8, 1861; *Clarksville Northern Standard,* April 27, 1861.

11. *Clarksville Northern Standard,* January 19, 1861.

12. *Austin Texas State Gazette,* November 23, 1861.

13. *San Antonio Weekly Alamo Express,* April 14, 1861.

14. *Clarksville Northern Standard,* April 27, 1861.

15. *Clarksville Northern Standard,* January 19, 1861.

16. *Tyler Reporter,* April 11, 1861.

17. *Clarksville Northern Standard,* September 13, 1862.

18. *Austin Southern Standard,* May 8, 1861.

19. *Clarksville Northern Standard,* September 13, 1862.

20. Rebecca W. Smith and Marion Mullins, ed., "The Diary of H. C. Medford, Confederate Soldier, 1864," *Southwestern Historical Quarterly* 34 (October 1930), 109.

21. Haynes, *Catching Shadows,* xiv.

22. Robert Gaston to "Dear Pa and Ma," July 10, 1861, in Robert W. Glover, ed., *"Tyler to Sharpsburg," The War Letters of Robert H. and William H. Gaston, Company H, First Texas Infantry Regiment, Hood's Texas Brigade* (Waco: Texian Press, 1960), 4.

Chapter 2

1. W. W. Heartsill, *Fourteen Hundred and 91 Days in the Confederate Army; or Camp Life, Day by Day of the W. P. Lane Rangers from April 19, 1861 to May 20, 1865* (Pine Bluff: Rare Book Publisher, n.d.), 2.

2. Houston quoted in Rupert N. Richardson, *Texas the Lone Star State* 2d ed. (Englewood Cliffs, N.J.: Prentice-Hall, 1958), 184.

3. Richardson, *Texas, The Lone Star State,* 185.

4. Shelby Foote, *The American Civil War, A Narrative: Fort Sumter to Perryville* (New York: Vintage Books, 1958), 295.

5. Ralph J. Smith, *Reminiscences of the Civil War and Other Sketches* (Waco: W. M. Morrison, 1962), 1–2.

6. Robert Hodges to Jackson Stubbs, October 27, 1861, "Robert Hodges, Jr.: Confederate Soldier," ed. Maury Darst, *East Texas Historical Journal* 9 (March 1971): 23.

7. John W. Rabb to "Dear Sister" [Melissa], December 5, 1861, "'We Are Stern and Resolved': The Civil War Letters of John Wesley Rabb, Terry's Texas Rangers," ed. Thomas W. Cutrer, *Southwestern Historical Quarterly* 91 (October 1997): 192.

8. Quoted in Patsy McDonald Spaw, ed., *The Texas Senate: Vol. I, Republic to Civil War, 1836–1861* (College Station: Texas A&M University Press, 1990), 315.

9. Quoted in Dudley G. Wooten, *A Comprehensive History of Texas, 1865 to 1897*, 2 vols. (Dallas: William G. Scarff, 1898), 2:105.

10. Quoted in B. P. Gallaway, ed., *Texas: The Dark Corner of the Confederacy: Contemporary Accounts of the Lone Star State in the Civil War* 3d ed. (Lincoln: University of Nebraska Press, 1994), 77.

11. Thomas North, *Five Years in Texas* (Cincinnati: Elm Street Printing Company, 1871), 95.

12. Richard Hubbard to Samuel B. Davis, December 10, 1861, Hubbard File, CRC.

13. Quoted in W. T. Block, "The Swamp Angels: A History of Spaight's 11th Battalion, Texas Volunteers, Confederate States Army," *East Texas Historical Association Quarterly* 30 (1992), 46.

14. Quote from note accompanying photograph, TSL.

15. Surgeon's certificate, E. P. Erath service record, National Archives, "Compiled Service Records of Confederate Soldiers who Served in Organizations from Texas." (Hereinafter cited as Compiled Service Records.)

16. John Simmons to "Dear Father," April 27, 1862, "The Confederate Letters of John Simmons," ed. Jon Harrison, *Chronicles of Smith County* 14 (summer 1975), 27.

Chapter 3

1. W. L. Alexander to Charles S. Taylor, May 31, 1862, "An Appraisal of the 1862 New Mexico Campaign: A Confederate Officer's Letter to Nacogdoches," Martin Hardwick Hall, *New Mexico Historical Review* 51 (October 1976), 332.

2. Quoted in Donald S. Frazier, *Blood and Treasure: Confederate Empire in the Southwest* (College Station: Texas A&M University Press, 1995), 144.

3. Quoted in Foote, *The Civil War*, 299.

4. Frazier, *Blood and Treasure*, 192.

5. Foote, *The Civil War*, 304–5.

6. Isaac Lynde to Adjutant General, July 26, 1861, U.S. War Department, *The War of the Rebellion: A Compilation of the Official Records of the Union and Confederate Armies*, 128 vols. (Washington: Government Printing Office, 1880–1901), series 1, vol. 4, 4–5. (Hereafter cited as *O.R.*, all citations to Series 1 unless otherwise indicated).

7. Martin Hardwick Hall, "The Court Martial of Arthur Pendleton Bagby, C.S.A.," *East Texas Historical Association Journal* 19 (1981), 65.

8. Letter of Charles Buckholts, January 13, 1862, in a private collection.

9. Quoted in Frazier, *Blood and Treasure*, 162.

10. Don E. Alberts, ed. *Rebels on the Rio Grande: the Civil War Journal of A. B. Peticolas* (Albuquerque: University of New Mexico Press, 1984), 48.

11. *O.R.*, vol. 9, 537.

12. Jno. P. Slough to E. R. S. Canby, March 29, 1862, ibid., 533.

13. W. R. Scurry to A. M. Jackson, March 31, 1862, ibid., 544.

14. Ibid.

Chapter 4

1. John W. Thomason Jr., *Lone Star Preacher*, (1938; reprint, Fort Worth: Texas Christian University Press, 1992), vii, 50–55, 276.

2. Harold B. Simpson, *Hood's Texas Brigade: Lee's Grenadier Guard*, (Waco: Texian Press, 1970), 25.

3. Ibid., 13–14, 67.

4. Simpson, *Hood's Texas Brigade*, 101.

5. *O.R.*, vol. 11, pt. 2, 973.

6. Ibid.

7. *O.R.*, vol. 12, pt. 2, 560, 606.

8. Ibid., vol. 19, pt. 1, 922–25.

9. J. B. Polley, *Hood's Texas Brigade*, (1910; reprint, Dayton: Morningside Bookshop, 1988), 133.

10. *O.R.*, vol. 30, pt. 2, 291; ibid., pt. 4, 652.

11. Simpson, *Hood's Texas Brigade*, 441.

12. Harold Simpson, *Hood's Brigade: A Compendium* (Hillsboro: Hillsboro Junior College Press, 1977), 533–34.

13. Polley, *Hood's Texas Brigade*, 17–18; A. V. Winkler, *The Confederate Capitol and Hood's Texas Brigade*, (1894; reprint, Baltimore: Butternut and Blue, 1991).

14. John Bell Hood, *Advance and Retreat* (New Orleans: n.p., 1880), 26.

15. Simpson, *Hood's Texas Brigade*, 122; Simpson, *Compendium*, 535.

16. "Capt. J. D. Roberdeau," *Confederate Veteran* 18 (September 1910): 439–40.

17. Ibid.; Simpson, *Compendium*, 535.

18. *O.R.*, vol. 19, pt. 1, 811, 932–33.

19. W. R. Hamby, "Hood's Texas Brigade at Sharpsburg," *Confederate Veteran* 16 (January 1908): 19–20.

20. *O.R.*, vol. 19, pt. 1, 811, 934–36.

21. Ibid., 936–37.

22. William H. Gaston to "Dear Ma and Pa," June 29 and November 28, 1862, William H. Gaston Letters (photocopies), CRC.

23. Polley, *Hood's Texas Brigade*, 142, 205, 225.

24. Simpson, *Hood's Texas Brigade*, 28; *The Countryman* (Turnwold, Georgia), April 28, 1863.

25. Rufus King Felder to "My Dear Mother," July 9, 1863, Felder Family Letters, CRC.

26. Mary Lasswell, ed. and comp., *Rags and Hope: The Recollections of Val C. Giles* (New York: Coward-McCann, 1961), 110, 178–82.

27. "Report of Major J. P. Bane, Fourth Texas Regiment," *Southern Historical Society Papers* 13 (1885): 190–91.

28. "Report of Lieutenant-Colonel Work, First Texas Regiment," *Southern Historical Society Papers* 13 (1885): 187–89.

29. Simpson, *Compendium,* 535.

30. Simpson, *Hood's Texas Brigade,* 299, 305, 308, 318.

31. Harold B. Simpson, "Whip the Devil and His Hosts," *Chronicles of Smith County, Texas* 6 (fall 1967): 11, 44, 46.

32. Polley, *Hood's Texas Brigade,* 230–31.

33. Winkler, *The Confederate Capitol and Hood's Texas Brigade,* 171–77.

34. Judy and Nath Winfield, eds., *War Letters of Tacitus T. Clay* (n.p), "Introduction," 7, 15.

35. Simpson, *Hood's Texas Brigade,* 440–41.

36. Polley, *Hood's Texas Brigade,* 274–77.

Chapter 5

1. *O.R.,* vol. 4, 412, 430, 524–25.

2. John Frederick Charles Fuller, *A Military History of the Western World* 3 vols. (New York: Funk & Wagnalls, 1956), 3:13, 15.

3. Joseph E. Chance, *The Second Texas Infantry,* (Austin: Eakin Press, 1984), 36, 38.

4. *O.R.,* vol. 10, pt. 1, 508, 560–63, 626–27.

5. Two of the units, namely the 6th Infantry and the 17th Cavalry, only served in Mississippi a few months before being transferred to Arkansas. Both later surrendered at Arkansas Post.

6. The regiment along with several other did manage to briefly seize the parapet of the battery, but they were thrown back by a Union counterattack. *O.R.,* vol. 16, pt. 1, 1108.

7. *O.R.,* vol. 31, pt. 2, 757.

8. William T. Sherman, *Memoirs of William T. Sherman* (New York: Library of America, 1990), 490.

9. Oliver P. Bowser, "Notes on Granbury's Brigade," *Comprehensive History of Texas, 1685–1897,* ed., Dudley G. Wooten (Dallas: W. G. Scarff, 1898), 750.

10. Sherman, *Memoirs,* 636–37.

11. Samuel B. Barron, *The Lone Star Defenders* (Washington: Zenger Publishing, 1983), 192–255.

12. *O.R.,* vol. 45, pt. 1, 666–67.

13. H. J. H. Rugeley, ed., *Batchelor-Turner Letters, 1861–1864* (Austin: Steck, 1961), 8.

14. Tom Burney, comp., "A Confederate Soldier's Recollection of his Experiences in Terry's Rangers," unpublished paper, CRC; *O.R,* vol. 47, pt. 2, 533.

15. *O.R.,* vol. 4, 524–25; ibid., vol. 7, 376.

16. Ralph J. Smith, *Reminiscences of the Civil War* (Waco: W. M. Morrison, 1962) 3, 5; Chance, *Second Texas Infantry,* 7, 25, 27.

17. *O.R.,* vol. 10, pt. 1, 508–10.

18. John K. Street to "Dear Minnie," March 3, 1862, John K. Street and Melinda East (Pace) Papers, Southern Historical Collection, University of North Carolina.

19. John K. Street to "Dear Minnie," April 12, 1862, ibid.

20. John K. Street to "Dear Minnie," April 9, and April 19, 1862, ibid.

21. *O.R.,* vol. 16, pt. 1, 936, 941–43.

22. Ibid., vol. 17, pt. 1, 185; Homer L. Kerr, ed., *Fighting With Ross' Texas Cavalry Brigade C.S.A., the Diary of George L. Grisom, Adjutant, 9th Texas Cavalry Regiment* (Hillsboro, Tex.: Hill Junior College Press, 1976), 44–47. Grisom put the total losses of the 9th Texas Cavalry for both Corinth and Hatchie Bridge at 149. Since the *Official Records* lists no officers wounded at Hatchie Bridge and casualties are relatively small at Corinth of the first day's fighting, Smith is likely wounded at the attack on Battery Robinett.

23. *O.R.,* vol. 17, pt. 1, 383, 398–99.

24. Eleanor Damon Pace, "The Diary and Letters of William P. Rogers, 1846–1862," *The Southwestern Historical Quarterly* 32 (April 1929): 260, 298; Chance, *Second Texas Infantry,* 74–78.

25. *O.R.,* vol. 17, pt. 1, 382.

26. James Henry Davis, *The Cypress Rangers in the Civil War,* (Texarkana, Tex.: Heritage Oak Press, 1992), 47, 125; Kerr, *Fighting with Ross' Texas Cavalry Brigade,* 53.

27. Jon P. Harrison, "Tenth Texas Cavalry, CSA," *Military History of Texas and the Southwest* 12 (1974): 96, 102, 104–6.

28. Lucia Rutherford Douglas, comp. and ed., *Douglas's Texas Battery, CSA* (Tyler, Tex.: Smith County Historical Society, 1966), 57–59, 164–65.

29. *O.R.,* vol. 20, pt. 1, 745, 749–51.

30. Douglas Hale, *The Third Texas Cavalry in the Civil War* (Norman: University of Oklahoma Press, 1993), 166.

31. Ibid., 166–67.

32. *O.R.,* vol. 23, pt. 1, 220–21.

33. Ibid., vol. 24, pt. 2, 358.

34. Ibid., vol. 30, pt. 2, 243.

35. Norman D. Brown, ed., *One of Cleburne's Command* (Austin: University of Texas Press, 1980), 43.

36. *O.R.,* vol. 30, pt. 2, 195.

37. W. W. Heartsill, *Fourteen Hundred and 91 days in the Confederate Army,* (Pine Bluff, Ark.: Rare Book, Publishers, n.d.), 79.

38. Ibid., 154.

39. *O.R.,* vol. 30, pt. 1, 233, 448.

40. "The Confederate Letters of Bryan Marsh," *Smith County Historical Society* 14 (1975): 42.

41. Judith Ann Benner, *Sul Ross, Soldier, Statesman, Educator,* (College Station: Texas A&M Press, 1983), 103, 107; Ezra Warner, *Generals in Gray,* (Baton Rouge: Louisiana State University Press, 1959), 264.

42. Kerr, *Fighting with Ross' Texas Cavalry Brigade,* 142–44; newspaper clipping from unidentified newspaper, 9th Texas Infantry File, CRC.

43. Brown, *Cleburne's Command,* 85; *O.R.,* vol. 38, pt. 3, 725–26.

44. "James P. Carver," *Confederate Veteran* 15 (January 1907): 36.

45. Brown, *Cleburne's Command,* 106, 129.

46. *O.R.,* vol. 37, pt. 3, 746.

47. James McCaffrey, *This Band of Heroes* (Austin: Eakin Press, 1985), 49.

48. *O.R.,* vol. 38, pt. 3, 748–49.

49. Ibid., 910–12.

50. Ibid., vol. 39 , pt. 1, 554–55.

51. Ibid., 823–24.

52. Ibid.

53. Rugeley, *Batchelor-Turner Letters,* 43.

54. Thomas Connelly, *Autumn of Glory,* (Baton Rouge: Louisiana State University Press, 1971) 502.

55. "Soldiers for the War," undated circular copy from Jenece Waid-Hurst.

56. Brown, *Cleburne's Command,* 151.

57. "A Confederate Soldier's Recollection of His Experiences in Terry's Rangers," unpublished manuscript, Tom Burney Papers, CRC.

58. H. W. Graber, *A Terry Texas Ranger* (Austin: State House Press, 1987), 237–44; "The reunion of the survivors of Terry's Texas Rangers. . . ," *Confederate Veteran* 5 (August 1897): 419.

59. Francis Taulman to "Dear parents," May 1864, Franklin A. Taulman Papers, CAH.

60. Francis Taulman to "Dear Father," [April] 12, 1865, ibid.

Chapter 6

1. Douglas, *Texas Battery,* 160–62. Hale, *Third Texas Cavalry,* 25, 52, 68.

2. Hale, *Third Texas Cavalry,* 77, 79, 82.

3. *O.R.,* vol. 8, 282–83.

4. Ibid., 776.

5. Ibid., vol. 13, 828–30.

6. Ibid., 43–44.

7. Michael E. Banasik, *Embattled Arkansas, the Prairie Grove Campaign of 1862* (Wilmington: Broadfoot Publishing, 1996), 515, 517, 524–25.

8. Edwin Bearss, *Steele's Retreat from Camden,* (Little Rock: Pioneer Press, n.d.), 29–37.

9. J. P. Blessington, *The Campaigns of Walker's Texas Division* (New York: Lange, Little, & Company, 1875), 11.

10. Stephen B. Oates, *Confederate Cavalry West of the River* (Austin: University of Texas Press, 1961), 44.

11. Quoted in Anne J. Bailey, *Between the Enemy and Texas: Parsons's Texas Cavalry in the Civil War,* (Fort Worth: Texas Christian University Press, 1989), xi.

12. Max S. Lale, ed., "The Boy Bugler of the Third Texas Cavalry: The A. B. Blocker Narrative," *Military History of Texas and the Southwest* 17 (1978): 148.

13. Ibid., 73, 81.

14. Douglas John Cater, *As It Was* (Austin: State House Press, 1990), 47, 59, 72, 103–4.

15. W. J. Lemke, ed., "Paths of Glory," *Arkansas Historical Quarterly* 15 (winter 1956): 349–59. Brown refers to recovering two ambrotypes of McCulloch, one of which he kept. He also had seven images made of himself, one of which he sent to his wife. The images of Brown and McCulloch that appear in this volume are part of the Brown Papers in the Barker Texas History Center at the University of Texas and are likely the images that Brown mentions in his diary.

16. William L. Shea and Earl J. Hess, *Pea Ridge: Civil War Campaign in the West,* (Chapel Hill: University of North Carolina Press, 1992), 99–103, 335.

17. Douglas, *Texas Battery,* 179.

18. Ibid., 184, 188, 193.

19. *O.R.,* vol. 13, 955–56.

20. Blessington, *Walker's Texas Division,* 41–42.

21. Heartsill, *Fourteen Hundred and 91 days,* 85, 88, 93, 96.

22. *O.R.,* vol. 22, pt. 1, 303.

23. Blessington, *Walker's Texas Division,* 66–75.

24. "Field and Staff Notes," 14th Texas Infantry, Compiled Service Records.

25. *O.R.,* vol. 22, pt. 1, 448, 460.

26. Ibid., vol. 34, pt. 1, 817.

27. Blessington, *Walker's Texas Division,* 250.

28. *O.R., vol.* 41, pt. 1, 789–92.

Chapter 7

1. *O.R.,* vol. 9 609, (quote) 619.

2. Ibid., vol. 15, 181.

3. Ibid., vol. 14, 149.

4. Ibid., vol. 14, 150.

5. Ibid., vol. 15, 211.

6. John S. Ford, *Rip Ford's Texas,* ed. Stephen B. Oates (Austin: University of Texas Press, 1963), 343.

7. J. W. Lockhart to "My Dear Wife," January 7, 1863, *Sixty Years on the Brazos: The Life and Letters of Dr. John Washington Lockhart, 1824–1900,* ed., Mrs. Jonnie Lockhart Wallis (Waco: Texian Press, 1967), 74.

8. *O.R.*, vol. 15, 218.

9. Charles P. Bosson, *History of the Forty-Second Regiment Infantry, Massachusetts Volunteers, 1862, 1863, 1864* (Boston: Mills, Knight, & Company, 1886), 114.

10. Wallis, *Sixty Years on the Brazos*, 74.

11. *O.R.*, vol. 15, 214.

12. Fred Tate to L. P. Walker, April 7, 1861, Sidney Sherman service record, Compiled Service Records.

13. Edward B. Williams, ed., "A 'Spirited Account' of the Battle of Galveston, January 1, 1863," *Southwestern Historical Quarterly* 99 (October 1995): 211.

14. Ibid., 212.

Chapter 8

1. *Rebellion Record* (New York: G. P. Putnam, 1863), 6:49.

2. David Paul Smith, *Frontier Defense in the Civil War: Texas' Rangers and Rebels* (College Station: Texas A&M University Press, 1992), 74.

3. Heartsill, *Fourteen Hundred and 91 days*, 37.

4. Quoted in Smith, *Frontier Defense*, 137.

5. Quoted in ibid., fn. 35, 214.

6. R. H. Williams, *With the Border Ruffians: Memories of the Far West, 1852–1868* (London: John Murray, 1907), 247.

7. Quoted in Carl L. Duaine, *The Dead Men Wore Boots: An Account of the 32d Texas Volunteer Cavalry, CSA, 1862–1865* (Austin: The San Felipe Press, 1966), 31.

8. John L. Donelson to H. P. Bee, September 8, 1862, John L. Donelson service record, Compiled Service Records.

9. Quoted in Smith, *Frontier Defense*, fn. 19, 200.

Chapter 9

1. A. J. L. Fremantle, *Three Months in the Southern States: April–June 1863* (Edinburgh: W. Blackwood and Sons, 1863), (first quote) 60; (second quote), 49.

2. Ibid., 68.

3. Rebecca W. Smith and Marion Mullins, "The Diary of H. C. Medford, Confederate Soldier, 1864," *Southwestern Historical Quarterly* 34 (October 1930): 122.

4. *O.R.*, vol. 48, pt. 1, 512.

5. Ibid., 79.

6. John Q. Anderson, ed., *Brokenburn: the Journal of Kate Stone, 1861–1868* (Baton Rouge: Louisiana State University Press, 1955), 332.

7. *O.R.*, vol. 53, 885.

8. Heartsill, *Fourteen Hundred and 91 days*, 198.

9. *The Old Flag*, March 15, 1864, Smith County Historical Museum.

Chapter 10

1. R. King to E. P. Turner, November 12, 1863, "'Let us have 500 good determined Texans': Richard King's Account of the Union Invasion of South Texas, November 12, 1863, to January 20, 1864," Bruce S. Cheeseman, *Southwestern Historical Quarterly* 101 (July 1997): 83.

2. Henry S. McArthur, "A Yank at Sabine Pass," *Civil War Times Illustrated* 12 (December 1973): 41–42.

3. Mintetta Altgelt Goyne, ed., *Lone Star and Double Eagle: Civil War Letters of a German-Texas Family* (Fort Worth: Texas Christian University Press, 1982), 111.

4. Quoted in Edwin B. Lufkin, *History of the Thirteenth Maine Regiment* (Bridgton, Maine: H. A. Shorey & Son, 1898), 64.

5. Goyne, *Lone Star and Double Eagle*, 114–15.

6. Ibid., 119.

7. *O.R.*, vol. 34, pt. 1, 648.

8. Ibid., 649.

Chapter 11

1. *O.R.*, vol. 26, pt. 1, 664.

2. Ibid., vol. 34, pt. 2, 55.

3. Ibid., pt. 1, 181.

4. Lester N. Fitzhugh, "Texas Forces in the Red River Campaign, March–May 1864," *Texas Military History* 3 (1963): 16–21.

5. John Dimitry, *Louisiana*, vol. 10 of *Confederate Military History* (Atlanta: Confederate Publishing, 1899), 142.

6. Alwyn Barr, "Texan Losses in the Red River Campaign, 1864," *Texas Military History* 3 (1963): 104–5.

7. Richard Taylor, *Destruction and Reconstruction*, (New York: D. Appleton, 1879), 176.

8. Ibid., 179, 192, 198; Alvin M. Josephy Jr., *War on the Frontier*, (Alexandria: Time Life Books, 1986), 70–71.

9. Blessington, *Walker's Texas Division*, 96–97.

10. *O.R*, vol. 26, pt. 1, 215–16.

11. J. S. Duncan, ed., "Alexander Cameron in the Louisiana Campaign, 1863–1865," *Military History of Texas and the Southwest* 12 (1975): 40–41.

12. George Guess service record, 31st Texas Cavalry, Compiled Service Records.

13. *O.R*, vol. 34, pt. 1, 130.

14. John Thomas Knight to "Dear Wife and Child" [March 10, 1864], letter in the possession of Gary Canada.

15. Alwyn Barr, "Polignac's Texas Brigade," *Texas Gulf Coast Historical Association Publication Series* 8 (November 1964): 29.

16. Joseph Garza to "Dear DeWitt," December 9, 1862, photocopy furnished by Martin Callahan.

17. John Samuel Bryan to "Dear Wife," April 7, 1864.

Mansfield State Commemorative Area, Louisiana Office of State Parks; Blessington, *Walker's Texas Division*, 188–89; Bryan quote from the Mansfield Historic Commemorative Area.

18. Lucille B. Bullard, *Marion County, Texas* (Jefferson: n.p., 1965), 79.

19. Blessington, *Walker's Texas Division*, 195–96.

20. Taylor, *Destruction and Reconstruction*, 169.

21. Ibid., 178.

22. Thomas O. Selfridge Jr., *Memoirs of Thomas O. Selfridge Jr.* (New York: G. P. Putnam, 1924), 103.

23. Taylor, *Destruction and Reconstruction*, 177–78.

24. Ibid., 178–79.

25. Woods's regiment is also often referred to as the 32d Texas Cavalry, but the Compiled Service Records uses the designation of 36th Texas Cavalry. I have arbitrarily chosen to use that designation to avoid confusion with Andrews's 32d Texas Cavalry, which served in the Army of Tennessee.

26. Duaine, *The Dead Men Wore Boots*, 80–83.

27. John Simmons to "Dear Companion," April 29, 1865, "The Confederate Letters of John Simmons," ed. Jon Harrison, *Chronicles of Smith County* 14 (summer 1975): 52.

28. E. J. Davis to C. T. Christensen, June 1865, *O.R.*, vol. 48, pt. 2, 621.

Chapter 12

1. *Confederate Veteran* 2 (May 1894): 136.

2. *Confederate Veteran* 4 (February 1896): 48; *Confederate Veteran* 4 (May 1896): 156.

3. *Confederate Veteran* 21 (September 1913): 420.

4. *Confederate Veteran* 22 (September 1914): 390.

5. *Confederate Veteran* 2 (September 1894): 328.

6. *Confederate Veteran* 2 (April 1894): 122.

7. *Confederate Veteran* 6 (July 1898): 299.

8. *Anderson County Herald*, October 10, 1902.

Select Bibliography

General and Reference Works

Boatner, Mark M. *The Civil War Dictionary.* New York: McKay, 1959.

Current, Richard B. *Encyclopedia of the Confederacy.* 4 vols. New York: Simon and Schuster, 1993.

Crute, Joseph, Jr. *Confederate Staff Officers.* Powhatan: Derent Books, 1982.

Davis, William C. *The Confederate General.* 6 vols. N.p.: National Historical Society, 1991.

Esposito, Vincent, J. *The West Point Atlas of American Wars.* Vol. 1. New York: Praeger, 1959.

Gallaway, B. P. *Texas: The Dark Corner of the Confederacy: Contemporary Accounts of the Lone Star State in the Civil War.* 3d ed. Lincoln: University of Nebraska Press, 1994.

Kerby, Robert L. *Kirby Smith's Confederacy: The Trans-Mississippi South, 1863–1865.* New York: Columbia University Press, 1972.

Long, E. B. *The Civil War Day by Day.* New York: Garden City, 1971.

Sifakis, Stewart. *Texas. Compendium of the Confederate Armies.* New York: Facts on File, 1995.

Simpson, Harold B., ed. *Texas in the War.* Hillsboro, Tex.: Hill Junior College Press, 1984.

Texas. Confederate Military History Extended Edition. Vol. 15. Wilmington: Broadfoot Publishing, 1989.

U.S. War Department. *The War of the Rebellion: A Compilation of the Official Records of the Union and Confederate Armies.* 128 vols. Washington: Government Printing Office, 1880–1901.

Warner, Ezra. *Generals in Blue.* Baton Rouge: Louisiana State University Press, 1981.

———. *Generals in Gray.* Baton Rouge: Louisiana State University Press, 1981.

Wooster, Ralph A., ed. *Lone Star Blue and Gray: Essays on Texas in the Civil War.* Austin: Texas State Historical Association, 1995.

Chapter 1

Haynes, David. *Catching Shadows: A Directory of 19th-Century Texas Photographers.* Austin: Texas State Historical Association, 1993.

Young, W. R., III. "A Capital View: Photography in Austin, Texas, after the Civil War." *Journal of the West* 26 (April 1987): 52–62.

Chapter 2

Buenger, Walter L. *Secession and the Union in Texas.* Austin: University of Texas Press, 1984.

———. "Secession and the Texas German Community: Editor Lindheimer vs. Editor Flake." *Southwestern Historical Quarterly* 82 (April 1979): 379–402.

———."Texas and the Riddle of Secession." *Southwestern Historical Quarterly* 87 (October 1983): 151–32.

Gage, Larry Jay. "The Texas Road to Secession and War: John Marshall and the *Texas State Gazette, 1860–1861.*" *Southwestern Historical Quarterly* 62 (October 1958): 191–226.

Hicks, James. "Texas and Separate Independence, 1861–61." *East Texas Historical Journal* 4 (October 1966): 85–106.

Maher, Edward R., Jr. "Sam Houston and Secession." *Southwestern Historical Quarterly* 55 (April 1952): 448–58.

Rutherford, Philip R. "To Hell with Black Republicanism: Texas Leaves the Union." *Civil War Times Illustrated* 20 (June 1981): 12–23.

Sandbo, Anna Irene. "Beginnings of the Secession Movement in Texas." *Southwestern Historical Quarterly* 18 (July 1914): 41–74.

———. "The First Session of the Secession Convention of Texas." *Southwestern Historical Quarterly* 18 (October 1914): 162–94.

Wooster, Ralph A. and Robert Wooster. "Rarin' for a Fight': Texans in the Confederate Army." *Southwestern Historical Quarterly* 84 (April 1981): 387–426.

Chapter 3

Alberts, Don E. "The Battle of Peralta." *New Mexico Historical Review* 58 (October 1983): 369–79.

Frazier, Donald S. *Blood and Treasure: Confederate Empire in the Southwest.* College Station: Texas A&M University Press, 1995.

Hall, Martin Hardwick. *Sibley's New Mexico Campaign.* Austin: University of Texas Press, 1960.

———. *The Confederate Army of New Mexico.* Austin: Presidial Press, 1978.

———. "The Formation of Sibley's Brigade and the March to New Mexico." *Southwestern Historical Quarterly* 61 (January 1958): 383–405.

Oder, B. N. "The New Mexico Campaign, 1862." *Civil War Times Illustrated* 17 (August 1978): 23–28.

Chapter 4

Fletcher, William A. *Rebel Private Front and Rear.* Washington, D.C.: Zenger Publishing, 1985.

Hood, John Bell. *Advance and Retreat.* New Orleans: n.p., 1880.

Lasswell, Mary. *Rags and Hope: The Recollections of Val C. Giles.* New York: Coward-McCann, 1961.

Polley, J. B. *Hood's Texas Brigade.* 1910. Reprint, Dayton: Morningside Bookshop, 1988.

———. *A Soldier's Letters to Charming Nellie.* New York: Neale, 1908.

Simpson, Harold B. *Hood's Texas Brigade: Lee's Grenadier Guard.* Waco: Texian Press, 1970.

———. *Hood's Brigade: A Compendium.* Hillsboro, Tex.: Hill Junior College Press, 1977.

Thomason, John W., Jr. *Lone Star Preacher.* Fort Worth: Texas Christian University Press, 1992.

Winkler, A. V. *The Confederate Capitol and Hood's Texas Brigade.* 1894. Reprint, Baltimore: Butternut and Blue, 1991.

Chapter 5

Barron, Samuel B. *The Lone Star Defenders.* Washington, D.C.: Zenger Publishing, 1983.

Benner, Judith Ann. *Sul Ross, Soldier, Statesman, Educator.* College Station: Texas A&M University Press, 1982.

Brown, Norman, ed. *One of Cleburne's Command.* Austin: University of Texas Press, 1980.

Buck, Irving A. *Cleburne and His Command.* New York: Neale, 1908.

Chance, Joseph E. *The Second Texas Infantry.* Austin: Eakin Press, 1984.

Connelly, Thomas. *Army of the Heartland.* Baton Rouge: Louisiana State University Press, 1967.

———. *Autumn of Glory.* Baton Rouge: Louisiana State University Press, 1971.

Daniel, Larry. *Soldiering in the Army of Tennessee.* Chapel Hill: University of North Carolina Press, 1991.

Davis, James Henry. *The Cypress Rangers in the Civil War.* Texarkana: Heritage Oak Press, 1992.

Dodd, Ephraim Shelby. *Diary of Ephraim Shelby Dodd.* Austin: E. L. Steck, 1914.

Douglas, Lucia Rutherford, comp. and ed. *Douglas's Texas Battery, CSA.* Tyler, Tex.: Smith County Historical Society, 1966.

Graber, H. W. *A Terry Texas Ranger.* Austin: State House Press, 1987.

Hale, Douglas. *The Third Texas Cavalry in the Civil War.* Norman: University of Oklahoma Press, 1993.

Harrison, Jon P. "Tenth Texas Cavalry, CSA." *Military History of Texas and the Southwest* 12 (1974): 93–107; 171–83.

Heartsill, W. W. *Fourteen Hundred and 91 Days in the Confederate Army.* Pine Bluff, Ark.: Rare Book Publishers, n.d.

Keen, Newton A. *Living and Fighting with the Texas 6th Cavalry.* Gaithersburg, Md.: Butternut Press, 1986.

Kerr, Homer, ed. *Fighting with Ross' Texas Cavalry Brigade, C.S.A., the Diary of George L. Grisom, Adjutant, 9th Texas Cavalry Regiment.* Hillsboro, Tex.: Hill Junior College Press, 1976.

McCaffrey, James. *This Band of Heroes.* Austin: Eakin Press, 1985.

Rugeley, H. J. H., ed. *Batchelor-Turner Letters, 1861–1864.* Austin: Steck, 1961.

Sherman, William T. *Memoirs of William T. Sherman*. New York: Library of America, 1990.

Smith, Ralph J. *Reminiscences of the Civil War*. Waco: W. M. Morrison, 1962.

Sparks, A. W. *The War Between the States as I Saw It*. Tyler, Tex.: Lee & Burnett, 1901.

Chapter 6

Atkinson, J. H. "The Action at Prairie De Ann." *Arkansas Historical Quarterly* 29 (spring 1960): 40–50.

Bailey, Anne J. *Between the Enemy and Texas: Parsons's Texas Cavalry in the Civil War*. Fort Worth: Texas Christian University Press, 1989.

Banasik, Michael E. *Embattled Arkansas, the Prairie Grove Campaign of 1862*. Wilmington: Broadfoot Publishing, 1996.

Bearss, Edwin. *Steele's Retreat from Camden*. Little Rock: Pioneer Press, n.d.

Blessington, J. P. *The Campaigns of Walker's Texas Division*. New York: Lange, Little, & Company, 1875.

Cater, Douglas. *As it Was*. Austin: State House Press, 1990.

Douglas, Lucia Rutherford, ed. *Douglas's Texas Battery, CSA*. Tyler, Tex.: Smith County Historical Society, 1966.

Hale, Douglas. *The Third Texas Cavalry in the Civil War*. Norman: University of Oklahoma Press, 1993.

Harrell, John B. *Arkansas*. Vol. 10 of *Confederate Military History*. Atlanta: Confederate Publishing, 1899.

Josephy, Alvin M., Jr. *The Civil War in the American West*. New York: Vantage Books, 1993.

Lale, Max S., ed. "The Boy Bugler of the Third Texas Cavalry: The A. B. Blocker Narrative." *Military History of Texas and the Southwest* 14 (1978): 71–92, 147–67, 215–27; 15 (1979): 21–34.

Oates, Stephen B. *Confederate Cavalry West of the River*. Austin: University of Texas Press, 1961.

Shea, William L. and Earl J. Hess. *Pea Ridge: Civil War Campaign in the West*. Chapel Hill: University of North Carolina Press, 1992.

Chapter 7

Barr, Alwyn. "Texas Coastal Defense, 1861–1865." *Southwestern Historical Quarterly* 65 (July 1961): 1–31.

Cumberland, Charles C. "The Confederate Loss and Recapture of Galveston, 1862–1863." *Southwestern Historical Quarterly* 51 (October 1947): 109–30.

Delaney, Norman C. "Corpus Christi—Vicksburg of Texas." *Civil War Times Illustrated* 16 (July 1977): 4–9, 44–48.

Fitzhugh, Lester N. "Saluria, Fort Esperanza, and Military Operations on the Texas Coast, 1861–1864." *Southwestern Historical Quarterly* 41 (1957): 66–100.

Frazier, Donald S. "Sibley's Texans and the Battle of Galveston." *Southwestern Historical Quarterly* 99 (October 1995): 175–98.

Jones, V. D. "The Battle of Galveston Harbor." *Civil War Times Illustrated* 5 (February 1967): 28–35, 38.

Chapter 8

Castel, Albert. "Quantrill in Texas." *Civil War Times Illustrated* 11 (June 1972): 20–27.

Elliott, Claude. "Union Sentiment in Texas, 1861–1865." *Southwestern Historical Quarterly* 50 (April 1947): 448–77.

Holden, William C. "Frontier Defense in Texas during the Civil War." *West Texas Historical Association Year Book* 4 (June 1928): 16–31.

Hunter, J. Marvin. "The Battle of Dove Creek." *West Texas Historical Association Year Book* 10 (October 1934): 74–87.

McCaslin, Richard B. *Tainted Breeze: The Great Hanging at Gainesville, Texas, 1862*. Baton Rouge: Louisiana State University Press, 1994.

Marten, James. *Texas Divided: Loyalty & Dissent in the Lone Star State, 1856–1874*. Lexington: The University Press of Kentucky, 1990.

Neighbours, Kenneth F. "Elm Creek Raid in Young County, 1864." *West Texas Historical Association Year Book* 30 (October 1964): 83–89.

Pool, William C. "The Battle of Dove Creek." *Southwestern Historical Quarterly* 53 (April 1950): 367–85.

Rutherford, Phillip. "The Great Gainesville Hanging," *Civil War Times Illustrated* 27 (April 1978): 12–20.

———. "Defying the State of Texas: German Immigrants Died at the Battle of the Nueces," *Civil War Times Illustrated* 18 (April 1979): 16–21.

Sawyer, William E. "Martin Hart, Civil War Guerrilla." *Texas Military History* 3 (fall 1963): 146–53.

Shook, Robert W. "The Battle of the Nueces, August 10, 1862." *Southwestern Historical Quarterly* 66 (July 1962): 31–42.

Smallwood, James M. "Disaffection in Confederate Texas: The Great Hanging at Gainesville." *Civil War History* 22 (December 1976): 349–60.

Smith, David Paul. *Frontier Defense in the Civil War: Texas' Rangers and Rebels*. College Station: Texas A&M University Press, 1992.

———. "Conscription and Conflict on the Texas Frontier, 1863–1865." *Civil War History* 36 (September 1990): 250–61.

Smyrl, Frank H. "Texas in the Federal Army, 1861–1865." *Southwestern Historical Quarterly* 65 (October 1961): 234–50.

Thompson, Jerry Don. *Vaqueros in Blue and Gray*. Austin: Presidial Press, 1976.

Chapter 9

Bowen, Nancy H. "A Political Labyrinth: Texas in the Civil War." *East Texas Historical Journal* 11 (fall 1973): 3–11.

Glover, Robert W. and Randal B. Gilbert. *Camp Ford, Tyler, Texas: The Largest Confederate Prison Camp West of the Mississippi River.* Tyler, Tex.: Smith County Historical Society, 1989.

Havins, T. R. "Administration of the Sequestration Act in the Confederate District Court for the Western District of Texas, 1861–1865." *Southwestern Historical Quarterly* 43 (January 1940): 295–322.

Oates, Stephen B. "Texas under the Secessionists." *Southwestern Historical Quarterly* 67 (October 1963): 167–212.

Ramsdell, Charles W. "The Texas State Military Board, 1862–1865." *Southwestern Historical Quarterly* 27 (April 1924): 253–75.

Tyler, Ronnie C. "Cotton on the Border, 1861–1865." *Southwestern Historical Quarterly* 73 (April 1970): 456–77.

Wilson, Gary. "The Ordeal of William H. Cowdin and the Officers of the Forty-second Massachusetts Regiment: Union Prisoners in Texas." *East Texas Historical Journal* 23 (1986): 16–26.

Wooster, Ralph A. and Robert Wooster. "A People at War: East Texans during the Civil War." *East Texas Historical Association Yearbook* 28 (1990): 3–16.

Chapter 10

Ashcraft, Allan C. "The Union Occupation of the Lower Rio Grande Valley in the Civil War." *Texas Military History* 8 (1969): 13–26.

Barr, Alwyn. "Sabine Pass, September 1863." *Texas Military History* 2 (1962): 17–22.

Block, W. T. "Sabine Pass in the Civil War." *East Texas Historical Journal* 9 (October 1971): 129–36.

———."The Swamp Angels: A History of Spaight's 11th Battalion, Texas Volunteers, Confederate States Army." *East Texas Historical Journal* 30 (1992): 44–57.

McCormack, John F., Jr. "Sabine Pass." *Civil War Times Illustrated* 12 (December 1973): 4–9, 34–37.

Muir, Andrew Forest. "Dick Dowling and the Battle of Sabine Pass." *Civil War History* 4 (December 1958): 399–428.

Oates, Stephen B. "John S. 'Rip' Ford: Prudent Cavalryman, C.S.A." *Southwestern Historical Quarterly* 64 (January 1961): 289–314.

Chapter 11

Blessington, J. P. *The Campaigns of Walker's Texas Division.* New York: Lange, Little, & Company, 1875.

Barr, Alwyn. "Polignac's Texas Brigade." *Texas Gulf Coast Historical Publication Series* 8 (November 1964): 1–72.

Dimitry, John. *Louisiana.* Vol. 10 of *Confederate Military History.* Atlanta: Confederate Publishing, 1899.

Duaine, Carl. L. *The Dead Men Wore Boots: An Account of the 32d Texas Volunteer Cavalry, CSA, 1862–1865.* Austin: The San Felipe Press, 1966.

Ingram, Henry L., comp. *Civil War Letters of George W. and Martha Ingram, 1861–1865.* College Station: Texas A&M University Press, 1973.

Josephy, Alvin M., Jr. *War on the Frontier.* Alexandria, Va.: Time Life Books, 1986.

Selfridge, Thomas O., Jr. *Memoirs of Thomas O. Selfridge, Jr.* New York: G. P. Putnam, 1924.

Taylor, Richard. *Destruction and Reconstruction.* New York: D. Appleton, 1879.

White, William W. "The Disintegration of an Army: Confederate Forces in Texas, April–June, 1865." *East Texas Historical Journal* 26 (1988): 40–47.

Williams, John Calvin. "The Fire of Hatred." *Civil War Times Illustrated* 17 (January 1979): 19–31.

Winters, John D. *The Civil War in Louisiana.* Baton Rouge: Louisiana State University Press, 1963.

Chapter 12

Bailey, Fred Arthur. "The Textbooks of the 'Lost Cause': Censorship and the Creation of Southern State Histories." *Georgia Historical Quarterly* 75 (fall 1991): 507–33.

Gaston, Paul M. *The New South Creed: A Study in Southern Mythmaking.* New York: Alfred A. Knopf, 1970.

Miller, Thomas L. "Texas Land Grants to Confederate Veterans and Widows." *Southwestern Historical Quarterly* 69 (July 1965): 59–65.

Moneyhon, Carl H. *Republicanism in Reconstruction Texas.* Austin: University of Texas Press, 1980.

Simpson, Harold B. *Hood's Texas Brigade in Reunion and Memory.* Hillsboro, Tex.: Hill Junior College Press, 1974.

Wilson, Claude R. *Baptized in Blood: The Religion of the Lost Cause, 1865–1920.* Athens: University of Georgia Press, 1980.

Index